STORMY PETREL

*Aaron Ernest Gompertz and the rise of
the South Shields Labour Party*

STORMY PETREL

Aaron Ernest Gompertz and the rise of
the South Shields Labour Party

IAIN MALCOLM

BROWN DOG BOOKS

Published under licence by Brown Dog Books and
The Self-Publishing Partnership Ltd, 10b Greenway Farm, Bath Rd,
Wick, nr. Bath BS30 5RL

www.selfpublishingpartnership.co.uk

ISBN printed book: 978-1-83952-603-9
ISBN e-book: 978-1-83952-604-6

Cover design by Kevin Rylands
Internal design by Mac Style

Printed and bound in the UK

This book is printed on FSC® certified paper

For my Mother and Father
their memory I cherish and presence
in my life I feel every single day

No man is an island entire of itself;
every man is a piece of the continent, a part of the main;
if a clod be washed away by the sea, Europe is the less,
as well as if a promontory were, as well as any manner of thy friend's
or of thine own were;
any man's death diminishes me, because I am involved in mankind.
And therefore, never send to know for whom the bell tolls; it tolls for thee.

John Donne

Contents

Acknowledgements

I am grateful to the staff of South Tyneside Libraries, with particular thanks to David Brooks for their patience, humour and encouragement; the Tyne and Wear Archive and Museum Service, in particular Iain Watson; the staff of Middlesbrough Library and also Hugh Alexander who undertook research work for me at the National Archives. I am also indebted to the staff of the British Library for their assistance. Transcription Services of the Isle of Man deciphered World War I military records and Towns Web Archiving in Surrey formatted the South Shields Labour Party historical records from microfilm into JPEG format which I have donated to South Tyneside Libraries in order to protect the fabric of the South Shields Labour and Trades Council Minute books. The staff of the Labour History Museum in Manchester allowed me to review records they have on the South Shields Labour Party – the Museum is well worth a visit by those interested in Labour and Trade Union history. I also acknowledge the support of the Working Class Movement Library based in Salford for their assistance in locating documents which referenced the South Shields Labour and Trades Council. The Surrey History Centre in Woking holds Chuter Ede's personal papers and diaries and they have been extremely helpful in establishing the strong bond and working relationship that existed between Ede and Gompertz.

I also acknowledge the support of my brother Ed Malcolm and brother-in-law, John Traynor for reading the draft and giving encouragement during the writing of this book and also Nick Davy for his invaluable comments on the final manuscript.

I have drawn on a number of local history books during my research but I particularly commend for further reading and insight, *In Excited Times* by Nigel Todd and *South Shields at War 1939–45* by Craig Armstrong. The former MP for South Shields, David Clark's book on the history of the South Shields Labour Party, *We Do Not Want the Earth* contains interesting recollections from a number of stalwarts of the period and Peter Chapman's book, *A Tyneside Heritage*, whilst concentrating on his grandfather Sir Robert

Chapman, provides further fascinating insights into North East politics of the time.

I have long been fascinated by the life of Ernie Gompertz, over the years I received many recollections about Gompertz from my father Billy, my great uncle also called Billy and local Labour stalwarts Jim Florence, Brian Howard and Ivor Richardson. Leslie Price and Brenda Robinson who as schoolchildren were presented by Gompertz with School Prizes when he was Mayor, kindly wrote and provided their recollections of the event. Stan Smith, a former Progressive Leader of South Shields Council kindly provided his personal recollections of Gompertz. I was also privileged in the early 1990s to meet Bessie Samuel, daughter of Ernie Gompertz's Aunt Rebecca and Ernie's niece Joy Winton, both of whom gave their own recollections of the family.

Surviving relatives of Ernie Gompertz have been kind to me particularly Melville Goldbaum – whose wife is Isaac Hush's granddaughter and has diligently recorded the Gompertz/Hush family tree for over fifty years. They have kindly reviewed my manuscript and provided me with anecdotal family history.

I hope they feel that the finished book adequately reflects the life of one of their remarkable ancestors.

Introduction

There was nothing inevitable about the Labour Party becoming the dominant political force within South Shields. Like all Parliamentary Constituencies at the turn of the last century, debate raged amongst the working class as to who they should coalesce around to support their interests. Since its formation as a Parliamentary Constituency in 1832, South Shields had never elected a Conservative MP, and Trades Unionists were understandably reluctant to sever their established links with the Liberal Party fearful that a third candidate on the ballot paper would split the anti-Conservative vote in the town. Endeavours by early pioneers determined to formally establish a Labour Party branch in South Shields, affiliated to the national Labour Party were continually rebuffed by leading Trade Unionists until Valentine's Day 1912. Even then the South Shields Trades Council continued to be controlled by Liberal supporting Trade Union branches – leading to Ramsay MacDonald when he visited the town in 1910 to remark that the Trades Council was *'Antiquated and needed modernising.'* By February 1918 it had merged with the Labour Party to create the South Shields Labour and Trades Council.

Electorally, although working class men were elected to the Council, albeit in small numbers as early as 1892, their loyalty remained with their respective Trades Union sponsors, as opposed to any political party. Whilst an active Independent Labour Party branch was established as early as 1892, South Shields would be one of the last on Tyneside to reject Liberalism; and the Parliamentary seat would not fall to the Labour Party until 1929 and then by just 40 votes – propitious circumstances aided that, including the death of the town's popular Liberal MP days before polling day, and the emergence of a third candidate which split the anti-Labour vote. Since 1935 however, the Labour Party has retained healthy Parliamentary majorities in the town. Taking power in civic affairs though would prove more laborious, South Shields County Borough Council would not see a working Labour majority in the Council Chamber until 1937, years after neighbouring authorities had witnessed the emergence of the Labour Party as the dominant force in civic life. Control was always a challenge for the Labour Party with a determined right-wing group from the Rent and Ratepayers (and latterly Progressive) Association occasionally seizing back control but since 1972 the Labour Party has always retained a majority within the local Chamber.

The fratricide which engulfed the Liberal Party following Lloyd George's ousting of Herbert Asquith from the Premiership in 1916, saw the Party become fissiparous and suffer a split between those loyal to either Asquith or Lloyd George, and the increase in adult suffrage enabled the Labour Party to eclipse the old divided Liberal Party hitherto seen as the Party of the working class and present itself as a new, modern Party – no more so than in South Shields. The Liberal Party never recovered from their schism.

The history of the rise of the South Shields Labour Party is the story of men and women from ordinary working-class backgrounds who looked around them, saw the appalling slums, living and working conditions their kith and kin were obliged to survive in, and refused to accept that it had to be the established order. Activists like the first working-class councillors, John Lisle, Joe Abbott, John Thompson and Joe Batey, the ILP firebrands Charles and Margaret Reynolds and Union activists Jim Curbison and Tom Mulgrew; and it was the local Labour Party that promoted the first woman JP, Sarah Noble in 1925, the first woman councillor, Elizabeth Ann Thorpe in 1927 and elected the first woman mayor, Jane Peel in 1947. Always central though to the rise of the South Shields Labour Party was Ernie Gompertz. A young man of only twenty-three when in 1912 he was elected Assistant Secretary of the new local Party, by 1929 he was working full time as Secretary to the Party and Agent to the newly elected Labour MP, James Chuter Ede. It was a position he would continue to retain, without serious challenge, until March 1960. Agent to Ede in eight general elections, Gompertz was the driving force as the infant Party matured and was an effective proselytiser for his beliefs to win the trust of the electors of South Shields. He without question created a powerful Labour Group on the Council and was central to the Labour Party becoming the dominant political force it was to become in South Shields.

Gompertz's downfall, when it came in March 1960, was swift and brutal, followed months later by the announcement of the long serving MP, Chuter Ede, that he would not contest the 1964 General Election. Despite the manner of his departure, Gompertz remained loyal to the Labour Party and his former comrades, never speaking an unkind word in public, remarking only that it was the future that counted not the past.

Born in Middlesbrough in 1888, proud of his Jewish ancestry, Ernie was a lifelong Trades Union activist, a conscientious objector in World War I, humanist, teetotaller, vegetarian and fanatically anti-smoking. Unlike Ede, Gompertz did not convert to Socialism from Liberalism, the principle of gradual social and economic reform was the cornerstone of his political beliefs, which led to a lifelong distrust of the Communist Party and indeed any political faction he felt undermined the Labour Party's efforts to present itself as the pre-eminent expression of working-class interests. He met Keir Hardie, devoured Socialist text-books and committed himself to one aim in life – that the Labour Party should become the dominant political force in South Shields. He passionately believed that only the Labour Party could create a new social and economic order and end the poverty he had witnessed daily as a pawnbrokers manager. He was not the only person of course to do so, numerous other men and women gave their time to help build the Labour Party into a formidable election machine, but it was Gompertz, as Secretary/Agent, who led them, gently cajoled them, encouraged them during times of defeat and spurred them on to do more in times of victory. The town's MP James Chuter Ede, relied upon Gompertz unhesitatingly and a close bond developed between the two men to the extent that when Gompertz was removed as Secretary/Agent in 1960, Ede knew it was time to go himself.

Writing a biography of a man who left no diaries, no papers and which, through the passage of time, those who knew him intimately have all since passed away, was always going to be a challenge, but because of his public record as an elected Councillor, and because he kept meticulous Labour Party minute books, a picture slowly emerged of his political views, his character, his commitment and at times how others viewed him. As I set out on this journey, my focus was primarily to record Gompertz's life, but it quickly became obvious that the rise of the South Shields Labour Party and Gompertz's life were entwined – you could not write one without recording the other. Neither could you provide an account without an appreciation of events taking place nationally and sometimes internationally which shaped and formed the South Shields Labour Party as it emerged over the decades.

Social change and economic improvements do not occur because a civil servant in London or a Town Hall public official decree that they must. In a democracy it can only be achieved through political agitation, electing politicians who are pledged to implement change and who have the stamina, patience and determination to drive through their vision for a better society. Gompertz had all three attributes and used every constitutional and procedural rule at his disposal to ensure Labour's manifesto was implemented across South Shields. He was frequently removed from Council meetings when Labour was opposition as his fiery temper was directed at right-wing reactionaries controlling the Chamber, but with guile and fervour ensured the Council implemented strategies the Labour Group wanted when they had a majority. He was never deliberately unfair, but he was a pugnacious tribal Labour politician and had contempt for the political opposition whose sole purpose, Gompertz believed, was to thwart the social improvements advocated by the Labour Party.

In writing this book I do not in any way seek to underplay or disregard the work of other pioneers: including the long-serving town's MP Chuter Ede or Joe Batey, Bill Blyton and Dick Ewart who went on to become MPs themselves elsewhere; Cuth Barrass who introduced Ede to South Shields or Charles Henderson; the fiery Margaret Gallagher; the redoubtable Margaret Sutton or the principled Sarah Noble. Jack Clark, who became the first Leader of the Labour Group or William McAnany who like Gompertz was a founder member of the Constituency Party and served as a long-standing Secretary of the Labour Group, retiring from the Council in 1965. All of them, amongst others, helped to make the Labour Party the success it became in South Shields, and I hope I have reflected their contributions within this book. Without their collective efforts, and the efforts of thousands of men and women across the country with new generations building upon the work of their predecessors, the Labour Party could never have dreamed of establishing itself as a Party of Government. Demographics alone did not determine that the Labour Party would succeed in South Shields: the collapse of the Liberal Party as a national political force; diligent campaigning, delivering social improvements when in power, articulating the aspirations of the people of the town as well as undertaking the more mundane work of raising finance for the Party to pay for the election's leaflets – all were crucial to encouraging the townsfolk to support the Labour Party.

In Chapter 1 I referred to Gompertz by his first name Ernie to save confusion with other members of his family. Within the wider Gompertz family he was known as 'Big Ernie' to avoid confusion with his cousin Aaron (Ernest) Hartog Gompertz who was known as 'Little Ernie'. To aid the reader, it is worth explaining that the South Shields Trades Council (sometimes referred to as The Trades and Labour Council) was initially established around 1872, Trade Union branches and lodges affiliated to it and sent Union Delegates to their meetings. The Independent Labour Party

(ILP) was a left of centre British political party, influenced by Socialist ideas, and established when the Liberals appeared reluctant to endorse working-class Parliamentary candidates. A branch of the ILP was established in South Shields on 31 August 1892. Members of the ILP who were nominated by their Trade Union could attend meetings of the Trades Council. South Shields Labour Party, affiliated to the newly created national Labour Party was formally established on 14 February 1912 with the active support of members of the ILP and local Fabian Society.

National Labour Party rules in January 1918 encouraged Trades Councils and local Labour Party branches to merge, this was achieved in South Shields by February 1918. However, there existed the anomaly that some Trade Union delegates were not Labour Party members, accordingly business was conducted in two stages. The *Industrial Section* was always conducted first which involved all delegates, followed by the *Political Section*, at which point non-Labour Party supporting Union Delegates were required to leave the meeting. As expected, the arrangement had a complex constitutional framework with the inevitable arguments always emerging as to who defined agenda items as 'Industrial or Political'. Non-Labour Party supporting Union Delegates were frequently critical that political business always took precedence and that the Labour Party was too controlling over the work of the Labour and Trades Council. Nevertheless, the arrangement remained in place until February 1970 when the two organisations formally split.

It is worth referring to the Labour Group's whipping policy because reference to it is frequently recorded in this book. The policy was not unique to the South Shields Labour Group. As at Westminster, all political parties in Council Chambers across the country operate a system that their group members will meet in caucus before the monthly Borough/County Council meetings to agree their position on business items being considered as part of the meeting agenda. Once a formal position is agreed, group members are expected to support the established line in any vote in the Chamber. Group meetings of all political parties will at times be turbulent with sometimes violent disagreement on the formal position to take in public, but if any political group is going to be able to implement their manifesto commitments, as presented to the public at election time, and given a Councillor would have been elected courtesy of their political party's colours then it is not unreasonable to expect their elected members to adhere to the agreed position. There is clear evidence that the South Shields Rent and Ratepayers' Municipal Association and latterly the Progressive Association also met in caucus and agreed their formal position. As in modern times, political groups during Gompertz's life did not mandate their respective members to vote a particular way during the numerous individual Council Committee meetings that Local Authorities operate under, and today Political Group whipping is illegal for key Committees such as Planning and Licensing.

Gompertz was a disciple of Keir Hardie, whom he met on several occasions. Iain McLean in his biography of Hardie wrote:

> 'He was too ready to let fly with his tongue at political opponents while sublimely confident of the rightness of his own views. In one sense this was his greatest strength, because it gave him reserves of stamina which forced him to persevere where any normal man would have given up in despair. But it did not show him in an attractive light to those who found themselves on the wrong side of him'.

Words about his political hero, which could equally apply to himself.

Ernie Gompertz would have liked that.

Chapter 1

The Early Years

I

Aaron Ernest Gompertz was born on Wednesday 20 June 1888 at 8 Gladstone Street, Middlesbrough, which was then part of the North Riding County of York.

Modern-day commentators reviewing Ernie Gompertz's ancestry always refer to his Dutch-Jewish parentage and maintain that his early relatives had emigrated from Holland to escape Jewish persecution. This though does not tell the full story. It is certainly true that his paternal great grandfather's family hailed from Amsterdam and were a well-established part of the Jewish congregation there. However, his maternal great grandparents Jacob Hirsch (born 1805) and Vogel Samuel (dob unknown) were Polish from the town of Szamocin located in the north west of the country which at the time was a centre of Poland's weaving industry and was also under Prussian occupation.

Jews had been living in Poland since the Middle Ages. When Crusaders moved through Europe in the thirteenth century, Jewish refugees sought safety in Poland. The 1264 Statute of Kalisz created legal protections for Jews that were extended by successive rulers, and within these protections, the Jewish communities in Poland began to thrive. Scholars have estimated that by the sixteenth century, 80 per cent of all Jews worldwide lived in Poland, enjoying relative autonomy and tolerance and developing a rich social and cultural life.

By the end of the eighteenth century however, in a series of diplomatic moves, this relative peaceful existence for Polish Jewry was threatened. In 1771 the first partition of Poland occurred which saw the country divided between Russia, Prussia and Austria. The town of Szamocin was initially annexed by the Kingdom of Prussia, before falling to the Napoleonic Duchy of Warsaw in 1807 with the town being restored to Prussian rule in 1815.

The fate of Polish Jews at this time invariably depended upon political decisions made in Vienna, Berlin or St Petersburg. In the Prussian zone, Poles were subjected to a policy of *Germanisation* and they experienced a repression of their Polish nationalism. Polish Jews were effectively reduced to the status of '*guests*', their autonomy was curtailed, and the beginnings of anti-Jewish sentiment began to emerge particularly amongst the commercial class who saw the Jewish community as unwelcome competitors leading to complaints about Jewish business practices and allegations of Jewish '*separatism*'. Political leaders began to regard Jews as a problematic group whose different religion, language and culture differentiated them from the rest of Polish citizenry.

Polish Jewry underwent extensive change, the population dwindled in the Prussian Partition as Jews began to migrate overseas or moved to the major cities in Germany seeking work.

It was during these turbulent times that Jacob and Vogel allowed their daughter Paulina to make the fateful decision to leave Poland to seek a new life at some point in the early 1850s. Family members insist that it was Paulina who made the journey westward first, not her younger brother Isaac. Whilst the treatment of Jews in Eastern Europe was the clear driver for the move away from Poland, we do not know why Paulina Hirsch chose England, still less why to Tyneside. It is probable that someone from Szamocin had already made the journey to the sailing ports on the Tyne and was able to secure for Paulina employment – family sources record as a housekeeper to a shipbuilding family – thus allowing her to settle with an established support network around her. It does seem unlikely that her parents would have allowed Paulina to make the journey without knowing either where she was headed or whether she would be looked after by friends upon her arrival into England. It is extremely likely she made the journey with her sisters Mina and Marla since they are recorded as marrying in South Shields in 1854 and 1859 respectively. Her parents remained in Poland, her father Jacob dying in 1888.

Ernie's paternal relatives the Gompert family – the z was added later in the family tree – can trace their Dutch ancestry back to the seventeenth century. His great grandparents on his father's side were Simon (Zimle) Solister Gompertz (born in 1773) who had married his second wife Rachel Aron Frijda (born in 1791) on 12 January 1820 – (his first wife Clara Hijmans having died in March 1819) in Amsterdam; Simon and Rachel had six children, Duifje, Simon, Rebecca, Rosette, Aaron Simon and Mozes (who died in infancy). Simon Gompertz appears in records as a *solliciteur* (solicitor) competent in the Amsterdam Courts. He remained in Office until his death in 1836 when Aaron Simon was just six years old. The wishes of the family were that there were to be no visible signs of mourning save an announcement in the local press from Rachel expressing the emotional blow she felt at the death of her husband – '... *leaving me behind with five children too young to realise their loss. All those who knew the godly and hardworking man will feel what I and my children lose in him.*'

Holland had always traditionally welcomed political and religious refugees and the country experienced the first major wave of Jewish immigration to escape the persecution of the Inquisition in Spain and Portugal at the end of the sixteenth century. The Netherlands' occupation by the French between 1795 and 1813 led to genuine attempts to emancipate the Jewish population. The problem though was that such legislative emancipation had not been the initiative of the Dutch government, but of an occupying power, so the Dutch were reluctant after the occupation ended in 1813 to extend genuine equality to the Jews.

The number of Jewish communities in Holland by the 1850s is believed to have numbered around 130 across the country with over 42 per cent of Dutch Jewry living in Amsterdam. The economic restrictions imposed on them by the Amsterdam authorities – they were excluded from joining the professional guilds for example – established a narrow occupational framework and contributed to their weakening economic position, particularly in the major towns. Jews in the main were required to work in low-paid, low-skilled jobs such as peddling, hawking and small trades such as fishmongers, tailors and barbers. Such was the dire economic situation for the Amsterdam Jews, that it was estimated that the Jewish poor relief in the capital numbered 20,000 out of a population of 25,000 Jews. During the 1840s, Jewish representations were made to the authorities expressing indignation at their total exclusion from Public and Civic posts and frustration at Dutch society that regardless of the Government's declaration to emancipate the Jews, their community were still not treated as equal citizens.

As Karina Sonnenberg-Stern has pointed out in her book *Emancipation and Poverty* which examined the Jewish community of Amsterdam at this time: '*Their exclusion from trades and crafts, their unequal share of public relief, and the difficulties in entering municipal schools, impeded their ability to progress at a similar rate to the non-Jewish inhabitants, and left them poorer and more backward than the rest of the Dutch populations.*'

Consequently, in common with other Jewish families in their local Congregation, the Gompertz family, experienced that being a Jew in the Dutch Republic, was a barrier to their occupational achievement and social advancement, and there was scant display from the Dutch authorities that they intended to make any discernible improvements in the foreseeable future. Further with the reconfiguration and upheaval of national boundaries across Europe during the eighteenth century – Poland's partitions, the aftermath of the Napoleonic Wars, the expansion of the German Empire, the Russification campaigns under the Romanovs – often violently executed, and with the successful invaders imposing their identity on their new conquests – many migrants and oppressed peoples sought to move.

Simon Solister's son, Aaron Simon Gompertz, living with his mother and siblings following the death of the father he had not really known, was not immune from these difficult circumstances and given the lack of opportunity for Jews in Holland decided, like his future wife Paulina, to make the journey to England.

Aaron Simon travelled from the Port of Amsterdam on the SS *Magnet* arriving into the Port of London on 3 September 1852, aged just twenty-two years old, he gave as his profession Kledesmaker (tailor). Any port can be viewed as a '*contact-zone*' for migrants seeking to establish themselves in a new country and wishing to meet fellow-countrymen as they sought to secure accommodation, housing and other support networks. The River Thames was a natural conduit for immigrants from the mainland Europe. We cannot be certain where he resided whilst he was in London, but he did attend as a witness his sister Rebecca's marriage to Hartog van Gelder on 26 February 1854 at the Hambro' Synagogue in Spitalfields.

Why Aaron Simon then moved north to settle in North Shields in 1854 before crossing the River Tyne to South Shields we can only speculate but arriving in to the town he was able to establish contact with Henry Kossick and Samuel Levy both of whom would become his brothers-in-law, and these families formed the nucleus of a new Jewish Congregation which initially travelled across the River Tyne to Linskill Street, North Shields to worship at the well-established Synagogue there. They made sure that they paid their ferry fares in advance so as not to desecrate the Sabbath.

Family sources have maintained that by chance, Aaron Simon met Paulina Hirsch at the Old Town Hall in South Shields Market Square, although given the closeness of the Jewish community it is likely Aaron Simon would have known who Paulina was, neither of them at the time spoke English so they communicated with a mixture of Yiddish and Hebrew. The courtship was short, they married on 18 December 1855 (Paulina's surname is registered as Hurst not Hirsch) and resided at 26 Church Street in Tynemouth before moving to South Shields in 1858 to reside at Wapping Street on the waterfront.

At some point Aaron Simon shelved using the surname Gompertz as he began to establish his business interests, using only his forenames. He had a tempestuous start in business since an examination of the local newspapers records several occasions when he appeared in front of the local Magistrates, on one occasion accused of defrauding a Dutch seaman, on another as a witness to thefts from his business and a further occasion where he reported a rival pawnbroker for a Breach of the Pawnbrokers Act. In July 1864, he was again required to appear in front of Magistrates, this time as a result of being involved in a quarrel with an Abraham Jackson another outfitter from the Holborn area, which resulted in the Police being called to a butcher's shop in Clive Street after Aaron Simon had apparently thrown meat at Mr Jackson. Clearly someone was not content with some business arrangement, whatever the reason, Magistrates fined Aaron Simon 10 shillings.

Aaron Simon also became a Member of the British Oak Lodge of Ancient Free Gardening, a Society whilst independent of, had a number of similarities to Freemasonry. A *Shields Gazette* public notice in 1869 bears Aaron Simon's name in which he exhorts fellow Brethren to attend the funeral of one of their Lodge members.

Paulina and Aaron Simon were by 1861 residing at 21 West Holborn before moving in 1871 to a larger property at 83 West Holborn in the East Holborn riverside area of South Shields where he had established a business as tailor and outfitter and where Census records indicate he employed a servant Maria Long aged just ten years who had been born in Whitechapel in London. The family then moved to a property at 22 Thrift Street, which was part of a crooked line of lanes which ran adjacent alongside the River Tyne towards Tyne Dock and the Jarrow Slake. East Holborn consisted of what the Medical Officer in 1876 described as '*wretched tenemented property*' and experienced high death rates. The Thrift Street area was regarded as the business centre of the town and with the adjacent Thames Street continued to rival the newly built King Street as the commercial centre of the town. The area was crowded with a twenty-four-hour bustle of commercial and retail activity from the butchers, bakers, ship-chandlers, boarding houses, warehouses and taverns, with no licensing laws, remained constantly open and received heavy custom from the steady stream of patrons from the merchant sailors docking at the Tyne.

Thrift Street serviced a diverse transient population given its proximity to the river port. Laura Tabili has observed that one property owned by a joiner, Patrick Clark, accommodated twenty men of various occupations, which included: '... *a troupe of five German musicians in a house in Salt Well Lane near the Market. Hawkers Alexander Levitt and Iman Arias from Austria and Poland, respectively, lived among 24 British-born men in a boarding house at 41 Thrift Street.*'

Buildings around the Market Place itself housed the professional classes and their offices and whilst this area was well maintained, most of the buildings in the surrounding area were poorly constructed and dilapidated with chronic overcrowding and residents living in unsanitary conditions. The extent of the problem was highlighted in the Chief Medical Officer's Report of 1876. He reported that the town centre housing, with a combination of industrial pollution and building on unsafe ground made from ballast emptied from ships contributed to the prevalence of '*damp, ill ventilated, uneven and dilapidated premises.*' Waterloo Vale was singled out for special mention with the Medical Officer observing that the sickly odour of organic decomposition made the area '*a source of menace to the health of the whole town*'.

Working class residents though did their best, even in the worst areas. Human effort, largely by woman of the household, who worked hard to improve their situation and make their living conditions as comfortable as possible – '*In Justice to the tenants, it must be said that the houses are clean, well-furnished and considering the state of the property, surprisingly well kept*' is how one Ministry of Health official in 1902 described the living conditions on Tyneside. The area though was one of the first to be cleared under a slum clearance programme before the local authority were able to begin clearing housing elsewhere in the town centre.

As Aaron Simon developed his business interests Paulina looked after their growing family – Simpson born in 1856, closely followed by Ernie's father Samuel (born October 1858), Rachel (born May 1861), Susannah (born 1863), Frances (born 1866), Moses (born 1868), Jeramiah (born 1870), Abraham (born 1872) and Rebecca (born 1878). At a time of high infant mortality, all the Gompertz children survived infancy, and Aaron Simon gave each child the middle name of Aaron, irrespective of whether they were male or female.

In February 1880, Aaron Simon made a public announcement via the *Gazette* Public Notices that in future he was again using his full name for all business transactions. Public records exist that reveal Aaron's business interests had been liquidated in 1874 and he clearly wanted to re-establish himself, as the town's first recorded Jewish resident he may have wished to utilise his Jewish connections, particularly considering his growing family. Whatever lay behind the *Shields Gazette* announcement, Jewish records indicate that by 1885 he became the first Secretary for Jewish marriages in South Shields, quite an honour within any Jewish congregation.

The Jewish population in South Shields whilst stable, was never large, at its height in the 1950s it is believed to have numbered no more than 300. There are records to indicate that Aaron Simon, together with Joseph Pearlman and Lazarus Joseph started conducting Jewish ceremonies in a private house in the 1880s and that by 1890 a Hebrew School had been opened consisting of thirty-five boys and five girls – without a doubt Aaron Simon and Paulina's children would have attended – and by 1897 the Jewish congregation had decided to purchase a house, Number 38 Charlotte Square to convert into a Synagogue.

Through a capacity for hard work, a fair number of knock-backs, shrewd (and probably at times dubious) business dealings, within twenty years, Aaron and Paulina's fortune would change once again. By 1891 Aaron Simon had established his own pawnbroking business and the family was on the move again, although in the same area, to 47 Thrift Street, a larger, more well-maintained property with Census records indicating he now also employed domestic servants. They do not appear to have lived there long, Burgess records for Newcastle indicate that by 1898 Aaron Simon owned a pawnbroking business at 50 Gosforth Street in the city and was residing at 11 Burrow Street in South Shields.

Having arrived, married and settled in South Shields, Paulina wrote back home to Poland and encouraged family members to migrate to England. Her brother Isaac and sister Bertha made the crossing with the 1861 Census records showing both Isaac and Bertha residing with Pauline and Aaron Simon at West Holborn. Meanwhile, her sister Mina Hirsch is recorded as having married Henry Kossick in Newcastle on 12 March 1854, her other sister Marla married Samuel Levy on 22 March 1859.

Isaac himself would eventually marry in May 1868, Henrietta Cohen from Newcastle, but who hailed originally from Winschoten in Holland. Isaac also became a naturalised British citizen in 1871, taking the opportunity to change the family name from Hirsch to Hush. Henrietta bore Isaac eight children, unfortunately two, Fanny and Sarah died in infancy. By 1874 the family took the decision to move from Stevenson Street in South Shields to 194/196 Cannon Street in Middlesbrough. Middlesbrough had a small Jewish community, it was not until as late as 1862 that the first Jew, Maurice Levy arrived there and is accredited with the distinction of founding the first Hebrew congregation. The Rev HP Levy noting at the opening of the town's first Jewish cemetery in 1885: '*About 23 years ago when Mr Maurice Levy settled in this town there were no Jews.*'

The move to Middlesbrough would have made business sense for Isaac. As an established and astute businessman, he would have seen the opportunity of a growing industrialised town with the associated poverty that had accompanied its growth presented him with. There were no established pawnbroking competitors in the district. Surviving family members assert that he started out as a pedlar or hawker selling goods to the inhabitants of farms and villages in Cleveland, it is unlikely this would have been his only source of income given he had a reasonable standard of living in North Shields. There is also historical evidence that upon arriving in Middlesbrough he immediately opened a pawnshop in Cannon Street whose surrounding houses accommodated the iron foundry workers and their families and that he later opened a second shop selling jewellery and fancy goods in Corporation Road. Both shops the Hush family would retain until slum clearance demolished the area in the late 1960s, and the welfare state helped to cushion families against the sometimes-harsh financial realities of life.

His wife Henrietta was not to enjoy a long life, she died in 1883 aged just 36, childbearing and the loss of her child Sarah less than a year earlier taking its toll on her physical and mental health. Isaac was left to care for his young family of five girls and one boy. Regular journeys to South Shields to visit his sister Paulina, had allowed Isaac to court his niece Rachel, and in 1886 Isaac asked for permission to marry her. The request clearly caused a scandal in the wider family because even today family members refer to the fact that Isaac was forty and Rachel would have been twenty-five years old when he sought her father Aaron Simons' permission to marry her. Her father consented, but whilst the marriage was legal under Jewish Law, it was not permitted under English Law, therefore Rachel and Isaac were required to travel to Hamburg in Germany and were married there on 12 July 1886 at the Herschel Hotel. They returned to Middlesbrough, where Isaac and Rachel eventually settled in The Brooklands, in Linthorpe and had a son named Phineas Aaron Hush (later called Ernest). Two other offspring died in infancy, Henrietta in November 1898 and Henry in July 1899.

Isaac's pawnbroking interests were certainly successful since the family moved to the imposing Norton Villa located in a desirable part of Park Road in Middlesbrough; the 1911 Census record indicates that he had both a housemaid and servant. By this time all his six surviving children to Henrietta had either married or left home.

Isaac was also acting as a mentor for at least two of Aaron Simon's children, Simpson and Samuel because both left Tyneside for Middlesbrough. Given he had no sons of age, Isaac probably needed support from the family network to manage his expanding business interests. Simpson and his wife Regina together with their daughter Rebecca were residing at 44 Wilson Street, and Ernie's father Samuel on his marriage certificate gave his address as 194 Cannon Street, the pawnbroking business of his Uncle Isaac. Samuel had married Rebecca Cohen on 10 August 1887 at the New West End Synagogue in Bayswater in London, Rebecca's parents had themselves emigrated from Amsterdam. The circumstances of Ernie's parents' meeting and subsequent courtship are unknown, but it is clear they were first cousins, Rebecca's mother Rosette being a daughter of Simon Solister and Rachel Gompertz. Samuel and Rebecca returned to Middlesbrough where he continued to be employed by his Uncle Isaac, managing the Cannon Street shop, whilst the young family resided at 8 Gladstone Street. It was not a residence they would remain at for long for by 1893 they had moved into the living quarters of the pawnbrokers shop at Cannon Street, in all probability due to Isaac moving his growing family into Norton Villa.

II

At the time of Ernie's birth in 1888, Queen Victoria had been on the throne since 1837, and was presiding over a nation enjoying high levels of relative peace and increased prosperity. The Great Exhibition of 1851 epitomised the country's new-found confidence and Victoria was crowned Empress of India in 1876. The Industrial Revolution had made Britain the most economically prosperous in the World, but the movement of people from the countryside to the new emerging industrial towns to satisfy the demand for labour saw the rise of slum dwelling and appalling poverty, in the second half of the century alone, the population of England and Wales was almost doubled from 16.8m in 1851 to 30.5m in 1901.

The late 19th century was a time of huge political uncertainty. Joseph Chamberlain and his supporters had split the Liberal Party over William Gladstone's Irish Home Rule proposals and contested seats in the 1886 General Election, with tactical support from the Conservatives, as Liberal Unionists' candidates. These political manoeuvres resulted in the Conservative Party winning the Election, albeit without an overall majority. Lord Salisbury became the last politician to serve as Prime Minister from the House of Lords, the support of Chamberlain's breakaway Liberal Unionists easing his passage to Downing Street. August 1888 also saw the passing – at the insistence of Liberal Unionist MPs, the Local Government Act in Parliament, which established uniformity across the Country of Local Government administration through the creation of County and County Borough Councils in England and Wales. This Act created a new South Shields County Borough Council in 1889 which Ernie Gompertz would serve as an elected Member and Alderman for over thirty years.

Gladstone Street in Middlesbrough where Ernie was born and spent his infant years, was part of a series of streets which ran alongside the main thoroughfare of the imposing Cannon Street, north of the new railway line which connected the town to the rest of the country and adjacent to the River Tees, it was very much the centre of Middlesbrough lined with scores of shops supplying the everyday needs of the close-knit community. Middlesbrough's population during the Industrial Revolution grew exponentially. A former small farming community with a population of less than fifty at the turn of the nineteen century, by the beginnings of the twentieth it had grown in excess of 100,000 people as Victorian entrepreneurs exploited the potential of the development of the town's natural resources, most notably iron.

So astonishing was the growth, that in 1862 Prime Minister Gladstone described the town as an '*Infant Hercules*' but like with so many other growing industrial towns, the Victorians became so preoccupied with economic growth, that no serious consideration was given as to long-term social conditions in which the new inhabitants were expected to live their lives. The housing district in which Gladstone and Cannon Streets were built had originally been marshland and had been inadequately drained to accommodate houses for the new workers who were expected to live in badly constructed and poorly maintained housing, cockroaches were the ubiquitous pest, outside toilet, no hot water and certainly no indoor bath except for a tin bath in front of the fire or if one could afford it, a trip to the 'slipper baths'. The residents were usually employees of the new ironworks, this led to the area being described as the 'Ironmaster District'. It is often said that Victorians constructed buildings to last, but the damp and insanitary conditions of this area, like so many other residential areas in urban areas constructed at this time, required the start of a massive slum clearance programme which did not conclude properly until Cannon Street itself was brought down in the 1960s.

Infectious disease would have been a constant worry to parents during Ernie Gompertz's childhood, smallpox, scarlet fever, diphtheria, typhoid, puerperal fever, croup and erysipelas the main culprits. Ernie's formative years in saw Middlesbrough saw the town hit by three outbreaks: pneumonia, typhoid fever and smallpox.

In 1888 there was an outbreak of pneumonia in the town, to what appeared an epidemic level, with the number of recorded deaths that year being 490. From February to July alone, 285 died from the disease with sixty-eight of those being under the age of five. To put the deaths into some perspective, there had been 480 deaths for the same six months during the entirety of the previous eight years. The Medical Officer for the area, Dr John Malcomson described the 1888 outbreaks as '*serious and very fatal epidemic*', with the key and alarming feature of this precise epidemic being its virulence, with patients often described as delirious by the second day, and the condition proving fatal by the third.

In 1890 an outbreak of typhoid fever is recorded with the source of the infection believed to have been the River Tees, with the river being polluted at the town of Barnard Castle (west of Middlesbrough) where poor sanitary conditions across the district saw public and private waste delivered directly into the water. Meanwhile, a smallpox epidemic of 1897/8 lasted nine months and forced the laissez-faire local Corporation into action. Obligatory hospital provision was given, Sanitary Inspectors were sent to visit each house where a case had been notified, and members of the household were offered free vaccination.

The underlying, but not the sole causes, of the outbreaks centred around poor sanitation, overcrowding, poor diet and lack of adequate medical health provision across the town.

Thus, the era into which Ernie Gompertz was to take his first steps was a precarious one, whilst his family were relatively comfortable in terms of financial security, due to Ernie's fathers moderate business interests, and certainly in a better financial position than their immediate neighbours, they could never entirely insulate themselves from indiscriminate diseases which affected the town.

III

Isaac Hush and his family would have been extremely close to and protective of Ernie's parents, Samuel and Rebecca. Isaac had not only arranged their employment and, by the standards of the time, a comfortable home, but he was also mentoring Samuel in the workings of the pawnbroking business, which would stand him in good stead for the future. Isaac was becoming extremely wealthy in Middlesbrough and was also taking a keen interest in civic affairs. Samuel Smith, a local resident recorded in *Lives and Reminisces*:

> '... *he filled the offices of Honorary President and Honorary Treasurer, (of the Jewish congregation ... authors addition) but as to this I'm not sure for without records one can't be definite, but it was a life's ambition with the Old Standards to occupy these positions which have now lost their glamour and hold no attraction.*'

Described as an earnest man, Isaac worked diligently with devotion, and was extremely modest he expected no honours and did not seek recognition for his charity work. He was also a well-read man with an extensive library of Hebrew books and was involved in charitable organisations across Middlesbrough not solely those connected with Jewish causes and was for several years a member of the Jewish Board of Guardians. Such was his benevolence that in 1908 he was presented with an illuminated address and appointed Life Warden, the highest honour which a Jewish Congregation can bestow.

Mr Smith also reminisces that Isaac was a quiet, mild, modest person '... *engrossed with business*' and was involved in a cottage property development with Benjamin Hyman.

Isaac died at the conclusion of Yom Kippur on 4 October 1919, records indicate that he left an estate valued at £41,408 (approx. £2.15m today). All his family were well cared for. He left his substantial business interests at 194, 196 and 198 Cannon Street to his son Phineas (Ernest), and directed that his wife was to have use of his household effects for life, and the sum of £6 per week; upon her death, he left property in Cannon Street and a further seven houses in Parliament Street, Middlesbrough in Trust for his other son Lipman and the residue of his property to his six daughters in equal shares. Isaac made it a stipulation of the terms of his will that any child marrying out of the Jewish faith would forfeit all interest in his estate.

IV

Ernie was the eldest of five children, Gabriel was born in August 1890, Alex in March 1897, Rosetta in March 1899, a fifth child Claude was born on 10 January 1894 but tragically died the following day.

The family would have been extremely close. Jews, whilst tolerated, would have still been viewed with some degree of suspicion, family life would have revolved around the father's work in the pawnbroking business, school and the local Synagogue based at Brentnall Street near to the new Municipal buildings which housed the new town hall, at which they would have been joined for religious observance by Uncle Isaac, Auntie Rachel and their extended family. The Jewish population in Middlesbrough was never particularly large, only around 100 in 1895, rising to a peak of 750 in 1934 before slowly declining.

When Ernie was eleven he was required to appear before a Coroners' Court hearing at Fleetham Street School. In early August 1899, whilst returning from a local park, he witnessed the tragic accident in which a two-year-old girl was run over and killed by a mineral water rolley on Cannon Street. He was required to give evidence to the Court where he gave a full description of the tragedy and whilst the Coroner recorded a verdict of 'Accidental Death' he severely reprimanded the driver for the carelessness he had shown, stating he could not envisage how the driver failed to observe the girl, Minnie Davison, playing in the street.

Fleetham Street Junior School where Ernie completed his formal state education stood imposingly on the corner of Fleetham Street and Union Street. This was one Victorian public building constructed to last, it was only demolished in 2003 to make way for housing, but the original structure was of solid design, large sloping roofs and a fancy spire, described as somewhat quaint.

It was clearly a popular school and Ernie must have enjoyed his time there, since he was determined during his Mayoral Year to revisit the school in 1954. Addressing a special school assembly, he recalled that his headmaster was a Mr Dixon, known as 'Slogger', who had a long ginger beard, a strict no familiarity rule, everyone knew he was in charge. He also remarked that the school had changed beyond recognition since he had attended fifty-two years earlier. Ernie explained that during his time at school, children were placed into small classrooms with poor ventilation and sometimes no heating at all, with the expectation that they were to learn to become good citizens.

'There's a lot to said for Fleetham Street School that out of such conditions so many important people have worked their way up in the world. What I have done is very small indeed compared with some other Fleetham Street boys and girls. I nearly brought with me the Deputy Chief Constable of South Shields – he is an old boy of this school,' Ernie said to the school audience.

Head Boy Leslie Price was presented to Ernie, who had attended the school in his South Shields Mayoral chains. He recalls that Ernie presented him with a collection of essays by Neville Cardus – *Cardus on Cricket* – which in later years he admitted may have seemed a little inappropriate for a boy of his age and background, although he fondly recalled he still had the book – '*So for me at least the occasion had lasting consequences, awakening an interest both in cricket and in the sort of essayistic literature I had hardly been aware of before.*'

Brenda Robinson was also presented to Ernie and recalled that she was presented with a book called *Our Everest Adventure* by John Hunt, a book she treasured.

V South Shields

It is unclear, why in 1902 when Ernie Gompertz was fourteen, his family decided to move back to South Shields. With his elementary schooling over, perhaps his father Samuel felt that the time had come to move on from managing his Uncle Isaac's business interests and to start managing his own business affairs. Given Ernie had become a Bar Mitzvah on his thirteenth birthday, Samuel may have wanted to go into business with his own son. Ernie's grandfather Aaron Simon was by this time seventy-nine years old, so perhaps Samuel believed he should assert his claim to a stake over the family's pawnbroking interests, it may even simply be that he felt the family needed to be nearer Aaron Simon and Paulina as they faced the autumn of their years. Whatever reason lay behind the decision, the family moved to Tyneside and resided at 100 Dacre Street, a row of newly constructed houses near to the towns thriving and lively Laygate Lane.

The Tyneside trades directory records for this period demonstrate that the extended Gompertz family in South Shields had an array of pawnbroking shops across South Shields. Ernie's grandfather Aaron Simon had his shop at 22 Thrift Street in partnership with his brother Abraham; Ernie's Uncle Simpson had properties at 8–10 Bede Street in Tyne Dock and at 50 Mile End Road, whilst his father Samuel now had his own business at 135–137 Palmerston Street, with Ernie assisting his father.

On 15 April 1909, tragedy struck the Gompertz family when aged just 51 years old Ernie's father Samuel died, leaving in his will goods and effects to the value of £685 (around £82,000 today). His wife was the sole beneficiary of the probate. Samuel's share of the pawnbroking business he owned with his brother Abraham was to be given to Rebecca so that she could benefit from the future income. His will stipulated that upon the death of Rebecca (or her remarriage) his estate should be converted into money and divided equally amongst his children. A proviso was included that anyone marrying outside the Jewish faith during Rebecca's life would forfeit a right to an inheritance. Given Ernie would marry outside the faith in 1923, and his mother did not die until 1944, we must conclude he received no share of his father's inheritance. Abraham himself would eventually leave the pawnbroking business to become a schoolmaster.

By 1911 Ernie, his mother and the rest of the family had moved to 20 Dean Road, which still stands today albeit as a shop. The house would have been viewed as more upmarket than Dacre Street given its location near to Westoe Village on the outskirts of the town. Ernie's brother Gabriel had trained as an electrician whilst Ernie himself worked in the pawnbroking business as a manager in the family shop. Life was comfortable to the extent that Census records reveal they were able to afford a live-in domestic servant called Alice Mack.

The family of Catherine Cookson were frequent visitors to Simpson Gompertz's Bede Street Pawnbrokers shop at Tyne Dock. In her autobiography, *Our Kate*, she revealed how the desperately poor Tyneside working-class communities were required to pawn their meagre possessions in order to scrape a living. Cookson wrote about how she would look through the shop window and whilst inside examine the watches, jewellery, clothes and moleskin trousers allowing enough time for onlookers to believe she was seeking to buy something before asking for her mother – '*… can she have five shillings on these.*' Even so, she recalled of Simpson: '*He was a kind man Bob, an understanding man. I look back upon him with affection, for he must have realised how I felt about this business.*'

Writing for his local newspaper in 1996 when he retired, Isaac Hush's son (also called) Ernie, who had inherited the family's business in Middlesbrough upon the death of his father, recalled how all members of the family had instilled into them by Isaac the importance of upholding the dignity of their customers, with the philosophy – '*Having no money is no sin – wasting it is … no matter who they are or how hard up they are, they still have dignity. They may be reluctant to hand over their belongings, but they do it with dignity.*'

VI

Ernie's Grandfather, Aaron Simon maintained his business interests all of his life, but in his final years, involved himself in the work of the local Synagogue as well as the South Shields Burial Board. The Boards had been established as part of the Burial Act of 1857, they were responsible for the management of the local cemetery, fixing fees and charges and the sale of grave slots. Parish Vestries elected the Boards and Aaron Simon had sought and won appointment, presumably to represent the Jewish community since in 1899 the community had purchased a plot for a Jewish burial via the Board located within Harton Cemetery, before this, members of the local Congregation were buried in Preston, North Shields. The Local Government Act of 1894 transferred the Board's duties to local government and in November 1901 the South Shields Burial Board, with Aaron Simon in attendance, met for the final time.

In February 1912, just three years after the death of his son Samuel, Aaron Simon, who had sought a new life in England and had founded a family dynasty on Tyneside died at the age of eighty-two years old. He was buried in the new Jewish burial plot at Harton Cemetery where his imposing memorial still stands. He left behind his wife Paulina, an extended and growing family and an estate valued at £735. To Ernie he left his silver spice box and a silver cup, Rebecca, Ernie's mother, was left the sum of £30. All of Aaron Simon's extended family were suitably provided for, save only that any who married outside the Jewish faith would forfeit their right to any proceeds from his estate. Paulina continued to reside at 11 Burrow Street, an imposing side street of town houses not far from the new Edwardian Town Hall which had opened in 1910 and Paulina maintained the family's pawnbroking business interests until her own death on 18 March 1920.

Ernie's mother Rebecca is recorded by a number of genealogy sources as having died in Cuyahoga County, Ohio in 1937 at the age of seventy-two but this is not correct. Rebecca married her second husband Abraham Harris on 9 November 1927 in Knaresborough, North Yorkshire and moved to Kelvin in Glasgow. Abraham died on 12 March 1932 in Scotland and the Scottish Death Index records Rebecca dying in Possilpark, Glasgow in 1944 at the age of eighty-one.

In later life, Ernie's brother Gabriel would marry Cissie Goldman on 10 March 1920 in South Shields and had two daughters, Joyce Ruby (Joy) and Audrey Rose, he opened an electrical shop before eventually opening a tobacconist and confectionary shop at 201 Laygate Lane in 1939. He was also an active member of the Readhead Lodge of the South Shields Freemason Fraternity. He died on 4 May 1986 aged ninety-six years.

As for Ernie's other siblings, Rosetta (Rosa) married Maurice Fink on 3 March 1926 and settled on Teesside where they opened a pawnbroking business on the South Bank, Rose died in 1982 aged eighty-three years old.

Alexander became a doctor and married Edith Harris (nee Bloch) in 1929 when he was thirty-one, her first husband Montague Harris tragically died at the age of thirty-three. Alexander and Edith had twins Kenneth and Clare. Alexander passed away in Wembley, Middlesex in 1971, whilst Edith herself moved to Tennessee and died at the age of ninety-one in 1988.

Ernie was proud of his Jewish roots. A new Synagogue in Ogle Street, South Shields was opened in January 1933, with a ceremony described by the Shields Gazette as one of the oldest religious rituals in the world, attended by the borough's Mayor, the local MP Harcourt Johnstone, other civic leaders and over 220 guests. At a formal dinner in the Hedworth Hall later that evening, Ernie, by now a Councillor, having been elected in November 1932 for the Tyne Dock ward, gave a heart-warming address on the achievements of the local Jewish community from the time of Aaron Simon's arrival into the town, to their work in securing a permanent home for their fellowship, worship and learning. It had taken some effort to find a venue suitable for their purposes. The congregation had initially travelled to North Shields for religious services before meeting in members' homes, subsequently acquiring a hall in Palatine Street, from there to Mill Dam, then to Mount Street and finally to a converted house in Charlotte Street before securing their new base in Ogle Terrace.

Harcourt Johnstone who had been elected as the town's Liberal Unionist MP in the 1931 General Election landslide for the National Government commented at the ceremony: '*Members of the Corporation will recognise that in the Jewish community they have as fine a body of citizens as in any part of the Country. It is one of the most ordinary commonplaces to say that Jewish communities, wherever they are settled in this Kingdom, provide a body of citizens second to none in public spirit, in generosity and in ability.*'

The early influences of Ernie's family had instilled within him a capacity for hard work and an analytical mind but his experiences working in the pawnbroking business would also have exposed him to poverty and awakened a sense of injustice as to how society was structured. He could easily have settled into the family business working alongside his Uncle Simpson or his grandmother Paulina, but he began to devour Socialist textbooks, became a disciple of the early Labour pioneer Keir Hardie and started to question how society could be changed to be more humane, just and equal.

A week after his grandfather's death in February 1912, he took his tentative first steps into politics becoming the Assistant Secretary of the newly constituted South Shields Labour Party.

Chapter 2

The Struggle for Unity

I 'Always Ready'

'Although the appearance of South Shields has little to recommend it, and its buildings are far from imposing, yet it is a place of very great importance.'

Henry William Tancred, the Parliamentary Boundary Commissioner who under the provisions of the 1831 Great Reform Bill considered the possible boundaries for a new Parliamentary constituency on the south bank of the River Tyne may have held a negative view of the South Shields in-built environment nevertheless its growing industrial importance could not prevent it from having its own Parliamentary representation. As a result, the town, after much lobbying by Civic leaders and business interests, was to be one of nineteen new Parliamentary constituencies created under Lord John Russell's Bill which eventually received Royal Assent on 5 June 1832.

The town's location at the mouth of the Tyne made it highly significant not only to the regional but also the national economy. Shipowners had become anxious that neighbouring districts were achieving Parliamentary representation and wanted to ensure they had a representative watching exclusively over their own business interests. Robert Ingham, a Liberal, was elected as the town's first Member of Parliament in December 1832, albeit with a franchise no greater than 540. Such was the pride of having their own Parliamentary Member, that attempts under Disraeli's 1867 Franchise Bill to include neighbouring Jarrow into the new Constituency were strongly resisted by the town.

Municipally South Shields was granted a Charter of Incorporation as a Borough in September 1850, with the town's industrial base, as noted by George Hodgson in his history of the *Borough of South Shields*, being composed of four glassworks, fifteen ironworks, four chemical and soda manufacturers, four oil, paint and varnish factories, a pottery and soap factory, a colliery, three ballast wharves, six timber yards, fourteen straits and two public railways. The new Borough Council's coat of arms contained in the centre, the lifeboat, manned by South Shields pilots, representing humanity, a sailor representing courage and a figure representing commerce. After much discussion, the Council also settled on the motto *Always Ready* which Robert Ingham had suggested.

Under the terms of the new 1888 Local Government Act, South Shields became a County Borough on 1 April 1889. This gave the municipal authority sole responsibility for all public services within their boundary including education, police and fire services, although geographically part of the County of Durham, South Shields as a County Borough administered its own affairs separate and independent from Durham County Council.

The Victorian years would witness a time of rapid expansion in the town. From 45,336 residents in 1871 it would grow to 104,228 by 1911 and like so many other new urban centres, the Victorian entrepreneurs were desirous to construct and develop their local towns as a demonstration of the wealth of the area. The sheer scale of the development was staggering, the Mechanics' Institute (later to become the public library and museum) was opened in 1860; the Marine School was founded a year later in 1861; the Customs House was established in 1864; the North Marine Park was laid out in 1869; the Ingham Infirmary was established in 1873; the Mile End Road Railway Station was constructed in 1879. Further developments included the Groyne Pier in 1882, South Shields operated its own electric company by 1891; the new Court Buildings in Keppel Street were opened to the public in 1892; further parks such as West Park were laid out and opened to the public in 1894 followed by the South Pier's completion in 1895. As municipal life was granted more responsibilities for the administration of civic affairs, ambitious plans were unveiled to construct an impressive new Town Hall in Westoe Road – with an architectural design to rival any regional counterpart, the foundation stone being laid in 1905.

Industrially, by 1894 coal was king, with the Port of Tyne Dock exporting 5.6m tons of coal annually from the north-east coalfield, the largest volume in the world; Harton Coal Company had purchased St Hilda's, Boldon and Whitburn (sometimes referred to as Marsden) collieries. By 1914, the company employed over 8,500 men. Shipbuilding followed the same trajectory as elsewhere in Britain. Smaller yards were amalgamated, expanded or taken over into concerns of sufficient size during the 1850s to build the ocean-going marine fleets or to service niche seafaring industries, of small boat construction and repair. As the shipbuilding yards expanded, it necessitated the demolition of poorly constructed and unsanitary housing and auxiliary business along the river front, particularly at Templetown and Wapping Street.

The innovations and wealth of the South Shields Victorian entrepreneurs whilst impressive, could not mask the social and health inequality, the appalling poverty and slum housing that also existed under their watch particularly in areas like Holborn and Tyne Dock. As early as 1851 one-quarter of working-class households lived in poverty and two-thirds in overcrowded housing. The prevalence of high infant mortality rates and tuberculosis in South Shields was statistically unmatched nationally except in parts of London's East End. Matters had hardly improved by 1903, with the Medical Officer's Report noting that high typhoid rates in Laygate could be attributed to the uneven and unclean streets and the building of houses without concrete foundations or wooden floorboards. Overcrowding was chronic, the 1911 Census found that 63.1 per cent of the town's population lived in flats compared to just 2.9 per cent of the population of England and Wales as a whole.

Typical of other industrialised urban centres across the country, the owners of local industry also controlled – due to the restricted elective franchise and lack of effective working-class organisation – municipal affairs, through membership of the Town Council, as Poor Law Guardians and they also administered local justice as Magistrates. This political monopoly also gave them unrivalled influence in determining who would be the Member of Parliament. Business oligarchs, walking into the citadels of civic power with their top hats, walking canes and astrakhan collared coats could reinforce control of their workforce and their wider communities given the scale of their influence.

As the franchise was extended, although only incrementally and with strict property qualifications, the homogenous nature of politics would slowly begin to be shattered as the working class began to organise themselves against this behemoth.

II Early struggles

At a national level over the course of two days, 26 and 27 February 1900, a special conference was convened which brought together trade unions and left-wing Socialist societies to debate a motion submitted a year previously to the TUC from the Amalgamated Society of Railway Servants, which called for the creation of a single body that would sponsor Parliamentary candidates.

The conference, held at the Congregational Memorial Hall, Farringdon Street London, was principally a reaction to the lack of progress in securing the election of working-class representatives to both municipal authorities and Parliament. Despite the extension of the franchise in both 1867 and 1885, the growth of working-class representation was slow. Whilst 'Progressive' interests composed of Fabians and Liberals had won control of the new London County Council in an election in 1889 and West Ham had elected the first ever Labour Council in 1898, there had been no discernible advancement in Parliamentary elections. This lack of a united platform witnessed the main trade unions still being supportive of the Liberal Party, whilst the left-wing Independent Labour Party (ILP) formed in 1893 secured only 44,325 votes in the 1895 General Election in the 28 constituencies they contested.

After intense deliberations, the 129 assembly of delegates agreed a motion formally proposed by Keir Hardie to establish: '... *a distinct Labour group in Parliament, who shall have their own Whips and agree their policy, which must embrace in promoting legislation in the direct interest of labour'*. Thus, the Labour Representation Committee (LRC) was born. By the time of the 1906 General Election, the LRC had won twenty-nine Parliamentary seats, and at the first gathering of the newly created Parliamentary Party they agreed to adopt the name *The Labour Party* with Keir Hardie as their first Chairman, in effect Leader.

The failure of the Liberal Party to embrace more working-class men as potential Parliamentary candidates made the creation of a distinct Party for the working class unavoidable. Early pioneers like James Keir Hardie, Ramsay MacDonald and Arthur Henderson had initially sought Liberal support to enter Parliament and in his famous by-election victory at West Ham South in 1892, Hardie, standing as an Independent Labour candidate, with Liberal support, was careful to explain there was much in the Liberal Party's programme that he supported. The Liberal Party contained radical elements who were keen to expand the number of working-class MPs, albeit taking the Liberal Parliamentary whip, but found too many local Liberal associations reluctant to adopt men like Hardie and Henderson because of the potential drain on local association funds at a time when MPs were not remunerated. More crucially by the turn of the twentieth century, trade union leaders became increasingly concerned that their hard-fought established legal protections were being systematically undermined by judicial attacks, with the Taff Vale Judgement the most infamous. The Company achieved notoriety in Labour movement history since they had successfully taken the Amalgamated Society of Railway Servants to Court in 1901, which held that at Common Law, trade unions could be liable for the loss of profits to employers that were caused by unions taking strike action. The judgement at the time caused national outrage and not just within the trade union movement. If anything, along with the Bryant & May matchstick factory workers dispute, the Taff Vale Judgement gave impetus to the need to establish an independent political party for the working class. If unchecked, judicial decisions like Taff Vale threatened not only their funds, but also the very survival of Trade Unionism. Their call to unite the working class, and secure their own direct Parliamentary representation was born more from the trade unions' need to protect legislative advances already secured still less from any visionary Socialistic ones.

Early stalwarts in South Shields for several years previous, had been endeavouring to establish a distinct policy platform separate from the Liberal Party in the town, who had dominated Parliamentary elections since 1832. As early as November 1869 pioneers had established a **Labour Representation League** in South Shields, but its aim was to register and mobilise working-class voters on behalf of favoured Liberal candidates rather than the promotion of a separate working-class political party. Politically, South Shields had one of the earliest Trades Councils, which was formed in 1872, and it was through this body that working-class sentiment initially expressed itself. It took another twenty years before the Trades Council in 1891 began to consider seriously how to secure independent representation locally and at a constituency level.

There were three main opportunities to secure working-class representation, the Town Council, the Schools Board and the Board of Guardians, responsible for poor relief. At their December 1891 meeting the Trades Council chose the January 1892 Schools Board for their first contest. They were successful with their Secretary, GT Scott winning a seat on the Board. We should not read too much into this success, Scott, whilst an active Trade Unionist was also immersed in Liberal Association politics. Candidates for public office at this time did not officially represent any political party, suffice that the candidates described themselves by their profession, he probably owed his election more to his Liberal connections, than Trades Council support.

Between 1880 and 1900 agitation also intensified amongst key activists within Trade Union and Socialist societies across the town as to how they could seize the Parliamentary seat for working-class interests. Some wanted to form a branch of the Independent Labour Party (ILP), an avowed Socialist organisation who wanted to field truly independent 'Labour' candidates, whilst others – particularly reactionary trade union branches like the St Hilda's Miners' Lodge – believed that the long established alliance with the Liberal Party should hold and they should perhaps consider a Lib–Lab arrangement which had seen working men like Thomas Burt elected in Morpeth in 1874, followed by William Crawford in Mid Durham and John Wilson in Houghton-le-Spring in 1885.

The establishment of a Fabian Society Branch in South Shields in March 1892, whose national policy was to support the creation of Independent Labour Party branches (ILP) across the country, gave much intellectual credence and drive to the formation of a South Shields ILP branch. The Fabians were extremely well organised, holding open-air meetings in the Market Place every Thursday evening during the 1892 summer months – their inaugural meeting however agreed to formally support the town's Liberal MP, JC Stevenson, at the next General Election. Notwithstanding that, the local Fabians' main aim was to see an ILP branch formed in the town which would coordinate the selection and election of working-class men to public office. The efforts of the local Fabians were rewarded since just a few months later on 31 August 1892 proponents met at Brown's Cocoa Rooms, Church Way (now the site of the National Centre for the Written Word) and established a local Branch of the ILP. The *Gazette* advised that there were a large number in attendance and within days the new independent Party had attracted over 4,000 people to an open-air meeting in the Market Place.

One of the key figures in the formation of the ILP Branch was Charles Henry Reynolds, who had moved to the town from Hull. A plasterer by trade, he had an ebullient personality and was an active correspondent to the *Shields Gazette* agitating for the formation of a new political body to challenge Liberal interests. Reynolds was initially the correspondence Secretary of the local ILP branch before becoming its President a year later. Along with other political agitators, Reynolds was the catalyst for much political activity during the 1880/90s. The establishment of an ILP branch in the town did not though lead to the unification of competing left-wing interests in agreeing either a policy platform or single 'Labour' candidates at municipal elections, still less an agreement as to whether to contest the Parliamentary seat.

Reynolds maintained the vision of a separate political Party, not one beholden to the Liberals and was fearless in his exposition of his Socialist beliefs and prodigious in promoting them. Aside from his regular correspondence to the *Shields Gazette* (with one critical correspondent describing him as the 'High Priest of the ILP'), in September 1893 he had helped form a South Shields Debating Society, with the aim of raising issues of local importance, the first meeting being held at the Brown's Cocoa Rooms on 28 September 1893. Reynolds stood unsuccessfully in Tyne Dock in the November 1894 municipal elections for the ILP, but in January 1895 he secured direct election to the South Shields School Board where the *Shields Gazette* observed that he would '*Introduce Socialism in his representation.*' Later that month he addressed a public meeting at the Mill Dam in support of unemployed seamen. He encouraged the ILP and the Trades Council to work together to form a Relief Committee to raise money to feed the children of the unemployed and addressed a further mass meeting in the Market Place demanding that the Mayor call a town meeting to discuss the plight of the unemployed in the Borough. In July 1895, despite much aggravation from the audience, he steadfastly sought to publicly hold to account William Robson, the Liberal Parliamentary candidate for the 1895 General Election at one of his public meetings, and in the November 1895 municipal elections he unsuccessfully contested the Laygate ward again for the ILP, although the Trades Council refused to endorse him, despite securing the support of his own the Plasterers Trade Union.

If evidence is required though of the difficulties in achieving local working-class representation, one only needs to review the antics of those opposed to Labour interests in maintaining their hold on civic power. Reynolds' election to the Schools Board had not been well received by the local establishment. Elections to the Board were always hotly contested, with candidates identifying themselves to the electorate as Church, Catholic or Unsectarian. Amongst the vicars, curates, solicitors, gentlemen and land agents seeking office, stood Charles Henry Reynolds as an avowed 'Socialist' and in the town-wide poll in January 1895 he was elected with 4,524 votes. In August 1896 Reynolds stood down from the Schools Board for reasons not recorded. Constitutionally, vacancies were not resolved by a Borough-wide by-election but rather the remaining Board members nominated a replacement until the next scheduled elections. Custom dictated that the replacement should be of '*the same class of representation as his predecessor*'. The local Trades Council, the ILP and the local Secular Society in good faith wrote to the Board to advise that Matthew Taylor, the Secretary of the Stonemasons' Society was their preferred nominee. The Schools Board ignored the correspondence and appointed Robert Reay who had lost his place in the January 1895 election, thus breaking their own long-held custom and practice and imposing one of their own standing.

III The Labour Electoral Association (LEA)

At the Trades Union Congress conference in 1885 calls were made for the establishment of funds to support Trade Union candidates to contest Parliamentary seats, and in 1886 Thomas Threlfall proposed the creation of a **Labour Electoral Association** (LEA) which would be linked to local Trades Councils. Marginally successful with the creation of a number of LEAs in key constituencies, its influence was hampered by disagreements as to whether they should enter agreements with the Liberal Party, contest municipal elections and what their overall policy platform should be. Threlfall himself favoured Lib–Lab candidates with the result that those Trades Councils with Socialist majorities would simply refuse to work with the LEA favouring to support an independent Labour challenge in their district.

As a political force, the ILP was never an electoral success either locally or nationally and in terms of membership it peaked at 10,000 across the country. Its distinctive avowedly left-wing Socialist agenda never really sat comfortably with Trades Councils, which tended to be dominated by pro-Liberal trade union delegates. The new South Shields ILP branch struggled to maintain the momentum for its agenda and there were clearly the usual clashes and disagreements over tactics with the local press quoting Reynolds following a meeting of the Trades Council in April 1894 as saying: '... *As to the ILP in South Shields it was dead as far as he was concerned in South Shields*'. In October 1895 the new nationally promoted LEA endeavoured to organise in the mid-Tyne Jarrow Constituency (only two members of the public attended, but the Branch was still formed), their regional Organiser observing that they had '*Stamped out the ILP in South Shields*'. Whatever lay behind both statements, the ILP in South Shields was certainly not finished as a political force, along with the Fabians it was giving serious thought to how to break the Liberal Party stranglehold on the town. The neighbouring Constituency of Jarrow was achieving greater success, they had already fielded James Johnston under the *Jarrow Radical and Labour Representation League* in 1885, and Jarrow would eventually become one of the first Constituencies in the country to successfully elect an MP under the new Labour Representation Committee banner, albeit briefly, at a 1907 by-election with Peter Curran.

Matters came to a head for Reynolds in early 1894 when the South Shields Liberal MP, James Cochran Stevenson announced he would be retiring at the next general election. Stevenson had been the MP since 1868, an industrialist, former Mayor of South Shields and one-time owner of the *Shields Gazette*, his daughter Hilda Runciman would eventually become an MP in her own right for St Ives in Cornwall. ILP members, with Reynolds as a driving force, clearly felt there should be an Independent Labour challenge.

Critical to the strategy was securing the support of the Trades Council who had access to much-needed finance for election purposes. By April 1894 there was criticism in the local press that the Trades Council had been infiltrated and taken over by key members of the ILP. *Shields Gazette* correspondents were complaining that the Trades Council headquarters was now only a base for the ILP to operate from. Reynolds who had become the Trades Council Financial Secretary successfully argued for resources to be allocated for a 'propaganda fund' to promote radical ideas in the town. It was too much for some Union Branches, notably the Harton Miners who resigned from the Trades Council. There were claims that the infiltration into the Trades Council by left-wing ILP members had resulted in the Trades Council losing credibly with the local Unions to the extent that they now spoke for only 12,000 affiliated Union members when previously they had spoken for 16,000. But the ILP did have their supporters, a resolution from the Tyne Dock Railway Servants branch demanded that no Trades Council Officer should be an Officer of any political party, following an intense debate which eventually agreed the motion, the Trades Councils long-standing Secretary, G Storey, who was also Secretary of the South Shields Liberal Association, promptly resigned and walked out.

With Storey gone, the ILP members sought to encourage the Trades Council to determine its response to Stevenson's retirement. Should they negotiate with the Liberals and other Radical elements and argue for a working-class representative under the so-called Lib–Lab arrangements or should they stand an independent Labour candidate in their own right?

The Lib–Lab route had its attractions. At its height, over twenty working class men had been elected under this arrangement. Reynolds though was opposed to negotiation with the Liberals, he wanted a truly Independent Labour candidate, but he needed Trade Union Branches' support to help fund a candidate.

As these events unfolded, a Parliamentary by-election was taking place in the Liberal seat of Sheffield Attercliffe in July 1894. The by-election caused a storm nationally because the ILP stood Frank Smith as their candidate, it was the first Parliamentary election contested by the ILP and there was a real danger that the anti-Conservative vote would be split. The 5 July by-election result was, however, a disaster for the ILP, the Liberals not only held the seat, but also, Frank Smith came third with only 13.5 per cent of the vote. Reynolds encouraged the Trades Council to write to Smith to invite him to be their candidate at the next general election. Records do not indicate whether Smith replied.

Reynolds though would be disappointed with the man who eventually emerged as a potential candidate.

IV

Thomas Threlfall, a member of Southport Town Council, President of the Southport Trades Council and the President of the TUC had encouraged the creation of Labour Electoral Associations which had gone on to support Keir Hardie's independent candidacy in the 1888 Mid Lanarkshire by-election. Threlfall eventually became the LEA national organiser and set his sights on being a Lib–Lab candidate for South Shields.

The local Liberals, together with their municipal partners, the Radical Party were having no truck with the notion of a Lib–Lab candidate. Their calculated response was to establish their own forum, the **South Shields Parliamentary Electoral Association (PEA)** whose principal aim was the keep South Shields for the Liberals and they brought together, what they believed, were the key stakeholders across the centre left political divide, Liberals, Radicals and representatives of working men. The PEA's first tactic was to urge Stevenson to rescind his decision to resign from Parliament at the next election, the Trades Council had made publicly clear that if Stevenson was the candidate, they would continue to support him.

Stevenson was adamant, he was resigning.

The PEA then approached a local man, Roland Philipson JP of Cauldwell to consider standing, Philipson declined. Their attentions finally turned to William Snowdon Robson QC, a former MP for Bow and Bromley in London who had caught the attention of the Liberal Party's national high command and who without question would have introduced him to the PEA as a potential candidate for South Shields.

Threlfall on the other hand had the critical support of the MP for Middlesbrough, Havelock Wilson (who was also the President of the Seamen's Union which boasted a membership of over 2,000 in South Shields) and encouraged Threlfall to submit his name to the PEA. The PEA, Secretary, W Osborne politely acknowledged Threlfall's interest. A selection conference was convened on 2 July 1894 at which Robson was invited, Threlfall was not, and the meeting 'unanimously' chose WS Robson QC, as the candidate to face the Conservatives at the next election. Threlfall and his supporters were outraged, believing the process had been deliberately 'rushed' for Robson. Threlfall in correspondence to Osborne on 4 July thundered that the Labour cause was too advanced '... *to allow of the working classes of South Shields or anywhere else having a barrister or anyone else being foisted on them by sharp tactics'.*

Further,

> *Allow me to state, on behalf of this Association (the LEA, author's insertion) that as Mr Robson's mandate to speak either directly or indirectly, on behalf of the Labour Party is in no sense admitted and as we are assured that no effective means have been taken to secure the opinion of local Labour parties as to the question of a Labour candidate, this Association will at once take all steps with a view to bring out a Labour candidate at the next general election for South Shields.*
>
> *I remain, yours very truly,*
> *T. R. Threlfall*

Havelock Wilson, who had defeated Robson at the 1892 General Election in Middlesbrough, was determined to use his influence to have Threlfall elected as the MP for South Shields. To demonstrate their strength, Labour leaders organised a mass meeting for Sunday 15 July 1894 – much to the chagrin of the *Shields Gazette* who complained at having to dispatch a journalist to the rally on a Sunday evening. The open-air meeting was held in the Market Place, Cllr Joe Abbott chaired the event at which Havelock Wilson and Thomas Threlfall addressed a large audience. Threlfall was clear, '... *an industrial centre like South Shields ought to be represented by a man who was conversant with the needs of the working classes.*'

South Shields did have a solid working-class base centred around the shipyards and its coal mines, but it also had a large middle-class demographic, in fact coal miners made up only 15 per cent of the burgess register. Wilson acknowledged that Robson was a Radical, and that he would be a worthy

Member of Parliament for the Borough, but Wilson wanted an open and transparent joint selection conference of Liberal, Trades Union and Labour interests to choose a Parliamentary candidate, and he wanted a Labour man to have fair consideration at such a conference. Failure to hold such a joint selection conference, would open the real possibility that the anti-Conservative vote in the town might be split at the 1895 General Election. Wilson didn't want to see this happen and told his audience that he had rejected the ILP's demands to ignore the Liberals and field an Independent candidate, he announced that a new local Labour Electoral Association Branch would be formed that evening in the Seamen's Hall. The Association would work with the Liberals and other radicals to keep South Shields free of the Conservatives, but they would first need to convene a fair open Parliamentary selection conference.

The months leading up to the July 1895 General Election saw frantic activity from both Threlfall and Robson supporters. Threlfall was anxious to have a special conference convened to consider both his and Robson's suitability to working-class electors, whilst Robson was desirous to prevent a split in the anti-Tory vote at the next election. Rival camps held mass meetings across the town during the summer months; at Tyne Dock, Threlfall was heckled that his behaviour would allow the Tories to win the seat, he had to deny he was standing as a representative of the ILP. At a rally in the Market Place on 2 August the President of the Cleveland Miners' Association supported Threlfall's claim for the seat. Rallies for both candidates were held on street corners as well as theatres, schools and memorial halls, the conclusion of which was always followed by a show of hands to indicate support for the guest speaker.

With neither Threlfall nor Robson preparing to back down, the Trades Council wrote to their Trade Union Branches and affiliates asking who they thought they should endorse at the next election. In response, the Coopers, Coal Ports, Glassmakers, Railway Servants, the Seamen's Union and the Marsden Miners all wanted to support Threlfall, but there was no response from ten affiliated Societies, including the Shipwrights', Plasterers', Tailors' or Plumbers' unions. Further, the Marsden Miners whilst endorsing Threlfall, urged the Trades Council to adopt a neutral position and proposed: '*That in the opinion of this Council, the question of Labour representation should be discussed at the Labour Electoral Association and not at this Council.*' In time-honoured Labour movement tradition, the Trades Council eventually decided to allow the motion to 'lie on the table' for a fortnight for further consideration – in effect making no decision.

Key South Shields ILP members like Charles Reynolds refused to endorse Threlfall because he was seeking to stand with the support of the Liberal Party and was not in their view truly 'independent'. After a 15 July 1894 rally in the Market Place, Reynolds' wife Margaret, wrote to the *Shields Gazette* quite indignant that they had suggested her husband had attended the rally in support of Threlfall and was distributing Labour Electoral Association pamphlets: She also was clear that her husband did not speak for Threlfall: *'Also I again most emphatically deny that my husband was on the steps in the Market Place on Sunday night.'* The local ILP Branch was also being encouraged by ILP's *Labour Leader* newspaper to maintain the fight for an independent working-class MP. The newspaper was of the view that the Liberals should *'… clear out of the way and let a good Labour man fight.'* The *Labour Leader* though did not support Threlfall, in one article dated 15 September 1894, they described Threlfall as the *'… wire-pulling liberal-radical-labour-socialist independent candidate'* and a *'Liberal-Labour poseur'*.

Fervent activity followed which became more heated as the months wore on, Robson accused Threlfall supporters of alleging he was Counsel to the North Eastern Railway Company with a remit to stop a rival Railway Company running a line to South Shields; Threlfall's supporters attacked Robson for suggesting Threlfall wasn't really a worker at all – given he was employed by the LEA, and that as the Secretary of the National LEA he had solicited financial donations from employers. At one pro-Threlfall Rally a member of the audience mounted the platform and demanded *'Three Cheers for Robson!'* before being dragged from the podium.

The whole saga was long drawn out and divisive and the Conservatives with their new candidate Henry Herbert Wainwright began scenting blood, although at one Conservative-organised rally in Tyne Dock, the audience, when asked if they endorsed Wainwright's candidacy cried out, *'No'*, to which the Platform Chair called the vote in favour of Wainwright and promptly exited the platform with his embarrassed candidate.

V

When Conservative Prime Minister the Marquess of Salisbury eventually called a July 1895 General Election, it was clear that the resolve of the South Shields Liberals and Radicals remained firm, and they would not convene a selection conference to resolve the issue of a Parliamentary candidate, Threlfall would either have to stand or withdraw, he accepted the evitable, he could not win in a three-cornered contest. The LEA held a 2,000 strong Market Place Rally on 4 July 1895 to explain why Threlfall had decided not to contest the General Election. The Chair, and ILP supporting Councillor, John Lisle explained that the LEA policy was to do nothing that benefitted the 'reactionary Party' (i.e. the Conservatives) and in a three-cornered fight there was no guarantee of securing the election of an independent Labour man. Joe Abbott, another ILP member, explained that they had to concede that Robson had demonstrated greater support than Threlfall by virtue of the sheer numbers of working-class people who had attended his regular rallies and therefore the local LEA would not risk handing the seat to the Conservatives. At the same time as the LEA were backing down in their Market Place rally, Robson was holding another enthusiastic rally opposite the Holy Trinity Church in High Shields.

With the defenestration of Threlfall, Robson won the July 1895 General Election contest in a straight contest with the Conservative Henry Herbert Wainwright, albeit by a majority of only 133 votes. It was the closest the Conservatives had ever come to winning the Parliamentary seat and demonstrates the negative effect the in-fighting between Threlfall and Robson had on the electorate. The LEA to their credit, staunchly supported Robson's campaign to prevent a Conservative victory, and to his credit once elected Robson worked hard to build bridges and develop a formidable political base in the town. He was never to experience again the bitter acrimony that overshadowed his introduction to the town. Robson was born and raised in the North East and had strong connections with the Tyneside conurbation. He amassed a strong following amongst Trade Unions, evidenced by the Marsden Miners' Lodge painting his portrait onto their new Lodge banner in 1900, and he took a keen interest in furthering industrial and educational legislation through the House of Commons.

In days before mass media when candidates relied upon open air meetings to promote themselves, Robson was noted for his oratorical skills on the public platform and he would frequently address crowds in the Assembly Rooms in Ocean Road, local theatres, union halls and in the solidly working-class district of Tyne Dock where he would speak to thousands of townsfolk. He was a diligent local Member of Parliament, and two of his notable local achievements included the removal of tolls on the town's pier and successfully lobbying for the right of townsfolk to fish for salmon within the limits of the mouth of the Tyne.

Threlfall had clearly been the victim of superior Machiavellian tactics amongst the established Liberal and Radical elite determined not to have a

Lib–Lab MP for the Town and they had finagled to ensure Robson was the nominee. Whether Threlfall would have won a special conference called to select the Parliamentary candidate is a matter of conjecture; given the support the Liberals still had amongst key working-class organisations like certain Miners' Lodges it was probably unlikely. He eventually became a Magistrate in his native Southport and took up a literary career. The Labour Electoral Association nationally was formally wound up in 1896.

There was the predictable backlash against Reynolds and his ILP supporters. They were removed from positions within the Trades Council, who made a point of actively supporting rival candidates to the ILP at municipal election time, even though the Trades Council always maintained that they were non-Party political.

Robson would always feel that his hold on South Shields was tenuous. Writing to his wife in October 1896 he noted that a trades body had advised Miners' Lodges that their members should only vote for Labour candidates at election times, Robson's full-time Parliamentary Agent, Russell Bransby, confidentially reassured his boss that there wouldn't be a single miner who would vote against him.

Bransby worked hard in the Liberal interests in South Shields, enabling Robson to forge a Parliamentary career in London. It was Bransby who developed Liberal Clubs in key districts, brought keynote speakers to the town to argue against independent Labour representation and helped fight a rear-guard action in the Trades Council to ensure their links with the Liberal Party were not easily relinquished.

Despite all Bransby's undoubted organisational skill, and Robson's growing popularity, the local MP accepted that the tide was slowly turning against Liberalism, not only in the town but also in the North East. In the same October 1896 letter to his wife, he wrote:

'Bransby also says that in his calls everybody has borne testimony to my popularity with all classes. That is my sheet anchor. Liberalism apart from the claims or personality of a Liberal candidate seems to have a very thin thread of life here.'

For now, the Liberals and their Radical Association partners had seen off attempts to dislodge them from the Parliamentary seat, they were determined to maintain their hold on civic affairs.

Chapter 3

Growing Pains

I Municipal challenges

Whilst the early ILP pioneers considered challenging for Parliamentary success, they were also determined to secure working-class representation on South Shields Town Council and other elected bodies like the Board of Guardians and the Schools Board. The process was frustratingly slow, with agreement on tactics falling foul of repeated personality clashes and failure to agree a common platform. The malevolent attitude of the Trades Council did not help matters but given the Liberal dominance in their ranks it was hardly surprising.

Before the 1895 General Election debacle a small group of ILP pioneers had been successfully elected to South Shields Council with the riverside working-class wards being their main battle grounds. John Lisle secured a seat in the Laygate ward in 1892, followed in 1893 by seaman Joe Abbott at Tyne Dock. Marsden miner John Thompson and Jack Cullen were elected in the Laygate Ward, in 1894. In addition to this, as we have noted, Charles Reynolds had been elected – as a Socialist – to the Schools Board, and Joe Batey, a St Hilda's Miners Official was elected to the Board of Guardians.

Building on their modest achievements though would prove laborious.

For John Lisle, regarded as a Labour standard bearer as he is acknowledged as the first working-class representative on the Council, 1895 would prove to be a tumultuous year. A tailor by trade he had been elected Secretary of the Trades Council following the resignation of the Liberal supporting G Storey earlier in the year. Lisle was aligned to the ILP grouping but following his decision to become a publican, Joe Abbott and Charles Reynolds demanded his resignation at the September 1895 Trades Council meeting held in the Seamen's Union Offices in North Shields. There was a mood amongst delegates that because of his new profession, he had ruled himself out of holding a Trades Council Officers position. Lisle argued his Union still supported his position, but a Seamen's Union delegate queried whether

Lisle, as a publican, would be able to – '... *act, and devote the same amount of attention to his duties as he would when connected with his own trade?*' Lisle was asked to resign.

The following meeting of the Trades Council was even more acrimonious. Lisle was due for re-election in his Laygate ward seat in November and was keen to ensure a clear run for himself. The ILP grouping wanted Reynolds to stand alongside Lisle in the two-member election. A furious row ensured which the *Shields Gazette* reported was '... *of a very personal character*', elements within the Trades Council, furious at Reynolds and his colleagues for conspiring against Lisle began manoeuvring against Reynolds and suggested they should support Trades Council-nominated candidates in the Laygate ward, potentially pitting candidates against the ILP. Joe Abbott moved that the Trades Council should stay out of the contest and allow the ILP a free run but his motion was defeated. In a further rebuff to the ILP, the Trades Council agreed that Lisle should stay as their secretary, but only until the end of the official year.

In the fervent political atmosphere of the time and the fact that there was no overarching political body maintaining discipline, the debate was conducted in an emotionally charged environment, the Trades Council agreed to support John Lisle's re-election campaign in the Laygate ward but steadfastly refused to support Reynolds as the second candidate. The dynamics resulted in a re-charged Radical Association, already emboldened by the election of their candidate William Robson as the town's MP, romping home in Laygate in the November Council election, in a ward which had proven in the past to be Labour's best chance of winning Council seats. Lisle came third and Reynolds a distant fourth.

Lisle was never to seek public office again. Reynolds was clearly disheartened, his correspondence to the *Shields Gazette* in 1896 became sporadic, as already outlined earlier, he resigned from the Schools Board in August 1896 and before the turn of the century had moved with his wife to Whitley Bay to open a boarding house, although he maintained a lifelong devotion to the Labour movement, the ILP's newspaper the *Labour Leader* references donations from him for election purposes as late as 1914.

The removal of Lisle and Reynolds allowed the more urbane and imperturbable Joe Abbott to become the Secretary of the Trades Council and his 1896 appointment witnessed the local union branches and lodges which had previously disaffiliated from the Trades Council slowly drifting back into the fold. Abbott was a friend of the fiery trade union orator Tom Mann who was regarded as one of the most successful union organisers of his generation. Mann was a regular visitor to South Shields and addressed crowds in the Market Place mostly notably in June 1894 when over 4,000 people listened to his address on '*Labour Representation*' at the height of the campaign to have Threlfall as the Parliamentary candidate. Abbott also became, in early 1897 a full-time Regional Union organiser for the International Federation of Sea, River, Dock and Railway Workers which demonstrates the high regard held for Abbott's administrative and organisational ability.

Endeavouring to assert itself amongst working-class voters, the Trades Council held regular public meetings in the Market Place, but it did not lead to any resurgence of municipal campaigning, the 1896 November Council election only saw a token effort made to stand Labour candidates in South Shields, and only in those seats which were proving to be fertile ground for the Labour cause and regarded by the *Shields Gazette* as 'Workingmen's wards'. Abbott, described by the *Gazette* as '… *an admirable representative of the ward and almost an ideal councillor*' topped the poll in Tyne Dock retaining a seat he first won in 1893, whilst the St Hilda's Miners Leader, Joe Batey, won in the Laygate ward in a seat previously held by John Thompson the Marsden Miners' Lodge Secretary who did not seek re-election. Batey had received the formal support of the local Liberal and Radical Association for his candidature and the canvassing support of the St Hilda's miners. In the days of multi-member elections, David Clements also stood in Laygate as a Trades Council Labour candidate on a joint ticket with Batey but was not elected. None of the candidates stood as ILP candidates, although the South Shields ILP at their meeting on 28 October 1896 agreed to formally support the Trades Council endorsed candidates. It is also worth noting that the Trades Council was also maintaining a watchful brief on the work of the Board of Guardians and had earlier secured the election of another of their stalwarts Joe Wake in a by-election at Tyne Dock in October.

The 1896 campaigning was very much focused on parochial community issues. Abbott for example called for a bridge to be constructed from the Deans Hospital to Stanhope Road which would allow his constituents to have safe access to the West Park, he also wanted more allotments, and a slum clearance programme. His political opponent Dr Gibbon believed that Tyne Dock had not achieved its fair share of council funding and wanted a lending library opened and improvements to the road infrastructure. Meanwhile in the Laygate ward, Batey was to lead on a campaign theme which would dominate municipal politics for some time, whether the Council should refuse to renew the lease to a private company or take over the running of the tramways themselves, similar to Birmingham and Glasgow, with any profit helping to keep the rates low rather than going to shareholders.

Another issue dominating municipal life was where a new town hall should be built. As South Shields grew and the local Corporation was assuming more responsibility for public services, it was becoming impossible to conduct civic affairs from the small Town Hall in the Market Place. Land had been purchased by the Corporation in Ogle Terrace to build a new town hall, but some opponents were questioning why the new town hall could not be built in Waterloo Vale in the heart of the town centre. The suggestion was eventually rejected, and the Corporation pressed on with the design and construction of the new building on Westoe Road. The idea of Waterloo Vale as an appropriate location for the new civic building was not as ludicrous as we may assume today. It should be remembered that at the time the Police and Magistrates' Courts, central Post Office, Fire Station, the School Board, the Board of Guardians and other imposing Victorian civic buildings were in close proximity together around the Keppel Street area, King Street was itself only just beginning to emerge as the town's main retail outlet. Opponents of the Westoe Road site genuinely felt it would mean a disconnect between the Borough Council and the rest of the central town amenities.

The November 1897 municipal elections would be contested under new ward boundaries which created three councillors per ward but with a third being due for election at any one time. The boundary review, whilst generally welcomed because it equalised the numbers of electors in each ward, required the Council to allocate existing councillors into the new wards until they were due for re-election. Hence the Labour representatives saw themselves shunted out of their seats into new areas, Abbott was moved to the new Rekendyke ward, Cullen retained Laygate but was required to face the electorate in that year's election, and Batey was displaced from the solid Laygate area to the more marginal Westoe ward.

The intransigence and punctilious nature of the Trades Council towards the ILP were again on display before the 1897 Council elections. Four working-class men had sought election to South Shields Council, a former councillor, John Thompson, was seeking election in Westoe, Joseph Wake of the Harton Miners' Lodge in the Deans Ward, and Matthew Taylor a stonemason seeking to win Rekendyke, whilst Joe Cullen as we have seen was required to seek re-election in the Laygate ward. The Trades Council were content to endorse Thompson, Wake and Cullen but were adamant they would not endorse Taylor, who was an ILPer and had received the South Shields ILP branch's public endorsement. The Trades Council maintained they would not support any political Party's nominee.

Their stance may seem hash, obdurate and difficult to appreciate today, after all the Trades Council was primarily a working-class organisation, it was the body which brought working-class interests together and articulated their aspirations, and it was natural for them to support working-class candidates for public office. The difficulty for the Trades Council stems back once again to the 1895 General Election fiasco. Deliberating as to whether to support the Liberal Party's Robson or support a working-class candidate had cost the Trades Council heavily. Their secretary at the time walked out, Liberal supporting Union branches and Lodges disaffiliated, their delegate numbers waned over perceived undue influence from left-wing ILP members within the Trades Council and Trade Union branches cut their financial subscriptions which, if not checked, would have placed the very viability of the Trades Council in jeopardy. They simply were not prepared to take the risk at local election time. The public endorsement of the Trades Council wasn't even mandatory for aspiring public servants, they didn't give financial support to an individual's election campaign and neither did they deliver a solid block vote at the ballot box despite their claims of representing over 16,000 Trade Unionists, but endorsement *was* important because it did give the candidate an air of respectability to the electorate in an era when there was genuine suspicion about supporting working-class representation to public bodies.

Cullen was alone in being re-elected in the solidly working-class district of Laygate although his colleague Thompson did poll a respectable 420 votes (as opposed to the victors' 538) in the Westoe ward.

As a result of the 1897 municipal ward boundary review, the Council now had forty members, thirty elected Councillors and ten appointed Aldermen. The fact that those who sought to represent Labour interests were still in single figures in the Chamber, was clearly of concern. Previous attempts to coalesce around agreed candidates under various forums were proving ineffective, in 1894 Abbott himself had led attempts to have a united slate of candidates for that year's Board of Guardians elections, without success.

The townsfolk though were concerning themselves with more than the fratricide behaviour of the Labour activists. Trouble was brewing in South Africa, whilst a little nearer home debates were ranging over the municipalisation of Council services. The Council was divided over whether to take over the operation of the tramways or extend the contract of the private operator, there was also much grievance as to the time it was taking to deliver electric street lighting to areas further away from the town centre and there was a debate about whether to monopolise the local gas company. The Trades Council agreed to establish an **Electoral Defence Fund** in readiness for the 1898 municipal elections, but the three candidates they supported, Wake in Tyne Dock, Tonge in Deans and Taylor in Laygate were soundly defeated. Meanwhile, in further evidence of the lack of discipline and failure to agreed election tactics, Joe Batey and Joe Abbott both backed rival candidates for the St Hilda ward.

II Municipal Labour League

By April 1899 it was the turn of the appropriately named **Municipal Labour League** established under the auspices of the Trades Council to try and bring the various competing working-class interests together. Abbott and Batey both had a vested interest in ensuring there was some resemblance of discipline in the ranks, as they were both facing the electorate in November, Abbott in Rekendyke whilst Batey would choose to contest the more favourable Laygate ward.

As part of their campaign, the Trades Council's attention turned to the directly elected South Shields Board of Guardians who had their own impressive offices in the Guardians Hall building in Barrington Street. Two leading members of Trades Unions now served on the Board, Joe Batey and Joseph Wake, and at the March meeting of the Board they endeavoured to have a fair wage clause initiative implemented. The Board, led by the elderly reactionary Alderman Bowman was having none of it, describing the principle of a fair wage clause as 'scandalous'. The same meeting considered arguments from Batey and Wake to increase the amount paid for outdoor relief. Again, Ald Bowman was apoplectic, he was supported by Ald Armstrong who insinuated that working-class people did not pay rates, and so they were quite disposed to having others paying for increased welfare. Ald Browell opposed any uniform increase, on the grounds that Committee members considered each case on its merits and had sufficient power already to increase any allowance to 3s if deserved. The Board voted 20–9 not to increase outdoor relief.

A few months later at their November meeting, the Board of Guardians having rejected any increase in support of the neediest in the town earlier in the year, in a ceremony which could have come straight from the pages of *The Ragged-Trousered Philanthropists*, presented the Assistant Clerk to the Board with a purse of gold on the occasion of his marriage, together with a silver-mounted Malacca walking stick. The Chairman of the Board spoke of the Clerks '… *excellent character and capabilities*' and that the whole Board '… *could bear testimony to his thoroughly sterling character.*'

The Municipal Labour League continued its campaigning up until the 1899 November elections, but the Labour activists were simply not gaining traction with the electorate, a major rally organised by the League in September attracted only a moderate attendance according to the *Shields Gazette*, with organisers expressing disappointment at the turnout. The election was a disaster for the Labour pioneers, their two leading lights, Joe Batey and Joe Abbott were ousted, Batey by only three votes in Laygate, Abbott's six years' service ended in Rekendyke by over 300 votes, William Tonge who was also supported by the League lost out heavily in the Deans Ward. Their one saving grace was the surprise election of Miner John Thompson in Westoe, returning to the Council in a seat he had diligently nurtured for several years. Following the elections, the enthusiasm of Joe Abbott, who by this time had opened his own shop as a tobacconist (he would eventually also become a pub landlord) seems to have diminished. He did not seek public office again, but he did attend a public meeting (along with John Cullen) on 18 October 1899 at the Royal Assembly Hall in the town, in support of Robson's candidature for the expected 1900 General Election.

The failure by Labour interests to make any significant breakthrough – or even to retain the advances they had already made – can be attributed to many factors. Firstly, the town's new MP, William Robson was proving to be an extremely diligent campaigner as well as a respected Parliamentarian, we have already seen how he employed an experienced full-time Agent in the Constituency, Russell S Bransby (who was eventually the Secretary of the Belgium Refugees Committee and died suddenly in 1917) and the reinvigorated Liberals were selling shares in their Ocean Road Club to improve the building and refurbish the interior, their municipal Radical Association allies had their own formal base in King Street.

Secondly, the country was at war with the South African Republics, the Boer War had commenced in October 1899 and would last until May 1902. A considerable number of men from the town signed up as volunteers and were accepted for army service. The conduct of the War was followed keenly across the country, no less so than in South Shields, with the relief of Mafeking provoking street parties and the Freedom of the Borough being conferred in May 1900 upon 107 local men who had fought in the War. Within this patriotic environment we have the Fabian Society procrastinating as to whether to support or oppose the war (leading to the anti-war Ramsay MacDonald resigning his Fabian membership), whilst the ILP nationally not only opposed the war but also supported self-determination for the Boer Republics and at their 1901 and 1902 conferences declared themselves 'pro-Boer.'

Thirdly, we must recognise that the electorate may have been comfortable with those long-standing individuals who were already serving as Councillors and perceived as conducting the town's civic affairs admirably. There was a great deal of regeneration being undertaken across South Shields, new libraries, museums, police and fire stations being opened, new schools being constructed, municipal parks at the foreshore being laid out, all giving a general feel that South Shields was a town on the move, led by 'gentlemen' and business owners who were at pains to express they were opposed to national politics being introduced into the Council Chamber (a sentiment that was still being expressed by their Progressive successors who controlled the Town Council in the late 1950s and 1960s).

Finally, we also have to conclude that the lack of a coherent strategy, their inability to provide the townsfolk with a candidate in every ward at election time, continuous disagreements amongst activists as to who they would support, the reluctance of some Trade Union branches to support anyone but their own members, activists like Joe Abbott being perfectly happy to chair public meetings of non-Labour Councillors seeking re-election, all were played out via a running commentary in the local media highlighting the inability of the Labour activists to unite, must have had a debilitating effect on the electorate's confidence in voting for working-class candidates.

As the new century dawned, the vision of the early pioneers had not diminished, though their political successes were few. The town still had active ILP and Fabian Society branches, the 1899 November Council election may have reduced them to only having Cullen and Thompson in the Council Chamber, but they did have some supporters on the Schools Board, notably Matthew Taylor and V Grunhut, both elected in January 1898 and the Board of Guardians had Trade Unionists like Wake and Batey amongst their number.

III The dawn of a new century

Robson's success in the 26 September–24 October 1900 first 'Khaki election' was a foregone conclusion. The Trades Council enthusiastically endorsed Robson when he met with them on 26 September. Following the meeting he travelled straight to a public rally in Tyne Dock where he was greeted by a standing ovation. Robson told the audience that he had just finished a meeting with the Trades Council and had received '… *an enthusiastic expression of approval.*' The support, he said, was gratifying considering the reception he had received when he had last met with them. Robson asserted that he believed the last trace of old differences had been removed and he explained he would be happy to be a '*Labour member as much as anyone the House of Commons*' and advised his enthusiastic supporters that he had actually been encouraged by the national Liberal Leadership to stand in Leicester – regarded as a safer Liberal seat – but he had declined. In an election dominated by the execution of the Boer War, Robson was clear, the Liberals had supported the Tory Government on the justification of the war, but they were entitled to demand a full and complete inquiry as to why the country was ill-prepared for it.

A further meeting organised for Robson in St Thomas Hall in the town centre days before the General Election, saw key Trade Unions represented such as the St Hilda's Miners, Marsden Miners, the Engineers, Trimmers' and Teemers' Association, Associated Union, even the Co-operative Movement. Robson joked that the last time he had met with Trade Unionists the turnout was very small, to which an audience member shouted out colloquially – '*Ah, but they didn't kn'aa ye then hinny.*' Meanwhile, an election rally in the Market Place on 2 October 1900 saw a crowd of nearly 10,000 assemble, which today seems incredible and must have been a tremendous sight to witness, even the declaration of the poll when it was announced saw Ocean Road and Fowler Street crammed with spectators awaiting the result. Robson would defeat his Conservative opponent, Robert Readhead by 7,417 votes to 4,119 but Lord Salisbury would lead the Conservatives and his Liberal Unionists allies to an impressive victory, securing a majority of 134 seats, Henry Campbell-Bannerman's Liberals securing only 183 seats.

Nationally the **Labour Representation Committee (LRC)** which had been formed earlier that year, with Keir Hardie at the head, contested the general election in just fifteen seats (eight of their candidates being formally chosen by the ILP), only Hardie (at Merthyr Tydfil) and Trade Unionist

Richard Bell (in Derby) were elected under the formal LRC banner, although other working-class MPs retained their seats under the formal Lib–Lab arrangements.

In South Shields the ILP chose not to contest the seat, given its public opposition to the Boer War it was probably a wise move. At their May 1900 branch meeting they had stubbornly insisted that their only genuinely elected representative, Matthew Taylor should resign from the Schools Board because he had supported the Board's decision to plan for festivities in schools on the occasion of the relief of Mafeking. Taylor refused but did eventually resign from the Board, due to moving from the town. The ILP Branch appears to have been reasonably strong in membership, the *Shields Gazette* reporting that their annual outing to Holywell Dene in July of 1900 was attended by sixty members, and they were still holding regular rallies from the Town Hall Market Place steps on Sunday evenings, Enid Stacy Widdrington the Socialist activist who worked full time for the national ILP being one of their regular speakers.

The Municipal Labour League continued to meet at the renamed Browns Café in Church Way, led by Joe Batey with key Unions such as the Harton and Marsden Miners, the Co-operative Society and the ILP being staunch supporters. Their attentions now turned to the need for a radical slum clearance programme, and they were desirous that the homes should be well built, Council owned and at an affordable rent to replace them. The question of increased powers for Municipal Corporations was of paramount importance to them and they wanted municipalisation of key public services such as the tramway system. The ILP Branch was now under the stewardship of Andrew Futers and they made repeated calls to the Town Council in 1902 drawing Councillors' attention to the effects on people's health of overcrowding and bad housing and urging the Council to consider implementing the Housing of the Working Classes Act.

But the Labour activists were still not united, nor even coordinated in their strategy for election success either locally or nationally. Municipally during the 1900–1902 election period, whilst Cullen continued to retain his Council seat, joined by Batey in the same Laygate ward in 1901, that was the limit of their success, although they were seeking to encourage more of their supporters to enter the electoral fray, they still did not contest every ward, restricting themselves to the deprived riverside wards.

IV

The lack of progress in securing strong municipal representation, as well as the failure of previous endeavours to forge a united working-class political movement in South Shields gave rise to much frustration amongst key political activists in the town. They now turned their attentions to the new **Labour Representation Committee** (LRC). The national Leadership of the LRC, which had held their Annual Conference in Newcastle in February 1903, was anxious to have an LRC branch established in South Shields, and matters came to a head on Saturday 5 September 1903, when a conference, organised by the local ILP Branch was held in the St Hilda's Miners Hall in Maxwell Street. In a circular, in advance of the meeting written by their Branch Secretary Robert Hearn, he advised:

> *'It is scarcely necessary to remind you that of late all over the Country the Trade Union movement has awakened from its apathy and is demanding a larger share of the representation both in Parliament and in the local bodies. Are we in South Shields to lag behind on this important question, or are we to step into line with the whole of the Trades Union movement? The answer rests with you and we trust that you will send two representations to the conference.'*

Twenty-four delegates were in attendance, from various branches including the Seaman, Glassmakers, United Machine Workers, the ILP, St Hilda's Miners, the Engineers and the Railway workers. In scenes which even today's Labour and Trade Union activists will recognise, arguments commenced about the validity of delegates in attendance and who should chair the meeting. Two nominations were accepted with Robert Morgan of the Municipal Labour League (and an ILP member) being elected. The conference then considered the business of the conference. Mr F Ash of the ILP addressed the conference and referring to the Taff Vale Judgement he made clear there was no time to lose in seeking to have candidates standing in the working-class interests. The local ILP were still of the strong opinion that they should be standing a Labour Parliamentary candidate against Robson at the next general election, but for Mr Ash, it was pointless seeking a 'big name' candidate until the local Trade Unions were onside. In relation to the local Town Hall, Ash was clear, how could they influence the municipalisation of services such as the Tramways with only Cullen and Batey being on the Council?

The Trades Union delegates in attendance were still not convinced. The Chair, Robert Morgan was concerned that some statements in the local press had suggested that their conference had been organised with the intention of running a Parliamentary candidate against Robson, and that Joe Batey's name had been mentioned as a potential Labour candidate. Other ILP members repudiated the public statements, their intention was simply to have an LRC Branch established, ready to field a candidate once Robson stood down, such statements giving further testament to the popularity of Robson as the town's MP.

The conference descended into opprobrium with procedural arguments and Union delegates alleging that the ILP did not have a clear purpose for the conference, and other delegates advising that Joe Batey had already written to the *Shields Gazette* making clear he felt the conference should only discuss municipal elections and not concern itself with Robson. A motion was moved to form a Branch of the LRC in the town, an amendment recommended that the matter be referred back to the respective organisations for discussion, the amendment was carried. In a further rebuff to the ILP, the Union delegates demanded that they should appoint an Executive Committee of five to arrange the next conference.

A further conference was convened six weeks later, on 17 October, held again in the Maxwell Street Miners Hall. In an indication of the indifference held by Trade Unions, the Number 14 Branch of the National Amalgamated Union of Labour (NAUL) made it publicly clear they would not attend the conference since they viewed any attempt to establish an LRC Branch as '*an insidious attempt (by a small section of the community) to disintegrate the progress forces of the Constituency, and thus render unsafe the seat of the present worthy Member of the Borough*'. To reinforce the point, the NAUL branch also passed a motion of confidence in William Robson sending a copy to Robert Hearn the Secretary of the ILP. Further disappointment was to follow. At the early October meeting of the Trades Council, delegates resolved not to support or send representatives to the reconvened conference, and the Tyne Dock Branch of the Trimmers' and Teemers' Association also refused to support the conference, expressing total opposition to the formation of an LRC in the town and moved a vote of confidence in William Robson MP.

The Liberal forces, with Robson's Parliamentary aide Bransby operating behind the scenes, were frantically seeking to demolish any attempt to create an LRC Branch in South Shields. When the conference eventually convened on that autumn Saturday evening in October only fourteen delegates attended the meeting.

In response to a letter, circulated by organisers to Trade Unions earlier, as to whether they supported the formation of an LRC Branch, the Coal Porters' Union Tyne Dock Branch said no; the Co-operative Bricklayers' Society were conducting a ballot of its members; the Associated Shipwrights, South Shields branch, described the timing as inopportune and said no; the Workers, Tenants and Lodgers Protection Society said they could not entertain the proposal; the National Amalgamated Union of Labour wrote and said no. It was clearly a disappointing response and the Societies that did attend were not much more supportive. The St Hilda's Lodge said that for them the ILP was an obstacle, the ILP's insistence that an LRC be formed with the clear intention of standing a Parliamentary candidate against Robson was preventing agreement on how to secure more Municipal representation, although delegates described it as a disgrace that only three workmen served on the Borough Council. The Railway Servants, whose original national motion to the TUC had created the LRC, expressed disappointment on the lack of progress but accepted that the low turnout was an indication that the time was not conducive to the formation of an LRC Branch in the town.

John Bell, Secretary of the Seamen's Union moved that the conference simply adjourn. There followed an explosive debate with ILP members expressing incredulity at the apathy in South Shields not only from the Union activists but also the electorate at large. William Tonge was clearly angry and remonstrated that the lack of support for an LRC Branch meant that for the Union Branches it was best – '… *to let them wallow in the mire that they seemed to believe in and were prepared to endure.*' James Johnson was equally dismissive of the Unions. Johnson lamented that the question of Labour representation was before every town in the country, but in South Shields they were doing nothing. The Chair, Robert Morgan accepted the issue was Robson's hold on the constituency, until he retired, there would be no LRC in South Shields. Following the outbursts, Bell amended his motion from adjournment to 'complete abandonment'. His resolution was carried unanimously.

V

In the 2 November 1903 municipal elections, conducted under heavy inclement weather, saw the Labour Municipal League support only three candidates who were all ILP members, James Johnson in the Shields Ward, who came last with only 65 votes in the poll, Robert Morgan in St Hilda who lost by 530 votes and James Dunlop who secured only 220 votes in Holborn.

The *Shields Gazette* reports that in Chairing the campaign meeting for Dunlop, Joe Batey criticised the Corporation for its obsession with allocating funds for implementing macadamised roads alongside the seafront, which benefitted only those who had cars, when the money should be spent on amenities which would benefit the majority, whilst Dunlop wanted music entertainment at the seafront. In a sardonic comment aimed at the number of publicans now entering the municipal arena, Dunlop was also clear, they should not be allowed to be members, if elected, of the Watch Committee (the Police Committee).

The failure to establish an LRC Branch in the town was a bitter disappointment, no more so than for ILP activists but also for the Municipal Labour League of which the ILP were leading players. The overall direction and purpose of the ILP was now questioned and the inevitable split occurred within the local ranks which saw in 1904 the establishment of the more left-wing **Social Democratic Federation (SDF)** in the town.

The SDF had been established nationally in 1881 as Britain's first Socialist Party, its fledging existence as a Marxist Party would see it survive numerous internal splits, which seems to characterise the history of the left in British politics, but it would always remain on the fringe. As Keir Hardie and his allies sought to unite the left into some form of coherent electoral force, the SDF was invited to join the LRC, but given that leading LRC, Co-operative, Fabian and Trade Union figures owed more to Methodism than Marxism for their politics, the SDF would always sit uncomfortably with the LRC and formally left in 1907.

The SDF branch in South Shields, under the stewardship of Joseph Rogers, was reasonably active, meeting fortnightly at 215 South Eldon Street, with Jimmy Dunlop a leading light and William Tonge also joining. Heinrich Fischer a Russian émigré who was arrested under suspicion of gun-running to Russia and JP Lloyd, a leading Marxist thinker of the time, visited the town to meet members and addressed public meetings in the Market Place.

Meanwhile, the remaining members of South Shields ILP maintained an active presence in the area, in 1904 Philip Snowden the General Secretary of the ILP, addressed one of their regular rallies in the Market Place, and in December, Keir Hardie paid a visit to neighbouring Jarrow to support Pete Curran the LRC's Parliamentary candidate.

In future, the municipal elections would witness candidates from the SDF opposing those supported by the Trades Council and the ILP, although the SDF electoral support was always minimal, their intervention was divisive. In the 1903 municipal election for example, Dunlop had opposed the ILP Branch Secretary Robert Hearn in the Holborn ward, whilst in the November 1904 election Dunlop's candidacy in the same ward, again on behalf of the SDF deprived John Bell from gaining the seat he was contesting with the active support of the Trades Council, even though Dunlop only secured sixty-seven votes. It was a similar pattern a year later in November 1905, Dunlop again stood against Bell in Holborn this time securing only twenty-seven votes but again depriving Bell of the seat who missed out on victory this time by only thirteen votes.

Dunlop was not the only SDF candidate, John Franks stood in the Shields ward in 1905 securing only twenty-five votes. It is worth noting that the 1905 municipal election saw Robert Hearn from the ILP elected in Tyne Dock and James MacDonald ousting a long-serving moderate councillor in the Deans Ward. It was progress, albeit painfully slow.

VI

Occasionally a general election is held which changes the whole direction of the country: the National Government's victory in 1931, Labour's in 1945, the Conservatives' in 1979 and arguably Labour's in 1997, elections which captured the mood of the era and defined national politics for a generation.

To that must be added the Liberals' victory in the January 1906 General Election.

It was an election which was precipitated by the resignation of the Conservative Arthur Balfour on 4 December 1905, the last Prime Minister to surrender office to his political opponents without suffering a defeat at the polls first. The Conservatives had governed since 1895, Balfour faced growing unpopularity and attacks from all sides. The conduct of the Boer War, and the issue of 'Chinese slavery' in South Africa mines (which had South Shields' Trade Unionists rallying in opposition at the Market Place) horrified the Conservative middle-class voters who viewed it as unethical that imported Chinese labour were treat almost like slaves. Nonconformists were also angry at the new 1902 Education Act which had abolished the elected School Boards and placed education they felt into the hands of high Church Anglicans. Rowntree's 1901 study of York had laid bare a city in which a third of the population lived below the poverty line, resulting in calls for social reforms. Added to this, and electorally the most damaging, was the Unionist Joe Chamberlain's resignation from the Government and the threatened backbench opposition to Balfour's free trade policies.

In a calculated risk, Balfour resigned, expecting the Liberal Leader, Campbell-Bannerman to soldier on without an election and assuming he would be unable to form a strong government given the Parliamentary arithmetic Campbell-Bannerman once installed in Number 10, simply called a general election for 13 January 1906.

The results were cataclysmic for the Conservatives, only 132 Conservatives were returned, 25 Liberal Unionists (Chamberlain's Party), 377 Liberal Members and 53 Labour Members (24 of whom were Lib–Lab MPs). The Conservative leader Balfour lost his seat in Manchester East and over 300 new MPs were elected who had never graced the Chamber of House of Commons before.

In South Shields, William Robson recently Knighted and promoted to Solicitor General in Campbell-Bannerman's Government, duly returned to the Constituency in late December and took up residence at Harton Grange ready for the rigours of the election campaign. As usual he conducted an energetic campaign. His Agent, Frederick Warden Newby was punctilious ensuring a committee room in every ward of the Constituency. Robson had little cause to concern himself, the unpopularity of the Balfour Government and the Liberal commitment to repeal the Taff Vale Judgement meant that the anti-Conservative vote was solidly behind him. When the ballot closed at 8 pm on the evening of Wednesday 17 January, the boxes were taken to the Congregational Hall in Ocean Road where thousands of people descended outside to await the result. Robson secured what would be the largest majority he would ever achieve in the Constituency and one of the largest Liberal majorities in the country, 6,286. Addressing the assembled orderly crowds Robson announced that his majority was a victory for free trade, his result had been a warning to politicians, to keep their hands off the food of the people. He then walked the short distance across Ocean Road to the Liberal Club, acknowledging the cheers and appreciation of the electorate as he entered the imposing Victorian building to thank his election team who were waiting for him inside.

A few days later Robson returned to his Eaton Gardens home in Belgravia, to be advised by the Prime Minister that he wished to retain the services of Robson as Solicitor General in the new Liberal Government.

And what of the Labour Representation Committee? In the euphoria of the Liberal landslide, it should be remembered that this election was also a pivotal one for the infant Party. Twenty-nine LRC Members were elected, alongside twenty-four who were classified as Lib–Lab MPs. Much of the success was due to a private agreement between the Liberal Chief Whip, Herbert Gladstone and the Secretary of the LRC, Ramsay MacDonald in 1903 in which the former agreed to stand aside in thirty-one of the fifty seats where the LRC was standing in order to allow the Liberals to concentrate on key Conservative marginals.

As Labour steadily gained Parliamentary seats in the North East of England, South Shields was now coming to the attention of the Labour Party national leadership. In 1906, following the General Election, a letter from the LRC was sent to Trades Council, as the principal organising body in the town for working-class interests, asking why Labour was performing so badly electorally in the town. The response of the activists was to convene a further conference on Tuesday 21 August to consider the desirability of joint action being taken to promote their cause in the November Council elections.

The Trades Council were in receptive mood, speaking oracularly, the conference Chair, Sam Robson, believed that single working-class candidates would have a greater chance of success, he advocated Trade Unionists stepping forward to seek Municipal honours under the banner of a **Trade Union Municipal Representation Committee**. Attempts by some delegates to resurrect the previous Labour Representation Committee were rebuffed, with James Dunlop declaring that unless the SDF locally was included in their final deliberations, he would field SDF candidates against them in November. Attempts to move a motion to ascertain from the ILP and SDF what steps they intended to take at the November Council election was ruled out of order, with one delegate protesting he was only interested in promoting Trade Union candidates not a debate about Socialism. The conference, which was well attended by several Unions – with the Boilermakers taking a particularly hard line on any attempt to involve political Parties like the SDF and ILP in the discussions – agreed to establish a committee to consider fielding Trade Union endorsed candidates.

The initiative though was ephemeral but was still marginally successful. In the November 1906 Council elections – conducted once again following a further boundary review to take account of the expanding township – agreement was reached between the ILP, SDF, Trade Union and Labour interests as to who should contest the various vacancies. The tactic resulted in some notable victories, Cullen was elected unopposed in Laygate; John Bell and John Toll were unopposed in Victoria and Dunlop secured election as a Councillor for the Tyne Dock ward with the SDF's *Justice* newspaper hailing his victory. Three other candidates stood unsuccessfully under Trade Union banner, two as Trade Union/ILP, R Vine as an ILP candidate in West Park missed out on one of the three vacancies by just twelve votes. There can be no doubt that leading Trade Union activists, irrespective of the 21 August decision, had spoken privately with the SDF and ILP to ensure working-class votes were not split at the election and had encouraged the National Amalgamated Union of Labour to withdraw two of their potential candidates on the strict understanding that they would be endorsed in any future Council by-elections occurring.

VII

1907 and 1908 saw little progress locally despite strides being made nationally to consolidate the position of the LRC. Robson continued to dominate the town's political thinking, the Council would pursue its laissez-faire approach to the housing and health problems facing the town as evidenced by the Chief Medical Officer of Health's report to June 1908 Town Improvement Committee which examined the quality of housing along the river front including Fairles' Quay, houses in Mitre Street and Heugh Terrace and land to the north of King Street and the Market Place (Thames Street and Long Row area). Under the Housing of the Working Classes Act the Medical Officer was clear that the houses were not fit for purpose and no new housing should be constructed in that area, but the Committee took more interest in the promises of landlords to repair their properties rather than seeking to undertake a wholescale demolition and regeneration area.

Outside of the Council Chamber, the SDF and the local ILP remained in direct competition with each other to secure political leverage and held their own rallies in the Market Place and propagated their own messages to the electorate, both Branches were extremely active with the ILP's *Labour Leader* and the SDF's *Justice* newspapers giving regular reports to testify as to the progress their comrades in South Shields were achieving. Of the two though, the SDF was making the most headway with the frondeur James Dunlop securing re-election to the Council in Tyne Dock in November 1907, whilst in Laygate, its position as a solid Labour ward was further displayed by the long serving Joe Batey being once again returned unopposed in the election.

Encouraged by the zeal of Colne Valley Socialist MP, Victor Grayson, the South Shields ILP and SDF branches worked together on the nationwide *'Right to Work'* campaign which focused action on rising unemployment and serious attempts were made to agree upon a single candidate to present to the electorate in future elections. The SDF was clearly the larger and more active branch at this time evidenced by the fact that in 1908 whilst mineworker R Vine of the ILP was allowed to stand successfully in the new Victoria ward, the SDF fielded candidates in Laygate, West Park, Tyne Dock and Simonside with the SDF's Ben Smith securing election in Laygate. Negotiations seemed to have faltered in the Deans ward though as both the ILP and SDF fielded candidates unsuccessfully.

1909 would prove to be a tumultuous year for the Labour movement, locally as well as nationally.

The Marxist SDF changed its named nationally to the **Social Democratic Party** (SDP) as it continued its break with mainstream Labour politics and the LRC to eventually become the British Socialist Party before it ended its journey as a founder member of the Communist Party of Great Britain in 1920. In April, at their Annual Conference in Edinburgh, Hardie, MacDonald and Snowden all resigned from the ILP National Executive following an explosive conference which saw delegates defeat a motion that recommended that the ILP should disaffiliate from the Labour Party, with the remaining ILP Leadership making the rhodomontade statement that the ILP was **not** the Labour Party. The fratricidal nature of the conference, in which Hardie described opposing delegates as *'snarling semi-disruptionists'* was bringing to a head the argument as to the effectiveness of the Labour Party's Parliamentary programme with some feeling the Party was too timid politically. Further controversy followed in September over disagreement as to whether Lib–Lab working-class MPs should sign the Labour Party constitution and abide by their Whip in Parliament. The fractious nature of the relationship between the ILP and the Labour Party would eventually see the ILP disaffiliate from the Labour Party in 1932.

Locally the ILP felt confident enough in January 1909 to hold a public meeting in the working-class district of Tyne Dock with the aim of establishing another Branch, unfortunately records do not remain which advise whether the ILPers were successful. Whilst relations were strained nationally between competing Labour factions as to the future direction of the movement, within the Council Chamber the small number of ILP, Trade Union and SDF Councillors were demonstrating that they could speak, and act, as one voice when required.

In 1909 the new imposing Edwardian Municipal buildings on Westoe Road were taking final shape but the escalating costs were the subject of a public meeting organised by the new centre-right Municipal Reform Committee at the Congregational Hall who argued it was time for new blood on the Council (although not Trade Unionists or Labour reformers), whilst in February, in a conflict with the contractors, the Council instructed their Clerk of Works to have part of the wooden flooring taken up in the new building. In what must have seemed surreal events, the aggrieved contractors guarded the entrances to the Town Hall and refused to allow the Council Officials admittance until assurances were given that the Council would honour the payment for the flooring.

At the August meeting of the Town Council, the costs of the new Municipal Building were again raised, this time with the right-wing Cllr Johnson criticising the costs in connection with the laying out of the forecourt and said it would be a '*resort for loafers and tramps who would smoke and spit about the place.*' Cllr Pritchard horrified at the comment asked: '*Do you mean middle class loafers?*' To which James Dunlop replied: '*No, he means the working-class man, Cllr Johnson is a loafer himself. He never does any work.*'

The Mayor was incandescent and demanded that Dunlop withdraw the comment. In chaotic scenes Dunlop was backed by Joe Batey and Ben Smith and the Town Clerk was asked to summon the Police. In the resultant melee, the Mayor demanded that Dunlop withdraw his comments or withdraw from the meeting. Dunlop announced he would not withdraw the comment but would go home. He left the Chamber and was joined by Councillors Pritchard, Ben Smith, Vine, Toll, John Bell and Batey. As he left Dunlop remarked: '*You can have peace now and go on with your business. You are all loafers now.*'

As Labour activists began to think strategically in terms of their candidates for Municipal honours, the Liberal and Radicals were beginning to formally organise themselves under the **Municipal Reform League** banner. It would however still be some time before Labour would pose a real threat to their hold on civic power. In the November 1909 municipal election, the SDF stood only one candidate T Pritchard in Laygate, but he was opposed by JE Plater a miner and noted temperance campaigner, Pritchard won the seat by just six votes. Elsewhere, the ILP contested only three seats, Simonside, Tyne

Dock and the Deans losing in all three contests. It seemed no matter how hard they sought to propitiate the electorate they simply could not make the crucial breakthrough at election time.

VIII

Occupying the minds of the nation was the unfolding drama at Westminster.

Herbert Asquith, following the aliment and eventual death of Campbell-Bannerman, had succeeded to the Premiership in April 1908. Despite the Liberals winning a conclusive election victory in January 1906, an obstructive Upper Chamber, overwhelming dominated by Conservative Peers, blocked a whole series of legislative proposals from the Commons including the Licensing Bill (designed to limit the number of public houses in any area), the Education Bill (designed to placate the non-Conformists concerned that the Church of England had assumed too much influence under the 1902 Act), a Bill for Old Age Pensions for the over seventies (which one Peer had described as '*so prodigal of expenditure as likely to undermine the whole fabric of Empire*') and finally Asquith's Chancellor, Lloyd George was seeking to have his Budget approved, considered revolutionary because it was the first in British history with the intention of seeking a limited redistribution of wealth amongst the British population.

Tensions were heightened between the Lords and the Commons, in which some MPs called for the abolition of the House of Lords, criticism was made in the Chamber that Churchill had attended one late night sitting in his pyjamas and Lloyd George told a Newcastle audience that '… *a fully equipped Duke costs as much to keep as two Dreadnoughts; and Dukes are just as great a terror and they last longer.'* The Lords – entitled to reject but not amend a finance bill – for the first time in over two centuries rejected a budget. It was clear that the intransigent behaviour of the Lords could not continue and would need to be resolved by a general election.

Robson, promoted to Attorney General in January 1908, and as diligent as ever, had made a visit to South Shields in June to lay a foundation stone for the new YMCA building being constructed on the corner of Burrow Street and Fowler Street. Following Prorogation of Parliament which occurred on 3 December, and with the General Election, as usual, being spread over a fortnight beginning on 15 January 1910, Robson arrived back to South Shields with his wife on 21 December, to be greeted by crowds outside South Shields railway station, he made his first appeal to the electorate in a statement to the press. Explaining how together they had comprehensively defeated those opposed to free trade, he said this time it was the *'Peers of England who are leading the attack'*. The Government, he advised, had proposed a budget to meet some of the costs for old-age pensions and for strong naval defences paid for by moderate taxes on land. The Peers owned the land but wanted to shift the burden of taxation onto the workers' food and trade which would *'... endanger and lessen your employment.'*

The MP would remain in the Constituency during the festive season, although he was required to speak in support of Liberal Party candidates elsewhere given his standing within the Government.

The Conservative Party, accepting they had never won South Shields, stood aside to allow their Liberal Unionist allies to contest the seat. They chose REL Vaughan Williams, after several prominent local worthies declined to stand. Williams requested that the South Shields Trades Council organise a meeting of Trade Unionists so that he could address them, the Trades Council politely declined on the grounds they were a non-Party organisation, but suggested he organise his own. He established his central headquarters at the Conservative Club, 9 Ocean Road, today occupied by an ice cream parlour. The Labour Party still not organised formally in the Borough was in no position to make a challenge, consequently Robson's hold on the seat was secure. The election rallies of Williams and Robson were fought on the national issues surrounding Lloyd George's budget, the obdurate behaviour of the unelected House of Lords and what was perceived as the growing menace of the German Navy. Williams ran an energetic campaign addressing frequent meetings across the Constituency and had a committee room in every ward of the town, but it would be to no avail. In scenes reminiscent of the 1906 General Election, crowds once again gathered in Ocean Road on the evening of 18 January to hear that Robson had won with a majority of 4,236.

Given the constitutional crisis in which the election had been called, the campaign nationally was not particularly exciting, public interest centred around Lloyd George's Budget and Tariff Reform, as Roy Jenkins points out in his book, *Mr Balfour's Poodle*: *'The Unionists got what they wanted: an election on the merits of the Budget rather than the propriety of the Peers' conduct.'* The Election was a stalemate, the Conservative and Unionists achieved a net gain of 116 seats and came within two seats of being the largest Party (given their 1906 performance this was astonishing change of fortunes) and the Labour

Party itself, under Arthur Henderson, sustained some exiguous momentum gaining eleven seats – although some Lib–Lab seats were lost.

Asquith's Government, with Robson remaining as Attorney General, was chastened but truculent and would continue with the notional support of the Irish Parliamentary Party and the Labour Party. Lloyd George's budget was eventually agreed, but the Constitutional crisis continued when the Liberal Government announced plans to implement a new Parliamentary Bill which sought to end the power of the House of Lords to veto future Government legislation. Given the Parliamentary arithmetic it was clear Asquith would be forced to go back to the country before the end of 1910.

Chapter 4

Division and Unity

I March of the women

The January 1910 General Election had centred around the constitutional issues of the respective rights and powers of the Commons and Lords but emerging as a social issue across the country was the question of women's suffrage. By 1869 women were eligible for election to the School Boards but the qualification to vote was still restricted to single women who were ratepayers. The right of women to vote was extended in 1894 to include some married women whilst the Local Government Act of that year removed property qualification as a requirement for women to be elected to the Board of Guardians. The emergence of women as wage earners, giving them some degree of independence helped give rise to the formation of organisations which campaigned for all women to have the vote of which the **Women's Social and Political Union (WSPU)** was one of the most prominent (and militant).

As early as December 1894 the South Shields Trades Council had agreed to formally support two women who sought election to the Board of Guardians, Miss Maxwell and Miss Kate Deans. Maxwell had already been elected three years earlier, leading to her male Guardian Board colleagues remarking in 1894 that whilst they had originally opposed a woman joining the Board, they had found her contributions thoughtful and insightful. Kate Deans was encouraged by Charles Reynolds to submit her name for consideration for the December 1894 election. The Trades Council enthusiastically supported both women's campaigns in the run up to the poll, with Deans securing a respectful 379 votes in the Deans ward but she was not elected (one assumes her campaign literature bore the slogan 'Deans for the Deans') whilst Maxwell topped the poll in Laygate.

The WSPU, as their national campaign became more militant and forthright, advocated a strategy of campaigning in any Parliamentary by-election against the Liberal nominee seeking to force Asquith's Government into allocating time in Parliament to debate (and support) a Women's Suffrage Bill. On 12 October 1910 William Robson was promoted by Asquith to a Lord of Appeal in Ordinary and elevated to the Peerage as Baron Robson of Jesmond in the County of Northumberland. His elevation necessitated a Parliamentary by-election in South Shields, giving the WSPU an opportunity to focus their attention on a town where the retiring Liberal MP had not been receptive to the idea of female suffrage. There had been rumours in the media and amongst national political circles for some time that Robson was destined for promotion. A strong supporter of Asquith, he had held firm during the 1910 Budget constitutional crisis and had been an accomplished debater in the House of Commons in defence of the Government.

The WSPU established an office in South Shields located at 44 Fowler Street and had been campaigning in the town for some time, the by-election presented an opportunity to raise their profile further and the WSPU immediately despatched two full-time organisers to coordinate the campaign, Annie Williams and Flora Drummond (known as 'The General'). They were determined to encourage an independent candidate to oppose both the Liberals and the Conservatives and if necessary were prepared to fund the campaign costs of the candidate.

The WSPU though was not the only active women's organisation in the town, following a split within the WSPU ranks, the **Women's Freedom League** had been formed nationally in 1907 and launched a local branch in South Shields in March 1910 with the inaugural meeting being held at the Ceylon Café. Twenty-six women were in attendance with the Secretary Mrs Miller of Langholm Road, East Boldon, the Treasurer Mrs Valons of 8 Morpeth Avenue and Mrs Robinson of 48 Morpeth Avenue as the Literature Secretary. The WSPU was run like an army by the dominant personalities of the Pankhursts, the League was more democratic and supported passive resistance as a tactic rather than attacks on people or property.

The Liberals moved fast following Robson's resignation. Robson would be instrumental in introducing his former Parliamentary colleague Russell Rea to the key players in the local Liberal Association. Rea a former MP for Gloucester had lost his seat in the January 1910 General Election and was regarded as a rising star, although of note is the fact that Rea had been a Deputy Chair of the Taff Vale Railway Company in Wales the cause of so much consternation within the Labour movement. He was a shipowner, with close links to the Tyneside shipbuilding industry. The Conservative Association stood aside to allow their Coalition partner, the Liberal Unionists, to once again field Vaughan Williams to contest the vacancy. The question though was whether the Labour movement felt sufficiently confident to contest the seat, given the popular Robson was now removed from the scene.

The Social Democratic Party (SDP formerly the SDF) considered fielding their own candidate, Jack Williams from London, with James Dunlop holding open-air meetings to advance his case. The issue for the SDP was money to meet the election expenses. As speculation increased about a third independent Labour candidate, names were emerging as to the potential nominee. The local Seamen's Union wanted their President, Havelock Wilson the former Middlesbrough MP to stand, the Miners were split between Alderman William House the Durham Miners' Association (DMA) President and John Johnson the DMA Financial Secretary who was also a former MP for Gateshead, whilst Will Crooks the former Labour MP for Woolwich was also mentioned as a possible candidate. The financing of the campaign was not going to be an issue for the local activists, if chosen, Crooks' expenses would be covered by the national Fabian Society whilst the Durham Miners' Association would cover the cost of whichever of their members emerged as the candidate.

Labour-supporting activists believed that even with a three-way contest, they had a good chance of securing the Parliamentary seat. There were an estimated 2,000 miners in the constituency, who had previously solidly voted for Robson, 1,000 railwaymen – whose Union was one of the main instigators for the creation of the Labour Party, and of course the shipyard workers, principally the traditionally moderate boilermakers, who were at that time involved in a lockout, with commentators observing that this would increase the likelihood of them voting against the Liberal candidate. The South Shields Liberals viewed the forthcoming by-election with much perturbation.

With the Liberals and the Liberal Unionists candidates in place, attention turned to the Labour Party. Their national Secretary, Ramsay MacDonald and the Chairman of the national Party, William Cornforth Robinson descended upon the town to convene a meeting of leading players within the Labour and Trade Union circles to determine whether to field a candidate. The fact that the two senior officials in the national Labour Party made the journey to review the matter is an indication of the seriousness with which a candidature was being taken.

National factors would play a crucial part in their deliberations.

Firstly, the Parliamentary Labour Party was part of the radical contingent which gave the Liberals and Asquith their majority in the House of Commons; and gave the Labour Party much gravitas in negotiations with their ministerial counterparts.

Secondly, Rea was a firm favourite of the Liberal Leadership, they saw South Shields as a solid Liberal seat, they would have felt they had every right to have a clear run at the by-election given they were the incumbents and the most likely to keep the Conservatives or their Liberal Unionist rivals out.

The national Labour Party was extremely anxious that the Osborne Judgement should be reversed. The Judgement delivered by the House of Lords on 21 December 1909 was brought by a railway worker, Walter Osborne, a member of the Amalgamated Society of Railway Servants (ASRS), a staunch Liberal, he objected to his Union subscriptions being used to fund the Labour Party. He brought a case against the ASRS to the High Court and lost, but an Appeal to the House of Lords was successful, whose judgement – that Union political funding was unlawful – caused uproar and disquiet across the Edwardian political world. The Judgement threatened the very financial existence of the Labour Party who relied upon the Union subscriptions to finance the salaries of their MPs.

There can be no doubt that the national Liberal hierarchy discussed the vacancy in South Shields with their senior Labour counterparts – even if no formal agreement was reached, recorded, or reported, given the volatile national political situation, the Liberals without question would have reached out in an attempt for an agreement.

II

During the whole of the week commencing Monday 10 October there was much discussion, debate and arm-twisting within Labour circles to decide whether to field a candidate and who the candidate should be. Media stories swept the country as the deliberations dragged on with much speculation as to the eventual outcome. On Friday 14 October a decision seems to have been reached. The Labour Party would indeed contest the by-election, and the candidate would be the former MP Will Crooks. National Labour figures were adamant though, his candidature would need to be endorsed by a properly convened meeting of key Labour and Trade Union figures within the Constituency. The delegates' meeting would be convened for

Monday 17 October, giving a weekend for last minute negotiations with local power brokers.

Arthur Peters, the Labour Party national organiser spent a few days in the town assessing the situation and was making it clear to the media that Will Crooks would be standing, finance would be forthcoming for the challenge and Peters believed the delegates' meeting would enthusiastically adopt Will Crooks. Peters' solecism would be misplaced. Reports were emerging in the press that a miner, Mr Heath, speaking at a public meeting in support of Russell Rea had voiced his concerns at a 'third candidate' – Peters met with the miner's representatives who gave reassurance they would support Will Crooks at the delegates' meeting. However, *The Daily Telegraph* reported that some Trade Unionists were animated by the '*high-handed action of a very small section of the Independent Labour Party*', leading Peters to make clear publicly that Crooks, if adopted, would be the Labour Party – not an ILP – candidate.

This latter reference may have been Ramsay MacDonald's influence following his visit to the town in which he met with the local ILP Branch and representatives of the Trades Council on 12 October. The meeting was tense and had been convened by the ILP to request the Trades Council to add their organisation's name to a circular calling a meeting of Labour and Trade Union interests in which the selection of a Labour Party candidate would be considered. The Trades Council representatives refused, stating they were non-Party political, replying to charges that the Trades Council had previously supported William Robson. Their Secretary WW Robertson replied that Robson had been the town's MP and they would do the same whoever was the Member of Parliament.

MacDonald is recorded as having replied that the South Shields Trades Council was '*antiquated and wanted modernising.*'

The Labour challenge was serious, Peters in a long interview with the press advised that the Fabian Society would financially support Will Crooks and that he would be fighting on the Osborne Judgement and reform of the House of Lords. Ramsay MacDonald, Peters asserted, was making arrangements to be in the Constituency, they had booked the largest hall in the town, the Royal Assembly Rooms, for a public meeting to be held the following Friday and that their headquarters would be the Plimsoll Hall, which was the base for the ILP and a number of Trade Union branches. Admitting that whilst there was no 'official' Labour Party in the town, Peters advised they would not suffer through lack of Party machinery.

The Liberals publicly called for Crooks to go back to London and contest his former seat at Woolwich – '*some of us would be glad to help him*' advised the Tyneside Liberal MP, John Mackinnon Robertson. Crooks has been described as having a magnetic personality and a speaker's gift of moving audiences, he was certainly a formable candidate. The Conservative and Liberal Unionists scented a chance of victory, launching Vaughan Williams' campaign to a packed meeting in the Victoria Hall, Fowler Street on 14 October, '*There is at the present moment ...*' Williams told his audience, '*... an ill-assorted alliance between the Liberal and Labour Parties. It is easy to see that each suspects the other and that each bullies the other. They may keep up appearances as far as they can for the outside world, but it needs but little intelligence to see that there is really the greatest disunion between them, and that neither trusts the other.*'

The autumn weekend before the special Labour and Trade Union delegate conference on Monday 17 October was far from calm, whilst Williams the Unionist candidate held no campaign meetings, the Seamen's Union released a telegram from Havelock Wilson advising he would visit the town to assess whether to stand as a candidate and the pertinacious WSPU matriarch, Emmeline Pankhurst, arrived in South Shields on Friday 14 October. The timing was fortuitous and probably designed to exert maximum pressure on Labour activists to field a candidate against the Liberal. Pankhurst addressed a mass rally in the Royal Assembly Hall. 'General' Drummond presided over proceedings at which Pankhurst declared their sole intention was to ensure the defeat of the Government nominee, Russell Rea. In an emotional peroration, she demanded assurance from Asquith that he would support the Women's Suffrage Bill and he had only to signal his intent that it would be before Parliament before the year's end and the WSPU would cease their campaigning. In an indication of how important Pankhurst viewed the by-election, she remained in the area over the weekend and addressed a further meeting on Monday 17 October at the Victoria Hall to be followed into South Shields by her fiery daughter Christabel Pankhurst who gave equally impassioned speeches in the town.

It was the oracular behaviour of the Marsden Miners which should have given cause for concern. At their usual fortnightly meeting held over that weekend, the Miners' Lodge was required to consider correspondence from Arthur Peters inviting them to send two delegates to a selection meeting on Monday 17 October for the purposes of determining whether to endorse Will Crooks as the Labour Party candidate for the by-election. The correspondence was not considered, and reports state they treated the invitation with the greatest contumely. Given this was the Lodge that had placed William Robson's image on their banner some alarm bells must have started ringing with the Labour Party's national organiser. Over the weekend, the Labour Party's National Executive Emergency Committee met to endorse Will Crooks and requested that William Robinson chair the meeting with the assistance of Peters.

As the media gathered outside the meeting hall on the evening of Monday 17 October, all expectation was that Crooks would emerge to announce that for the first time, the Labour Party would contest the South Shields Parliamentary seat.

The meeting though was a disaster.

Around 100 people attended the Plimsoll Hall at the Mill Dam, of whom around forty-four were delegates representing twenty-three different trade union branches, the ILP and the Fabian Society. Cllr Joe Batey moved the motion to contest the seat and to invite Will Crooks to be their candidate. A debate followed, with several trade union delegates intimating that they did not have instructions from their union branch as to how to vote and therefore would be neutral.

Following a ballot, the result was:

For a third candidate (Will Crooks)   16
Against   7
Neutral   21

The meeting lasted three hours and exasperated national officials advised the waiting media that in the absence of unanimity they were unable to recommend Crooks' endorsement by the National Executive of the Labour Party, '*It is impossible to go on with the forces divided*', Peters laconically explained to the journalists.

What was the explanation for the vote? Given that the finance was available, endorsement and support from the Labour Party National Executive had been given, that a credible candidate had come forward, support provided by the WSPU, the fury felt by Trade Unionists at the Osborne Judgement and the Liberal Government's delay in resolving the matter, why no unanimity?

There were perhaps several factors at play, some alluded to in a *Daily Telegraph* article of 19 October 1910. Firstly, Arthur Peters, Labour's national organiser believed that local activists had acted egregiously and said he felt '*grossly misled*' by the South Shields ILP branch who had given reason to believe that they had sounded out the local Trade Unions, when in fact it transpired, they had only spoken to three or four Union branches. Secondly, we cannot discount that William Robson was lobbying his network of local Trade Union leaders to ensure no third candidate emerged. Rea was at pains in the lead up to the Labour selection conference to make clear he wanted the Osborne Judgement amended so that Unions could make donations to political Parties, but that individual members should have a right to determine which Party they wanted their subscription to go to. Thirdly, nationally the Liberals would have made clear to the Labour Party that if they entered the fray in South Shields, then they would be under no obligation to stand aside in Woolwich (Crooks' former seat) at the next election. Locally, Cllr Ben Smith probably best expresses the views of those Labour activists desperate for a challenge – the selection conference in his view was simply held too quickly and did not give delegates enough time to seek the instructions of their various Trade Union branches and Lodges, allowing them to remain neutral in the meeting.

On 23 October Havelock Wilson having visited the town and addressed several open-air meetings, chose not to contest the by-election which was just as well because the election was held on 27 October and it would not have left much time for a formal and energetic campaign from the Seamen's leader. Further, elements of the local SDP were still intent on fielding an independent Socialist candidate. James Dunlop announced that William Gee would stand as a Revolutionary Socialist Candidate, a Committee Room was procured in the Market Place and leaflets began circulating across the town, but on the day that nominations closed, no papers were submitted. Dunlop attended the Town Hall but his candidate failed to materialise. Gee eventually made a statement that he simply could not raise the funds for the Returning Officers' fees, a promise of support from the SDP in London was not forthcoming and he could not himself raise the funds.

III

The election, held on a dull cheerless Thursday, saw the Liberals fight in blue colours, the Liberal Unionists in red. Due to lockouts the shipyards were closed, Suffragettes stood outside the polling stations exhorting electors to '*Vote the Liberal out.*' The Mayor, Town Clerk and Police Chief visited the WSPU Offices on Fowler Street on polling to congratulate them on the organisation of the WSPU campaign, which was high profile but not militant.

An estimated 20,000 people were excitedly perambulating the evening streets in what was regarded as a party atmosphere (although shopkeepers barricaded their windows), as electors (and non-electors) were joined by residents from neighbouring towns waiting to hear the result declared. The result when it came shortly after 10.30 pm was a triumphant for Russell Rea but with a reduced Liberal majority of 3,019. Rea would rejoin his son who was the MP for Scarborough in the House of Commons.

The Suffragettes claimed some success in that the Liberal majority had decreased by 1,000 and the campaign had brought together a nucleus of thirty-six new members for their cause, with regular meetings being arranged in the Ingham Hall. They were in buoyant mood and arranged several further open-air meetings across the town to promote their cause.

The townsfolk though would face two more polls before 1910 was out. In November in uneventful Council elections, Joe Batey was once again returned to the Council unopposed in Laygate, his mining colleague John Toll did the same in Victoria, whilst in a tough contest, Jim Dunlop of the SDF was re-elected for the third time in Tyne Dock. The last Council meeting to be held in the Town Hall in Market Place was held on 5 October, a month later the Annual Council meeting was held in the new Council Chamber of the newly opened civic buildings on Beach Road.

But it was to the Parliamentary crisis engulfing national politics that was uppermost in people's minds. The Conservative dominated House of Lords was still refusing to pass Liberal Government Legislation without significant amendment. Parliamentary arithmetic forced the Liberals to go back to the country to secure a mandate for their new 1911 Parliament Act which would in future prevent the House of Lords from blocking legislation from the elected Chamber. As rumours swept the country of a potential January 1911 General Election, Asquith caught the opposition off guard and sought the King's permission to dissolve Parliament early with an election taking place between 3 and 19 December, the last General Election to be held over several days.

The South Shields ILP branch was still desirous of fielding a candidate, but the issue for the ILP, remained the question of finance. Without the support of the Unions or organisations like the Co-op or the Fabians they simply could not afford the Returning Officers' fees which at the time saw all election costs being borne by the candidates seeking election. Figures show that a staggering proportion of the infant Labour Party's expenditure was spent on this single item in the two general elections of 1910, £7,192 (worth around £853,000 today), which accounted for around 31 per cent of the Party's national budget that year.

Talks were held between the ILP and the increasingly active local Suffragette branch as to whether the latter could fund the election costs, indeed there were detailed negotiations between the ILP branch and the Northern Representatives of the Women's Suffrage Societies with agreement that funds would be provided. The talks went no further, the short time frame for the election gave little scope on agreeing a candidate and preparing for the campaign. Nationally, Labour's leaders would not have been keen for the contest, their experiences of the town in the October by-election would not have helped and they would not sanction a candidate. Following their decision, the Conservatives and Unionists announced they would not contest the seat at the general election either, they had been awaiting the decision of Labour interests before making their final decision. Records do not indicate why the Conservative/Unionists felt unable to field a candidate, but the most likely reason is again finance. Having financed two elections already in January and the October by-election, and with little chance of winning they probably felt financially it was impossible to justify a candidate.

Russell Rea returned to the Constituency for the election, relieved that he would face no challenge. He was formally adopted by the Liberal Association at the Congregational Hall in Ocean Road on 28 November. The general election though was once again a frustrating stalemate, Will Crooks returned to Woolwich and regained his seat lost in January, nationally the Liberals gained one more seat than Balfour's Conservative and his Liberal Unionists allies, Asquith, with the support of the Irish Nationalists and the conditional support of the Labour Party's forty-two MPs, could return to Downing Street, and was able, with the threat of the creation of 500 new Liberal Peers, to curtail the power of the House of Lords with the Passing of the 1911 Parliament Act.

IV Great unrest

The pre-war years of 1911–14 have been described invariably as the years of 'Labour unrest' or 'The Great unrest' marked by several crises which the Asquith Government was required to contain; the question of Irish Home Rule, the increasing militancy of the Suffragettes, the Constitutional crisis with the House of Lords and the explosion of bitter strikes, most of them national disputes, which threatened to paralyse the country. South Shields was not immune from the influences of these issues, the Borough had a rising Irish immigrant population and as we have seen the Suffragettes regarded the town as fertile ground for recruitment and activity. However, its strong industrial base also meant that during this period it was affected by strikes, lockouts, disputes over 'black-leg' labour and reports that in February 1911 outside militant influences were even considering the establishment of a new District Trades Council to rival the pro-Liberal entity that already existed in the town. Coal mines, shipyards, blast furnaces, steel works and railways all stood idle at one time or another during this period of great uncertainty.

The workers' agitation saw some 3,000 strikes during the period and would cost three million workdays by the railwaymen, seamen and dockworkers in 1911 alone, with the next year seeing forty million workdays lost, mainly from coal miners, the prospect of a general strike was a real threat.

The Asquith Cabinet received a report from their Industrial Advisor, Sir George Askwith as to the reasons for the increase in industrial strife. He laid out several potential causes: the rise in the cost of living, the failure of wages to keep pace with inflation, the growth of the press and improvement in communications which made for greater national Trade Union coordination of activity as well enabling the conspicuous display of luxury by the affluent to a mass audience.

The ILP, Trades Council and the SDF all had a ringside seat as these events unfolded. The SDF organised open-air meetings to support the Seamen's Union during their industrial disputes whilst within the ILP one new interesting member to emerge was Cuth Barrass, a schoolteacher, who became Secretary of the ILP Branch and took over the organising of their Sunday evening lectures in the Labour Hall at Chapter Row. Key to their activities was to maintain a working relationship with the Women's Suffrage movement in the town, with the ILP nationally calling for the Government in November 1911 to withdraw the Manhood Suffrage Bill in favour of an Adult Suffrage Bill. Women were also beginning to come to the fore in Labour politics in the town with the ILP establishing in January 1911 a new Women's League Branch with Mrs Curbison of 1 Corney Street at Tyne Dock acting as the Branch Secretary.

Nationally, the Labour Party was rewarded for its support of the Liberal Government through the decision to grant an annual salary to all MPs of £400, and whilst the Osborne Judgement was not repealed in its entirety, it was significantly modified (one provision was that individual Trade Unionists could opt out of paying the political levy) to enable Trades Unions to give financial support to the Labour Party.

The November municipal elections in South Shields saw the ILP, and Labour interests consolidate their position marginally. Cullen had been appointed to the Aldermanic Bench, which given their in-built majority in the Chamber could only have occurred with the express support of the anti-Labour Councillors, an indication of the significant respect in which Cullen was held. Elsewhere, Jim Curbison was elected in the Laygate ward, following the decision of the sitting Labour supporting Councillor Ben Smith to retire given his appointment as a trade union official in Scotland, the ILP's R Vine and J Henderson were also returned unopposed in respectively the Victoria and Bents wards. Harton Lodge miner James Howe, with the support of the railway workers won in Simonside but his mining colleague, JR Surtees failed once again to be elected in the West Park ward. The SDP failed to contest any of the wards possibly because local members were in a state of flux, earlier in 1911 the SDP nationally had formed with other left groups the short-lived, British Socialist Party.

V Unity at last

Leading figures within Labour Party circles were determined to progress with the formation of a Labour Representation Committee in the town. They met at the Labour Hall to establish a branch in South Shields, appropriately enough on Valentine's Day 1912, elected as Assistant Secretary for the new South Shields Labour Party was Ernie Gompertz who was at the time twenty-four years old and rapidly emerging as a driving force within political circles. He was making a name for himself, both as an ILP member and as a Trade Unionist. In an interview, published in *The Journal* newspaper in December 1954 under the headline '*The Eternal rebel*', he recalled leading a delegation of shop assistants to the steps of the Town Hall demanding that the Council exercise its powers in appointing a Shop Inspector to ensure fair wages and workers' conditions. Gompertz recalled that this happened in 1907, but given he mentioned that they met the Mayor, Ald Robert Readhead, who told the fiery Gompertz – *All right young fellow, don't over egg the pudding'*, it must have occurred during 1910–12 when Readhead was Mayor. Even so, the protest, Gompertz recalled, was a success with the Council appointing a Shop Inspector not long after. He was certainly instrumental in the negotiations between the various competing left-wing groups in the Town to forge the creation of the South Shields Labour Party and was rewarded with a senior position in the Party's new structure. One can only imagine the intense discussions that must have occurred at the time bringing together disparate groups and competing interests before a final agreement on a constitution was reached.

Despite his relative youth, Gompertz had a ringside seat in these discussions by virtue of his membership of both the ILP and the Shop Assistants' Union but events in his personal life would have caused some pain since his grandfather Aaron Simon Gompertz was nearing the end of his life. Aaron Simon died on 7 February 1912 just days before the fateful inaugural meeting of the new South Shields Labour Party. The Shop Assistants' Union played a pivotal role in the creation of the Labour Party in the town, along with the more powerful coal miners, railwaymen and shipbuilders, since the first President of the local Labour Party was one of their leading members, Councillor Jim Rowden Curbison newly bestowed with civic honours following his election in the previous year's municipal elections.

The forty-four-year-old Curbison was twenty years older than Gompertz and acted as his mentor. He was a primitive Methodist lay preacher, the Manager of the local Co-operative Society's shoe and boot department, and one of the leading architects in the formation of a local Branch of the Shop Assistants' Union in November 1897, he was also a dominant figure in the local ILP Branch.

The *Shields Daily News* recorded the momentous occasion with a small article published on Friday 16 February 1912 which advised as follows:

South Shields Labour Party

At the first annual meeting of the South Shields Labour Party under the Chairmanship of Coun. JR Curbison it was decided to apply for affiliation to the National Labour Party. The following officers were elected: – President, Councillor JR Curbison; Hon. Secretary, Mr Charles Johnston; Assistant Secretary, Mr AE Gompertz; Financial Secretary and Treasurer, Mr RH Noble; Vice Presidents, Mr G Budd and Mr R Morgan. Deputations were appointed to meet Trades Unions and Societies not yet affiliated with a view to drawing all into the Labour Party ranks.

Affiliating to the Labour Party nationally, the local Party's next task was to establish a political base, raise funds and prepare for the next set of Council elections due in November 1912. The Party also took immediate steps to establish a Women's Labour League in the town. The new Party was determined to perform well and contest as many Council seats as possible.

The minutes of the nascent Party testify to the tenacity of the early pioneers; union branches were the key to establishing the Party's long-term future and central to this were the mineworkers. Deputations met with the Harton, Marsden and St Hilda's Lodges who were initially reluctant to affiliate but following subsequent 'pit-head' ballots of their members, agreed to affiliate a proportion of their membership and were thus entitled to send delegates to the Constituency Labour Party meetings.

In March 1912, just two months after being appointed Assistant Secretary of the Party, Gompertz was required to resign his position since the town centre Shopworkers Union Branch declined to affiliate to the Constituency Party and Gompertz lost his delegate's credentials. His absence though would only be temporary as he found a more willing Shopworkers Branch at High Shields who did affiliate in June 1912 and thus restored his right to attend Party meetings. The same meeting also discussed the issue of whether Labour Councillors in the Town Hall should be entitled to attend the Constituency Party meetings, without seeking a delegate's position from their Trade Union. In an indication of the dominance of the trade union movement within the Labour Party at the time, the South Shields Labour Party voted decisively 17–3 against the proposal.

The Party was careful not to overstretch themselves financially in fielding candidates for the local Council and in November the local Party agreed to send a delegate to the national Labour Party conference but only on the proviso the delegate paid their own travel and accommodation fees.

In response to the establishment of a Labour Party branch in South Shields, the remnants of the SDP, which had become the British Socialist Party, sought a merger with the ILP in the town. The ILP were reluctant to agree to the request. Replying to the BSP, Joe Wake the ILP Secretary wrote: '… *the South Shields branch of the ILP, whilst appreciating the motives of our comrades of the BSP, cannot see their way clear to abandoning the present alliance with the Trades Unions, etc., forming the Labour Party, and cannot therefore agree to join the British Socialist Party.*'

The Labour Party was given an early opportunity to establish itself with the electorate when a Council by-election was held in the Shields Ward on

21 June. Although their candidate, George Linney, a miner, came bottom of the poll, the fact that they fielded a candidate in a ward they had hitherto shown little interest in, was an indication to their opponents that the Labour Party was determined to campaign in all areas of the Borough and that in future there would be nothing pusillanimous about the new Party. By September, a joint meeting of the South Shields ILP and the local Labour Party agreed a slate of candidates for the November Council elections, but they only managed to field six candidates in the fourteen available contests with Labour's T Pritchard being returned unopposed in the Laygate ward. Long-serving John Bell was returned in Victoria, and George Linney, this time contesting Tyne Dock, missed out on the seat by just five votes. No alternative candidates from the British Socialist Party were fielded.

The infant Party also maintained its public presence by arranging a summer lecture tour across the town for Russell Williams, a radical Trade Unionist, Socialist and aspiring Parliamentarian. But the issue of securing their own Parliamentary candidate was never far from the early pioneers' minds. By January 1913 at the Constituency Annual Meeting (which saw Gompertz safely returned as the Assistant Secretary), a long discussion ensued about fielding a Labour Party Parliamentary candidate in the town. Delegates agreed to write to Party's headquarters asking for advice and consideration. Correspondence from London was clearly non-committal, not least because the Party nationally would only support candidates who had significant financial backing to fund the constituency campaign and no regional Union was prepared to bear the financial burden, without some assurance of electoral success. Nevertheless, local activists continued to press their claim. In April 1913, the Constituency Party wrote to Ramsay MacDonald the Party's Leader and in June there were further discussions at the monthly delegates' meeting.

Accepting that they needed to demonstrate to Labour's national leaders significant support for a Parliamentary candidate in South Shields in November 1913 they convened a conference of Trade Unionists and Socialist Societies in the town's Labour Hall based on Chapter Row to consider the issue further. Party Chairman, Cllr Jim Curbison, officiated at the meeting with over forty delegates, representing over twenty-two various organisations in attendance. The meeting considered several potential candidates and shortlisted four for consideration, Cllr Joe Batey, the St Hilda's Lodge Union activist (nominated by the railway workers but not by his own Durham Miners' Association), WC Anderson an ILP member and Shopworkers Union official from London, Ben Tillett of the Dock Labourers' Union from

London and the journalist Bruce Glacier another ILP member from Cheshire. The meeting adjourned with a commitment to reconvene in February 1914 to make a final choice.

Curbison reported back to the South Shields Labour Party's monthly delegates' meeting in December on various discussions he was conducting with key stakeholders. The same meeting supported correspondence from the Women's Suffragette Movement asking for the Party's support in their *'Votes for Women'* campaign and local activists were already beginning to think strategically in terms of consolidating their position as the leading voice for the working class in the town writing to the South Shields Trades Council suggesting a formal merger between the two organisations. Similar arrangements existed elsewhere in the country and a merger would prove less of a financial drain to affiliates (who were required to pay subscriptions to the two organisations) and give a clear formal point of reference for Trade Unions seeking support for their members who were anxious to be considered as Council candidates.

The Party also noted at their December meeting that they had gained another seat within the Council seat, gaining Simonside in November's municipal election. It seemed as if the momentum, at last, was with the emergent Labour Party in South Shields.

VI

1914 began with exceptionally wet and inclement weather across the country, but the enthusiasm the early stalwarts of the South Shields Labour Party felt could not be dampened. As the new year unfolded, they had much of which to be proud. They had consolidated their position on the Council, the sentimental hold which the Liberal Party held on Trade Union branches was weakening, evidenced by the number of Union Branches affiliating to the local Party; they were promoting their cause across the town (although inviting Russell Williams the previous summer had proven a serious financial challenge), they were making their presence felt nationally by ensuring they were represented at the Labour Party Annual Conference and a delegation from the Constituency met the Party Leader, Ramsay MacDonald when he visited Tynemouth in July 1912. They were also making moves to ensure working-class people were considered for the local Magistrates' Bench and they had united many working-class organisations into a single unit to the extent that they were looking forward to their Parliamentary selection contest in February.

Whilst building up the Party machine, they had also discussed policy issues, the Minutes record that in September 1912 they wrote to the Town Clerk and objected to the '*ineffective and dilatory manner*' in which the Council had put into operation the 1912 Shops Act; recorded a resolution at their March 1913 meeting in support of coal miners striking for a minimum living wage and in December 1913 they supported the Women's Suffragette campaign.

The 16 February 1914 Annual Meeting of the Constituency Party, held at the Labour Hall witnessed a good turnout of delegates, with Joe Batey becoming the Chair of the South Shields Labour Party, Jim Curbison moving to the position of Secretary, Harry Smith as Treasurer/Financial Secretary and Gompertz retaining his role as Assistant Secretary. The meeting was in good spirits and once again requested the Secretary to approach the Trades Council in relation to an amalgamation between the two bodies.

Two days later, the Constituency Party would convene once again to consider a Parliamentary candidate, records do not indicate if any of the other shortlisted candidates invited from the November meeting attended, the local media merely reports that Cllr Jim Curbison presided over a large meeting of activists including the Women's Labour League and that Cllr Joe Batey was invited to address the meeting on 'political matters', at the conclusion of which he was unanimously adopted as the Labour Party Parliamentary candidate for the Borough.

Batey was in many respects the obvious choice. Born in 1867 in Killingworth, he moved to South Shields at the age of nineteen to work as a putter at St. Hilda's Colliery where he was eventually elected by the miners as a Checkweighman in 1896 before also becoming the Secretary of the St Hilda's Miners' Lodge. By 1914, he had served on the Area Executive of the powerful Durham Miners' Association and was a member of the Durham Miners' Conciliation Board. He had also been a member of South Shields Town Council since 1898 – often returned unopposed at election time, a member of the local Board of Guardians since 1894, even being appointed Chairman in 1906 (quite an achievement for what was a reactionary Board membership) and was also a Justice of the Peace. He was clearly immensely well respected and had helped guide the local stalwarts in building the infant Labour Party. Both the Durham Miners' Association and the local railwaymen endorsed his candidature.

His endorsement though needed to be ratified by the Labour Party's National Executive Committee, who were anxious not to stretch their infinite resources contesting Parliamentary seats where there was little chance of success. The two issues of concern to Labour's leaders were ensuring financial support for the campaign and a demonstration that the proposed candidate could unite Labour and working-class interests in the Constituency. The first point was covered by the Miners who formally endorsed Batey and advised they would appoint an experienced full-time election Agent for the Constituency, and the second point was covered in April, when the South Shields Trades Council voted to end its long emotional attachment to the Liberal Party and endorsed Joe Batey's Parliamentary bid.

All that remained was for the National Executive Committee of the Labour Party to give their final endorsement.

While excitement about a Parliamentary contest raged, the Party was jubilant when in March a Council by-election in Tyne Dock saw Miner George Linney of Readhead Road secure a further seat for the Labour Party in the Council Chamber. The Party was beginning to demonstrate that it was rapidly becoming the focal point for working-class expression within the town. In March it agreed to hold a public meeting to welcome two South African mine deportees to the Borough, whilst the same meeting welcomed a representative from the National Union of Women's Suffrage Societies to talk about how they might work together to develop a campaign in the town. Finally, delegates were also beginning to turn their attentions to establishing an annual May Day Rally to develop working-class solidarity in South Shields.

The Party was anxious to maintain a strong presence on the Board of Guardians and agreed to support a Mrs Brock and Mr Tetley in the next scheduled elections – in supporting Mrs Brock the stalwarts were putting into action their vocal support for the right of women to seek public office.

However, it was not only this last point in which the local Party demonstrated it was ahead of its time. At the turn of the twentieth century, the Labour Party had no individual membership base, supporters were only allowed to play a part in their deliberations if they were an appointed delegate from a Union affiliated to the Constituency party. In May, following a long discussion the Party passed the following resolution:

> 'That we admit persons as individual members of the Party, who are members of an organisation, until such time as their organisation becomes attached to the Labour Party.'

An amendment specified that the members' fee would be 2/-.

South Shields Labour Party became one of the first in the country to introduce individual membership, although the member would still be required to be a member of a Trade Union eligible for affiliation to the local Party.

As spring gave way to the summer of 1914, there were two final projects for the South Shields Labour Party to complete before they contemplated the enjoyment of the warm weather. The Party undertook a registration of voters campaign in the town under the auspices of the Constituency Party Secretary, with an agreement to pay him £5 for five weeks' work, with the expectation that the fee would be paid by the Durham Miners. Finally, a special conference was organised for 9 June at the St Hilda Miners Hall attended by representatives of forty-one Union Branches to consider the need to construct more housing for working-class families across the Borough. The urgency for new housing had not been lost upon civic leaders given a recently published report by the Council's Medical Officer, D Morley Mathieson which outlined in detail the conditions of dwellings across the Borough.

Using the 1911 Census returns, Morley advised that with a population of 108,647, residents in South Shields were predominately living in 'flats' as opposed to 'family dwellings', statistically only 31.1 per cent of the population lived in a family dwelling (as opposed to the England and Wales national average of 86.6 per cent) whilst 63.1 of the population resided in blocks of flats or individual rooms within a house (as opposed to the national average of 2.9 per cent). Further, Morley highlighted the chronic overcrowding – which by Census returns meant *an average of more than two persons to a room.*' Morley estimated that 32.9 per cent of the residents lived in overcrowded accommodation. Almost half of the number of children in the town (47 per cent) were living in overcrowded housing conditions. In addition, the rental rates across the town were found to have been statistically higher than corresponding Boroughs across England. Morley was clear the situation could not continue, he noted that the population since 1911 had increased due to the amount of immigration into the town because of economic and trade prosperity which saw an influx of workers.

The Report concluded that the existing housing stock had outgrown the needs of population, that the Council needed to undertake an expansion – and that '*Owing to its peculiar natural position, South Shields has practically only one direction for expansion namely Southwards.*' Morley though was clear that such expansion should not be a repeat of long monotonous rows of featureless houses and '*dreary back-lanes with yards as substitutes for gardens*';

rather greater thought should be given to the construction of dwellings, a restriction on the number of houses built per acre with the provision of open spaces. Morley concluded his Report by acknowledging that the issue of housing provision was inseparable from the problems of '... *public morality and public health*' and that the weight of resolving the problem in the Borough could not be reconciled purely by the Town Council.

The local Labour Party organised a housing conference presided over by Joe Batey and considered the report in some depth agreeing to support the Council's decision to seek to expand the Borough's boundaries southwards with the aim of constructing new housing development. Gompertz spoke at the meeting and seconded the motion. The conference wanted the Council to accept the shortage of good quality 'working class housing' and urged the Authority to use its powers under the Town Planning Act of 1890 to ensure the creation of such housing in the future. Gompertz moved a further resolution that the meeting should write to the Local Government Board in London seeking financial support considering the high death rate, overcrowding and unsanitary conditions of the existing housing provision across South Shields.

The Party would meet again in July before the summer recess, to approve arrangements for the campaign to register electors onto the Burgess Roll and to hold an open-air meeting '... *to give Councillor Batey a hearty send off as Labour candidate*' for the next general election. No mention was made of fateful events in the Balkans at the meeting.

The motion would prove to be premature on two accounts – world events would result in the next general election not being held until December 1918 and Joe Batey wouldn't be their candidate.

Chapter 5

Conscientious Objector

I

On 28 June 1914, the Archduke Franz Ferdinand, the Heir Presumptive to the Austro-Hungarian throne, was assassinated in Sarajevo by Gavrilo Princip, a young Bosnian member of the Black Hand movement, whose aims were the creation of a Yugoslavian State, free of Austro–Hungarian rule. The turn of the twentieth century had seen a diplomatic build-up of complex Foreign Treaties between European States suspicious of each other's expansionist plans and with it an equally dangerous arms race, the assassin's fatal bullet brought these complex alliances into play which ultimately led to a war spanning the globe. Under the 1839 Treaty of London, Great Britain pledged to protect Belgium's neutrality, Germany's invasion of the Benelux country saw Great Britain declare war on Germany on 4 August 1914.

The onset of war presented the Labour Party with a particular set of problems. It had supported the concept of a Socialist International Movement in which workers would reject the narrow confines of naked unnecessary nationalism, which was, they believed, designed to keep workers divided, but the war merely witnessed Socialists volunteering in the interests of their own countries, the class struggle would have to wait. Further, the Labour Party was still very much a coalition of disparate groups and found itself unable to speak with one voice. It also led very much to an acrimonious, though not terminal split within the Party, in which the founding father, Keir Hardie opposed the war and Ramsay MacDonald resigned the Party Leadership declaring, '… *this country ought to have remained neutral.*' At Westminster, most of those MPs who had campaigned under the Labour banner supported the Government's declaration of war with Labour's National Executive Committee following suit. As Labour historian Martin Pugh has noted, much of the rank and file of the Party supported the war and leading Labour politicians such as Arthur Henderson, George Barnes and William Brice served as Ministers under first Prime Minister Asquith, and subsequently his successor Lloyd George.

II The DMA withdraws support

In South Shields, whilst the town was gripped in jingoistic fervour, the local Labour Party minutes record a membership that was practical rather than robustly endorsing the outbreak of war. At their meeting on 23 September 1914, they agreed not to contest the local elections (save only to defend their existing seats) and following correspondence from their new national Leader, Arthur Henderson (who had assumed the Leadership following Ramsay MacDonald's resignation) they agreed to nominate three members to serve on the local army recruiting committee – Batey, Cozens and Curbison.

Gompertz, who eight days before the assassination of the Archduke had turned twenty-six years old, and by now a humanist, teetotaller and vegetarian moved that the local Party write to Arthur Henderson urging the Parliamentary Party to ensure adequate financial provision for the dependants of soldiers, pensions for those servicemen disabled in the war and pensions for soldiers' widows. The resolution was agreed without dissent. It would not be the only occasion in which the local Party frequently raised the plight of servicemen and their dependants.

It is clear that Gompertz was a rising star within the Labour movement in South Shields, records bear testimony that Gompertz was beginning to assert himself within Labour's ranks. He chaired meetings of the local Party when the Chair himself was absent, and frequently moved resolutions on issues of concern to him, but as a humanist and a pacifist he was opposed to war and became one of the early members of the **No-Conscription Fellowship** formed in November 1914 to counteract national arguments urging Asquith's Liberal Government to conscript male adults for the war effort.

In May 1915, Gompertz, now residing at Westoe Crescent on Horsley Hill Road, submitted his name, via his ILP membership, as a potential council candidate for the November elections. The Party agreed to endorse Gompertz for the Tyne Dock ward (regarded as a promising seat for the Labour Party and an area Gompertz had strong connections with due to his family's pawnbroking business), although for some reason by July the ILP asked the Labour Party to stand Gompertz down and support J Surtees for the nomination, this was subsequently agreed. Whilst the reasoning behind this is not recorded, Gompertz, despite his pacifist views was well respected within local Party circles. Although he was not yet to enjoy municipal battle honours the decision by Jim Curbison to stand down as the Party Secretary (due to work commitments) at the same meeting in July, saw Gompertz elected unopposed as Secretary of the local Party and thus occupy one of the senior Labour and Trade Union positions in the Borough.

Gompertz wasted no time in using his position to espouse his pacificist views, within weeks the Labour Party agreed a lengthy motion that opposed compulsory military service on the grounds that it undermined the principle of civic freedom, it was a theme Gompertz would continue to encourage the local Labour Party and Trade Unions to pursue during numerous Labour Party meetings held over the course of 1915/16.

The Coalition Government, formed at the outbreak of World War I, introduced the Elections and Registration Act which received Royal Assent in July 1915, the Act halted Council elections for the duration of the war with any Councillor vacancies being dealt with through Borough Council appointment. Consequently, the South Shields Labour Party used the time to engage in community activity which included campaigning for greater working-class representation on the local Magistrates' Bench, organising public meetings against rising food costs and helping to establish in November 1915 a **Tenants' Defence League** which sought to oppose excessive rent increases by private landlords during wartime. The outrage across the country at what was seen as unpatriotic landlords forced the Government to introduce a Rent Act to prevent further excessive increases.

South Shields was on war footing, at least 13,000 men served in either the Army, Navy or its auxiliaries during the war, with some 2,000 men laying down their lives, the town itself was subjected on at least four occasions to Zeppelin raids and the Town Council led efforts to raise money for ambulances and supplies to be sent to the Western Front. In January 1917 the Borough contributed over £650,000 towards 'Tank week' and even children were involved with schools establishing War Savings Associations.

As the war became a stalemate with trenches being dug along the Western Front, the local press reported in August 1915 that the Durham Miners' Association had decided to withdraw their support for Joe Batey as the Parliamentary candidate for the Borough. Mr Gilliard the DMA's full-time Agent in the town was moved to Chester-le-Street to undertake campaign work in that district, a Constituency in which Labour already had Parliamentary representation. The decision by the DMA Executive caused great consternation within local Labour and Trade Union circles with Batey's St Hilda's Miners' Lodge sending strong correspondence to the DMA demanding their reconsideration. Arthur Henderson, Labour's national leader, seems to have been involved in forcing the DMA's decision. There was much concern amongst the national leadership that the Miners' Union in the North East of England had exerted too much influence and achieved too much success in securing Parliamentary candidatures for their own members. The *Shields Daily News* on 5 August 1915 reported that Labour's national headquarters were adamant that the proper procedure in selecting Batey as the South Shields nominee had not been followed. The decision by the DMA Executive to fall into line with Henderson's wishes came as a surprise to local Labour Leaders. Gompertz reported to the Constituency Labour Party meeting on 10 August that he had been approached by the press for comment and had insisted that as far as they were concerned Batey was still the Parliamentary candidate; the local miners' delegates were requested to use their influence to seek clarification from the DMA.

Whatever lay behind the decision of the DMA Executive, it was an act of solipsism and they had clearly shown discourtesy to a Constituency Party which had, in good faith, supported one of the Union's leading lights as their Parliamentary candidate. For the local stalwarts to learn of his removal via media enquiries rather than a formal explanation from the DMA clearly hurt. It was not until their September meeting when the DMA sponsored Election Agent handed the Party Officers a letter from the DMA confirming the decision not to support Joe Batey for South Shields.

The Constituency Labour Party was not prepared to let matters stand. Whilst the decision by the DMA Executive was irrevocable, Gompertz wrote to remind them that the local Party had undertaken campaign work in connection with Batey's candidature at the behest of the DMA and requested them to honour invoices for expenditure. The Labour Party was due to hold their Annual Conference in Bristol in January 1916 and local leaders fired off a resolution demanding that the national leadership appoint a special committee to enquire as to circumstances surrounding the decision not to endorse Batey, Gompertz would be attending the conference as the delegate from South Shields. The local Labour Party minutes record that the DMA wrote back to Gompertz in a visceral manner advising that they had no intention of honouring the invoices and considered the affair closed, matters came to a head in December when the St Hilda's Mechanics Lodge disaffiliated from the South Shields on the grounds that their members showed '… *a lack of interest* …' in the work of the local Labour Party. In the same month the Marsden Miners' Lodge submitted a resolution to the DMA area Executive which condemned the '… *weak and indefensible actions of the Executive Committee* …' in withdrawing Batey from South Shields and insisted that inference from the national Labour leadership in Parliamentary selections must end.

III

The withdrawal of Batey as the Parliamentary candidate was not the only issue which occupied Gompertz's time. As the war unfolded Gompertz was fastidious in his devotion to the anti-conscription cause. Whilst initially there was no shortage of willing volunteers seeking to wear khaki and fight at the front for King and Country, the realisation that the war would not be over by Christmas led, by 1915, to an acute shortage of new recruits for the British Army. A campaign was being orchestrated across the country for military conscription to be introduced for the first time in the country's history. Led principally, though not exclusively, by the *Daily Mail* it also attracted the support of the ambitious Liberal politician and former Chancellor of the Exchequer, David Lloyd George, who threatened to resign from the Government unless the Prime Minister supported the measure. Asquith was sufficiently concerned that he agreed to implement the Military Service Act of 1916, which came into force on 2 March 1916.

The Act specified that men from eighteen to forty-one years (subsequently increased to fifty-one years) old, were liable to be called up for service in the army unless they were eligible for exemptions. The exemption included men who were married (although the Act was amended to include them in May 1916), those widowed with children, those already serving in the armed forces, ministers of religion or men working in one of several reserved occupations. The Act specifically included conscientious objection as a reason for exemption, an early success of lobbying by the No-Conscription Fellowship. In the jingoistic atmosphere which existed during the war, this Clause of the Act was never fully adhered to by the Civil or Military powers charged with the Act's implementation.

Gompertz was one of the leading lights in South Shields against conscription, to such an extent that his patriotism was questioned at a meeting of the local Recruiting Committee, Gompertz felt compelled to give a personal statement at the Labour Party meeting in December 1915. His comrades endorsed his personal views even suggesting that they should demand an apology from the Recruiting Committee Chairman.

The anti-conscription movement was not without its strong opponents locally, no more so than within the local Trades Council where in January

1916, Gompertz sought their support for a motion that protested against compulsory Military service and, '... *rejoicing at the magnificent success of the appeal to the voluntary principle and expressing the opinion that no case has been made out for any measure of limited or temporary compulsory service.*' During a heated and ill-tempted debate, reference was made to '*slackers*' and '*If a country is fit enough to live in, it's fit enough to die for*', insinuations were also made that the anti-conscription cause was being funded by '*German gold*', and an amendment was moved and successfully carried that, '... *Compulsory service for all eligible citizens is the only just way of raising an army adequate to the present national danger*'.

Gompertz had more success with the South Shields Labour Party who defiantly maintained their opposition to compulsory Military service, perhaps in part to their Secretary's skilful advocacy of the voluntary principle. Nationally the Trades Union Congress had expressed their opposition to any compulsory service and Labour's new Leader, Arthur Henderson, despite being Labour's first Cabinet member in history, was urged to resign from the Government and remove the Labour Party from Asquith's Coalition-led administration. Matters came to head at a special Congress held in London on 6 January 1916, at which over 1,000 delegates assembled to consider the issue. Gompertz had been chosen to represent the South Shields Labour Party armed with a mandate to oppose Military conscription. The conference was fractious, but decisive in its rejection of compulsory Military service, demanding an end to Labour's involvement in the Coalition Government and insisting upon the resignation of Henderson and other Labour MPs from the Asquith Ministry.

Travelling back from London, Gompertz would have taken satisfaction that his deeply held convictions had been shared by the colleagues across the country. To prevent the Labour Party from dividing, Henderson and his colleagues submitted their resignations from the Government but made clear they would still support Asquith's Conscription Bill on grounds of military necessity. Asquith, determined to retain Labour (and by implication the trade union movement's) support, met with senior representatives of the Labour Party and pledged to make amendments to the Government's Bill which would remove the requirement for married men to be conscripted and disavowing any intention of introducing industrial conscription. The Labour Party Leadership mollified by Asquith's concessions rescinded their resignations and agreed that the matter would be further considered at the Labour Party Annual Conference to be held in Bristol due over 26–28 January 1916.

Gompertz duly made his way to Bristol determined to raise two resolutions authorised by the South Shields Labour Party. The first dealt with the refusal of Labour's national leadership not to endorse Batey as their Parliamentary candidate for South Shields. This was swiftly dealt with by national Officials who referred the issue to a special Committee of the Labour Party's NEC. The special Committee never met although by March the matter had become academic, Batey had been appointed to the full-time Agent's post for the DMA which necessitated him resigning from the Council, the Board Guardians and residing in Durham. Batey would eventually be elected to Parliament for Spennymoor in 1922.

The second resolution from the local Party referenced their objecting to Labour being part of the Coalition Government.

The Bristol conference was a classic political fudge designed to keep activists content whilst giving their leadership as much room for political manoeuvre as required. It was the first Labour Party conference since they had entered the Coalition Government, but Gompertz would be on the losing side as a motion to endorse Labour being part of the Coalition Government was agreed by 1,622,000 votes to 495,000. However, the conference reaffirmed their opposition to compulsory military service by 1,716,000 votes to 360,000, but the resolution was amended so heavily so as not to bind its Parliamentary representatives to demand the repeal of Asquith's Bill, which had been approved by Parliament a week before the Bristol conference. Once the Bristol conference was over, Asquith maintained his agreement with the Labour leadership for only six months before amendments were placed before the House of Commons to allow for the conscription of married men.

IV

As a single man aged twenty-eight years, Gompertz was now eligible for conscription. He advised the local Labour Party at their May 1916 meeting that he was due to be called up by the Military authorities at any moment and that arrangements should be made to appoint another Secretary in his place. Pacifist and humanist beliefs saw Gompertz, when the call-up papers arrived at his Westoe Crescent home, exercise his right of Appeal against military service to a Local Military Tribunal. The Tribunals were appointed by local Councils and made up of prominent men who undertook aggressive questioning to ascertain whether conscientious objection beliefs were deeply held pacifist, political or religious beliefs, or whether the applicant was simply a coward seeking to avoid military duty. Newspaper records for this period indicate that Ald Readhead, Ald Richardson, the Town Clerk and Lt Annard usually sat to hear Appeals with the Mayor Ald Taylor presiding. In Gompertz's case, the Tribunal refused to award an exemption certificate, so he subsequently took his case to the County Appeal Tribunal who, no doubt due to the force of Gompertz's arguments, overturned the judgement of the Local Tribunal.

The hostility towards those who refused to serve in the army and the sometimes chaotic civil and military administration that can exist during wartime resulted in many people who had been given Certificates of Exemption, finding themselves arrested as an '*absentee*' before their exemption certificate had been issued. Such was the fate of Gompertz.

He was arrested on 4 July 1916 and appeared in front of the local Magistrate who summarily tried, fined and handed him over to a military escort, where he refused to answer any questions on the Army Enrolment Form B2513 and declined to be medically examined. He must have looked younger than his twenty-eight years, because the Recruiting Officer, in the absence of a response listed Gompertz's '*apparent age*' as twenty-two. He was ordered to be sent to Richmond Castle but later that day he was taken to the Newcastle Barracks and enrolled in the 4th Northern Non-combatant Regiment enrolment number 2100. By 1916 there were more than 14,000 conscientious objectors across the country, most agreed to undertake non-combat duties, but a hard core of around 1,500 '*absolutists*' objected to undertaking any work associated with military work. Gompertz was an absolutist, and no doubt confident his military exemption certificate would eventually be acknowledged by the Authorities, refused to co-operate, six days later he was court-martialled for refusing to wear a military uniform, disobeying orders and for conduct to '*the prejudice of good order and military disciple*' he was sentenced to six months' imprisonment, later commuted to 112 days. He served his time at Richmond Castle.

Conscientious objectors were originally sent to military prisons on the grounds that the Courts considered them soldiers, the Army's response was often harsh and brutal and certainly without sympathy for those they regarded as cowards. Routinely beaten, abused, forced to stand for hours in their underwear on freezing parade grounds, humiliated, dunked into cold water and put on half rations. Following extensive lobbying, again by the No-Conscription Movement, objectors were eventually sent to civil prisons, but their treatment was no less severe and during the war around seventy-three men died as a direct result of the maltreatment they received.

The arrival of Gompertz's exemption certificate to his home on 14 July 1916, was to prove of no use. The Military Authorities insisted he was now required to serve out his military sentence. By October 1916 he had been moved to Brampton, where he again refused military orders. Sentenced on 13 October 1916 to one year's further imprisonment with hard labour but this was reduced to six months' hard labour to be served at Wormwood Scrubs. Gompertz steadfastly refused to obey orders, so his sentence was increased in early April 1917 by a further two years this time to be served at Leicester. Although this sentence was again commuted to twelve months without hard labour, upon release from Leicester Prison and returned to his Unit, he again refused military orders and in February 1918 was sentenced again to two years' hard labour to be served at Leicester.

Family and friends examined all ways of raising his plight and the Anti-Conscription Movement succeeded in having his case heard on 27 July 1916 in the House of Commons by the anti-war Labour MP, William Anderson, who represented Sheffield Attercliffe, and who had close links with both the Shop Assistants' Union and the Independent Labour Party.

Mr Anderson asked the Secretary of State for War:

'Whether his attention has been called to the case of A. E. Gompertz whose application on the grounds of conscientious objection to participating in war was refused by the South Shields Local tribunal but subsequently admitted by the Appeal Tribunal, who granted him exemption from combatant service and promised that his certificate would be forwarded to him; whether he is aware that this man, his certificate not coming to hand, was arrested as an absentee, handed over by the Magistrate to a military escort, taken to Newcastle Barracks, placed in a combatant regiment, court martialled, and sentenced to four months' imprisonment; and whether he will cause inquiry to be made into the facts of the case?'

The reply from Henry Forster, the Financial Secretary to the War Office was that he would need to review the particulars of the case and write to Mr Anderson. But it was merely gesture politics and stalling for time. Gompertz was by no means the only case raised in the House, Hansard reports that every afternoon proceedings would commence with questions from Parliamentarians to the War Office pleading the case of their Constituents.

The response was always the same, that the Minister would review the individual issue and reply direct to the Member of Parliament, but in the pro-War, patriotic hysteria that had gripped the country, Ministers were on safe ground simply providing an obfuscating response to the MP.

The South Shields Labour Party at their 25 July 1916 meeting agreed to make representations to the Local Government Board, South Shields Council and the Lord Chancellor's Department in relation to '… *the illegal arrest of our late Secretary Com (rade) Gompertz'* although Minutes of subsequent meetings make no reference to any replies having been received and the plight of Gompertz seems not to have been raised again by his comrades.

The relatives of conscientious objectors would also have had a difficult time, not only the constant worry and anxiety about loved ones serving a prison sentence, but also because the local community would tend to shun those neighbours whose relatives had refused to serve. This would not have been helped by the fact that South Shields, although escaping the destruction wrought on Hull and Hartlepool, nevertheless experienced four Zeppelin raids one of which bombed the fairground near the Market Place. Further, like the rest of the country, the town was enthusiastically supporting the war effort with the townsfolk raising money for two motor ambulances for the Western Front, a War Savings Movement being formed which involved local schools, flag days being organised and the local Authority contributing to the January 1917 Tank Week fund. Gompertz's family would in some parts have been insulated from the criticism of Gompertz's encasement given his younger brother Alexander was serving in the 47th Field Ambulance Unit of the Royal Army Medical Corps in France and being formally recognised in the British Jewry Roll of Honour whilst his cousin, Ernest Hartog Gompertz was a Lance Corporal in the Durham Light Infantry and his other cousin Ernest Hush from Middlesbrough, served with distinction in the battlefields of Europe being twice decorated and rising to the rank of Sergeant in the Yorkshire Regiment.

Like all objectors, Gompertz would have begun any sentence with one month in solitary confinement on bread and water, performing arduous tasks like breaking stone, hand-sewing mailbags and picking oakum. Keeping their spirits up, the *Labour Leader* newspaper on 23 November 1916, records prisoners at Leicester occupying themselves by staging a 'mock Parliament' where the wooden beds were arranged to resemble the House of Commons. Guardsmen were invited to listen to the debate on the continuation of war. Gompertz took on the role of the MP for Leicester and condemned '*with the utmost vigour*' the policy of the Foreign Office in having involved the country in obligations to other countries which had made the war inevitable. Following a lively debate two soldiers voted to continue with the war, whilst sixteen soldiers and nine conscientious objectors voted for immediate peace negotiations.

Whilst at Pontefract Barracks Gompertz was also one of seven men who signed a letter on 31 October 1916 to Labour MP Philip Snowden and pacifist Liberal MP, RL Outhwaite MP describing the forcible undressing, and haircutting of three of their fellow conscientious objectors. As part of a strategy to disorientate conscientious objectors and ensure what was termed *Equality of Sacrifice* the Authorities tended to move conscientious objectors as far away from their home as possible.

The final part of Gompertz's prison sentence was served at Armley Prison in Leeds, during which he was subjected to punishment of such a brutal and harsh nature that he was released on medical grounds on 5 August 1918, as a Class W Reserve. Reservists received no emoluments, were not required to wear a uniform and were not subject to military discipline, they were deemed to be more valuable to the country in civil rather than military employment. His discharge papers made clear he was not to be '*medically boarded*' thus making clear Gompertz and his family would themselves be responsible for nursing him back to health. The Class W Reserve was clearly the mechanism used by the Military to release Gompertz, they had not broken his resolve but they had broken him physically, for several months he would only be able to walk with the aid of crutches. Three months later the war ended.

V Labour's 'rebirth'

Russell Rea's hold on the South Shields Parliamentary seat, which he won at the 1910 by-election following Robson's elevation to the Peerage was resilient, but his public service was cut short by ill health. He died in February 1916 from heart failure at the height of World War I. Lloyd George attended his funeral at St Margaret's in Westminster. The South Shields Labour Party received clear instructions from their headquarters in London that the political truce meant that there would be no Labour Party opposition to the Liberals' chosen successor. Cecil Cochrane, a forty-six-year-old ironmaster from Middlesbrough was adopted as the Liberal Party candidate, he was returned unopposed in the March 1916 by-election.

The enforced absence of Gompertz from the local scene saw the Party in some state of flux. The Secretary's position could not be filled on a long-term basis, several members were approached who declined nomination but eventually Mr Cozens was encouraged to undertake the onerous administrative burden in August 1916. The absence of Gompertz also saw the local Party, whilst maintaining its opposition to conscription, at its January 1917 meeting refusing to consider a motion on the question of appealing to the Government to enter peace negotiations.

Cozens, although now a largely forgotten figure in the development of the local Party, deserves some credit for steering it through the next stage of its journey.

In November 1916 the local stalwarts were again turning their attentions to ensuring an amalgamation of working-class interests in the town. Since the formation of the South Shields Labour Party in February 1912, there still existed, quite separate from the Labour Party, the South Shields Trades and Labour Council which was comprised of affiliated Union branches from across the town. Nationally, Trades and Labour Councils could affiliate to the National Labour Party in their own right, but this position would change at the Labour Party's Nottingham conference in January 1918.

In what has been described as the '*Rebirth of the Labour Party*' by Herbert Tracey in his tome, *The History of the Labour Party*, the conference agreed a new Constitution and clear aims and values (which included the new Clause IV commitment to nationalisation of industry). The Party moved to regulate its structures and encouraged the amalgamation of the Trades Councils with established local Divisional Labour Parties. The new Constitution also realised that its rigid membership structure, which only permitted membership of the Labour Party via an affiliate such as Trade Union, was outdated given there were eight million newly enfranchised women the vast majority of whom neither had the opportunity to join a Trade Union nor were prepared to be associated with a Socialist organisation affiliated to the Labour Party. The conference agreed that individuals could, for the first time, join the Labour Party direct.

With the national Labour Party agreeing a new constitution it seemed a fortuitous moment to merge the South Shields Labour Party and the South Shields Trades and Labour Council into one body with monthly meetings dealing with political and industrial business. There was clearly pressure for the amalgamation from the local Unions because Cozens reported to the South Shields Labour Party just four weeks after the Nottingham Conference that the Trades and Labour Council had met and agreed to talks in relation to a merger.

The desire to merge though was not without its challenges, there were initial talks between the two organisations from as early as November 1916, the local Party Minutes indicate that discussions were protracted but it was not until their July 1917 meeting that the South Shields Labour Party agreed to 'dissolve' itself and formally agree to merge with the South Shields Trades and Labour Council. The new constitution would still need to be ratified by Labour's London headquarters which meant that it was not until 21 February 1918 that the first meeting of the newly merged organisation came into being.

The first Annual Meeting of the South Shields Labour and Trades Council saw the election of Cllr Curbison as Secretary and Cllr George Linney from the Marsden Miners as Chairman. Given their numerical strength it is interesting to note that the Chair was the only senior position occupied by a Miners' Lodge (although St Hilda's Lodge refused to initially affiliate to the new body), further still that not one woman was appointed either as a Constituency Officer or as a member of the Executive Committee (although they sought to rectify this relatively quickly by agreeing at their March meeting to consider establishing a Women's Section). The meeting was required to amend its Constitution at the insistence of Arthur Peters, the Labour Party National Agent. This centred around the important point that individuals were not required to be a member of an affiliated Union before they could join the Labour Party.

New political activists were clearly coming to the fore and the sentimental attachment to the Liberal Party in the town was unravelling. The Liberal Party were in many respects the victims of their own misfortune, the splitting into factions nationally between Lloyd George's National Liberals and Herbert Asquith's Liberals would have caused some difficulty for the Liberal Party in the town. The final act of the South Shields Labour Party before it merged with the Trades Council was to ensure they began the process of choosing a Parliamentary candidate who would replace Joe Batey. Given the split in the Liberals' ranks, they had a high expectation of winning the Parliamentary seat once the war was over. In their final act as a standalone organisation in December 1917 and with the support of their national headquarters, the South Shields Labour Party agreed to invite Mr John Hill (Boilermakers), Mr R Young (Engineers) and Mr Jones (Engineers) from Sheffield to a selection conference to be held at the Marsden Miners' Hall in Imeary Street in early 1918. Local Councillor, Jim Curbison considered seeking the nomination but chose not to enter the race. Added to the Official Minutes in the side column though was added *Cllr Rowe (Boilermakers)*, the reason for his late inclusion is unexplained but the name was clearly added after the formal Minutes had been written.

George Rowe had developed a tough reputation in the trade union movement. A Tynemouth County Borough Councillor, he had joined the Boilermakers' Society in 1891 and became a full-time Society Official representing men in pay negotiations and seeking to improve their work conditions. By all accounts he was well respected, a fluent orator, and given the importance of the shipbuilding industry on the Tyne during this period, he would have been well known across Tyneside. He was originally from London's East End, but the family had moved to the North East when Rowe was in his early teenage years. Rowe had also been an enthusiastic supporter of the war and served as a member of the Armaments Committee for the Northern region before joining the Munitions Board in 1917.

The selection conference to choose the Parliamentary candidate took place on 9 March 1918. George Rowe won the nomination by fifty-five votes to John Swan's vote of twenty-two. Swan had been supported by the Durham Miners and one cannot help speculating that his heavy defeat was in part due to some of the long-serving local activists recalling the behaviour of the DMA in withdrawing Joe Batey three years earlier. Swan though would eventually be elected to Parliament for Barnard Castle.

Rowe had a strong base amongst the shipbuilders, and because of the financial assistance from the Boilermakers' Society, the Party was able to advertise for a Parliamentary Organiser and quickly recruited George McNamara of Blackburn, who took up residence in the town and with the Party being financially secure, rented a political base at the Edinburgh Buildings in the centre of town.

The decision by the local MP, Cecil Cochrane to resign from Parliament after only two years' service, forcing a further by-election in the town in 1918 gave the Labour stalwarts an electoral opening. Cochrane, his Parliamentary career never having taken off, wished to return to business and had also renewed his interest in academia becoming Chairman of Armstrong College and the Honorary Treasurer of the Durham College of Medicine, the two institutions which later merged to become Newcastle University.

The local Party wired their national headquarters following a meeting on 17 October, requesting permission to field a candidate. Arthur Henderson discouraged the breaking of the national truce between the national political parties and requested a meeting with representatives of the local Party when he was next in the region. Rowe's Boilermakers' Society, who were providing funding to the South Shields Labour Party, were also of the view that contesting a by-election when a general election was imminent was impractical and financially undesirable. The *Newcastle Journal* on 17 October 1918 reported that if the Labour Party were honourable, they would abide by the wartime truce and not treat it as a '*scrap of paper.*' The delegation from South Shields, which included the Chair, Cllr Linney and the Agent, McNamara, duly met Henderson in Newcastle, he was adamant that no authorisation to contest the by-election would be given and urged the local Party to save their finance for the impeding general election. On the afternoon of Sunday 20 October, the delegation reported back to a specially convened meeting of the Constituency Party and in a fraught and tense atmosphere agreed the following statement for the press:

> '*That this meeting expresses its unabated confidence in Councillor G J Rowe as the Labour candidate for the Borough of South Shields, and that we take more active steps in furthering the candidature of Mr Rowe for the General Election; and further, that we do not contest this by-election.*'

Given the national truce, the vacancy should have been filled by a Liberal Party nominee, but it wasn't. When nominations closed, neither the Conservatives nor the Liberal Party nominated a candidate and the only declared candidate for 28 October 1918 by-election was Havelock Wilson, who described himself as a Trade Union Coalition candidate.

Havelock Wilson **had** been formally supported by the town's Liberal Association who wrongly assumed they had his agreement at a meeting in the Liberal Club in Ocean Road in August that year, to contest the seat as a Liberal–Labour candidate, however on Tuesday 15 October, two days before nominations closed he again met the Liberal Association and the Women's Liberal Association in the Queen Street Assembly Rooms, to advise he now intended to stand as a Trade Union Coalition candidate. Given that the close of nominations was only hours away they had no option but to agree. Wilson accused the Labour Party of '*a cowardly act*' for failing to field George Rowe and said he was looking forward to the election campaign, he was though elected unopposed in the Parliamentary by election.

Wilson had a chequered career in the Labour movement. He stood in an 1890 by-election in Bristol as an Independent Labour candidate, and lost; he fought Middlesbrough in 1892 as Independent Labour, defeating the Liberal William Robson (who went on to become the MP for South Shields); he quickly realigned himself to the so called Lib–Lab pact of MPs for the 1895 General Election in Middlesbrough ensuring he had a straight run against the Conservative Party and won, but by 1906 he was standing in Middlesbrough as a Liberal, defeating a future Labour Party Leader George Lansbury in the process, before losing his seat in 1910.

VI

It was not just in the political world where Wilson acted as a lone and divisive figure. Born in Sunderland in 1859, he was a seaman by the age of ten. In 1879 he had become involved in the Sunderland Seamen's Union eventually rising to become President by 1885. But Wilson saw the potential the Union offered him and pursued a policy of building the organisation along nearby ports on the North East coast. By 1887 after a series of disagreements with the Sunderland Seamen's Union he left and established his own National Sailors' and Firemen's Union regarded as the first national Trade Union for seafarers remaining the Union's President until he died.

Organising and representing a membership that was in the main at sea and working across the globe was always difficult, Wilson ruled the Union with an iron rod brooking no opposition from within. He had no sympathy for those seeking to create a working-class-based political Party, he encouraged his Union not to affiliate to the Labour Party and he refused to support the 1926 General Strike, viewing it as '*revolutionary plot.*' In the main, he showed total antipathy towards Labour's early leaders like Keir Hardie and Arthur Henderson, was pugnacious and held extreme right-wing views, but he was more than content to use the Labour name when it suited his political purposes. Indeed, he had attended a special Labour and Trade Union conference in September 1918 seeking Labour's support to contest South Shields in any future election but was rebuffed on the grounds the local Party had already selected George Rowe. His aggressive recruitment style saw his Union grow, and the shipowners were relaxed about dealing with a Union leader who could control the waterfront membership without too much disruption to their operations.

We can measure Wilson's political and jingoistic outlook through his own words, recorded in the *Newcastle Journal* on 17 October 1918:

'Our day has finally arrived with startling rapidity. It is opportune that it should have come at this moment when the Huns are crying out for peace, although they are still murdering innocent people at sea as is the case at Leinster. I am a thoroughly win-the-war man, one who does not believe in a patched-up peace which would result in more bloodshed, outrage and murder in the future and I shall fight primarily as one who believes in punishing the Germans. In so doing I am confident that I shall have the support of every right thinking – every British elector in the Division.'

So, this was the man whom the political power brokers of all political Parties in South Shields stepped aside for. In hindsight the decision taken by the local Labour Party was unfortunate since it allowed Wilson, following the by-election, to enter the 1918 General Election held just eight weeks later with the status as the town's Member of Parliament.

As the guns fell silent across the battlefields of France, Prime Minister Lloyd George wasted no time in seeking a fresh mandate from the British people. Within twenty-four hours of the Armistice on 11 November, he called a General Election scheduled to take place on Saturday 14 December 1918. It was the so-called 'Coupon Election' in which candidates, pledged to support the Liberal Lloyd George and his Coalition supporters the Conservative Party, were given official endorsement for their election address. It was the first General Election since 1910 and the first held after the passing of the Representation of the People Act 1918 which saw all women over the age of thirty, and all men over the age of twenty-one being entitled to vote. It increased the voting electorate in South Shields from 18,500 at the 1910 General Election to over 50,000.

In South Shields there would be no repeat of the by-election fiasco. George Rowe was nominated as the official Labour Party candidate, the first occasion on which the Party contested a general election. The new enfranchised electorate in the town were faced with two choices, Rowe and Havelock Wilson. Wilson needed to secure the new working-class men and women's vote, so continued to describe himself as a Trade Union Coalition candidate, receiving Prime Minister Lloyd George's 'coupon' and public endorsement.

In returning to South Shields after his ordeals in prison and after recuperation, Gompertz was anxious to assist the local Labour Party. However, in a final piece of political spite against conscientious objectors the Law was changed to deprive them of the right to vote for five years from the date of the end of the war. We can safely assume that Gompertz, physically incapacitated, and denied a vote in the general election, would have only played a minor role, if any role at all, in the election campaign. He was a recognised Labour activist in the town and his prison record was well known publicly, George Rowe, given his jingoist opponent Havelock Wilson was criticising Labour's response to war at every available opportunity, would have been keen to restrict Gompertz's public involvement with the campaign.

Reviewing the chronicles of the North East regional media, Wilson's campaign was fought entirely on his support for the war and anti-German vituperation. He ridiculed those in the Labour Party locally like Ernie Gompertz who had been conscientious objectors, he denounced the Labour Party nationally for not being patriotic enough during the war years and called for a boycott of all German shipping. He warned that Labour supported '*red revolution*' in the country and told one crowded public meeting at the Empire Palace that the Labour Party: '… *had captured the leading positions in our Trade Unions and were going to use them in a way which would shackle the people as slaves.*' With the mood not just in South Shields, but across the country being extremely anti-German, Wilson played the war years for every vote he could muster.

Rowe, despite his own exemplary war record – he had received the Order of the British Empire for his wartime work on the Munitions Board – was unable to withstand the populist onslaught that centred around Wilson's entire campaign. Rowe's speech at the Palace Theatre in High Shields on 9 December 1918, endeavoured to highlight social policy surrounding better housing, better wages and fairer taxation with his call that incomes over £5,000 a year should be confiscated by the state. His message was simply drowned out by a war-weary public's desire to show their support for Lloyd George's handling of the war and Wilson's fervent support for it.

The *Newcastle Journal* on Monday 16 December 1918 wrote:

'*Probably no contested Parliamentary election in South Shields ever took place with less fuss or show than that which was held on Saturday, notwithstanding the fact that never hitherto had there been anything like the number of votes to be recorded. Party colours were absent, no vehicles by arrangement between the Parties were used to convey voters to the poll and everything passed off in quiet and orderly fashion.*'

The general election had been called during an influenza epidemic, and in agreement with the town's Medical Officer, the candidates had agreed to keep canvassing and campaigning to a minimum, except for public meetings in the local theatres and meeting halls. This could not have helped the Labour Party as they fought their first Parliamentary election. Wilson on the other hand was a political campaign veteran. On Friday 13 December the day before the poll, Wilson addressed two mass rallies, one in the Market Place and one at Mill Dam before addressing a meeting of women in the Victoria Hall, Fowler Street. Meanwhile, it was noted in the media that Rowe was enjoying considerable success in the '*thickly-populated labour district at the western part of the Borough*', clearly Tyne Dock, Simonside and surrounding streets, holding final rallies at the Marsden Miners' Hall in Imeary Street and in a large auction tent.

Both candidates declared themselves in favour of Irish Home Rule, an issue that had split the Liberal Party nationally with the result that the Irish Nationalist Party in London wired to the Irish community in South Shields – '*Standing Committee will leave action of Irish electors in this election entirely in their own hands.*'

There was an anxious wait over the Christmas period since the ballot papers across the country were not counted until 28 December to enable the Armed Forces ballot boxes overseas to be added to the final tally. When the result was declared a jubilant Havelock Wilson had triumphed with 19,514 to Rowe's 6,425.

Lloyd George's National Liberals, with his Conservative Coalition partner achieved a landslide, Asquith's Liberals saw their strength drop from 272 MPs to just thirty-six with even Asquith being defeated in his East Fife seat. The Labour Party, with just fifty-seven MPs faced the Government benches of 520 MPs and although larger in number than the Asquith Liberals ceded the role of the Leader of the Opposition to the Liberal Party because of the failure of experienced Parliamentarians like Henderson and MacDonald to secure a seat at the general election.

Perhaps the final word should be left to Curbison, the local Labour Party Secretary who recorded in the Party Minute book:

'*Labour was defeated, as the counting of the votes on Dec 28th 1918 revealed, defeated by votes, it is true, but not disgraced, nor yet discouraged, but filled with hope that possibly before very long, when the dazzle and the glamour of the cheap patriotism has passed away and things resolved to their normal conditions, we would again face the electorate with the same candidate (George Rowe) and win the seat for organised Labour. We accept the temporary defeat but our hopes for coming days are bright and cheery.*'

George Rowe though would not contest the South Shields seat again.

Aaron Ernest Gompertz's paternal grandparents Aaron Simon Gompertz and Paulina Hirsch. *c.*1890. (*Courtesy of Melville Goldbaum*)

Rebecca Gompertz (nee Cohen) and
Aaron Ernest Gompertz, *c.*1888.
(*Courtesy of Melville Goldbaum*)

Samuel & Rebecca Gompertz with
their sons Aaron Ernest Gompertz
(standing) and Gabriel, *c.*1893.
(*Courtesy of Melville Goldbaum*)

Aaron Ernest Gompertz with his mother Rebecca Gompertz (nee Cohen). (*Courtesy of Melville Goldbaum*)

The Gompertz Family c.1886

Jeremiah   Paulina   Abraham   Simpson   Regina   Maurice
                                   Samuel   Aaron Simon   Susannah
                       Fanny   Rebecca

Gompertz family, 1886. (*Courtesy of Melville Goldbaum*)

Gompertz gathering taken c. 1927-1932

| Rosa Fink (nee Gompertz) | Annie Gompertz (nee Thompson) | Abraham Harris | Gabriel Gompertz |
| Cissie Gompertz (nee Goldman) | Rebecca Harris (nee Cohen) | Maurice Fink | Alexander Gompertz |

Gompertz family gathering, *c.*1927–32. (*Courtesy of Melville Goldbaum*)

Samuel Aaron Gompertz, before 1909.
(*Courtesy of Melville Goldbaum*)

Hudson Street, Tyne Dock, *c.*1920s, at the time Gompertz represented the area. (*Courtesy of South Tyneside libraries*)

Chapter 6

The Interwar Years

I

In 1923 at the age of thirty-five, Gompertz married Annie Thompson, the eldest of three daughters and two sons of William and Susannah Thompson. The marriage certificate states that Gompertz was living at 42 South Eldon Street in South Shields and his profession was a Shop Assistant – as opposed to manager – in a jewellery shop. Gompertz also records that his late father Samuel's profession was a jeweller not a pawnbroker.

Annie's family originally lived at 180 Eldon Street in South Shields where her father was a chemical labourer. By 1901 the family had moved to nearby 191 Alice Street but by the 1911 Census the family had relocated to a six-roomed house at 53 Bewick Street in a more prosperous part of the town but within walking distance of the local shipyards. Her father by 1921 is registered as a plater one of the senior skilled occupations in the shipyards. Annie was born on 15 June 1885 and by the time of her fifteenth birthday in 1901 was working as an Assistant in one of the Gompertz family pawnbroking shops. Annie was still working for the family in 1921 but Census records show she had risen to become the Manageress of the shop at South Eldon Street. The Thompson family fortunes must have changed rapidly from the 1921 Census since her marriage certificate indicates that by 1923 her father William had become the Secretary to a Friendly Society (Annie is recorded as a spinster with no profession indicated) and the family unit had moved to a pleasant estate house, Howard Cottage, in the small village of Wetheral located in Cumberland. Gompertz clearly kept in regular contact with Annie since by the time of her thirty-eighth birthday she had accepted his marriage proposal. They were married at Carlisle Registry Office on 28 June 1923.

During this time, Gompertz was also the Secretary of the South Shields Hebrew Congregation based at 14 Ogle Street. He was always proud of his ancestry and on no occasion sought to hide his Jewish origins, but in later life rejected the strict religious ordinances. Summer holidays for Gompertz and Annie were always taken in August, when Council and Labour Party meetings were in recess and always two weeks in the same boarding house in Allendale in Northumberland, where both would read, relax and go for long walks over the hills.

Gompertz and Annie made their home together at 31 Quarry Lane, South Shields where they remained for the rest of their lives. They had no children, but Annie would have been tolerant of the endless Council and Labour Party meetings her husband attended on an evening, and proud of his work as the Parliamentary Agent to the town's MP, James Chuter Ede. Annie played her own active role in the life of the South Shields Labour Party becoming the first woman delegate to the South Shields Labour and Trades Council from the Shopworkers Union and although she never sought public office, as the spouse of a senior and well-respected political activist she would have undertaken her fair share of work at election time, supporting her husband in his own Council election campaigns as well as ensuring she gave support at general election time. She entertained at their Quarry Lane home many prominent Labour figures who visited the town and became a close confidante of Ede's wife Lilian. A shy and reserved woman, she came into her own in 1953, when she became the Mayoress of South Shields supporting her husband during his Mayoral year. She died in 1967.

II

The interwar period saw the Town Council, under the direction of the Addison Housing Act, make strident efforts to tackle some of the appalling housing that existed in the centre of South Shields. The Town Clerk, Harold Ayrey, described housing conditions in the town as the worst slums he had ever seen. The Council began to implement their former Medical Director's 1914 recommendations by creating a Town and Planning Committee under the Chairmanship of the Mayor, Andrew Anderson. Across the North East, Councils were under increasing pressure from Labour and Trades Councils to tackle the housing crisis and it is not surprising that the Council agreed to appoint a Labour Councillor, James Dunlop as the Vice Chair of the Housing Committee. The Council sought to expand the town southwards with the creation of the town's first council estate, Cleadon Park. A Parliamentary order would be required to transfer the area to South Shields Council, since it lay outside the Borough boundary, this was followed by a new housing development in Simonside. Once constructed, whole swathes of the inadequate town centre housing were demolished, Waterloo Vale, Catherine Street and Maxwell Street as well as at Tyne Dock. It was an ambitious programme which continued until the outbreak of World War II in 1939, with new housing estates under construction at Horsley Hill and Marsden.

The regeneration was not without its controversy not least that the farmland at Cleadon Park had been privately bought by the Mayor, Andrew Anderson, who had originally advised that he was concerned the Corporation may not complete the transaction and had purchased the land himself to sell back to the Council at no additional cost. As the Town Clerk endeavoured to negotiate the transfer of ownership, communication with the Mayor ceased. In the resultant fury, it was discovered that the Mayor had been working privately with the Smith's Dock Company who wished to build houses for their own workers with the eventual intention that the workers would be able to buy them. A subsequent Council Inquiry in October 1919 saw Anderson resign as Mayor and from the Council. The Council eventually purchased the land on behalf of the Corporation and the new Cleadon Park housing estates would quickly be connected by electric trams and benefit from significant road improvements. Clearance of the dilapidated town centre housing along the river allowed for the expansion of new industrial sites most notable Brigham & Cowan's shipyards at Middle Docks, where they were able to modernise their operations, thus enabling further job creation. The tourist potential of the seafront was also of interest, particularly to Jim Curbison who urged the local authority to establish a working group to consider ways of improving the recreational offer afforded by the seafront.

In early 1919, the Boilermakers' Society advised the South Shields Labour Party that they would not renew McNamara's contract as the Party's full-time Agent, thus withdrawing their interest in the Parliamentary seat. The Constituency party considered ways in which they could raise the £200 annual salary to retain his services but by February 1919 had reluctantly concluded that they needed to let McNamara go. The Constituency Party was also turning attention as to how it may consolidate their position within the local Council where elections were to be fought in November 1919 for the first time since the Armistice with the Tyne Dock branch of the Irish Labour Party requesting that their members be considered for West Park, Tyne Dock and Simonside. The local Party also undertook an ambitious plan to form a Labour Club with a working party established in February 1919 to consider how such a Club could be self-financing. Finally, the advent of individual membership of the Labour Party, saw the emergence of an active Women's Section, with the February delegates' meeting welcoming '*the three lady delegates approved by the Women's Section.*'

III

The local Party also took advantage of the new Labour Party constitution to restructure itself. In April 1919 following a request from the newly formed Durham County Council Labour Group of Councillors, they agreed to request that their own Labour Councillors on South Shields Council formally constitute themselves into a Labour Group. The recommendation was carried through, but the Labour Group made clear that the local Party could not mandate or instruct Councillors how to vote in Council meetings. Further, the Party's growing membership base saw the creation for the first time of individual branches across the town based on Council electoral wards.

The initiative to create individual branches was not without its detractors, notably the trade union delegates (loyal to the pre-merger Trades Council) who asked how 'industrial business' would be considered at such meetings and whether the Party branches would be delegate based rather than organised around individual party membership. The Labour Party Executive were adamant they wanted local branches formed with the full involvement of individual members residing in the area, who would form a campaigning nucleus in wards they were keen to win at the local elections. In an exiguous recorded response to the Trade Union delegates the Executive declared at their June meeting, '*That the Executive Committee are of the opinion this Party is a political organisation only*' but they maintained that the central Constituency Party would still be structured as a delegate-based body. Individual members would be entitled to attend the constituency meetings and speak but not vote (a system that would endure nationally until the Labour Party's 'one member one vote' reforms in the 1990s).

The town's MP, Havelock Wilson was displaying erratic behaviour in the House of Commons which caused concern to his Liberal supporters in the town. Within days of being re-elected in December 1918 he supported the formation of the short-lived **National Democratic Party (NDP)** which had a decidedly anti-Socialist and anti-Communist ethos, and which sought to manipulate and exploit the genuine grievances of former front-line soldiers whom he described as '*True British Patriots.*' He joined an NDP Group in Parliament along with ten other MPs but still pledged to support Lloyd

George. The Liberals locally were becoming weary of Wilson's unstable behaviour and there was every likelihood of them standing a separate Liberal candidate at the next general election.

From their new base at 14 King Street, the Labour Party considered the matter at their May 1919 meeting.

Curbison was still keen for George Rowe to contest the Parliamentary seat and recommended that approaches be made to the Boilermakers' Society to secure their support, an amendment to his proposal though was approved with the Party instructing the Secretary to write to all affiliate Trade Unions asking for Parliamentary nominations. With the previous decision by the Boilermakers' Society not to support Rowe for South Shields in future, the local mineworkers exerted their authority once again and lobbied for a miner to be considered for the nomination, with all the financial and logistical support from the DMA such support entailed.

In December 1919, the *Daily News* carried reports that Will Lawther, the Secretary of the Chopwell Miners' Lodge in Gateshead, a village in Labour folklore described as 'Little Moscow' was being discussed as a possible South Shields candidate. Whilst there was a body of opinion that believed the Miners were the obvious choice (with the local Party requesting the local Miners' Lodges in August 1920 write to the DMA Executive urging them to make South Shields one of their constituencies), they did consider other potential candidates. Given its strength in South Shields, they approached the National Union of Railwaymen and the name of a respected local man, Cllr Charles A Henderson, a member of the NUR National Executive was mentioned, in addition so was a London Engine Driver, Cllr P Black (who eventually declined given he was being considered as a Parliamentary candidate elsewhere). A further potential candidate considered was Charles Trevelyan and a deputation went so far as to meet him, but he declined the invitation, becoming a Labour MP for Newcastle Central in 1922 and subsequently the President of the Board of Education in Labour's first Government.

IV

Global events saw the British Government send troops to Russia as part of a 'White army' contingent to restore the previous Tsarist regime which had collapsed in 1917 following the Russian Revolution. South Shields Labour Party at its September meeting expressed its '*disgust and alarm*' at the attempt to '*suppress free people*' and urged the return of their '*Sons and brothers*'.

Although in a demonstration of the moderate approach that has always characterised the local Party, by October they rejected a suggestion that they should affiliate to the **National Committee Hands off Russia** and vetoed any moves to have the matter discussed at future public meetings organised by the Party. Mindful of the reaction of the public to their stance against military conscription – which still drew critical correspondence in the local press – the Party stalwarts may well have been concerned at appearing to the public too sympathetic to the new Russian Government.

The local Party was not to enjoy a successful November municipal election, despite much central planning, finance being allocated (including the loan of £30 from a sympathetic supporter) and a full slate of candidates contesting all seats, the Party was not to enjoy sweeping municipal success. They gained only three seats giving them a strength of fifteen on the Council, although they suffered no net loss of seats. It was a disappointing result given that nearby Gateshead Labour Party had enjoyed nine gains, Durham County Council fell to Labour whilst Bradford, the birthplace of ILP was captured by Labour and in London, the Party led by Herbert Morrison, secured control of twelve Boroughs. The local elections did though see the local Labour Party fight a well-managed and coordinated campaign, there was no significant vote splitting between rival working-class candidates and a Labour manifesto was produced which had as its mainstay improvements in housing and education provision.

Much credit should be recorded to Mr W Tetley, an ILP member, who with his wife devoted their time to the organisation and campaigning aspects of the Constituency Party. Mrs Tetley was a founder member of the Women's Section, served on the Constituency Executive and appears to have been the first woman nominated to contest a Council seat on behalf of the Party; Mr Tetley was Literature Secretary and despite having an obvious claim for standing for election in a Westoe Ward by-election in January 1920, he humbly stood aside and acted as the Agent for the unsuccessful campaign when the Marsden Miners insisted on fielding one of their own. The Tetleys also instigated a prize-draw to raise funds for the local Party. Being a sole trader, he had no trade union base, and consequently was overlooked for the Secretary's position when it became vacant in May 1920, losing to the Railwaymen's nominee Henry Donnelly. He did secure the position of Financial Secretary on the casting vote of the Chair.

V

The new Labour Group of Councillors in South Shields Town Hall, as requested by the Labour Party, met and constituted themselves into a formal unit. Attempts by the local Party to impose Constituency Party Chair, Linney as the Chair of the new Group with Curbison as Group Secretary were rebuffed with the Labour Councillors making clear to the local Party that the decision would be for the elected members in the Town Hall to make. We cannot underestimate the importance of the creation of the Labour Group, previously an array of working-class candidates had been elected under various banners and there was no collective decision making against the opposition when they met at Council meetings. There was historically, friction as working-class Councillors, nominated and financed by their Trade Union would instinctively feel their first loyalty was to their trade union not the Labour Party. Two miners, Cllr Edmondson and Watson from the St Hilda's Lodge (which still refused to affiliate to the local Labour Party), and Cllr Amos Ayres of the River Pilots Society refused to join the Labour Group. Matters came to a head by July 1920 with the local Party writing to the St Hilda's Lodge requesting that their Council representatives join the Labour Group, and in an attempt to ensure firm discipline in their ranks following the failure of Curbison to vote with the Labour Group on the appointment of the Borough's Chief Engineer, the Group made clear that all members must vote on the majority decision reached by the Labour Group or face expulsion.

The Party, despite its numerical weakness on the Council was determined to propagate their causes within the Council Chamber. They argued furiously against what they regarded as excessive salary increases for senior Borough Officials, endeavoured to have women Labour Party members co-opted onto the Housing and Planning Committee and wrote to the Lord Chancellor expressing concern that not enough working-class people were being appointed to the local Magistrates' Bench. Meanwhile, the Labour representatives on the Board of Guardians also constituted themselves into a formal Labour Group and maintained pressure on ensuring financial support was given to those facing hardship in the post-war years with some success since they reported in July 1920 that following their lobbying, *Out Relief* had been raised from nine shillings to twelve shillings. Although the work of the Guardians was not without controversy, Trade Union Affiliates reported to the local Party of the injustices of some of the Guardians' decisions, including the refusal to grant relief in respect of two children because their grandparents refused to guarantee that they would receive religious instruction.

National issues during the Labour Party meetings in 1919 centred around the 'Irish Question' with the April meeting supporting a motion that the British Army should leave Ireland and extolling the rights of self determination for the Irish people. The meeting was not without controversy with the Chairman, Linney and two colleagues walking out of the meeting when the motion was agreed.

As the November 1920 municipal elections approached, two issues arose both of which were pragmatically dealt with.

Firstly, the newly formed Co-operative Party in South Shields wanted an agreement with the Labour Party that they would not contest the Bents and Hadrian wards at the November polls and allow the Co-operative Party a clear run in those seats. The Co-operative Party began its existence following the creation of a Joint Parliamentary Committee in 1881, to lobby for *Co-operative principles* but it was not until their Congress at Swansea in 1917 that the Co-operative Party was formed. Contesting national and local elections they achieved mediocre success but given they shared the same values as the Labour Party, arrangements were made to enter into a formal pact and in 1927 the **Cheltenham Agreement** was reached that allowed the Co-operative Party to stand candidates with Labour Party support on the understanding that they would accept the Labour 'Whip'.

South Shields Co-operators Mr Marshall, Mr Hopper and Mr Willis met with the local Labour Party in June 1920 and made clear they had no desire to run candidates against the Labour Party, indeed Mr Marshall was himself a member of the Labour Party, and the delegation were perspicuous that they would assist the Labour Party in other wards not contested by Co-operators and if elected would work with the Labour Group on the Council. The local Party agreed not to contest the Bents and Hadrian wards.

The second issue centred around Amos Ayres who was anxious to receive the Party's endorsement given he was due for election in the Beacon ward. Ayres had met with senior representatives from the Party and had secured approval from his Society, the River Pilots Association to seek endorsement from the Labour Party on condition that if he were unopposed and returned to the Council, he would support the Labour Group in the Council Chamber. There was an acrimonious debate within the Constituency party but eventually the Party agreed not to oppose Ayres.

Both episodes highlight the fact that, whilst the Labour Party may not have achieved significant electoral success in the past, there was a recognition that the Party was now the central body for working-class expression and that its support was becoming crucial at election time.

The Party manifesto for the November elections included supporting the development of a new Cleadon Park housing estate; the need for a more modern sanatorium; the extension of the tram system to Cleadon; to review the rates and the need for improvements to the seafront. Under the instruction of the Typographical and Printers Union, the local Party was required only to the use printing firms who were trade union organised and they appointed Cuth Barrass as the Assistant Central Agent to oversee the elections.

November's municipal election, despite the preparations, was an anti-climax, only seven of the fifteen wards were contested, Labour withdrew a number of candidates due probably to the lack of finance. Ayres had secured election unopposed in Hadrian and the Co-operative Party failed to win the only seat they eventually contested, the Bents. The election did not see the Labour Group increase its numbers and the turnout was down on previous years. The Party recorded that – '*The opponents of Labour, as having excelled themselves in low down electioneering …*'. There followed a period of introspect discussion as to why the Party was not performing better, the recriminations led to arguments that the Labour Group on the Council was not as effective as it should be, with criticism of a number of Group members not attending meetings and the majority of the work in holding the Council to account being left to a minority of Labour members.

Matters rumbled on during the winter before finally coming to a showdown in January 1921, when the Labour and Trades Council demanded a meeting with the Labour Group to discuss their performance. The Group Secretary, Cllr Chapman said average Labour Group attendance was only five/six, despite the Group being fifteen strong, and proceeded to name the worst offenders. The meeting became more hostile and bad tempered with Alderman Dunlop stating: '*Once we had three members who did something, now we have fifteen who do nothing.*' Some Councillors antagonistically made clear they were answerable to their Trade Union not the Labour Party, whilst another belligerently retorted that certain Labour representatives '*suited the enemy*'. Whilst the members were extremely truculent, they did coalesce around a resolution in a display of comity which stated the Labour Group should start again, keep a record of attendances and a note of work done by members with a view to ensuring the Party had a record to refer too when the members were next due for re-election to the Council. To enforce discipline, it was made clear, again, that the decisions of the Labour Group were '*absolute*', and members should vote as a bloc in the Council Chamber.

VI

By 1921 Gompertz, now fully recovered from his prison ordeals, was beginning to return to active campaigning both within the Shopworkers Union and the local Party. Gompertz was elected President of the North East Federation of the National Union of Shop Assistants in 1924/25 and served a term as Vice President in 1925/26.

The 1920s for the UK economy were a period of depression, deflation and steady decline in the country's former economic pre-eminence. By 1920 unemployment rose steadily to over 10 per cent with returning servicemen being particularly hit hard. A key cause was the economic policy of the Government which endeavoured to keep the value of sterling at pre-war levels – a political view held that a strong pound was a key feature of Britain's former economic prosperity. However, with the exorbitant costs of the Boer War, the First World and the War Loans from the USA ceasing, the only way to maintain a strong pound was to pursue a fiscal deflationary and monetary policy. The Government between 1918 and 1920 severely cut public spending and actually ran budget surpluses for most of the 1920s. The effects though were felt harshly in the industrialised areas of the country. Shipyards, required for war shipping, found a shortage of orders; the extraction of coal and manufacture of steel required to fight the war, was not in such high requirement in peacetime – unemployment began to rise and reduced to desperation, people were driven back on to Poor Law relief.

The scale of the problem is evident in figures of the time. In December 1920 the number of people across England and Wales on poor relief was 568,000 by September 1921 it was 1,243,042. So appalling was the situation that the local Board of Guardians were required either to demand a rise in the local rates or borrow the money (which still saddled the ratepayer with a longer-term cost) to finance the cost of poor relief. The situation led to one deprived East-End London Council, Poplar, deciding not to place a greater burden on their residents by refusing to collect the rate precept for the London County Council. It led to twenty-nine Councillors in the Borough being imprisoned for contempt of Court, including George Lansbury, a future Leader of the Labour Party.

Trade Unions for their part fought to retain their national pay agreements on behalf of their members with bitter employment disputes following and the three big Trade Unions creating a '*Triple Alliance*' to support each other, with marginal success. The reduction in coal exports in 1921 saw the coal owners 'lock out' the miners, including the collieries in South Shields, after miners refused to accept wage reductions, leading to a threatened national rail and transport strike and the potential of more than two million men stopping work. As history records, the Triple Alliance collapsed on 15 April – Black Friday – following unresolvable disagreements amongst national Union leaders. The miners fought bravely on through the summer of 1921 only to be forced back to work, their wages reduced by 34 per cent over the next nine months. Labour representatives on the South Shields Board of Guardians, like William McAnany, successfully argued that loans should be secured to help local miners locked-out by the coal owners, whilst the town's MP, Havelock Wilson, who was still President of the Seamen's Union, called for the Triple Alliance to be scrapped. Meanwhile, the 1921 May Day Rally on Sunday 7 May, would be a speculator and large affair with four Colliery bands and union banners assembling at Westoe Parade marching down Laygate Lane, Green Street, through the Market, King Street and Fowler Street before holding a rally at the Marsden Miners Hall in Imeary Street, Will Lawther being a key speaker. In an indication of the possibility of social unrest and volatile atmosphere the Chief Constable reminded the local Party that any such parade would need the consent of the local Police, as would any future open-air meetings the Party frequently held in the Market Place.

Against a backdrop of the economic slump and rising unemployment the Government implemented the 1920 Unemployment Insurance Act which extended unemployment benefits to all workers who earned less than £250; but this was followed by the 1921 'Seeking Work Test' which stated that to receive future benefits the unemployed were required to provide evidence that they were actively seeking work. The Government further required Councils to establish Unemployment Grants Committees which subsided wages to encourage employment and South Shields Council used part of the resource to hire men to lay out the new Readhead Park in the Westoe area of the town. South Shields, reliant upon the coal mines and shipyards for economic stability, was to experience appalling hardship and deprivation. Gompertz was asked by the local Party to lead a deputation to the Town Council in May 1921 and he took the opportunity to address Council members in the Chamber on the need for more to be done to alleviate the plight of the destitute within the town. He informed the Council that 6,626 men, 800 women and 300 boys were unemployed in the Borough, some being out of work for over six months. More needed to be done, he argued, in creating work through an extension of public works within the town as well as ensuring the children of the unemployed were being adequately fed.

The Council explained they could not do more without sanction of the Ministry of Labour or the Ministry of Transport whose approval would be needed to use the Unemployed Grants money to fund proposed new works such as an extension of the tram system to Cleadon Park. This was eventually given later in 1921 and saw new roads laid out at Green Lane, Harton Lane, Grosvenor Road to Bents Park Road, as well as an expansion of Mortimer Road. The plight of the unemployed was a cause which Gompertz and the Labour Party locally would continue to crusade and highlight in order to maintain constant pressure on the Council, Gompertz's deputation to the Town Council would prove to be the first of many during the early 1920s.

Meanwhile, the quest to secure a suitable Labour Parliamentary candidate for South Shields continued and the Party also began to prepare for 1921 municipal elections. Lawther advised the Party that he was prepared to stand in the general election with the full support of the DMA and arrangements were made to hold a Parliamentary selection conference in January 1922 after they had fought the November local elections.

The usual tussle of deciding municipal candidates and what wards to contest followed. For the first time the Party interviewed aspiring candidates with the Boilermakers' choice of a Mr Scott being subject to criticism because he was a member of the Property Owners' Association (POA). Scott met the Party officials and explained he owned two properties but would follow the Labour whip, his candidature was still rejected because the POA had publicly objected to Labour representation on the Council and Scott refused to rescind his membership of the POA. The Party did though support a request for the National League of the Blind to field one of their members, Mr RK Wilson in the Shields ward.

Despite the social unrest, poverty and the work the local stalwarts were doing to help mitigate the worst excesses, the Council election results in November proved a disappointment for the local Party. They contested ten seats, and whilst they secured the election of Mr Wilson in the Shields Ward, they lost their former long-serving Party Chairman, George Linney in Tyne Dock. Worse still, due to the growth of the town, three independent

Councillors were elected for the new Harton ward, increasing the anti-Labour majority still further against the Labour Group in the Town Hall.

Gompertz's services were required again in October 1921, following a request from the Marsden Miners' Lodge that the local Party investigate a complaint raised by the Musicians' Union against two of their members. The issue centred around allegations that some members of the Marsden Miners band were not Trade Unionists. The decision to recommend Gompertz for the investigations panel is an indication of the respect he was held by the local Party. Inter-Union disputes are always difficult for local Labour Parties to deal with, and only those considered trustworthy, beyond reproach and who have the confidence of all sides are recommended to serve. It was also to Gompertz that the Party turned to when they sent a delegation to the Council's Watch Committee to meet with Chief Constable. Complaints had been raised as to police heavy tactics on 11 July 1922 against striking St Hilda's miners who had assembled in Spohr Terrace, outside a quarter of a mile police cordon around the Colliery, following rumours some men were seeking to break the strike and return to work. It was alleged striking miners had been arrested without access to legal representation. Gompertz reported back that the Chief Constable had refused to discuss the issue at the Watch Committee leading to the Party requesting that the Labour Group on the Council press for the Chief Constable's resignation.

VII

On Saturday 14 January 1922, twenty-three affiliated bodies of the South Shields Labour and Trades Council met with the approval to hold the meeting from Labour's national headquarters, to interview the only person nominated for the Parliamentary candidacy, Will Lawther of the DMA.

Following his address – in which he referred to the need for Parliament to be a sounding board for working-class opinion – the obligatory questions followed. Would he accept the Parliamentary whip? 'Yes'; Could he suggest a cure for unemployment? 'Under capitalism there was no cure'. Did he think the Key Industries Act was responsible for unemployment? 'Yes'; and of course – will the Durham Miners' Association finance the campaign? 'Yes'.

The vote to endorse Lawther was unanimous.

Lawther would in many respects be an unusual choice for the local Party. By his own admission he was a militant left-wing firebrand; he was a Durham County Councillor and had opposed World War I. He had, at various times, described himself as '... *a Marxist, syndicalist, anarchist and member of the ILP'*. Lawther did have some links with the town, not just through the Mineworkers' Union but also because he had helped to establish the left-wing debating club, The Plebs' League in South Shields before 1914.

Will Pearson, a local miner, who told the local Party at one prospective council candidate interview, that he was on the 'extreme left' was appointed as Lawther's Parliamentary Agent and they began to consider how they could raise his profile in the town in preparation for the next general election. The following week Lawther was introduced to the townsfolk at a public meeting at the Scala Theatre in Ocean Road arranged by the ILP and addressed by Bertrand Russell. Russell attacked the US-led Washington Conference, which aimed at reducing the naval arms race in the Pacific, Russell argued it was not achieving its aims and denounced international capital for exploiting the workers. It was an interesting choice of speaker for a town which had the anti-Communist, pro-war, jingoistic Havelock Wilson as its MP.

The maverick Wilson though was again on the move politically.

A week following Lawther's selection, the Prime Minister, Lloyd George, despairing at his failure to seize complete control of the Liberal Party from Herbert Asquith simply broke ranks and on 22 January 1922 established his own National Liberal Council. Across the country Liberal Associations and their members were required to choose which Liberal leader they would support. Meanwhile, the Conservative Party in Westminster was becoming weary of the Lloyd George Premiership. His national Liberal Group had always been very much the junior partner in the Coalition, and there was emulating from the Tory Parliamentary backbench a feeling that too much Government policy was being seeded to the junior Liberal partners at the expense of their own. The Honours Scandal, in which it was exposed that Lloyd George had been selling Honours and Peerages to finance his national Liberal Party was for many, the final straw. It was only a matter of time before the Conservatives would resign from the Coalition, install their own Leader, Bonar Law, as Prime Minister and seek a fresh mandate from the country through a general election.

Within these national considerations, the perfidious Wilson was ever mindful of the need to keep the anti-Labour vote in South Shields united, he announced that at the next general election he would stand as a Lloyd George supporting national Liberal candidate (having already relinquished his links with the NDP), and approached the local Conservative Unionists for their support. The Conservative Association met and agreed to endorse

Wilson but only because one of their own, a prominent local businessman Sir James Readhead declined the nomination. Unfortunately for Wilson, the Local Liberal Association members, like their counterparts across the country – remained bitterly divided with the South Shields Asquith-supporting Liberals announcing they would field a candidate against Havelock Wilson at the next general election.

If Wilson could not get the Asquith Liberals on board, he faced potential defeat at the next general election with the anti-Labour vote in the town being split.

Chapter 7

Unstable Times

I

The economic depression in the 1920 and 1930s that enveloped areas like Tyneside, Merseyside, South Wales and Clydeside was not shared by other areas of the country whose regional employment was not centred around heavy industry, it is for those areas the phrase '*The Roaring Twenties*' belongs. It was a time of unbridled consumerism, the rise of middle-class suburbia with the detached house, garden and car, the spread of Marks & Spencer, Sainsbury's, the annual holiday to the coast, whilst the fall in infant mortality rates saw the average family become smaller, suburban women becoming more empowered and enlightened and mass communication through cinema and radio bringing the country together.

It was a time of great social contrasts epitomised between the jaunty plays of Noël Coward and P G Wodehouse and novels like *The Great Gatsby*, opposite the works of writers like George Orwell who examined in detail the life of the working classes in his novel, *The Road to Wigan Pier* – it seemed the country had not moved on from Disraeli's observations in his 1845 novel, *Sybil, or The Two Nations* in which he declared there were – '*Two nations, between whom there is no intercourse, no sympathy; who are as ignorant of each other's habits, thoughts and feelings, as if they were dwellers in different time zones ...*'

It is not surprising that the social divisions gave rise to great political uncertainty. Lloyd George's Coalition Government which had promised a '*Land fit for heroes*' was characterised by a laissez-faire mentality and the Ministries populated by politicians who were ideologically anti-big government. There were no moves to extend health provision, no radical overhaul of the failing education system, no long-term economic planning which would have overhauled the country's inefficient working and management practices. Even the lauded new housing provision was too expensive for some Ministers, with housing not being constructed in the numbers required to remove the slums in the industrialised areas. The Government was losing credibility following events like the Amritsar massacre in 1919 and the creation of an Independent Ireland (albeit without the six Protestant northern counties and the new State holding only Dominion status within the British Empire) which caused fury amongst Conservative politicians. Alongside public spending being reduced dramatically whilst income tax remained at 33 per cent for high earners – by the autumn of 1922 the Conservative backbenchers which sustained the Lloyd George Government had had enough.

Their decision to meet at the Carlton Club in St James in October 1922, saw the Conservative backbenchers openly revolt against their own leadership, Lloyd George resigned, with the Conservative Bonar Law becoming the new Prime Minister. The Liberal Party still split between their official Leader Asquith, and those supporting Lloyd George under his 'National Liberal' banner, failed to reach any accommodation between the warring factions and the electorate would be presented with two Liberal policy platforms, as a consequence, the November 1922 General Election would prove to be a decisive moment for the long-term electoral fortunes for the Labour Party.

II The Communist Party

The Russian Revolution of 1918 would witness the rise of the Communist Party throughout Europe. On 31 July 1920, following a merger of several small Marxist Parties, the Communist Party of Great Britain was formed. Critical to its development and appeal was determining their response to the Labour Party which had become an established outlet for working-class expression and agitation with the support of the Trade Unions. The Labour Party operated a federal structure allowing Socialist societies like the Fabians to affiliate both locally and nationally, the Communist Party submitted a request to affiliate.

Lenin believed that the Communists should support the Labour Party as a 'rope supports a hanged man' and encouraged affiliation given the Labour Party's organisational strength within the Trade Union and wider Labour movement. A request for affiliation to the national Labour Party quickly followed in August 1920, it was swiftly rebutted by the Labour Party National Executive on the grounds that the Communist Party's programme did not concur with the Labour Party's. Not to be deterred, the Communist Party sought direct affiliation to local Constituency Labour Party's and pressed their claim for national affiliation once again at the 1921 Labour Party conference, it was once again rejected, but the Party Leadership chose not to take any defensive action against Communist influence within local Constituencies, leaving the matter for local activists to determine. The matter was again before the Labour Party conference in 1922 only this time the National Executive not only recommended refusal to the Communist Party to affiliate but also to instruct local Labour Party's not to accept any Trade Union delegate to their meetings who was a Communist Party member.

The delegate ruling proved difficult to enforce. The merger of Labour and Trades Councils in areas like South Shields meant that non-Labour Party activists were entitled to be appointed as delegates by their Trade Union, but only to debate, and vote upon on what was regarded as 'industrial issues' relevant to trade unions; once the 'political business' of the local Party was discussed, non-Labour Party members were required to leave the room. Following pressure from the Trade Unions the 1923 Labour Party Conference rescinded the ban on Communist delegates, but still refused to allow the Communist Party to affiliate to the national Labour Party.

South Shields Labour and Trades Council was not insulated against the debate which was raging nationally. As early as October 1920, just three months after it was formed, the Communist Party requested the right to affiliate to the local Party. Labour delegates discussed the matter at their October meeting, but following the advice of their national headquarters, rejected the request, although by only two votes.

The issue was discussed again by the South Shields Labour Party in March 1921 when the local Party agreed to submit a resolution to that year's Labour Party Conference expressing '… *with alarm the dictatorship of the National Executive in refusing admission to the Communist Party without submitting the matter to the affiliated bodies.*'

Despite the Labour Party Conference rejecting the motion, a body of local activists were determined to encourage the local Labour Party to accept the Communist Party affiliation to the local Party and by November 1921, the Communist Party once again approached the local Labour Party with a request to affiliate. The meeting agreed to refer the matter to the local Trade Union branches for their views, with the subsequent meeting of the local Labour Party rejecting once again the Communist Party's overtures for affiliation. The local Communists were furious and offered to debate publicly with the South Shields Labour Party, on the issue of 'Working class emancipation, the Labour Party v the Communist Party' – local stalwarts resolved not to '*entertain the offer*' by a large majority.

The issue though would continue to fester; the February 1923 Annual Meeting of the local Party saw Gompertz return to the powerful Executive Committee after an absence of more than six years. Gompertz would prove to be a formidable opponent of the Communist Party. By early April a resolution from the Marsden Miners' Lodge requested that the Communist Party be allowed to affiliate locally '... *on the condition that they adhere strictly to the constitution of the Labour Party*'; given that the strongly left-wing Will Lawther had been selected by the Party in January 1923, one cannot help speculating that attempts were being made to politically reposition the normally moderate local Party. If that was indeed the tactic it met with marginal success because the 17 April meeting of the Party, by just one vote accepted the Marsden Miners' resolution to allow the local Communist Party to affiliate. Gompertz, in attendance at the meeting, was clearly agitated and had it recorded formally in the Minutes that he intended to raise the matter again at a future meeting.

Announcing he intended to raise the matter again was a delaying tactic by Gompertz, one he would deploy throughout his Labour Party career. By the time the Party met again on 1 May, Gompertz had organised support amongst moderate Trade Union branches and the meeting was heavily attended. As the meeting was opened by the Chair, Gompertz moved that the previous decision to admit the Communist Party be rescinded, several Trade Union delegates spoke, making clear that their Union branch would disaffiliate from the local Party if the decision was not reversed. Gompertz with unbridled ebullience would no doubt have reminded the meeting that the Labour Party Conference had made clear the Communist Party could not affiliate either nationally or locally and therefore the question of affiliation by the Communists was not a matter for the local Party to determine. The debate clearly became heated and fractious but Gompertz's plotting had paid off, the meeting voted heavily to rescind the previous meeting's decision.

The question of the Communists' affiliation though would again be discussed a year later in July 1924 when the local Party considered which resolution to send to that year's Annual Labour Party Conference. A suggestion was made that they submit a resolution supporting the right of the Communist Party to affiliate. The meeting became explosive and Gompertz used every debating and procedural tactic at his disposal to have the meeting reject the motion. Attempts to have the matter considered as 'Industrial business' (at which non-Labour Party Trade Unionists would be able to remain in the meeting and vote) was disputed, Gompertz demanded the matter be considered 'political' and as such, only Labour Party members should remain in the meeting to discuss the matter. Questions of procedure, repeated points of order and repeated challenges to the Chairman's rulings were made and arguments as to the validity of the meeting itself were the hallmarks of a bitter meeting until the Chairman, Councillor Linney simply rose from his Chair, closed the meeting without conclusion and the delegates departed.

A section of Trade Union delegates was furious at the behaviour of Gompertz to the extent that the Patternmakers' Union Branch submitted complaints to the local Party requesting that Gompertz be removed from the Constituency Executive. In one of the largest meetings of the local Party held on 22 July 1924, Gompertz was called a '*Cad*' by one delegate resulting in Gompertz promptly leaving the room. Delegates demanded action on what they called Gompertz's '*disobedience*' at their previous meeting and eventually a resolution was moved – '*That this Party and Council write to the Shop Assistants Branch complaining of the conduct of their delegate in holding up the last meeting, and ask the Branch to withdraw this delegate, unless we receive an apology from him*' the vote was thirty-nine votes to twenty-six in favour.

Gompertz had made political enemies, his fiery temper had irked those delegates supportive of the Communist Party affiliation. The Marsden Miners' Lodge, which had become more militant in its outlook, wrote and advised the local Party that they believed Gompertz had verbally attacked Trade Unionists, in particular the Miners, and that as a consequence, the Marsden Miners' Lodge had voted not to allow the Labour Party to use their hall for future meetings. In an indication of Gompertz's standing within the local Party hierarchy however, they resolved merely to ask the Marsden Miners to meet with them and to supply evidence of '... *persons pouring contemptuous and scurrilous odium upon Trade Unionists.*'

The matter was eventually resolved through the emollient approach adopted by the Party Secretary, Harry Donnelly. Gompertz's Union advised the Party they were supporting him and would not remove him as a delegate, the Marsden Miners, to their credit, accepted they were not acting in the best interests of Party Unity and agreed to rescind their previous decision and continued to allow their Miners Hall to be used by the local Party. The Labour Party Conference later that year resolved that the Communist Party would be allowed to affiliate nationally but only after they had agreed to change their Constitution to reflect Labour's aims and values and to agree to take part in an inquiry creating a united Party. The cleverly worded motion made it impossible for the Communists to accept.

Sidney Webb remarked, rather unkindly, in 1930 that it was *'fanatics and cranks and extremists'* who dominated and maintained the Labour Party at a Constituency level. Gompertz, years before Webb made those remarks had demolished any attempts to include Communists into the South Shields Labour Party even to the extent that the local Party voted heavily against having a Communist Party speaker at their 1926 May Day Rally. The issue of the Communist Party affiliating to the local Party was never raised again.

III

It seemed as if fortune would favour Will Lawther, he was a charismatic and forceful speaker and with the DMA financial backing, he was able to assemble a well-organised campaign team in the South Shields Constituency spending as much time as possible on the stump in 1922 meeting the electorate and speaking at numerous public meetings across the town.

Aside from the potential of the anti-Labour vote in South Shields being divided, another issue would give the local Party confidence that they would win the seat at the next general election.

The Sunderland and South Shields Water Company announced plans in late 1921 that they were applying for Parliamentary approval to increase dramatically the water rates across the area. They faced obloquy from households since the water rates were being unevenly applied regardless of the type of housing tenure. Over 9,000 men across the town were unemployed, and industrial unrest saw this number increase at intermediate periods. There was already pressure from the Board of Guardians for the Council to increase their financial support for the administration of the Poor Law, any increase in water rates would therefore have a huge detrimental effect on whole sections of the community.

The local Labour Party was already heavily involved in campaigns to agitate for more public work schemes to be initiated by the Municipal Corporation and one activist emerging as their champion was Tom Mulgrew, a miner who lived in John Williamson Street. He was active in the Unemployed Committee and had stood unsuccessfully in the December 1921 Hadrian Ward Council by-election at the request of the Unemployed Committee with the blessing of the Labour Party. An elected member of the Board of Guardians it was Mulgrew who was the driving force for Labour on the

Board of Guardians and gave comprehensive accounts of their work at Party meetings. Although the Labour Party was always in a minority, the vocal Group was able to secure concessions and additional poor relief support. It was also Mulgrew who led protests against any proposed increase in the water rates. Labour's 7 February 1922 Constituency delegates meeting was adamant, they condemned the proposed water rate increase, they wanted the local Council to examine municipalising the water supply and they were prepared to organise a campaign of civil disobedience, encouraging residents not to pay the increased water charges.

The campaign took root across the town, hardly surprising given that the 25 per cent increase at a time of economic hardship and high unemployment would drive even more residents onto poor relief. The Party raised a 5,000 name petition which obliged the Mayor to call a town meeting to discuss the matter. The Water Company shareholders were denounced as '*dividend hunters*' with demands that any Councillor or Alderman who was a Company Shareholder must not take part in the Council's deliberations on the matter.

Having raised the required number of petitioners, on 14 February 1922 the Mayor, Edward Smith, hosted a Town Meeting at St Paul's Church Hall on Westoe Road, the sheer number of residents arriving required organisers to arrange an overflow meeting at St Michael's Church Hall. Linney, on behalf of the Labour and Trades Council spoke of his opposition to what he described as an iniquitous increase and alleged that a shareholder in the Water Company had advised him that even he thought the charges excessive. Linney listed Labour's demands to applause from the audience, they wanted opposition from the Council to the Parliamentary Bill and they demanded the Council seek to take control of the town's water supply. If the charges were implemented, Linney pledged that they would encourage residents not to pay the increase. Labour speakers dominated the proceedings and Mulgrew had moved the same demands at the overflow meeting at St Michael's Church Hall.

Ald Lawson, Chairman of the Council's Sunderland and South Shields Water Company assured the audience that the Council opposed the increase, that they saw no reason for such a high increase and that in partnership with other local Councils they were examining how they might oppose the Parliamentary Bill but as far municipalisation of the water supply, it was not within the Law for them to implement such a measure. Both meetings endorsed the Labour Party motion without dissent. Arrangements were made to lobby Havelock Wilson, but astonishingly when questioned at a public meeting on Saturday 18 February at the Empire Theatre he admitted he was unaware of the Water Bill or its implications, following heckling from the audience, he vowed to oppose it.

The anger was not just felt in Sunderland and South Shields, other Water Companies were also seeking to increase their rates dramatically, and before Parliament considered the matter, a Select Committee heard evidence from interested Parties in March 1922. Travelling to London to give evidence from South Shields was the Mayor, Edward Smith, William Bell of the Property Owners' Association and John Rowley, the Secretary of the South Shields Tenants' Defence League. The Mayor gallantly fought his corner. Under cross-examination from MPs he was admonished for presiding over a public meeting that had suggested withholding any proposed increase in the water rates, the Committee Chairman explained everyone wanted a better water supply, even his water bill, he exclaimed, had increased from £4 to £10. John Rowley was challenged as to whether he really believed 3.5d was an excessive charge, to which he responded: '*Some of our men believe that water, being one of nature's products is dear at any price*'.

The Water Company's Counsel explained that any increase would be for three years, and that they could not be held responsible for the change in economic and industrial conditions. The Committee recommended Parliamentary Approval for the increased water rate charges.

The local Party became nervous, like their national counterparts, they were anxious to demonstrate that they were moderate and competent to run public bodies, leading a civil disobedience campaign, however worthwhile, would not have sat easily with local Councillors, some of whom were seeking to become local Magistrates. The May Labour Party meeting voted by a large majority to advise their membership and affiliated bodies that further grand remonstrance against the water charge increase was futile given it had received Parliamentary approval. The meeting agreed to maintain pressure on the Chair of the Board of Sunderland South Shields Water Company who had made a commitment not to enforce the Law in matters of extreme hardship. Residents though did maintain defiance with over 2,000 receiving Court Summons for non-payment, Gompertz, at the request of the Party, attended local Court proceedings to support residents.

Irrespective of the climbdown, the local Party had demonstrated to the public that they were supportive of their claims whilst the Moderate Council members were perceived as being in the pocket of the Water Board shareholders. In a heavy November Municipal poll, the Labour Party gained three Council seats, in the Shields, St Hilda's and Laygate wards. With Lawther's Parliamentary Agent, William Pearson securing a Council seat in Laygate – the local Party had every right to feel confident of a positive result at the forthcoming 15 November General Election.

IV 1922 General Election

The Honourable Edward Augustine St Aubyn Harney KC was born in Waterford in 1865, following his education at Trinity College Dublin, he emigrated to Australia, was elected in 1901 to the first Senate of the Australian Commonwealth as a 'Free Trader', was made a King's Counsel there in 1905, returned to England and was called to the Bar at Gray's Inn taking Silk in 1920 – by 1922 he had Parliamentary ambitions but was resigned to accepting that he was unlikely to find a winnable Parliamentary seat to contest in the forthcoming General Election.

Fate would deal him a winning hand.

Havelock Wilson's increasing erratic political manoeuvres never sat comfortably with long-established Liberals in South Shields, he had served his purpose in 1918 by standing as a Coalition 'coupon candidate' preventing Labour winning the Parliamentary seat in a straight contest, but with the Coalition at an end, and with the Liberal Party split, they were determined to secure the seat for an Asquith supporter. Parliament would be dissolved on 26 October and the close of nominations for the General Election would be 4 November, but as late as 22 October the local Liberals were still awaiting confirmation from Ald Brown of Sunderland Council as to whether he would stand as their Parliamentary candidate. By 27 October with Parliament formally dissolved, Ald Brown advised the South Shields Liberal Executive he would not stand. Frederick Newby, the local Liberal Agent was despatched to speak to the Northern Federation of the Liberal Party, and to seek their support in securing a candidate. Tyndal Anderson, a local shipbuilder and Chair of the South Shields Liberal Association pushed for consideration of Edward Harney, who had no connections with South Shields but was known to Asquith's London supporters. Harney received a telegram from the Northern Liberals, he caught a train to Newcastle and with just days before close of nominations submitted his papers as the Liberal Party candidate into the Town Hall.

The General Election campaign was intense, backed by Newby's undoubted organisational capabilities, Harney immediately addressed numerous public meetings across the town, one in the Scala Theatre witnessed an audience of over 2,500 townsfolk and he also took time to speak at a regional rally in Newcastle addressed by Herbert Asquith. Standing on a platform of free trade, repeal of the Industries Act (which he claimed prevented greater investment in the shipyards), strengthening the League of Nations to secure world peace and supporting sex equality, he opposed any future Coalition with the Tories. The local media gave Harney a sympathetic press, reporting that he was rapidly gaining support with every public meeting he addressed, Lawther, they asserted, was offering an impossible manifesto platform and Wilson was merely preaching to audiences of the converted. The *Shields Daily News* noted that Harney – '*Has rightly banned personalities from his platform. In one notable instance, he has refused to answer a question because it cast an aspersion upon one of his opponents.*' The pugnacious Wilson however was not helped when during the short campaign he caught bronchitis, rendering him unable to conduct a full campaign.

The eve of poll saw all three candidates frantically mobilising their supporters, the *Shields Daily News* recording that any of the three candidates could emerge victorious. The town, it acknowledged had a Liberal tradition scanning over ninety years and Harney, despite his late entry into the contest and with no major national speakers supporting him, was endearing himself to the electorate with every public meeting he addressed. Lawther held three mass meetings in the various Miners' Hall's before addressing a mass meeting in Coronation Street supported by colliery bands whilst Wilson's final appeal was before 3,000 supporters at the Casino. All candidates made overtures to the town's 21,000 women voters with the press reporting that election day itself witnessed a great deal of campaigning being undertaken by women, supporting each of the three candidates.

The General Election saw Bonar Law's Conservatives secure a landslide victory with 344 seats, due in part to the Liberal Party fratricide. Lloyd George's National Liberals secured just fifty-three seats, Asquith's Liberal Party sixty-two. The Labour Party planted itself firmly as the alternative Government, securing 142 seats and receiving over four million votes across the country, they gained an impressive ninety-one seats, but South Shields would not be one of them.

It took eight-and-a-half hours to count the votes in South Shields as crowds waited nervously outside the Congregational Hall in Ocean Road. A full recount of the votes was ordered as only two votes separated the leading candidates, but when the result was verified and announced by the Mayor it was a remarkable victory for Harney and the Liberals by just twenty-five votes. Harney had secured 15,760 votes, Lawther 15,735. The town's retiring MP, Wilson was reduced to 8,121 votes. He returned to London with bronchitis and heart issues troubling him again and rested in a convalescence nursing home.

Lawther had fought an energetic campaign, Labour's discipline had held, although internally there was some animosity as to who had overall control of the candidate – the Miners or the local Labour Party, with Lawther's campaign manager, Harry Bainbridge defiantly replying he was a servant of the DMA not the local Party. Lawther's campaign had though given encouragement to Labour supporters in the town, but the collapse in Wilson's vote had been to Harney's benefit.

Nationally, the divided Liberal Party politicians would spend the next year reconciling their policy differences with an agreement on 13 November 1923 which saw Lloyd George re-enter the Liberal fold. But the electoral damage was done, the Labour Party had replaced the Liberals as the alternative to the Conservative Party and the years following the 1922 General Election would witness the gradual decline of Liberal representation in the House of Commons.

V

Local Labour Party activists were obviously despondent but could take some consolation that the Parliamentary seat was within their grasp, they settled down to what they imagined would be a five-year Conservative Government and renewed their efforts both on the Board of Guardians and the local Council. Attempts by reactionary Guardians to preclude local Co-operative Societies from their food voucher scheme for those on poor relief had been rebuffed, whilst the Labour Group on the Council was thinking strategically about the borough's long-term economic requirements and was campaigning for a South Shields–North Shields 'Tyne Tunnel' arguing that the usage of local labour would help alleviate unemployment in the town, the local Party also kept a watching brief on Harney, going so far as to ask their headquarters in London to secure information on his political activities during his time in Australia. They also maintained their close working relationship with the Unemployed Committee and the Tenants' Defence League. The local Party was growing in confidence. In a sign that it had become the predominant working-class organisation, further local Unions affiliated such as the

Railway Clerks' Association and the National Union of General Workers. Also, the number of women activists was increasing to the extent that women members in the west of the borough clustered around Tyne Dock and led by Jim Curbison's wife, established their own Women's Section Branch securing the right to send voting delegates to Labour and Trades Council meetings in the process.

Given the closeness of the General Election result, South Shields was now a key election target for the national Labour Party, it is not surprising that local activists were able to secure visits by luminaires such as the new Seaham MP and Party intellectual Sidney Webb; the victor of the July 1922 Pontypridd by-election Mardy Jones and the June 1923 Morpeth by-election victor, Robert Smillie, as well Manny Shinwell and George Lansbury. The intention was always to raise the profile of the local Labour Party and to demonstrate that for them, South Shields should become a 'natural' Labour seat. The highlight would be the visit to the town of the Leader of His Majesty's Opposition, Ramsay MacDonald in July 1923. The meeting held at The Queen's Theatre in King Street on 29 July was a sell-out with Gompertz acting as the Platform Stewart and long serving stalwart Jim Curbison moving a vote of thanks, seconded by Cuth Barrass. The Party also requested the Mayor to hold a Civic Reception.

A week before the meeting, the local Party met to endorse unanimously Lawther as their Parliamentary candidate for the next general election. A candid discussion followed with Harry Bainbridge the DMA's full time Agent for the Constituency making clear to the Executive Committee that he wanted a proper understanding that he oversaw campaigning and desired no repeat of internal complaints that had marred the 1922 General Election efforts when there was frequent debate over who had final control of the candidate.

MacDonald's visit to South Shields took place against a backdrop of a change in Premiership. Bonar Law, suffering from throat cancer and unable to speak resigned as Prime Minister on 20 May 1923, he was replaced by Stanley Baldwin. Law would have the unfortunate distinction of being at that time the shortest reigning occupant of Number 10, and following his death in October that year, was buried in Westminster Abbey, Asquith remarked that they were burying 'The unknown Prime Minister next to the tomb of the unknown soldier'. The change in leadership though would have significant ramifications for Government policy, not least on a question that had split the Tory Party so many times in the past, free trade or protectionism.

Law had been a classic Free Trader, he considered that it was more advantageous for the consumer, he believed foreign competition reduced prices by eliminating tariffs on imports and required local industry to be innovative and modernise against global competition. Baldwin though, in the face of stubborn unemployment and demands for immediate support for home-grown industries like wool, wanted to a pursue a Protectionist agenda, this policy, he gambled, would protect domestic jobs and was a better strategy for overcoming the balance of payments deficit. The respective merits of both policies had been debated frequently in the past and had divided the Tory Party between its traditional rural farming base and its emerging urban business interests. The conundrum for Baldwin was that the Tories had won the 1922 General Election on a free trade platform, he felt duty bound that any change in Government policy should receive a mandate from the public through a General Election. The poll was called for 6 December 1923.

As a Liberal, Harney was pro-free trade, as was the national Labour Party who felt it kept down the cost of living for ordinary workers. Lawther though made clear that for him it wasn't a question of free trade or protectionism but the need for Socialism and buoyed by a further three gains for the Labour Party on the Borough Council in the 1923 November municipal elections, commenced his election campaign in the town which included visits by George Lansbury and the victor of that year's Morpeth by-election Robert Smillie. The local Conservative Unionists though were in a quandary, do they stand a protectionist candidate in support of Baldwin – this course of action would in all probability hand the seat to Labour – or do they stand aside and allow Harney a clear fight with Lawther? They chose the latter option, and with it went Labour's chances of securing the seat.

Lawther secured 15,717 votes to Harney's 22,912 giving the Liberals a majority of over 7,000. It was a bitter blow to the local activists but not entirely unexpected. Three days later on 9 December 1923, with thousands of townsfolk lining the streets leading into Mile End Road, Harney arrived at Low Station at 9 pm, crowds cheered, clapped and threw their hats into the air, as he boarded the train back to London. Labour activists would have more to cheer though in the national results, Baldwins strategy to secure the country's support for Protectionism was a disaster losing his Party eight six seats, whilst Labour solidified its position as the alternative party of Government winning 191 seats, the unified Liberal Party secured 158 seats. Baldwin accepted that the new hung-Parliament had a Free-Trade majority when the combined forces of the Opposition voted against the King's Speech in January 1924. He immediately tended the Government's resignation, King George V summoned for Ramsay MacDonald as the Leader of the second largest Party and the first Labour Government was formed.

VI

The electoral map of the North East of England following the 1923 General Election saw the singular Liberal seat of South Shields surrounded by a block of Labour constituencies, South Shields activists were clearly frustrated that their campaigning efforts were not being rewarded at the ballot box, although no blame was attached to Will Lawther. The local Party wrote to him immediately after the General Election to reassure him of their *'confidence and appreciation'* for his *'gallant fight'* in the Parliamentary election. Notwithstanding, Lawther wrote back to the Party indicating that he did not intend to seek nomination as their candidate in the future. His intention not to seek re-nomination was leaked to the *Shields Gazette* who ran an article, much to consternation of local Party officials who responded that no final decision had been taken. By March the Harton Lodge of the Miners' Union had again proposed Lawther as the Parliamentary candidate. Lawther had discussions with national Labour Party officials as to his next course of action; acknowledging that MacDonald led a minority Government at Westminster, it was clear a further general election was imminent, it was critical therefore that the local Party had an established candidate in place as quickly as possible. Lawther wrote to the local Labour party Secretary advising that he was prepared to contest the seat again, with the full support of the DMA.

Lawther's attraction as the Parliamentary candidate though was beginning to wane amongst some sections of the Party. The ILP advised that they wished to nominate Alderman Smith of Durham County Council, whilst the Engineering Unions were supportive of David Adams a shipowner who had lost his Newcastle West seat in the previous General Election. The Party agreed to invite the three candidates to a selection conference held on 1 May at which thirty-nine affiliated bodies were represented along with the two Women Sections. Adams declined to appear, indicating he had decided to seek the nomination for Newcastle West again (he who would not actually return to the House of Commons until 1935, for Consett), Alderman Smith though did appear.

Lawther was forthright and in a bullish mood, he told the meeting that he had personally felt the DMA had spent enough finance seeking to secure South Shields for Labour, but they had agreed to finance the campaign for a further General Election, he answered questions in relation to the control of the General Election campaign, with delineation he stated that if the DMA financed the Agent, then they had the right to appoint the Agent and that the Agent would be a member of the DMA. Smith on the other hand gave a lacklustre performance. He wasn't, the Minutes report, desperate to go to Parliament but he was prepared to offer £150 towards the election campaign, a suggestion Edwin Gribbin the Labour Party Regional Organiser ruled out of order. When the delegates' votes were counted Lawther had won the nomination, forty-six votes to thirteen; but it was clear that divisions were appearing within the Party, centred largely around the appointment of the Election Agent. Indeed, the next meeting of the Executive Committee wanted a deputation, including Gompertz, to meet with the DMA to discuss the issue but a subsequent meeting of the full Constituency Party delegates moved against the recommendation.

VII Insane miracle

It was not a foregone conclusion that MacDonald would accept the King's request to form a minority Government in January 1924. Following the December 1923 Election key figures including MacDonald, Henderson, Snowden, Clynes and Thomas met at Sidney Webb's London home to consider their next steps. It was clear that the pro-Protectionist minority would not be able to deliver a King's Speech and, in the circumstances, it was constitutionally certain that MacDonald would be prevailed upon to form a Government. There would be risks of course, they rejected any suggestion of a Coalition with the Liberal Party which would almost certainly mean the Government would not last a full term in Office.

MacDonald once described the first Labour Government as an '*insane miracle*' but its nine months in Office demonstrated that Labour *could* govern, that its strategy was social democratic and gradual as opposed to revolutionary and despite the overwhelming numbers against them, they did secure some important, albeit moderate, legislative changes for their supporters across the country. As Francis Williams recalls in his book, *Fifty Years' March*, they abolished the 'gap' between periods of benefit under the unemployment insurance scheme, the 'Means Test' was abolished, increased support for public works schemes, increased rates of unemployment benefit and children's allowances and improved support for old age pensioners. New infant welfare centres were opened, and the number of health visitors increased. There were improvements in education provision with Local Authorities empowered to improve school buildings; maintenance allowances were increased and grants for adult education trebled. All of which would have had a direct impact on the residents of South Shields, but perhaps none more so than the Wheatley Housing Act which saw rapid Council housebuilding through the provision of subsidies for Local Authorities – a provision which the local Labour Group on South Shields Council actively encouraged the Council to exploit. The Government also secured a second Reading of a Bill designed to extend the Women's Franchise to all women at the age of twenty-one, enthusiastically supported by the South Shields Labour and Trades Council, but Parliamentary time prevented its implementation.

It was, though, the media attacks and a united Conservative onslaught on the perceived 'red Communist' threat that derailed the Government. Central to this was the Government's decision to open diplomatic relations with the Soviet Union and suggestions that Britain might loan money to the USSR. It led to media hysteria with the former Liberal MP, Winston Churchill contesting the March 1924 Westminster Abbey by-election as a Constitutionalist candidate on a strongly 'anti-Socialist' platform attacking what he called, 'Our bread for the Bolshevist serpent' and losing to the Official Conservative by just forty-three votes. Matters were not helped when later that year, the Communist columnist John Ross Campbell was arrested over an article he had written in which he implored troops not to fire at strikers. The inexperienced Wallsend MP and Attorney General, Patrick Hastings first refused to intervene, but following attacks from Labour's left-wing MPs, the Prosecution was withdrawn, leading to Conservative MPs accusing him of abusing his position. A further heightened right-wing media frenzy followed, Asquith in an effort to buy the Government time, suggested an enquiry be established to look into the matter, such an enquiry would in all probability of exonerated Hastings and allowed the Government to survive. MacDonald, irritated, misjudged the offer, he advised he would have none of it, if Parliament voted for an enquiry the Government would resign, a General Election would follow.

The decision left the Liberal Party with no room for manoeuvre, the subsequent Parliamentary vote 364–198, brought down the first Labour Government.

VIII

Despite MacDonald becoming Prime Minister in January 1924 and leading the first Labour Government, the Minutes of the South Shields Labour and Trades Council record no discussion or the placing on record of their evident satisfaction of the event. That is not to say the matter was not considered, it seems inconceivable that such a momentous event would not have been. Although that year's May Day Rally did agree an open motion which congratulated the Labour Government on its international work (particularly recognition of the USSR), and believed that the International Labour movement would eventually abolish the capitalist system. The keynote speaker was Will Lawther.

Local activists during 1924 did though deal with two contentious issues – one constitutional and one of policy, but both of which would continue to be debated at regular intervals, even to the modern day.

The first related to what influence and power should the local Labour Party be able to exert over the elected Councillors who coalesced into a formal Labour Group in the Town Hall. Labour councillors were clear, they had been elected, albeit on a Labour platform, but they were legally responsible for the decisions they took and could not (and would not) be mandated by the local Party. Matters were not helped that some Councillors, such as the St Hilda's Miners' Lodge Secretary, Jimmy Edmondson had repeatedly failed to attend Group meetings whilst there were frequent claims other Labour Councillors did not vote along Group lines at meetings of the Borough Council.

The tension between the local Party and the Labour Group needed to be resolved somehow. As Mr Stoker, one Party delegate retorted, it was no good seeking national Government office, if locally they could not get their act together. Matters came to ahead in April 1924 when a joint meeting between the local Labour Executive Committee and the Labour Group met to consider *'Rules for the control and guidance of Labour representation on public bodies'*.

The document was quite explicit – any elected representative who had secured election with the support of the Labour Party must agree to abide by the majority decision of a Labour Group meeting; any policy decision taken should be based on the local Labour Party manifesto; no member shall speak or vote against the collective decision making of the Labour Group, the penalty for infringement would be *'repudiation'* by the Labour Group and local Party; regular attendance at Labour Group meetings was required for future endorsement as a Council candidate and all future candidates for public office must sign their agreement on the above principles.

The document set out how the local Party felt Labour Group decision making should be maintained, and no one raised any serious objections to the overall principles. An attempt by the Constituency Executive to add to the printed document a new Rule 7 – that the local Labour Party would be directly represented on the Labour Group was lost. It was clear the Labour Group would not accept what they considered interference in their decision making by non-elected representatives. When the Executive Committees deliberations were considered by a full meeting of the local Labour Party, delegates overturned the Executive and voted to add Rule 7 to the printed constitution in clear defiance of the express wishes of the Labour Group.

The issue became more fraught, Labour Councillors met in May and out of thirteen in attendance, ten were adamant they would not accept Rule 7, but in a heavily attended meeting of the local Party delegates voted by thirty-six votes to twelve to keep the Rule. The local Party Vice Chair, Mr Hutchinson was instructed to attend the next Labour Group meeting which he did, but one elected member, Cllr Watson, stormed out of the meeting in protest and the Group Chairman, Curbison offered to resign his post. Watson explained at the June Labour Party meeting that he would not apologise and felt that the issue of Rule 7 should have been referred to the Trade Unions for their consideration. The meeting successfully encouraged Curbison to rescind his threatened resignation, and in an attempt to assuage matters, noted Watson's objections.

Attendance by Labour Party officers at future Group meetings was accepted.

The episode is worth recording because it was a sign of the local Labour and Trades Council maturing. Local activists were becoming politically confident in their outlook, whereas previously working-class candidates for municipal honours felt their first loyalty was to their trade union, the local Party was making clear that in future their loyalty would be to the Labour Party. They were seeking public office, not as a member of their respective trade union, but as a Labour Party member, and as such the local Party had a right to ensure they were adhering to Labour Party principles and acknowledging elected members had a responsibility to vote with the collective will of the Labour Group. Even today, under national Labour Party rules, Labour Groups of Councillors, are required to have in attendance representatives of their local Labour Party who can speak – but not vote – on matters being considered by the Labour Group, and tensions do still flare up on occasion between a policy decision taken by the local Party which may be at odds with the will of the elected Councillors.

The second issue, centred around policy, was a contentious one which frequently divided the local Party, right up to the modern day, whether to support the sale of council housing.

IX A land fit for heroes

The issue of housing supply was a central theme for Lloyd George's 1918 election manifesto, in partnership with his Conservative Coalition partners. Britain's dilapidated housing stock, particularly in heavy industrial areas needed to be tackled but ideologically both the Liberals and Conservatives were opposed to subsided state housing. The Treasury was also against any subsidies but using the pretext of the '*Bolshevik threat*' Lloyd George convinced his Cabinet to implement the 1919 Housing, Town Planning, &c. Act which empowered local Councils to build local authority housing for rent.

The Act delivered over half a million new homes, including Cleadon Park and Simonside developments in South Shields, but despite this success, political and economic pressures saw the Geddes Committee abolish the subsidies (except for slum clearance) in June 1921 and also a policy to support the sale of council housing. The attempt was as much political, as economic. Conservatives (every much as Lloyd George) were keen to develop a new body of public support in an attempt to semi-detach the 'respectable' working man – or the 'good class artisan' from the wider Labour movement. Alongside this, the Government also made moves to restore the market in private rented housing, allowing landlords to increase their rents, a policy of 'decontrol'.

The South Shields Labour and Trades Council were enthusiastic supporters of the 1919 Housing Act, to the extent that they made repeated representations to the Town Council to use the Act's full powers to eradicate and accelerate the clearance of town centre slum housing. By 1923, the Labour Group had gained sufficient influence in the Council Chamber (although not overall control) that they were able to have one of their members, Alderman Dunlop, a former leading light of the fledging left-wing Social Democratic Federation (SDF), elected as the Chair of the Housing Committee. The Committee's main focus was on the development of the new Cleadon Park estate – land which was being incorporated into the borough's boundaries under Parliamentary Statute. Following a change in Government policy, which vigorously encouraged the selling of council houses, the Housing Committee recommended to the Borough Council that 290 of the additional 600 which were being constructed should be for sale.

The recommendation was controversial, not least because there was a prevalent view amongst some in Labour circles that to sell housing when the slum clearance was nowhere near completed was morally indefensible. Dunlop moved the proposals at the 17 December 1923 Council meeting arguing that it was one of the *'finest advantages they could offer the working man'* to become the owners of their own home. He was supported by Jim Curbison. Despite the Labour Group agreeing to support the sale, four Labour Councillors rebelled, Noble, Cheeseman, Linney and Pearson who moved an amendment to block the sale, in the case of Noble because he objected to *'private landlordism'*. The Council voted 42–4 to approve the sale.

There was the predictable uproar within the Labour and Trades Council, the Tenants' Defence League wrote to the local Party expressing opposition to the sale of the houses, the Party voted by a large majority to instruct the Labour Group of Councillors to support the letter of protest from the League when it was discussed at the next Borough Council meeting and a letter of protest was also to be sent to the Minister of Health. The local Party interviewed all potential candidates for the 1924 November municipal elections with the predicable question being asked, *'Would you be against the sale of Council housing?'*, with one potential candidate Mr J Parker being refused a place on the candidates panel because he believed *'A man should own his own home.'* Labour Councillors due for re-election in November 1924, accepted the principle that no further council house sales should be approved, and were adopted as candidates for the local elections.

Whilst the respective merits of the sale of the Cleadon Park housing simmered down, the overall policy of whether it was right to sell council housing would be a recurring argument within the ranks of Labour activists, but the Conservative and Liberal Parties strategy of dividing the Labour movement on this central issue would prove to be a long-term policy success.

X 1924 General Election

An unstable political situation meant that the country faced its third general election in less than two years, the poll was fixed for 29 October 1924. Baldwin and the Conservatives scenting victory, changed their economic policy and fought the election on a free trade platform. It would be a short election campaign for the battle-weary political troops, and MacDonald had not given up his belief that Labour may deliver an election upset and win an outright majority. The media though sought to play on the electorate's fears of a Communist conspiracy, particularly since the Labour Government had endeavoured to normalise relations with the Soviet Union. The 'red menace' fears, in part explains the determination of Gompertz and his allies in the local Labour Party not to allow the Communist Party affiliation to South Shields Labour and Trades Council.

The town's MP Edward Harney faced two challenges. Firstly, he had caused a stir in 'polite society' by divorcing his wife, Clarissa Crewdson Benington in 1923. Harney, as a Roman Catholic and representing a constituency with a significant Catholic influence would have had his private life under scrutiny by a certain section of the electorate. Secondly, holding onto one of the few non-Labour seats in the North East of England would require the anti-Labour vote to be united behind him, but as he arrived back to South Shields to launch his election campaign, he was advised that the Conservative and Unionist Party in the borough were determined to field a candidate in the election. By Friday 10 October they had one found one in William Nunn, a prominent member of the Conservative Newcastle Central Association, an Election Agent was appointed, and Committee Rooms established in Charlotte Terrace. The Marquess of Londonderry was invited to address a public meeting in the town in support of Nunn but no public meeting occurred. Londonderry did though meet senior Unionists privately and advised that the interests of the country would not be best served by splitting the anti-Labour vote in South Shields and allowing Will Lawther to potentially win the seat. He urged them to withdraw Nunn's nomination. By Friday 17 October a public statement from the Unionists was given to that effect, advising the electorate that having sought and received Harney's guarantee that in the event of his re-election, he would '*strenuously oppose Socialism*' they had decided not to contest the seat.

The following day, Saturday, when nominations closed, it was announced that it would again be a straight contest between Harney and Lawther.

The Prime Minister, MacDonald, would be buoyed by the reception he was receiving at public meetings across the Country during the eighteen-day campaign. The Conservatives – and Liberals – ignored the prevalent issues of the day such as unemployment, housing and how to maintain world peace, and chose to fight the election solely on the question of the 'red menace,' backed up by a daily press onslaught against the Labour Government's loans policy to the Soviet Union. The devasting climax for Labour's campaign though would come through the 'Zinoviev' letter.

Just four days before the 29 October poll, the *Daily Mail* published a purported letter from the Head of the Communist International Grigory Zinoviev to the Communist Party of Great Britain urging them to engage in '*seditious activities*' and boasted that the resumption of diplomatic relations with the Soviet Union by the Labour Government would '*hasten the radicalisation of the British working class.*' The letter appeared to be genuine, and the Foreign Office in an official note to the Prime Minister stated that they had no cause to doubt its authenticity. MacDonald hesitated in providing a robust response – with historians suggesting he may himself have believed the letter to genuine – and Labour candidates across the country had their campaigns derailed.

In South Shields, the usually polite and urbane Harney delivered his own 'red menace' threat by loquaciously alleging that Will Lawther had himself sent a telegram message of goodwill to the Communist Party a few months earlier – Lawther's retort, that it was actually sent to the Communist Congress, was somewhat lacklustre in the febrile anti-Communist atmosphere. The *Shields Daily News* records that Lawther's public meetings had been subjected to disruption and interruption. Harney hammered home the message at every public meeting – whether it was sent to the Communist Party or to a Communist Congress was irrelevant, Harney told his audience, the sender of that telegram was a Communist.

The unpropitious circumstances of the Zinoviev letter would see the Labour Party lose forty Parliamentary seats, returning 151 Labour MPs, although its national tally of votes would actually increase by over one million. Baldwin's Conservatives secured a landslide winning 413 constituencies. The Liberal Party though were decimated, returning just forty-two MPs.

In South Shields, Lawther went down to his third defeat in less than two years, securing 16,852 votes as opposed to Harney's 23,171. Lawther would not contest the seat again and went on to become the General Secretary of the Miners' Federation.

As for the Zinoviev letter itself, it would continue to be an infamous chapter of Labour history, to such an extent that in 1998 the Labour Foreign Secretary, Robin Cook, asked the Foreign Office Chief Historian to review all available evidence and determine whether the letter was a fake. The conclusion from Gill Bennett was that the letter was the work of 'White' Russian émigrés with encouragement by rogue elements within the Secret Intelligence Service and leaked to *the Daily Mail*.

The Zinoviev letter had been a fraud.

Chapter 8

Victory …

I

The Conservative and Unionist politician, Sir Arthur Sackville Trevor Griffith-Boscawen or 'Bosey' was not a 'lucky' politician. Elected for Tonbridge in 1892 at the age of twenty-seven he subsequently lost the seat at the 1906 General Election; he then lost the East Denbighshire by-election in August 1906 and promptly lost the Dudley by-election of January 1910. He was elected for Dudley in the December 1910 General Election but when in February 1921 he was promoted to the Ministry as Minister for Agriculture by Lloyd George he was required under Law to resign and re-contest his seat, unfortunately for him he lost the ensuring 'Ministerial' by-election to the Labour candidate, so the MP for Taunton – Sir Dennis Boles, was elevated to the Peerage and Bosey fought the inevitable by-election in April 1921, winning only to lose it at the October 1922 General Election.

Whilst he wasn't electorally lucky, he was incredibly well connected and despite not being an MP, he remained a Member of Lloyd George's Coalition Government and set about promoting an unpopular Parliamentary Bill on the reform of local government finance. Following his promotion to the Cabinet as Minister of Health by the new Prime Minister Bonar Law in early 1923, an impregnable Conservative Parliamentary constituency was needed for him. This time, Sir Thomas Cato Worsfold, the MP for Mitcham, duly applied for the Chiltern Hundreds (he was elevated to the Peerage a year later) and Bosey fought the March 1923 by-election.

Misfortune though would follow Bosey to Surrey, with minutes to spare, nomination papers were submitted on behalf of a renegade Independent Conservative candidate, who shared concerns of middle-voters across the Country, alarmed by the Conservative Government's proposals to decontrol rents and their failure to resolve the housing crisis. It led to Pathé News describing the by-election as '*The housing problem by-election*'. Despite Bonar Law sending an open letter to the constituents of Mitcham imploring them to support Bosey, a split Conservative vote sealed his fate. When the votes were counted on Monday 5 March, and in what they regarded as an act of moral turpitude, allowed a forty-one-year-old Surrey County Councillor and National Union of Teachers official, James Chuter Ede to secure an unprecedented victory for the Labour Party in one of the Conservative Party's safest seats, winning a majority by just 833 votes. It caused a media sensation across the country, in the Vestry Hall, Mitcham Green where the count took place, Lady Boscawen graciously congratulated Mrs Ede on her husband's victory whilst her own resigned from public life later the same day.

Chuter Ede had now come to the attention of the national Labour Leadership in Eccleston Square in London. His remarkable performance and campaigning style in securing such a safe middle-class Conservative seat, claiming the scalp of a Cabinet Minister and helping to destabilise the Government in the process, won him many platitudes. Although he would lose the Mitcham seat just nine months later at the 1923 General Election, and he would again fail win to win Mitcham at the 1924 General Election – his name was made, a distinguished Parliamentary career without question would soon follow. It was just a matter of time before he secured a promising Labour seat.

With the Governor of the Bank of England, Montagu Norman and his new Chancellor, the recently elected (now Conservative MP) Winston Churchill, by his side, Baldwin's new Conservative Government, elected at the October 1924 General Election was required to deal with a still sluggish UK economy, widespread industrial unrest and the country's diminishing influence in the world. Central to their discussions was whether Britain's economy should return to the Gold Standard.

The Gold Standard was the pre-war financial system in which, as the name suggests, fixed global currencies to a set amount of gold. The system had seen Britain dominate the financial world before World War I, but the high cost of the conflict saw Britain, and other European nations, leave the Gold Standard in order to freely finance rapidly escalating military expenditure and in Britain's case go cap in hand for a loan from the US to meet its financial obligations. The result was that the US economy would grow exponentially, leaving them with nearly 40 per cent of the world's stock of gold and New York rivalling London as the financial capital of the world. By 1925, Montagu Norman wanted Britain back on the Gold Standard, and at a price set at pre-war levels. He believed that the austerity measures undertaken by the Treasury (which had resulted in bitter industrial disputes) and the need to curtail rising inflation – as well as the international prestige it would give the country – justified and necessitated returning to Gold. The risk though was that returning to the Gold Standard would make British goods more expensive and would expose heavy industry, upon which much employment depended, to their globally more efficient rivals who, unlike Britain, didn't have a vast Empire to manage and defend. Churchill initially held out, but under Treasury pressure, who were impervious to the views of industry, agreed to return to the Gold Standard in his April 1925 Budget – with disastrous consequences.

II

By January 1925, the Labour Group of Councillors within South Shields Town Hall had increased their number to such an extent that they were just three seats short of having a majority of Councillors, twenty-five moderates opposed to twenty Labour Councillors – and with it the power to appoint the unelected Alderman – a number of whom were due for reappointment in November.

The growth of the Labour Group caused anxiety amongst the non-Labour Councillors, who had continued to describe themselves as 'Independent' although they organised themselves through the South Shields Municipal Association, which brought together an array of right-wing municipal interests to coordinate their nominations to the electorate. Nearby Gateshead Council had fallen to the Labour Party in the 1924 Council elections, and the Municipal Association was determined to halt what they regarded as the '*Socialist and Communistic advance*' within the Town Hall. On 21 September 1925, they gathered at the Regent Café in Ocean Road to hear reports from Gateshead Municipal Association representatives and to consider their actions for the forthcoming November polls. Mr J Weir, the Chair of the meeting was in no doubt as to the urgency for stronger campaigning – '*The local Labour Party was dominated by Communists, the position is one of real peril to the town*'. Speakers from Gateshead spoke of the '*apathy*' of middle and better class of voters who simply didn't appreciate the financial extravagance that Socialists brought to municipal affairs. The local Labour Party was determined to turn the Town Hall Chamber into a '*Moscow bear garden*' run by a '*caucus of extremists*' who would operate through '*intimidation and dictation.*' The meeting agreed to increase their efforts and contest every seat to defeat the '*local Communist and Socialist plot to seize control of the town's finances*'.

The Association was clearly in an agitated state, the election of the local Labour Party Secretary Harry Donnelly to the Council in a Rekendyke by-election in June 1925 cemented unity between the local Party and the Labour Group of Councillors, whilst the election of Tom Mulgrew to the Council in a further by-election in Rekendyke in July saw the Labour Group not only secure a vital gain in numbers in the Council Chamber but also an accomplished and eloquent speaker of the unemployed who would bring a forensic debating style to the Council Chamber. There was more encouraging news for the Labour Party when the April 1925 Board of Guardians elections witnessed the local Labour Party field no less than seven women for Office and secure further inroads into their membership of the Board with the election of Maria Curbison, the wife of Jim Curbison. The Labour Guardians Group was exiguous but highly effective. The Municipal Association also noted with some alarm that the Labour Party had been able to secure further nominations to the Magistrates' Bench in May with the appointment of Cuth Barrass, Jim Curbison, George Linney and the town's first woman Magistrate, Sarah Noble, wife of a long-serving Labour Councillor.

The Labour Group on the Council was beginning to operate as a cohesive force, in part due to the discipline of a well administered local Labour Party and the unqualified support of the local Unions. In January 1925 the Labour Group argued unsuccessfully for the Labour Party to oversee the provision of relief work provision in the borough and they repeatedly forced Chamber votes on proposed increases in salaries for Borough Official's, but it was an off-the-cuff remark that demonstrated the simmering underlining tensions between the growing Labour Group and the Moderate councillors.

At the August 1925 Borough Council meeting, Curbison on behalf of the Labour Group moved that the Authority refuse to accept a tender for sanitary works, this led to a Moderate member, Councillor Brock asking if Curbison would have rejected the tender if the second supplier on the list had not been submitted by the Co-operative Wholesale Society. Uproar ensured, with the fiery Curbison demanding the withdrawal of the comment and the Mayor repeatedly calling for order, as a packed Public Gallery bellowed its support for Jim Curbison. The meeting became impossible to manage for the Mayor and elected members agreed that the meeting should be abandoned without resolve. The matter would not drop though, at the September Borough Council meeting as proceedings commenced, Curbison rose and demanded an apology from Councillor Brock for impugning his character. The Mayor refused to discuss the matter, uproar again followed with Labour members demanding Councillor Brock apologise and the public gallery erupting into repeated applause and cheers when Labour members spoke. Eventually the Mayor took the unprecedented step of calling for the Police, who upon arrival '*forcibly dragged*' Curbison out of the Chamber, upon which the Labour Group followed out in support. Pandemonium broke out in the public gallery, before further police officers arrived and cleared the gallery.

The Labour Group was furious at the antics of the Moderate Councillors and in an act of defiance submitted a number of resolutions for the next meeting of the borough seeking to overturn previous Council decisions. The move was designed to thwart and harass the Moderate Councillors and to disrupt the business of the Council. Eight resolutions were proposed ranging from expanding unemployed works provision, Brinkburn Recreation Ground, a request to rescind approval to send South Shields Police Officers to other districts when called upon, a demand to build an infectious diseases and tuberculous hospital, that a direct labour force be used to construct the new houses in Sunderland Road and finally to demand that in future tenders should be opened in front of the Town Clerk. All were defeated heavily with the Moderates inbuilt majority thanks to the unelected Aldermanic Bench.

The Labour Party's hopes of controlling the Council rested on securing a crucial three seats in the November 1925 municipal elections, this would have secured them a majority of the Councillors and the ability to appoint Alderman from the Labour side.

It was not to be.

In a high turnout the November poll saw Labour lose one seat. The Moderates ruthlessly reappointed supportive Alderman to the Council, strengthening their tentative hold on municipal power. The *Shields Daily News* lamented the increasing influence of Labour in local Government and the emergence of '*class politics*' in Council Chambers, not just in South Shields, but across the North East region, believing local affairs were best served without the involvement of national political parties.

Neither the *Shields Daily News* nor the Moderate Councillors in South Shields could though ignore the growth and influence of the Labour Group, nor could they refuse to acknowledge that the position of the ceremonial Mayor was usually afforded to the longest serving Councillor or Alderman. It was one civic position – strictly apolitical which they could not deny to the Labour Group. James Rowden Curbison had been a Councillor since 1911, although he had a quick temper, he did play a constructive role in the work of the Council and as a result of a private meeting of the Council – in which assurances would have been sought about his future conduct by the Moderates – he was supported for the position of Mayor of the Borough for the 1925/26 municipal year. He would be the first Labour Mayor nominated and supported by the official Labour Group, although even then the Labour Group meeting on 5 October, after debate, only allowed Curbison to accept the nomination by five votes to six. It was a role he was to rise to with increasing respect and even his Moderate opponents were moved to publicly acknowledge the fairness in which he conducted Council meetings and the professionalism that both Curbison and his wife conducted Civic Receptions. Council business, they believed, had been carried out more expeditiously with him in the Chair than when he was prominent in debate on the floor of the Chamber. It was not a view shared by his Labour Group colleagues, who following their March 1926 meeting wrote to Curbison protesting at his *'harsh enforcement of the standing orders of the Council'* and objecting to him voting against the Labour whip.

The Chains of Municipal Office though still took second place to the main issue facing South Shields during the 1920s, the high rate of unemployment. By December 1925, Curbison, as Mayor, convened a special meeting of the Borough Council to consider the rising unemployment figures, now reaching over 10,500 and the financial hardship facing so many of his townsfolk. The Council considered further schemes which could be undertaken to help alleviate the problem with the Unemployed Grants Committee being instructed to direct further monies to the Brinkburn Recreational Scheme of improvement works, and the Council debating the construction of a tunnel or bridge over the River Tyne, to connect South Shields with Tynemouth using the Government's Unemployed Grants resources to finance the scheme.

Meanwhile, the Board of Guardians, administering financial support to the hardest hit was under severe pressure due to the sheer scale of applicants seeking support. By December 1921 Guardians across the country were relieving around 1.5 million people, almost 4 per cent of the English and Welsh population. Not only were Local Authorities inundated by requests for aid, but the question was also what to do with able-bodied men out of work. As Lynn Hollen Lees observed – *'The familiar choice between the workhouse and the stoneyard had not gained in appeal after the experiences of military service or years of full employment.'* The Government though were concerned that too many Boards across the country were now Labour controlled and defying the Government by allocating support to able-bodied men whom they felt did not fully meet the requirements of Poor Law assistance. The Health Minister,

Neville Chamberlain, announced in December 1925 that he was proposing major changes to local government finance which would eventually see the Board of Guardians abolished and their functions transferred to County and County Borough Councils in 1929.

Whilst maintaining pressure in the Council Chamber, the South Shields Labour and Trades Council would also, in early 1926, turn their attentions once again to seeking a Parliamentary candidate.

III

'It is a triumph of sheer brain power. He has a disciplined mind, great capacity for work, a smashing logic and a wonderful power of mastering and marshalling hard facts' so advised a friend of James Chuter Ede to the *Daily Herald*, upon his by-election success in Mitcham in 1923.

Born in September 1883 in Surrey, Ede's father was a lower middle-class grocer who along with his wife Agnes were Gladstonian Liberals with strong religious Nonconformity traditions manifested in Unitarianism which they impressed upon their family. Friends recall Chuter Ede was a passionate Liberal in his youth, seeking to convert the farm labourers to Liberalism with a ferocious debating style. He won a scholarship to Dorking High School and a further scholarship took him to Christ's College Cambridge to study natural sciences, but lack of finance meant that he left university before securing a degree.

Having chosen teaching as his vocation, he returned to his native Surrey and taught in a number of schools around Ewell, Mortlake and Tolworth and was elected to Epsom District Council in 1908 where it was observed he was an assiduous attender of meetings, missing only four meetings in six years. The residents of the borough duly elected him in 1914 to Surrey County Council whereupon he was required to resign his post as a teacher. During World War I he served as an Acting Regimental Sergeant Major with the Royal Engineers in France where his experiences converted him to Socialism and the emerging Labour Party. While on leave in 1917 he married Lilian Mary Williams, a teacher herself, and became a member of the Labour Party, making him the sole Labour member of Surrey County Council. After the war he was appointed Assistant General Secretary of the National Union of Teachers.

Organising the Union's National Executive Committee meetings, Ede became acquainted with the North East Executive member, Cuth Barrass, a prominent member of the South Shields Labour and Trades Council. Following Ede's defeat in Mitcham at both the 1923 and 1924 General Elections, Barrass encouraged the ambitious Ede to consider allowing his name to be considered for the South Shields Parliamentary seat. The failure of the Miners official and firmly left-wing Will Lawther to secure the seat for the Labour Party, led Barrass to believe that a new style of candidate was required to secure the more moderate and middle-class elector within the town, crucial to winning the Parliamentary seat from the Liberal Party. With the blessing of his Union, who agreed to sponsor him if selected, Ede took the train to Tyneside.

Ede was not assured of the South Shields nomination. The local Labour Party wrote to twelve aspiring Parliamentarians on the Labour Party's national panel, Ede wasn't one of them. In a sign of the growing influence of the women within the South Shields party, Dr Marion Phillips (who would eventually become the MP for Sunderland) was considered, and approaches were made in April 1925 to Ellen Wilkinson (who would eventually become the MP for Jarrow, synonymous with the Jarrow March). The Minutes do not record any attempts to approach any particular Trade Union for support, rather potential candidates themselves were asked their 'financial status' in essence, who would fund their campaign.

Ede's name first appears in the February 1925 Minute Book, as being asked to confirm his financial status, along with Col Arthur Lynch. Both were asked to speak at that year's May Day. Lynch had an interesting career in his own right. Described by Geoffrey Serle as a '… *hefty man, strikingly handsome of charm, courtesy and even temper … although erratic in his grasp of public affairs*', he was born in Smythesdale, Victoria, Australia. Following qualification as a Civil Engineer he emigrated to London to take up journalism and then to Ireland to take up politics. He served as an MP for the Irish Parliamentary Party in 1901/02, was admitted to the Royal College of Surgeons in 1908 and was re-elected to Parliament in 1909/18. Pro-Boer, he fought in South Africa and upon his return to Britain was sentenced to be hanged which was commuted to life imprisonment, but in 1904 he was released 'on licence' by the Balfour Government, eventually being pardoned in 1907. A prolific writer, he wrote a 40,000-word novel during his incarceration but is quoted as saying, that because he was permitted no pen or paper in prison, he was required to memorise it. One of his publications sought to refute Einstein's theory of relativity. Lynch supported the British war effort in World War I and raised his own Irish Battalion and at the end of hostilities, unsuccessfully contested Battersea South for the Labour Party in the 1918 General Election. In later life he practised medicine in London, and for good measure he was also descended from Rob Roy MacGregor on his mother's side.

The Labour Party selection conference was held on 2 May 1926, attempts were made to delay the selection meeting because Lynch was detained in Athens. These were rebuffed and saw Ede eventually defeat Lynch by forty seven votes to twenty-eight votes.

Several factors would undermine Lynch's candidature.

Whilst Lynch was Catholic and would have received a body of support from some sections of the audience for his religious affiliation, Lynch's failure to reach South Shields did not help although he did wire a commitment to support the local Party with a £100 annual grant towards the cost of his campaign. Whilst his military service in World War I was exemplary, his pro Boer views may well have counted against him, and by 1926 he was sixty five years old; Ede was only forty-four. Finally, Ede's fellow National Union of Teachers activist, Cuth Barrass was working the numbers for him with the delegates who would make the final choice. Despite all these drawbacks, Lynch still polled a respectful vote which indicates a degree of nervousness by some delegates towards Ede.

Barrass, who had intellectual acuity was fastidious in his determination to secure the nomination for Ede, not only because they shared the same devotion to the value of education, but because Barrass was convinced Ede's background, his campaigning abilities and his moderate politics would turn those sections of the electorate which had rejected their previous candidate Will Lawther's 'class view' of the world. The support of Barrass was critical for Ede because he was immensely well respected within Party circles. Born in 1878 and thus a contemporary of Gompertz, he was a schoolmaster at Deans Road and a decorated World War I veteran, gaining the Military Medal in August 1917 with the 9th East Yorkshire Regiment for his work as a stretcher bearer, he had also been a prisoner of war being captured on 25 April 1918 and serving out the rest of the war at Friedrichsfeld POW Camp north of Cologne. Barrass was an accomplished speaker in his own right and was in high demand to address rallies across the North East region on behalf of the ILP.

There can be not a scintilla of doubt that Gompertz would have been an enthusiastic supporter of Ede. They unquestionably shared the same political outlook, Ede's municipal work in Surrey would have impressed Gompertz and as a senior member of the Constituency Party, Gompertz would have had access to vital information, such as the names of delegates eligible to vote as well as a full list of affiliated Unions to the Constituency Party. This administrative intelligence would have been critical to Barrass securing the eventual numbers for Ede. Gompertz from the moment of Ede's selection was very much his eyes and ears in the Constituency, protesting at the Labour Party's January 1927 meeting that inappropriate comments were being made by members about Ede and that their main focus should be on securing the Parliamentary seat.

As Ede and supporters spent the weekend celebrating his selection, they would have been conscious of the unfolding events nationally which would, two days later, see the industrial heart of South Shields in the grip of the national strike.

IV The 1926 General Strike

The decision by the Baldwin Government to return to the Gold Standard resulted, as some experts like JM Keynes had predicted, to the British pound being too strong for effective exporting. The impact was devastating for Britain's coal mining communities.

Demand for coal had reduced following the war effort, the Dawes Plan had allowed German coal mines to provide both Italy and France with free coal as part of their reparations for World War I and the industry suffered from poor management which had refused to modernise production allowing Poland and America to supply coal more cheaply and at a faster pace. Over a seven-year period the wages of coal miners had reduced from £6 to just £3.18s by 1926. The failure to make a profit from the industry forced mine owners to demand not only a further reduction in the wages of the million mine workers across the UK, but that they should also work extra hours. The Government sought to ease tensions in July 1925 by establishing a Royal Commission to examine the industry and in the process provided a nine-month financial subsidy to the mine owners to prevent industrial unrest. However, when the Samuel Commission presented their report in March 1926, they were resolute that the wages of miners would need to be reduced by 13.5 per cent. Following the collapse of protracted negotiations, the TUC called a General Strike and by 4 May over 2 million workers, mainly in the heavy industries, transport sector and docks, were out on strike, the *Shields Gazette* reported that a third of the workforce across South Shields was supporting the strike with the coal miners and transport workers being particularly solid.

The Government, well prepared and with the full apparatus of the State, were able to successfully challenge the strike, whilst commentators like WR Garside, noted that the TUC leadership was not only unprepared mentally for the strike, but also openly feared its consequences, with the Derby Labour MP, and a former senior National Union of Railwaymen official, JH Thomas, declaring in a speech in Hammersmith on 9 May that: '*I have never disguised, and I do not disguise now, that I have never been in favour of the principle of a General Strike.*' The Government, publishing their own newspaper *The British Gazette*, appealed to the country and condemned the dispute as subversive – '*The General Strike is a challenge to Parliament and is the road to anarchy and ruin.*' For Prime Minister Baldwin, whilst having some sympathy for the miners, it was the principle that Parliamentary democracy was supreme and could not be dictated to by a minority, however worthy their case.

The Durham Coalfield was solid in their support for the strike with Will Lawther, the former Parliamentary candidate for South Shields arrested and detained under the Emergency Powers (Defence) Act accused of interfering with food distribution and Police intimidation, and on 13 May was fined £50 with the alternative of two months' imprisonment, he chose prison. However, the Government's preparations kept food supplies and docks functioning, and the nervousness of the TUC Leadership, ultimately meant that the General Strike was destined to fail. Frantic efforts were made by the TUC to secure some compromise via Government intermediaries, and by Tuesday 11 May, attempts were being made to encourage the miners to accept a settlement, which always involved a reduction in wages, a red-line bargaining position for the miners which they could not accept. On 12 May, the TUC informed Baldwin it was calling off the strike, an unconditional surrender which was greeted with fury in the Durham Coalfield. '*Never in the history of workers struggles – with one exception of the treachery of our leaders in 1914 – has there been such a calculated betrayal of working class interests*', thundered *the Newcastle Workers' Chronicle*.

Not for the first time, the miners were expected to battle alone. Despite community support, families were required to seek the support of the Board of Guardians, but the strike continued throughout the summer and into autumn. The national leadership of the miners under AJ Cook were adamant that there should be no negotiation on the principle of wage reduction or an increase in hours. So determined were the miners that even the highly respected regional miners' leader, Peter Lee, was shouted down and told to leave the platform at a rally in Tyne Dock on 2 June 1926, when pointing to a banner exclaiming: *'No reductions, no increased hours and no district settlements'* advised the audience of hardened striking miners that that would never be in his case, because anyone could shout a motto, what they needed was settlement. The Government was in no mood for compromise and on 28 June proposals under the Coal Mines Bill were laid before the House of Commons to enable mine owners to increase the hours miners worked, in direct contravention of even the Samuel Commission which had reported the year before on the problems faced by the coal industry. In a heated debate, the South Shields MP Edward Harney made clear he would oppose the Bill, insisting that whilst the miners in his constituency were *'not revolutionaries'* neither were they *'ignorant of the factors that go up to make the present problem with which we are faced.'* Harney pointed out that every enquiry into the coal industry since 1919 had made clear that an increase in hours was not the solution. The Bill was approved in a House of Commons division.

Whilst mineworkers across South Shields remained loyal to the strike, one colliery in the town experienced an early drift back to work: St Hilda's. By early November over 350 men marched into the colliery with a Police escort, led by their Lodge Secretary, Councillor John Edmondson. Demonstrators jeered and jostled with the Police along Victoria Road as the miners marched back to work. Picketing and social ostracism followed, with one striking miner, James Philips of Rosa Street being fined £5 for *'intimidating'* one miner returning to work.

The situation for coal miners in South Shields was exacerbated by the fact that they had been on strike since the summer of 1925 in a dispute with the Harton Coal Company over weekly wage agreements. Boldon, Marsden, St Hilda's and Harton collieries had invariably remained idle for long periods in 1925 and through to early 1926, with the town's Mayor, Curbison hosting meetings in the Town Hall in an effort to secure a resolve to the situation. Gompertz was appointed as the Chairman of the Miners' Relief Fund in the town, South Shields Labour Party was represented on the short-lived Central Strike Committee, whilst the Member of Parliament, Edward Harney had also used the opportunity of a House of Commons debate in February 1926 to raise the issue of the dispute criticising any attempts by the Government to change the entitlement of striking miners to receiving financial hardship assistance during trade disputes, particularly when men were *'locked-out'* by the colliery owners. It seemed that no sooner had one dispute reached a conclusion then the men were called out again.

Chuter Ede as the prospective Labour candidate gave support when he was in the town, folklore has it that on one occasion when he travelled from Surrey, the train journey was hampered by the strike, and he duly walked the rest of the way to South Shields. At their 6 November 1926 meeting the local Party resolved to hold a protest meeting on 14 November with Ede as the main speaker demanding the Government reach a '*settlement through negotiation not starvation*' but the protest was pointless. Literally destitute, the miners could not hold out much longer, in the face of a significant return to work in the Midlands, Derbyshire and Nottinghamshire, and hunger and despair driving a quarter of the workforce back to work, AJ Cook coined a new motto – '*Back to work we go on the status quo*', but the mine owners, backed by a Government reluctant to involve itself in a private industry (but quite prepared to change the law to allow for a longer working day), were in no mood for compromise. The *Newcastle Journal* reported on 18 November, that all four collieries that made up the Harton Coal Company had voted to return to work, but in Boldon's case they did not return to work until 6 December. The long bitter dispute had achieved nothing for the miners, they were forced to accept district wage settlements, longer hours (in some cases a forty-nine-hour week) and their wages were often lower than those they earned for a seven hour day. For good measure the Government the following year implemented the 1927 Trade Disputes and Trade Union Act which banned sympathy strikes, limited the right to picket, required trade unionists to 'opt-in' to a trade union political fund and banned civil servants from being a member of a trade union affiliated to the TUC. The Act caused outrage in Labour and Trade Union circles and within certain sections of liberal society leading to great personal resentment to Baldwin who used the Government's overwhelming majority to force the legislation through the House of Commons.

Locally, the aftermath saw St Hilda's Lodge vote to leave the DMA in January 1927 and help establish the Northumberland and Durham Miners Non-Political Union. Prominent in the manoeuvres was Councillor Edmondson, who as early as October 1925 had been expelled from the Labour Group on South Shields Council for not adhering to the Labour whip. He was elected Area President of the new non-political union which inevitably came under the influence of George Spencer's breakaway union based around the Nottinghamshire coalfield which received enthusiastic support from the right-wing Seamen's Leader, Havelock Wilson. There was no such breakaway in Boldon, Marsden or Harton.

V Aftermath

Hardship payments to striking families had a devastating impact on the finances of local Councils across the North East. The Board of Guardians who administered the fund, were required to request further support from Councils in order to meet their obligations. At the time of the General Strike in the summer of 1926, nearly 2.5 million people were assisted under the Poor Laws. The Guardians were inundated by requests for aid whilst at the same time were required to support men who were unemployed.

At the October 1926 meeting of the South Shields Council, Ald Lawson reported that the Authority was near to bankruptcy. As a member of the Board of Guardians, Lawson stated that they were working to prevent any attempt to avoid a supplementary rate to pay for the relief, since it would inevitably lead to further warrants being issued to residents who simply would not be able to pay the increase. The Labour Councillors sought to allocate further expenditure on the new King George Road extension to enable unemployed men to have work during the winter months, it was rejected as too costly by the Moderate civic leaders.

The Mayor, Jim Curbison, had his own idea as to how to save public money, he announced he was arranging a meeting in the Town Hall on 21 October inviting the relevant political parties, with a view to agreeing not to contest any seats in the November 1926 municipal elections. Curbison argued that given the febrile and volatile atmosphere of the industrial unrest, and the costs of the elections, they should be seeking to create some unity whilst saving money at the same time. His subsequent meeting was attended by the Moderate leading lights but not a single Labour representative attended the meeting, and the suggestion was aborted.

There was no question that the local Labour Party was determined to contest the elections, the Moderates had a majority of only five on the Council and with the volatile industrial situation and the support they were rendering to the striking miners they had every reason to believe they would be successful. The campaign was not without rancour, a meeting to promote Labour's Municipal candidates in the Marsden Miners' Hall in late October 1926 descended into acrimony when the Socialist firebrand, Tom Mann arrived uninvited to speak. The Labour Party Secretary, Harry Donnelly advised he had no knowledge of who Tom Mann was, which enraged Mann to the point he refused point blank to join the platform leading to complaints from the Miners as to Donnelly's conduct. The election would prove though a false hope, in the eleven November 1926 contests, not a single ward changed hands, save in Laygate where St Hilda's rebel miners official, Councillor John Edmondson stood as an Independent Labour candidate and was soundly defeated by the Official Labour candidate, Thomas Proud, a fellow St Hilda's miner, loyal to the DMA.

With a weakened Labour and trade union movement following the failure of the General Strike, Neville Chamberlain, the Health Minister on 29 March 1927 declared in the House of Commons that '*It is a deliberate policy of the Socialist Party if they obtain majorities on the Board of Guardians to use the money of the ratepayers to assist their political friends. They would distinguish between one working man and another according to his Trade Union.*' Whilst Chamberlain had in his sights the Labour dominated Chester-le-Street Guardians (whose remit he was seeking to terminate) by 1927 the Labour Party in South Shields could count on twenty members on the Guardians as opposed to twenty-one Moderates with every prospect of securing control at the next Board of Guardians election. Chamberlain set about implementing changes to the administration of Poor Law relief as well as changes to unemployment benefit. The changes to entitlement to unemployment benefit in particular had the effect of shifting responsibility for financial assistance onto the local Boards of Guardians who faced the task of adjudicating on 'out relief' support to those denied assistance from the Labour Exchange. It placed additional financial pressures on already overstretched local budgets, to the extent that the Boards began considering scaling back their financial support. The changes were met with fury as protesters stormed meetings of the Guardians in Newcastle and Gateshead when they met to consider the recommendations, whilst on 29 September 1927, in South Shields over 100 unemployed men marched through the town to lobby a meeting of the Board at their offices in Barrington Street but were prevented from parading outside the Guardians Hall by a heavy police presence.

The South Shields Guardians faced real difficulties, they provided assistance to over 16,650 families, 1,400 who were in institutions or homes, they also had a financial deficit mainly due to the support they had given to striking miners during 1926. Whilst the miners had agreed to have six pence of their wages deducted each week to clear the £106,000 commitments to the Board (considered by the Minister of Health as a totally inadequate repayment plan) the fact that there had been changes to unemployment benefit entitlement meant that there were potentially over 10,000 men seeking, at some stage, support from the poor relief. The Guardians precept from the local rates had increased from £30,870 in 1914, to £163,800 by 1927. Even Labour's Councillor Tom Mulgrew, a longstanding Guardian member accepted the position was going to become even bleaker. The solutions were laid before them, either the Government provided support or rates would need to increase (running the risk of tipping low wage ratepayers over the financial edge and potentially making some businesses unsustainable thus increasing unemployment further) or they would need to scale back the amount of relief payable per household. Their 31 August meeting, which lasted over four hours, agreed to scale back support, leading to a predictable fury which culminated in unemployed workers representatives pleading their case at the Guardians Board September meeting. In a rare victory for Labour representatives, George Linney successfully moved (twenty votes to eighteen) that they revert to the former scale of support but that they request the Council to apply for additional Government support for the local authority to implement further public works schemes to relieve pressure on the Guardians. In response the Government and the Banks, whilst not agreeing additional support, did allow further time for the Guardians to repay their loans but an increase in the local precept was inevitable. South Shields Council considered any further public work schemes for the unemployed a financial risk, leading to one Moderate Councillor, John Wood, who had recommended support for the unemployed, declining to seek re-election for the Council in the November polls.

The unemployed demonstration to the Board of Guardians on 29 September 1927, was not without controversy, Police were accused of being heavy handed and the South Shields Labour Party made a formal complaint to the Council's Watch Committee who refused to consider the matter.

VI

At the conclusion of his Mayoral Year, Curbison, as tradition dictated, was appointed Deputy Mayor to his successor Councillor Ranson. In April 1927 following the death of Labour Alderman JW Henderson, Labour's Richard Vine was elected by the Council to replace him on the Aldermanic Bench. Although a significant number of Moderate Councillors supported one of their own – Councillor John Wilson – there were enough Moderate abstentions (on the principle that a Labour representative should replace a departing one on the Aldermanic Bench) to secure Vine's eventual victory. Curbison, now residing at Lossiemouth in Harton Lane, broke ranks, probably aggrieved that as the longer serving Councillor he was not chosen by the Group for the vacancy and stood for election himself receiving just one vote. The inevitable by-election in the Victoria ward to replace Vine upon his elevation was uncontested and saw another miner, Richard Longstaff elected to the Council.

In a demonstration of how important women were becoming within the Labour ranks of the local Party, they agreed to select the wife of a trade union official, Elizabeth Ann Thorpe, a member of the Board of Guardians, as their candidate for Tyne Dock in the 1927 November Municipal poll. Although the election saw no change to the overall composition of the Council, Thorpe secured a stunning victory in Tyne Dock and has the distinction of being the first woman Councillor on South Shields Council. Along with a large group of Labour women members on the Board of Guardians, Elizabeth Thorpe joined an illustrious line of women activists who were steadily making their mark on civic affairs.

Chuter Ede also saw the importance of encouraging women within political life. They would form an important voting bloc in future elections given that the voting age for women had been reduced to twenty-one, in line with men, in 1928. But for Ede it was more than simple political expediency. As a Unitarian, Socialist and educationalist, Ede believed fervently in equal rights and the emancipation of women. His own wife Lilian, was elected to Surrey County Council in November 1928, joining her well-established husband in the Council Chamber. In addition, Ede encouraged the political activist and author, Helen Keynes to contest the July 1928 Epsom by-election. Keynes was a member of the Fabian Society National Executive, and agreed to stand, so long as Ede acted as her election agent. The choice made sense. Ede knew Epsom well, given he had been the Labour Party candidate there in the 1918 General Election, but his Union duties, as well as his campaigning commitments in South Shields, prevented him undertaking the role. Keynes was unsuccessful at the poll, but Ede did give some assistance in the campaign using his networks to encourage leading lights such as Margaret Bondfield to visit the Constituency. Further, as an MP he would make frequent interventions in the House of Commons supporting the emancipation of women, most notably when as the Member for Mitcham he spoke in support of women being admitted to Oxford and Cambridge Universities.

Like all political parties and organisations, new recruits and activists constantly emerge and there are manoeuvres to replace the old guard. The local Party's 1927 Annual Meeting held in February saw a number of changes with Cllr Pearson confirmed as the new Chair of the Party following the decision earlier by long-standing stalwart, George Linney, to step aside to concentrate on his Municipal work. Harry Donnelly lost the Secretaryship to Alex Stephenson and the existing Treasurer William Hibbett saw off a strong challenge for his post by just two votes. Gompertz, now residing at 38 Bertram Street – which he would eventually purchase and rent out – did not seek any positions and for a further year was also absent from the powerful Constituency Executive although he did accept a nomination to serve as a lay member of the Council's Assessment Committee, which considered business rate qualifications in the borough.

VII Abolition of the Board of Guardians

Although Neville Chamberlain's contribution to politics would be defined by his appeasement strategy to Nazi Germany in the 1930s, he had previously built a solid reputation as a reforming Health Minister who within a month of his appointment in 1924 submitted no less than twenty-five pieces of social reform he wished to enact. Ranging from local government finance reform, an expansion of council housing and owner occupation, planning and local government boundary reform. Twenty-one would eventually make it to the Statute Book and laid the basis for the operation of local government for a generation. As someone with a solid background in Birmingham municipal politics he instinctively appreciated the value of strong local civic leadership and received garlands of praise. His reform of the Poor Law though was driven by his desire to abolish what he regarded as unaccountable bodies, who in many cases were over exercising their powers in providing poor relief to the able-bodied unemployed.

The South Shields Guardians Board would be abolished on 1 April 1930, with the local Council being required to establish a Public Assistance Board. Cynics – usually members of the Guardians or their senior employees – would criticise the move as creating Guardians of the Rates as opposed to Guardians of the Poor and saw the move in some way as the nationalisation of local government. The Labour Party though gave support to the proposals particularly since it abolished workhouses, the workhouse test and ended the demeaning term 'pauper'.

As Chamberlain implemented Poor Law reform nationally, South Shields and the North of Tyne Councils were continuing their campaign to have a Tyne Tunnel crossing constructed, possibly a short tube railway and appeared before a House of Commons Select Committee in June 1928 to argue for the finance to implement the scheme. We should recall that the number of pedestrians seeking to travel between the north and south of the Tyne would have been greater than today given the number of waterfront workers who would have been employed in the various shipyards. Whilst the Select Committee were supportive, the two Councils could not agree on the final design, Tynemouth insisting that the Tunnel should cater for all modes of transport, South Shields preferring a tube railway. The proposals were opposed by the Tyne Improvement Commissioners who were clearly concerned that such a scheme would reduce the usage of the Tyne Ferries and impact severely upon their budgets. Local authorities were nevertheless encouraged to press on with design work, but the final proposals would eventually fall due to lack of public finance for the scheme and the onset of World War II. A Tyne Crossing would not be constructed – for road traffic and pedestrians – until 1967.

The potential sale of council housing caused friction again during 1928, when the Moderates sought to sell newly constructed bungalows on the Cleadon Park estate, arguing that no resident in the borough should be excluded from a potential purchase, so long as they only purchased one property. The proposal was opposed by the Labour Group but endorsed by the Borough Council thirty-one votes to nineteen.

In April the Party lost one of its most effective Council Chamber performers, Tom Mulgrew, who relocated to Horden for work, and eventually became Chairman of the Horden Miners' Lodge and President of the Seaham Harbour Labour Party. The Moderates in the Chamber would have been quietly pleased that one of Labour's most effective debaters would not be able to hold them to account in future.

Whilst local issues were predominant in the minds of activists in South Shields, there were still occasions when national policy concerns were debated, most notably when considering their motions to the Annual Labour Party Conference. As tensions began to rise again across Europe, the local Party was anxious to support international endeavours to prevent any arms race developing and to support moves for worldwide military disarmament. In addition, they fervently opposed the Simon Commission on the future constitutional reforms of India because the membership of the Committee did not have Indian representation on it. Motions on both issues were agreed by South Shields Labour Party for submission as resolutions to that years Labour Party Conference.

The municipal elections would see no change in November 1928, the Labour Party contesting only eleven of the Councils fifteen wards. The Annual Council meeting saw Ald James Dunlop assume the Mayoralty, expelled from membership of the Labour Group in February 1927 for consistently voting against the Labour whip, he had been opposed by Labour's George Linney but had gained the Mayoralty with the support of the Moderate Councillors. It was a political journey which had taken Dunlop from the Marxist SDF to the Labour Party to becoming a pillar of the civic establishment.

VIII 1929 General Election

By the beginning of 1929, Baldwin's Government would be nearing the conclusion of its 1924 electorate mandate and a new General Election would be required. Britain was faced with mounting unemployment as its decision to revert to the Gold Standard undermined attempts to stimulate the economy. A string of by-election defeats and the country still reeling from the after-effects of the General Strike should have been a warning to Baldwin, but the Conservative Party believed that they could win the election essentially on the question of their slogan '*Safety First*' which was primarily a reaction to the Keynesian economies being espoused by the Lloyd George Liberals as much as seeking to exploit what they believed was Baldwin's appeal to the public. Lloyd George, with the slogan '*We can conquer unemployment*' wanted a massive public investment across the country and with a personal war chest (built through the sale of honours), was determined to field over 500 Parliamentary candidates.

The Labour Party, even though it was the main opposition Party, was not perceived as a threat. The country, Baldwin gambled, was naturally anti-Socialist (though not necessarily Conservative), the Machiavellian Lloyd George held private talks with senior Conservative politicians, principally Churchill, about the need for a united front against the Socialists in the event of a hung Parliament – with proportional representation being a key priority for the fledging Liberals. Baldwin and the Health Minister Chamberlain though would have none of it, their tactic was to smash the Liberal Party and revert to a two-Party system, but this time built around the Conservatives and Labour. This tactic they believed had paid off at the 1924 General Election when the Liberals won only forty seats.

The Labour Party went into the election under the slogan '*Labour and the Nation*', it was a lacklustre manifesto, Harold Wilson recalls: '*On unemployment and the worsening economic position, Labour and the Nation was virtually innocent of anything except platitudes'.* MacDonald had withstood the desire of some in the higher echelons of the Labour movement to take a radical turn after 1926, although he stuck rigidly to his belief in free trade principles and the document was careful to appeal to women voters with a promise to implement legislation to ensure equal treatment between men and women.

Historians have observed that in relying upon Baldwin's appeal, as opposed to promoting concrete policies to tackle rising unemployment, save a proposal to 'de-rate' industry from the burden of rates, the Conservatives seriously misjudged the mood of the country. Little was done to promote issues which might appeal to the new women voters, the 1929 '*Flapper election*' saw women from the age of twenty-one being allowed to vote for the first time (as opposed to the previous age limit of thirty), and the, for once, united Liberal Party making an ambitious pitch for the working-class vote, contesting nearly 450 seats, splitting the anti-Labour vote in key marginal constituencies.

The election was a disaster for Baldwin. Although the Conservatives won the majority of votes, it suffered a net loss of 140 seats, winning just 260 MPs. Labour became the largest party with 287 seats, the Liberals took only 59 seats (although gained 23.4 per cent of the vote), but they held the Parliamentary balance of power.

Baldwin to his credit, resigned immediately – he would countenance no deal with Lloyd George (although Baldwin would have been unlikely to carry his Parliamentary Party with him if had suggested such a course of action) – he had appealed for the trust of the electorate and had been rejected. To seek to carry on would have offended his moral sense of fair play and belief in the Parliamentary democratic process.

Labour's Ramsay MacDonald was called upon to form his Second, minority Government – it was a bittersweet victory, sixteen weeks later the Wall Street Crash plunged the World into further economic and political crisis, MacDonald had no Parliamentary majority to deal with it.

IX

The May 1929 General Election which propelled MacDonald and Labour back into power came at a fateful time for the South Shields MP, Edward Harney.

His wife Kathleen had given birth to their son, Desmond on 14 February 1929, but Harney had been required to undergo two operations in London for internal complications before he was able to travel to South Shields to be formally adopted as the Liberal candidate for the pending General Election. Recuperating at his father-in-law's townhouse in Logan Terrace (now part of Beach Road), Harney developed double pneumonia, requiring his London physician, Dr Abraham, to journey to the Constituency to examine Harney. The Physician advised that whilst the condition was serious, Harney would eventually recover. On the strength of this advice, the press was informed that Harney would contest the General Election, but by Tuesday 14 May further complications developed, and the family announced that Harney would not contest the election. Harney tragically died three days later at 4.15 pm. Whilst his family grieved, the local Liberal hierarchy, given that nominations for the Parliamentary contest would close on 20 May, had already agreed to meet on the Friday evening to consider a new candidate. Harney's father-in-law, Tyndal Anderson had been suggested in some quarters as a possible candidate, but given the family circumstances, it was firmly rejected by Anderson. Later that evening the Liberal Association announced that they had asked Harold Robson, the only son of the former Liberal MP for town, William Robson, to be their standard bearer. He agreed to the request, whether it was an act of filial piety on his part we will never know.

Harold Robson had tried unsuccessfully to secure a Parliamentary seat in previous elections at Berwick-upon-Tweed. A Barrister, he had served as an Officer in the Northumberland Hussars Yeomanry receiving the Croix de guerre. Following the war, he had maintained his military connections, being appointed a Lt Col commanding the 7th Battalion of the Northumberland Fusiliers (TA). He arrived in South Shields the following day and addressed his first public meeting at St Michael's Hall the following Tuesday knowing that he would have a serious challenge to hold the seat for the Liberal cause.

Chuter Ede had nursed the constituency since his own selection as the Labour candidate in May 1926. His Parliamentary Agent was Gompertz, although the choice was not Ede's alone to make. The Constituency Party, recalling friction between the members and the DMA sponsored agent under Lawther, were clear that they should have a say in the final decision. Applicants were invited to an interview with the Constituency officers, and three appeared in January 1929, Gompertz, Cllr McAnany and Mr Hutchinson. In the final ballot, Gompertz secured the post, six votes to Hutchinson's one. Whether Ede had indicated any preference before the meeting we cannot ascertain, but Gompertz hit the ground running with regular reports to the Party and cajoling the Party to work in ensuring supporters were registered to vote. In recognition of his position as Agent, he returned to the Executive Committee at the 1929 Annual Meeting in February. As part of his campaign, Gompertz also recognised that the Party needed to secure control of the Council, Labour Group minutes record that in April 1929 Gompertz met with Labour Councillors to impress upon them that thought needed to be given as to how they could begin to penetrate Moderate held wards, it was not enough simply to take a defensive position and hold on to the working-class riverside wards, they needed to branch out if they were ever to seize municipal power.

Unfortunately for Robson, the anti-Labour forces in the town were, for the first time split, with the Conservative Party determined to field their own candidate, a Civil Servant called William Nunn. The combatant Ede was confident of success. Fighting on the local Party's traditional green and white colours, he addressed one public rally, organised by the Labour Party in the Harton Miners' Hall in Bede Street, Tyne Dock on the evening of Sunday 24 February 1929. He described the '*old parties*' as '*discredited*' and said that even *The Times* newspaper accepted that the return to the Gold Standard had in the coal industry produced a situation where the owners were unable to pay the Gold Standard rates as well as a minimum wage. '*Inasmuch as human activity produced this state of affairs, human activity must be used to produce contrary effect, and the Country will be compelled to turn to the Labour Party as the only one that is not under the domination of the financiers to bring about a better state of affairs.*'

South Shields Rural Council lay to the south of the South Shields County Borough Council boundary, and comprised the Whitburn, Cleadon, Boldon and Monkton areas, together with farmland that encompassed Biddick Hall, Whiteleas and Hedworth. It had previously included Cleadon Park, but in August 1921 the South Shields Corporation Act was approved, much to consternation of the Rural Council, which incorporated the Cleadon Park estate and Harton Village into the County Borough boundary under the auspices of a new Harton Ward. The Rural Council's Parliamentary boundary though did not change and remained Houghton, and as such, being a resident of the new Cleadon Park estate in Quarry Lane, Gompertz and his wife Annie, found themselves within the South Shields County Borough area for municipal purposes, but within the Houghton Division for Parliamentary elections. Both Gompertz and Annie enthusiastically signed the nomination papers for Labour's candidate in that division, Robert Richardson for the 1929 General Election.

Gompertz may have resided in the Houghton Constituency, but his heart was in South Shields and as Ede's Parliamentary Agent devoted all his energies to the South Shields campaign. Key members were assigned as ward agents, including Charles Henderson at Simonside and Ede undertook an impressive speaking engagement across the constituency, including supporting Houghton-le-Springs May Day Rally at Whitburn on farmland owned by J Colley and despite facing a difficult contest, took time to visit Seaham Harbour to speak in support of the Labour candidate there, Ramsay MacDonald. One incident though saw Ede cautioned by Police that he was in breach of Wartime Regulations in taking photographs whilst taking a stroll along the pier. It was a restriction he would successfully later ask the Tyne Improvement Commissioners to lift.

The election result, when it was declared outside the Town Hall, saw Labour win the Parliamentary seat in South Shields for the first time. Ede had secured 18,938, Robson 18,898 whilst the Conservative William Nunn secured 7,110 votes. Ede was carried on the shoulders of two stalwarts Councillors McAnany and Thompson into the enthusiastic and ecstatic crowd waiting outside. The *Shields Gazette* was unimpressed and did not even acknowledge the victory with a photograph or suitable banner headline, declaring in their Comment section: '*With others who believe in Liberalism we deplore, frankly, the South Shields result and the passing, for the time being, of the Boroughs representations in Parliament to the Socialist.'* Labour, they maintained, had managed to pull out their maximum vote, the Conservative received their sternest criticism for splitting the anti-Labour vote. Ede was unmoved, he placed an advert on the front page of the *Shields Gazette* thanking the townsfolk for their support, signing off, *James Chuter Ede MP.*

Labour had finally won South Shields, their majority was just forty, the cost of the election for the local Labour Party, Gompertz would later remark, was one of the lowest of any candidate in the country. Ede's victory opens up some interesting matters of conjecture. Had the highly respected and well entrenched Harney lived, it is highly likely he could have won the seat, even with a Conservative opponent. Had the Conservatives not contested the seat, the new Liberal candidate, Robson without question would have secured the Liberal hegemony that had existed for so long in the Constituency. politics though is not conducted on the 'what ifs' but on the cold realities of present-day circumstances. A new Labour candidate, facing a divided opposition, with an expanded electorate, had positioned the local Party in the most advantageous way to secure the widest appeal to the people of South Shields and had finally secured the Parliamentary seat for the Labour Party.

The Constituency Party minutes record the evident excitement of winning the Parliamentary election for the first time with a statement to the press extolling, *'We re-affirm our belief that British progress depends upon ensuring for every worker the means of life, without fear of unemployment, or dread of poverty and that the Labour Party can be depended on to work steadily and persistently for the abolition of the present conditions and the establishment of universal welfare, through the re-organisation of our social system'.*

Appreciation was also recorded in the Minutes to those Surrey teachers and personal friends of Ede who had journeyed to South Shields to support the election campaign. Gompertz received special mention with a host of speakers thanking him for his valiant work in securing victory for the Party. In response Gompertz advised there was no time to waste, and that he was already seeking an office for Chuter Ede and a headquarters for the local Party, this would eventually be above Martins Bank Chambers, 91 Laygate Lane.

The faith the local Labour Party had invested in Chuter Ede was well rewarded in terms of his standing within Parliamentary circles. Described by the journalist M J Landa as a man of *'real ability and knowledge'*, his early Parliamentary interventions were inevitably on educational matters and in particular the need to increase the school leaving age to fifteen, and the establishment of a system of maintenance allowances, a commitment given by the 1924 Labour Government but held up by Baldwin's Ministry. In early July 1929 he was placing questions on the Commons Order Paper, and in one interjection, with his own line in raillery, said that they would not have to raise the school age by that much for the new Chancellor of the Duchy of Lancaster to be required to return to school – the young and dashing Sir Oswald Mosley. Ede lobbied Ministers repeatedly and was pushing very much at an open door since the responsible Government Minister, Sir Charles Trevelyan announced on 18 July that the Government would implement the long-standing commitment to raise the school age on 1 April 1931 together with a new system of educational maintenance allowances.

The commitment would prove controversial with the Roman Catholic schools insisting that they would need additional funding to implement the measure, a move supported by other religious denominations. Matters came to a head in January 1931, as the Parliamentary Bill's final proposals were submitted to the House of Commons for agreement. Labour MPs had been bombarded with postcards from mainly Catholic voters demanding that the measures should be delayed until agreement for funding for Church schools had been approved. In a heated Parliamentary debate on 21 January, over thirty Labour rebels joined opposition benches to defeat the Government and delay the implementation of the School Attendance Bill. Reports circulated that a furious Ede had told his Party Whips that he would not seek re-election to Parliament on the grounds he could not remain a member of a Party which allowed its MPs to place religious considerations above economic and political objects for which he believed the Party existed. The rumour though was swiftly rebuffed by Ede who sent a telegram to Gompertz advising that his Agent should issue a categorical denial that he intended to resign at the next election and Ede wrote a formal letter to the *Shields Gazette* making clear he had every intention of fighting the next General Election in South Shields. Following further defeats in the House of Lords, the Government announced it would need to postpone the Bill's implementation. This was not the first occasion rumours circulated that Ede was unhappy in Parliament. Stephen Hart in his biography of Chuter Ede recalls that in May 1930 Ede had written to the Labour Parliamentary Chief Whip advising that given his civic duties in Surrey (he was soon to be elected Chairman of Surrey County Council), there may be a conflict of interest and he was considering taking the Chiltern Hundreds. The Chief Whip, fearing a by-election in a highly marginal seat, worked with the NUT General Secretary, Frank Goldstone, to convince Ede to remain in Parliament.

The South Shields Labour Party campaigned anxiously but with some confidence for the November 1929 municipal elections, supported at rallies by Ede. Politically the Council was now comprised of thirty-seven Moderates (twenty-four Councillors and thirteen Aldermen) and twenty-three Labour representatives (twenty-one Councillors and two Aldermen). Crucially, seven Moderate Aldermen were due for reappointment following the elections, and given only Councillors could vote on their appointment, if Labour gained two extra seats in the Council elections, the balance of power would switch to the Labour Group who would be able to appoint seven Labour Aldermen and thus control the Council. The fact that the Council was assuming new powers under the Local Government Act of 1929, with in particular the creation of new Public Assistance Bodies, meant the stakes for Municipal success were incredibly high.

The Labour Government's moderate legislative successes did not though result in municipal success locally. The November 1929 poll saw Labour lose a seat in the Holborn to the Moderates, whilst they also ran Labour close in two other seats, the Shields and St Hilda's wards. The allocation of municipal spoils would be with the Moderates, and with it, the right to the Chairmanship of the new important Public Assistance Committee. The elevation of Curbison to the Aldermanic Bench following the elections, with the Moderate Groups support, necessitated a by-election in his Laygate ward. Gompertz was nominated, but declined to stand, presumably because he wished to concentrate on securing Ede's Parliamentary base, Jane Peel was eventually selected and secured the seat in the subsequent election, commencing a political journey that would see her become the borough's first woman Mayor in 1947.

As the 1920s came to a close, South Shields Labour and Trades Council had much to proud. They had secured the Parliamentary seat, the Labour Group of Councillors was solidifying into a cohesive force within the Council Chamber, prominent members served as Magistrates and they now had their own political home, courtesy of Ede, in Laygate Lane.

Within the space of two years, events would see national political disaster for the Labour Party and political fratricide grip the local Party.

Chapter 9

... And Defeat

I National Minority Movement

As a thriving seaport, South Shields had always attracted migration and during World War I, as British men were conscripted into the Army and Navy, the numbers of migrants arriving from the Yemen, Aden and Somalia was encouraged as the country needed merchant seamen to keep the country's food supplies open. Accommodated in the East Holborn and Laygate area, with its boarding houses and lively street cafes, the Arabs played a crucial part in maintaining Britain's supply lines, with the town losing one of the largest proportions of Merchant Navy sailors in the war, it is estimated that one in four men killed were Yemeni. The end of hostilities, the return of white men from the war and the economic downturn which followed the peace, saw tensions arise at Mill Dam with fierce competition for seafaring jobs. The shipowners exploited the situation, preferring to hire Arab men, because they were able to pay them less, have less regard for their welfare and required them to work longer hours. The situation came to a head on 4 February 1919, when Arab men, recruited from the riverside boarding houses, owned by Arabs, arrived at Mill Dam to sign for work on the SS *Trowalland*. National Union of Seamen Officials objected, arguing the Arabs, like other men, should have been 'picked' at Mill Dam that morning giving everyone a fair chance of work. Violence ensured with Yemeni men being pelted with stones as they sought refuge in their Holborn boarding houses. The inevitable arrests and court cases followed but tensions remained.

The situation was not helped by antics of the right-wing NUS Union, still led by Havelock Wilson. The Union was content to take subscriptions from Arabs but displayed little empathy for their plight, in 1923 the Union made representations to the Government against '... *the employment of Arabs to the detriment of British seafarers.*' A view was developing nationally, amongst the Labour and trade union movement that the NUS was corrupt and because of Wilson's close relationship with the shipowners, they were not negotiating effectively enough for their members, who had seen their wages decline since the onset of the 1920s. The implementation of a new system called PC5 required any seamen to receive a card from the NUS before they could work, the system was clearly discriminatory because unemployed men usually allowed their Union subscriptions to lapse. It was also open to abuse because local Union Officials were able to determine who was a member of the Union and when they would receive a card allowing them to work.

The Communist Party in August 1924 established the **National Minority Movement** (NMM), their aim was to convert the revolutionary minority working class into a majority sensing that there was great dissatisfaction amongst certain sections of the workforce with their Unions. Whilst there was a lack of enthusiasm for joining the Communist Party, the workers could be organised they believed by Communists through an independent front, the NMM. No more was this true than in the Seamen's Union with organisers from the NMM being detached to South Shields to begin a campaign against the PC5. Supporting them in organising the Arabs was Ali Said, a boarding house owner.

In early 1930, the NUS agreed with shipowners a rota system which applied only to Arab seamen in South Shields, Hull and Cardiff. Under the system, those who had been on shore the longest would be at the front of the queue for work. The system was clearly discriminatory because it was an attempt to only employ Arab's whose wages were lower. A letter to the *Shields Gazette* from Ahmed Alwin made clear – '*As they are British subjects they are entitled to all the rights of British seamen. They do not desire preferential treatment over white seamen, and do not intend to take part in any scheme that may come into conflict with them.*' But his views were not universal, with some Yemenis and Somalis supporting the scheme.

As the rota scheme was introduced on 2 August 1930 violence again erupted at Mill Dam as the NMM picketed the offices of the NUS and the Board of Trade. Although later dubbed the 'race riots' or 'Arab riots', this is not a true reflection of events. Peter O'Donnell one of the NMM Leaders addressed around 150 Arabs and 100 white men advising them not to sign on under the rota system. As the Shipping Federation and NUS called out for men, there was a rush from white men and Arabs wanting work, but they were held back by a strong NMM picket, serious violence followed. Knives were drawn, policemen were injured with nineteen Arabs and two NMM officials being arrested. Later that day marauding gangs of white men patrolled the waterfront streets of East Holborn attacking Arab men and raiding their lodging houses. One NMM official, William Harrison, was eventually imprisoned for eight months at Durham Assizes in November 1930. Harrison announced that he had every intention of standing at the next General Election in South Shields as an Independent Labour candidate, although the threat never materialised. Ali Said received sixteen months' imprisonment and was recommended for deportation. Little though was done to alleviate the real cause of tensions, the NMM was beginning to achieve some success in uniting Arab and white seamen against the unfair practices of the shipowners whilst the NUS preferred to divide and rule. Resistance to the rota system though collapsed, 100 Arabs – not implicated in the riots – were deported and scores of unemployed Arab seamen were required to seek poor relief much to chagrin of local ratepayers who complained in letters to the *Shields Gazette* that it would be better to repatriate them. The South Shields Labour Party distanced itself from the episode, correspondence sent to them in July 1930 (presumably from the NMM, the Minutes do not record) in relation to the operation of the PC5 was merely noted as being a trade union issue for the Seamen's Union to resolve, although they did write to the TUC General Secretary requesting guidance as to whether the TUC felt the PC5 was a fair way for the shipowners to operate.

Meanwhile the local Labour Party were in buoyant mood, the country's first woman Cabinet Minister, Margaret Bondfield had visited South Shields in March 1930 in her capacity as Minister of Labour and Ede addressed the May Day Rally. Bishop Auckland MP, Hugh Dalton, the Under-Secretary of State for Foreign Affairs was the keynote speaker. It was standing room only in the Marsden Miners' Hall with Dalton giving a denudation of Churchill's handling of the economy, which he claimed had left the budget £14m in deficit meaning no tax cuts were possible, but Dalton reassured his appreciative audience that new taxes would be levied on high earners and those with the greatest ability to pay.

II Tuberculosis outbreak

The 1929 Local Government Act abolishing the Board of Guardians and transferring their powers to County and County Borough Councils also empowered the Ministry of Health to withhold grants from local authorities if they believed they were not providing efficient health services. Consequently, local Medical Officers were required to undertake audits and surveys with the results being sent to the Ministry of Health.

The release in March 1930 of the borough's Chief Medical Officers report to the Council's Health Committee into tuberculosis levels in South Shields outlined appalling statistics which showed that the borough since the 1920s consistently had one of the highest rates of death from the pulmonary disease across the country. Between 1922 and 1929 alone there had been 3,733 reported deaths. The disease was more prevalent in the working-class riverside areas, where housing density was high, chronic overcrowding rife and workers, for fear of losing employment, would not report their symptoms until it was too late to resolve. Campbell Lyons, the Medical Officer was scathing in his condemnation of the housing conditions making clear he regarded the housing conditions in South Shields as one of the main factors in the high incidence of morality from tuberculosis. Nationally, 9.6 per cent of families were living in overcrowded conditions, Campbell Lyons noted that the figure in South Shields was 36.5 per cent.

A list of recommendations contained in his report outlined the need for medical practitioners to make clear to their patients that the illness was treatable if notified early, that their employers would not be notified of the illness (unless they worked in the milk industry) and that all precautions to prevent the spread of the disease should be taken, potentially by admitting patients into hospital accommodation but advanced cases would need to be treated by the town's sanitorium. Poor Law relief should not be reduced where a family member was suffering from tuberculosis and the Council's tuberculosis extra nourishment scheme payments needed to be enhanced, he was clear this should not count towards the family's income when calculating poor relief. The town's tuberculosis scheme also needed to be reorganised with a more efficient administration system in place to track patients who had been diagnosed. Increased publicity highlighting that the disease was treatable if detected earlier, as was the need to enforce the by-law to stop spitting. The need to progress at greater speed with slum clearance though was not highlighted in the Medical Officers report.

The report caused a storm, not least because in submitting it to the Ministry of Health, the Government's Chief Medical Advisor, George Newman referenced the appalling statistics in his own report, noting also that South Shields had one of the highest infant mortality rates in the country. The local Labour Party's June meeting considered the report and demanded that the Government hold a Public Inquiry into the tuberculosis rates in the borough. Ede raised the matter with the Ministry of Health who agreed to send a Medical Inspector to meet with interested parties to discuss the situation with the aim of advising the Government of further measures to be undertaken. A deputation of eight, including Curbison and Gompertz were authorised to prepare evidence and meet with the Inspector. The Party Minutes do not record the outcome of their deliberations, but by January 1931, the Council reported that the Ministry of Health was prepared to organise a regional conference in the North East to consider further measures to tackle the question of high tuberculosis rates in the region. The process though was slow, by the March meeting of the Borough Council, Curbison objected to the Health Committee's report on the grounds that it contained insufficient recommendations to deal with tuberculosis other than mentioning that they were awaiting details of the Regional Conference to be organised by the Ministry of Health. *'It seems to me that it is matterless if people suffer pain, it is matterless if we bury them because we can bury them cheaper than it costs to house them in our sanitoriums. This report from month to month is a most disconcerting report so far as this vital question is concerned'* Curbison told the elected members. Col Chapman for the Moderates objected on the grounds that the Council was dealing with the root cause of the disease, clearing the slums.

As the controversy dragged on, the November 1930 municipal elections in the town saw notable swings against the Labour Party across the North of England. On the principle that whoever controls Whitehall will lose the town halls, the Party suffered a string of defeats, losing Leeds to the Conservatives and Hull falling to a Conservative/Liberal alliance. South Shields produced no overall change although Labour did gain a seat in the Shields Ward but lost a seat in Holborn where NMM activist William Harrison, before appearing in front of Durham Assizes, stood as a Workers Candidate, he only polled forty-five votes, but it was enough to allow a Moderate candidate to seize the seat.

III The Great Betrayal

Although MacDonald had no Parliamentary majority in the House of Commons, the Labour Government did succeed in implementing much of its Legislative programme. The Old Age and Widows' Pension Act was amended and improved, subsidies to local Councils for housebuilding was maintained and an improved Unemployment Insurance Act was passed. Slum clearance measures were enhanced, a new Roads Bill was introduced, and a Coal Bill sought to improve the efficiency of the industry whilst Labour also took the opportunity to amend the divisive and, in many cases, spiteful 1927 Trade Disputes and Trade Union Act. Internationally, they also began the first steps towards eventual Indian Independence with a Round Table Conference set for the autumn of 1930.

Their policy successes however could not disguise their failure to tackle the rising unemployment figures. MacDonald entrusted his Chancellor of the Duchy of Lancaster, Oswald Mosley, a former Conservative MP who had returned to the Commons as the Labour MP for Smethwick in a December 1926 by-election, with the responsibility for solving the unemployment problem. The urgency was underlined by the London Stock Exchange crash on 20 September 1929 which aggravated the unemployment figures further and the Wall Street Crash in November which exacerbated the problem further still. Mosley's plans centred around increased state intervention, including the control of imports, the public control of the banking system, large-scale public borrowing for infrastructure works, the school leaving age raised further and the retirement age cut. Mosley's Memorandum to the Cabinet was attacked by his Ministerial Cabinet head, Jimmy Thomas whilst the inflexible Chancellor Philip Snowden and Treasury were openly hostile to the idea of further public borrowing. Mosley's ideas were hardly revolutionary, writing in 1961, Richard Crossman observed: '*This brilliant memorandum was a whole generation ahead of Labour thinking*'. South Shields Labour Party had initially invited Mosley to address the 1930 May Day in the town, he declined, but they did purchase 100 copies of his speech which outlined his interventionist platform. Despite the support of a significant number of Labour MPs including Joe Batey MP and Nye Bevan MP as well as the Miners Leader AJ Cook, the memorandum was rejected by the Cabinet in May 1930, Mosley took his ideas to the October 1930 Labour Party Conference but was again defeated. Within months, Mosley, impatient with the democratic process launched his own **New Party** and began a journey which would eventually lead him to Fascism.

By December 1930, unemployment had reached 2,500,000 nearly 20 per cent of the population. Rather than suspend the Gold Standard to enable British exports to find their true level in world markets, or even to accept that in times of depression it is feasible for the budget to be unbalanced and wiped out by a surplus in more prosperous times, Snowden stuck rigidly to the Treasury conservative orthodoxies and established in May 1931 a Committee under Sir George May with an express remit to recommend reductions in national expenditure. Francis Williams has observed that the

Committee's investigation was deliberately designed to frighten the country by presenting a picture of financial disaster. But it did more than that, when the report was submitted to Cabinet it damaged Britain's credit abroad and started a speculation on Sterling which made a large-scale financial crisis inevitable – but still neither MacDonald nor Snowden would abandon the Gold Standard. Without a change in this policy, the only way the Government could secure vital loans was to balance the budget books, by implementing the recommendations suggested by the May Committee.

By 19 August, MacDonald now in talks with the opposition Party leaders, agreed to meet a delegation from the Parliamentary Consultative Committee along with the TUC. The delegation, which included James Chuter Ede, met MacDonald in Downing Street for frantic talks to reach a settlement, but the meeting lasted less than an hour a sign that the Prime Minister was in no mood for compromise.

The Cabinet met in constant session in late August 1931, against a background of a further run on Sterling, to consider the May recommendations, amongst them were wage reductions for the police, teachers and pre-1925 entrants to the armed forces, cuts to social services and public work schemes all unpalatable but accepted as necessary, but the recommendation that unemployment benefit should be cut by 10 per cent with a suggestion that the Means Test would be reintroduced caused fury. In the days before the welfare state or NHS, unemployment reduced families to the edge of starvation, living in underheated and almost threadbare houses. It was a cut too far for many of the early pioneers of the Labour movement such as Arthur Henderson, Lansbury, AV Alexander and Arthur Greenwood, who saw the cut as an attack on the poorest in society and wanted an examination of tax raising proposals as an alternative. On 24 August, the Cabinet split eleven votes to nine to accept the cut in benefits but with the threatened resignations from the Cabinet by senior Government Ministers, MacDonald now accepted he could not keep his government in power.

Offering his resignation to the King, he was implored to establish a government of national unity given the financial crisis faced by the country. It was a strategy supported by Baldwin and the Liberal Party's acting Leader, Herbert Samuel when they met in conference with the King the following day. Meeting his shocked Cabinet colleagues later that same day, who had expected Baldwin to establish a government perhaps with Liberal support or even for MacDonald to call a General Election, MacDonald advised them that he had agreed to head a Government of National Unity. It was an act described by the ILP as a *'great betrayal of trust'*, and in many respects a pointless one since a few weeks later the National Government suspended the Gold Standard, despite being formed to preserve it and called a General Election for the 27 October 1931.

IV

Whilst tumultuous events unfolded at Westminster during 1931, the South Shields Labour Party was dealing with constitutional difficulties within its own ranks which would lead to the expulsion from membership of its first Chairman, James Curbison.

The issue centred around the appointment of members to the Magistrates' Bench, an appointment made by the Lord Chancellor on the recommendation of local Advisory Committees which submitted suitable names for consideration. The local Labour Party had always felt the Bench was weighed against working-class interests and that the names of potential working-class Magistrates were not taken seriously. It was a concern that the local Party had over the years repeatedly raised with the Lord Chancellor's Office in London. By December 1930 a host of new Magistrates were to be appointed across the County of Durham and the local Labour Party worked hard to encourage and promote a number of local supporters for potential membership. None of the twenty names submitted were accepted, although four Labour members who were already on the Magistrates' Bench served on the Advisory Committee, Ald Curbison, Councillor Henderson, Sarah Noble and Cuth Barrass. The local Party remained dissatisfied and immediately began to ask questions at their December 1930 meeting of the four appointees as to the process and on what grounds the Labour nominees had been rejected. Curbison refused to acknowledge the questions advising their deliberations were confidential and to discuss the process would, for him be a breach of trust with his fellow Magistrates. Henderson refused to meet the Party to discuss the issue, whilst Barrass and Noble gave some explanation, advising they had tried to promote Labour nominees, but they had been unsuccessful.

Senior members of the South Shields Labour Party were incandescent with outrage. Curbison, who was increasingly becoming detached from the local Labour Party as evidenced by his voting record in Council meetings, felt the full force of the wrath of his comrades. Gompertz moved that Curbison should be expelled, whilst Henderson, if he refused to meet the Party to discuss the matter should be asked to resign. The saga followed into January

1931 when the local Party agreed to write to the Lord Chancellor requesting the removal of the four members from the Magistrates Advisory Committee and providing alternative names for consideration. As news filtered into the press, and with Curbison giving interviews attacking the position of the Party, the 10 February 1931 monthly meeting of the Constituency Party reaffirmed Curbison's expulsion and resolved to formally ask Henderson, by now the Mayor of South Shields, to resign. Henderson refused and was subsequently expelled. The expulsions caused a sensation, not least because Henderson, as a member of the NUR National Executive was well-known figure nationally. Curbison immediately filed an appeal to the national Labour Party, whilst Henderson's NUR Trade Union wrote disaffiliating from the local Party in his support. Still the issue rumbled until June, when the Party, following the refusal of the Lord Chancellor's Office to remove Curbison, Henderson, Barrass or Noble from the Advisory Committee, decided to expel both Barrass and Noble from membership.

The episode may seem trivial today, but there was genuine concern, and not just in South Shields, that Advisory Panels were biased against appointing working-class people on the Magistrates' Bench. The local party was so animated by the episode that their motion to the 1931 Labour Party Conference centred around these concerns demanding greater transparency by the Lord Chancellor's Office when Magistrates were being appointed.

Following interviews in South Shields by national officials, Labour's National Executive Committee, when their report was published in June, was clear. There had been no breach by the gang of four, it was unreasonable that the four serving on a civic body should be asked to break a confidence, no matter how strongly the local Party felt. Curbison's appeal was successful. However, the NEC did acknowledge their disappointment at the derisory number of Labour Party members who had been recommended for appointment to the Magistrates' Bench, particularly given the work the local Labour Party had undertaken to secure potential candidates for nomination. They advised the local Party: '*At the same time, the National Executive Committee were of the opinion that it should be intimated to you and your colleagues that when a local section of the Movement takes considerable trouble to compile lists of men and women deemed to be competent to fulfil the duties of magistrates, it is desirable that Labour members of Advisory Committees should seek to discharge their loyalty to the movement by promoting such appointments in every legitimate way.*'

The NEC's recommendations, requesting the local Party to lift the expulsions were rejected by the Constituency Party, the matter was then reported to the Labour Party Conference held at Scarborough that year, and following the Conference endorsement of the NEC recommendations it was accepted *without reservation* by a meeting of the South Shields Labour Party Executive Committee at their September meeting to readmit the gang of four. Whether Curbison sought readmission is unknown, but by July 1932, following further complaints about his voting record in the Council Chamber it was noted that he was no longer a Labour Group or Labour Party member and was not associated with any Union affiliated to the local Party. The episode must have been particularly concerning to Sarah Noble because in 1933 her request that the Minute relating to her expulsion be expunged was rejected. Following her public resignation from the Magistrates' Bench in January 1936 following her refusal to accept the decision of two fellow JPs to authorise the birching of two juveniles she again asked the Party to expunge the Minute at their meeting in January 1937, this time it was agreed by the Party, Gompertz subsequently covered over the episode in the Minute book.

V 1931 General Election

As the Labour Party came to terms with MacDonald's actions, attention focused as to how many Labour MPs would follow him. Chuter Ede is reported to have been the first backbench MP to refuse to support the National Government. Writing from Penzance where he was on vacation, he advised his local Constituency Labour Executive that the Government should have met the financial crisis created by the banks with a '… *bold enunciation of a Socialist programme for dealing with the emergency … attacks on wages and the local social services will aggravate the evils from which we are suffering, and the throwing of large numbers of persons off the unemployment fund must overwhelm the local resources of their industrial areas.'* His position was supported by the South Shields Labour Party at their meeting on 25 August 1931. The same meeting saw the Party also agree to create a new post of Organising Secretary and Hon Agent. Three candidates stood for the position, James Yates of the Marsden miners, Cllr Watson from the St Hilda's miners and Gompertz, on a card vote Gompertz was elected with a large majority.

As the political crisis unfolded nationally, by September, Ede addressed the local Party, this time accompanied by the Liverpool Labour MP and Whip, Jack Hayes. Both men were heard at length and the meeting supported the stance they had taken in refusing to join MacDonald's National Government.

Harcourt Johnstone (affectionately known as 'Crinks') was no novice to Liberal politics. Described by TD Nudds in the *History of the Liberal Party* as an '*aristocrat to his fingertips, but a radical of the first water*' he had played a key part in the Liberal Party infighting during the interwar years, spending much of his immense personal wealth to subside the cash-strapped Asquith wing of the Party. A former MP for Willesden East, but losing his seat in the 1924 General Election, he was a central figure in the Liberal Candidates' Association, vetting Parliamentary candidates and seeking winnable seats for leadership favourites. He failed though to secure himself a safe seat, being twice defeated by small margins in Westbury at a by-election in 1927 and at the General Election in 1929.

He sensed that South Shields, with its long Liberal tradition, was a seat he could win. Coalition leaders allocated South Shields to the Liberal Party, despite the Liberal Party again splitting at a national level this time in three directions (**Sir John Simon** forming the Liberal National Party, essentially in opposition to the main Liberal Party policy under **Herbert Samuel** which had advocated maintaining MacDonald in Office following the 1929 General Election, and thirdly **Lloyd George's** Independent Liberals concentrated in Wales who in 1931 opposed the concept of a National Government).

Chalmers Kearney, an Engineer with significant business interests was also seeking the Liberal nomination for South Shields. Kearney was keen to build the Tyne Tunnel link between South and North Shields. Attempts were made to influence the local Liberals with a telegram in early October being sent to them by the International Trust Company advising that, subject to Kearney being the Liberal candidate and subsequently elected, they were prepared to finance a Tyne Tunnel project, '*subject to usual conditions*'. Mr Pattison the Liberal Agent replied curtly, '*Your telegram, Liberals last night adopted Harcourt Johnstone as Liberal supporter of National Government. Conservatives officially supporting him. Kearney's name was not considered – Pattison, Liberal Agent*'.

When nominations closed, it was announced that it would be a two cornered contest, between Ede and Harcourt Johnstone. A *Shields Gazette* editorial urged Conservative voters to vote Johnstone to support the National Government.

In the closing days of the contest, Viscount Grey was dispatched to South Shields and warned his audience at the Spa Skating Rink that a Labour win would collapse the credit of the country. Johnstone also secured another senior Liberal figure, Walter Runciman, the Liberal MP for St Ives, to speak on his behalf. Runciman, the son of a shipping magnate had been educated at

South Shields High School. Whilst MacDonald aimed to project himself as a national leader, and eschewed personal attacks on his former associates, the former Labour Chancellor Philip Snowden had no such misgivings saving the worst of his verbal venom for his former Socialist comrades describing Labour's manifesto as '*Bolshevism run mad.*'

Across the country excited audiences paid for picture house seats to watch the national results, whilst others were able to listen into special radio broadcasts giving updates through the evening. Ede's well documented voting record in the House of Commons, in which since 1929 he had voted in all 948 Parliamentary divisions was to prove of no avail. As townsfolk crowded into the Queen's Theatre and Scala to receive news of the results across the country, they were advised Johnstone had secured 30,528 votes to Ede's 20,512. In the face of a gruelling anti-Labour media onslaught nationally and with the Labour Party divided, Ede was out, although he did improve on Labour's overall vote from the 1929 General Election. Labour also lost the neighbouring Houghton constituency to Col Robert Chapman, who was a long-serving Moderate Councillor in South Shields Town Hall and would combine his role with being Mayor of the borough during 1931/32.

Nationally the result was an unmitigated disaster for the Labour Party, their Leader Arthur Henderson lost his Burnley seat, and they were reduced from 289 MPs to just forty-six. MacDonald and his national Government had secured 554 seats – although MacDonald's National Labour faction accounted for only thirteen of that total. MacDonald was the titular head of the Government but with the Conservatives making up 470 of the national Government's tally. Given the sheer scale of the victory for the National Government, many political commentators feared that it placed effective Parliamentary democracy in danger.

Days following the General Election defeat, the Party met to record its gratitude to Ede for his sterling work as the borough's first Labour MP and his '*brilliant work*' in Parliament. Ede returned to his Tamworth Farm Hall home in Mitcham to concentrate on his Aldermanic work at Surrey County Hall and his employment with the Surrey County Teachers Association, whilst Gompertz prepared the campaign work for the November Council elections. He agreed to stand as a candidate in Westoe ward but throughout the town it was an unexciting and lacklustre campaign, a turnout of 52 per cent saw the culminative vote for Labour across the town being only 5,904 as opposed to 13,957 for Moderate candidates. Gompertz went down to a crushing defeat in the Westoe ward. Given the national political situation, the local Party did well, losing only one seat, in its traditional Rekendyke heartland. With support riding high for the new National Government, it could easily have been much worse.

VI

The South Shields Labour Party was despondent, but also defiant. As the new National Government began to implement its policy of reducing support to the unemployed, it was left to the newly created Public Assistance Committees (PACs) to enforce the measure. There was the predictable backlash in the industrial heartlands, particularly on Tyneside. On Saturday 19 December 1931, the Tyneside Federation of Trades Councils met to consider their response to the Government's decision to reimpose the Means Test. Chaired by South Shields stalwart, Alex Stephenson and attended by Gompertz on behalf of the South Shields Labour Party concern was expressed that the Government was seeking to 'pauperise' those genuinely seeking work. Gompertz spoke passionately against the Means Test, and ridiculed one delegate from the South Shields Boilermakers, for suggesting there needed to be some fairness in the application of unemployed support, otherwise someone with £1,000 worth of savings could claim support. Gompertz advised the meeting that the delegate was not affiliated to the South Shields Labour Party otherwise '... *his education would be far more advanced*'. In the face of an overwhelming majority for the National Government there was little the meeting could do other than propose motions to the TUC. Gompertz though was determined to go further.

The Labour Party and Trades Unions held mass demonstrations across the country demanding the end of the Means Test. Locally, a meeting at Barnes Road School in February 1932 attracted an audience of 400 at which Gompertz spoke, and a further demonstration on 13 March in the South Shields Market Place was attended by 15,000 residents. Gompertz endeavoured on several occasions to be nominated as a lay member of the new Public Assistance Committee but was rebuffed by the Moderate majority in the Council Chamber.

The Board of Guardians before their abolition had always met in public, the transfer of their operations to the PACs in 1930 meant that the scope of their work was now under the guidance of Local Councils who were not required to admit the press to their meetings. Ede sought to change this with his Local Authorities (Admission of the Press) Bill which passed the crucial

Second Reading in the House of Commons in December 1930. Although pressure of time, and the calling of a General Election resulted in the Bill not progressing, it did have significant cross-Party support.

Gompertz was not prepared to allow the South Shields PAC to operate 'in camera' without challenge. The South Shields PAC was due to meet in the Town Hall on Wednesday 23 December, Gompertz led a delegation of trade unionists which included Bill Blyton of the Harton Miners, as they stormed the meeting of the PAC demanding, to startled Civic Leaders, that their concerns about the cutbacks in the relief for the unemployed be heard. Tempers were raised as the Chairman for the meeting Councillor Lawlan ordered the delegation to leave the meeting on the grounds it was not a public meeting. George Linney protested that the delegation was respectable and represented Trade Unionists across the town who had a right to be heard. Curbison also voiced belief that the delegation should be admitted. Gompertz in the absence of public seating, sat down at the Committee table and advised he felt '*quite comfortable*' when ordered to remove himself. A vote was taken as to whether to hear the delegation, the fourteen Committee members divided equally, and the motion was deemed lost. Protesting that there were '*undesirables*' in the room who needed removing, the Chairman asked the Committee Clerk to fetch for a police constable. Gompertz retorted '*I know we are undesirable; I recognise that the people we represent are undesirable unless they pay their rent.*' The arrival of the police saw the delegation leave quietly but not before further angry exchanges between Labour's Councillor Watson and the Committee Chair.

The South Shields Labour and Trades Council continued their action and organised a mass demonstration on 6 January 1932 when the Borough Council was due to meet. The *Shields Daily News* carried a front-page story advising that a procession which included four colliery bands and a crowd of several thousand people had occupied the open space in front of the Town Hall. Negotiations had taken place during the previous week between Gompertz, Bill Blyton and the Mayor, Robert Chapman, who made clear the Council could not repeal the Economy Act, the PACs were required to enforce a Means Test, but that he would allow them to address the Council meeting. The Moderate Councillors in the face of such protest could do little else but allow a deputation to address the Council meeting and in doing so instructed the PAC to meet with the Labour and Trades Council delegation to listen to their grievances as to the application of the Means Test in the town. An attempt by the Labour Group to have Gompertz elected as a lay member of the PAC was defeated by just one vote, indicating that some Moderate members must have voted for Gompertz.

As the Labour Party nationally came to terms with its depleted Parliamentary numbers and faced an impossible task of holding a Government with a Parliamentary majority of over 490 to account, there was the inevitable tensions as to how to respond. Sir Oswald Mosley formed his British Union of Fascists, the ILP disaffiliated from the Labour Party in July 1932, whilst the Communist Party, through their control of the National Unemployed Workers' Movement organised hunger marches and portrayed themselves as the only truly left-wing Party capable of defeating the Government. In what was clearly a coordinated tactic the 1932 May Day Rally's across the country were disrupted by Communist Party members. The Rally in Hyde Park, London, descended into street fighting, whilst in South Shields, as the local Labour Party and Trade Unions held their own rally in the Marsden Miners' Hall, members of the Minority Movement disrupted the meeting when Jack Lawson the Labour MP for Chester-le-Street spoke, only leaving the meeting when Police arrived.

VII

At the Labour and Trades Council meeting of 7 February 1932 it was agreed, by acclamation, to endorse Ede as the Prospective Parliamentary candidate for the next General Election, but with a strong Parliamentary majority for the National Government, it was unlikely voters would go to the polls for some time. Nationally, the ageing George Lansbury assumed the Labour leadership, with the youthful Clem Attlee as his Deputy. Attlee offered to visit South Shields in December 1932, but the invitation was acutely turned down on the grounds that a Friday evening was not the most propitious time for a public meeting. As the Labour Party became more insular, the National Government imposed iron economic measures of reductions in unemployment benefit, the Means Test, cuts in pay for public servants and no real economic strategy for which to bring back confidence in the traditional northern industries such as textiles, coal mining or heavy engineering, giving rise to the epitaph 'the hungry thirties'.

By November 1932 Gompertz was forty-four years old, he was no longer associated with the pawnbroking business and his entire life centred around being the Organising Secretary and Hon Agent of the South Shields Labour and Trades Council he had also secured membership of the Labour Exchange

Committee. Residing at 31 Quarry Lane with Annie, his main source of income was his from his political actives.

Labour Party financial records indicate that Gompertz received no renumeration from the local Party during Ede's short tenure as the MP, we can safely assume that his salary was paid direct from Ede. Following Ede's defeat, the Party was anxious to maintain a full-time Organising Secretary, and in 1931 paid Gompertz £58 in salary following Ede's defeat at the October General Election. In 1932 he was paid just under £190 and in 1933 £174, no records could be found for 1934, but in 1935 he received again just under £174, out of the renumeration Gompertz was required to pay his own tax and insurance stamps, so the wage, whilst generous, wasn't particularly exorbitant. In addition, in later years, Gompertz had two properties from which he received a rental income, 38 Bertram Street and 40/42 South Eldon Street. Financially, it was always a challenge for the local Party to continue to maintain their base in Laygate Lane and to pay for a full-time official, but they successfully managed it thanks to an annual grant from the DMA of £100, and in 1931 Ede provided the Party with a donation of £39 (around £2,500 in today's money). Gompertz was fastidious in his duties, and even though Ede was no longer the MP, constituents would arrive at the Labour Office seeking support with matters particularly around the PAC, Labour Exchange and housing, Gompertz gave regular updates to the Party on the constituent-facing work he had been involved with.

Following his defeat in the Moderate stronghold of Westoe in November 1931, Gompertz was chosen by the Party to stand in Tyne Dock for the November 1932 municipal elections following the retirement of (John) Henry Cheeseman. Signing a statement, as all candidates were required to do, that he would abide by Labour Group decisions if elected, he nevertheless asked for it to be recorded that the only time he would break the Whip would be over the question of supporting or condoning war, a request he would make each time he was due for re-election.

Tyne Dock was well known to Gompertz, his family had a pawnbroking store in the heart of the ward and as Ede's Agent he would have campaigned in the working-class district enthusiastically both in the 1929 and 1931 General Elections. Applying his trademark energy for campaigning, he used the announced increase in water charges by the Water Board as a central plank of his campaign organising a series of public meetings against the increase. Gompertz was rewarded with a decent majority of 849 over his Moderate and Communist opponents. His was a youthful age for a Councillor in those days, but Labour's victory in Holborn saw an even more youthful twenty eight-year-old Richard Ewart (who would eventually become a Sunderland MP) wrestling the seat from the Moderates.

The Labour Group now had twenty-two Councillors, facing twenty-four Moderate Councillors, although the unelected Aldermanic Bench gave the Moderates an edge in the Council Chamber.

The stormy petrel had finally achieved his municipal dues, the Moderate Councillors would do all in their power to thwart Gompertz's advance.

Chapter 10

Municipal Honours

I Stormy Petrel

The *Secret Document* affair, as it was to become known, would establish Gompertz as a stormy petrel, a public servant beyond reproach and a politician who would give no succour to his political opponents. It also demonstrated the fear in which the Moderate Group of Councillors in South Shields Town Hall held Gompertz and laid open their determination to thwart their young Labour opponent's endeavours to hold them to account.

The majority over their Labour opponents in the Town Hall was tight for the Moderates, but their control over the appointments to the Aldermanic Bench ensured them a comfortable margin. The Bench was made up of fifteen appointees, one for each ward in the town, and their appointments were for a four-year term (as opposed to a three-year term for elected councillors) the appointments to the Bench were also staggered, so Aldermen 'retired' at varying times in the municipal cycle. As a consequence, whoever had the greatest number of Councillors at the time of an Aldermanic vacancy, could appoint one of their own side to the Aldermanic Bench. The Aldermen were able to undertake all duties in similar fashion as Councillors, except vote on Aldermanic appointments, and they did so from the luxury of not having to contest a Council election. The system, which was an established feature of local government across the country, was clearly undemocratic but the Aldermanic Bench was not eventually abolished until the 1973 Local Government Act.

In the Town Hall the Labour Group now had a strength of 22 Councillors as opposed to 24 Moderate supporting Councillors. The unelected Aldermanic Bench though, still gave the Moderate group a healthy majority in the Chamber. Gompertz personified the utter frustration of the local Labour Party at their failure to control the Chamber and although he was new to the Council, he was apt at using every procedural and constitutional manoeuvre possible to harass and frustrate the long serving Moderate Group facing him.

The Shields Gazette, whose editorials were usually biased towards the Moderates, within days of his election had marked Gompertz out as '*the new Leader of the opposition in the local Parliament*' and urged the Mayor to ensure a '*happy medium*' in the length of his speeches – '*Surely three hours is enough in which to dispose of business …*'

Councillors and Aldermen assembled after the November 1932 local elections for their Annual Council meeting. As usual, the Annual Meeting began by thanking the retiring Mayor for his services and in a civic ceremony that has changed little over the decades, proceeded to appoint a new First Citizen of the County Borough. Following the Oath of Office and signing the Official records, the new Mayor, Labour's George Linney, took the Chair and proceeded to oversee the election of members to the various Council Committees for the ensuing municipal year. Tactically, Labour Councillors and Aldermen met in caucus to determine who they would support in any contested election for positions and voted accordingly as a bloc. Moderate Councillors and Alderman had long prided themselves on having no such Whip holding the view that Party politics had no place in the Chamber – such public sentiments and indiscipline were possible when the Moderates had a large majority in the Chamber, and a stray vote by one of them to a favoured Labour representative would still mean the Moderate nominee invariably won. But the Moderates didn't have a large majority in 1932 and faced with a well-disciplined and clearly 'whipped' Labour group of Councillors and Alderman, they needed to change their tactics in the Chamber if they were to maintain their positions of influence.

They were utterly determined that Gompertz should not be appointed to the Public Assistance Committee.

The Labour Party vehemently opposed the concept and operation of the Public Assistance Committees and viewed them as little more than an attempt to embarrass and belittle those who sought the Committee's welfare. The Committee had powers under the Act to introduce alternative local schemes of poor relief, but the exemption was rarely used and was certainly not the case in South Shields. At the forefront of the campaign to harass and hold the Committee to account was Gompertz, who on every occasion whether in Labour Party, public or trade union meetings or indeed via correspondence to the *Shields Gazette*, objected to the decisions reached by the Moderate Party led Committee. Gompertz, given his interest, understandably sought membership of the Committee and was determined to change the Committees operation from within.

Two moderate Councillors though were adamant he should not serve on the Committee. Councillors Robert Bainbridge and the Chairman of the Public Assistance Committee, Edwin Thompson, both long-serving Moderate Party councillors, who appreciating that the Moderate majority on the Council was precariously tight, prepared a 'slate' of names for whom the Moderate Councillors and Aldermen should vote for at the Annual Council meeting and circulated it to their colleagues. Added to the circular were the clear instructions – '*On no account vote for Ernest Gompertz*' and '*Labour members should not be allowed to retain their seats on spending committees but that they should be put on committees that have no power at all.*' Unfortunately for Councillors Bainbridge and Thompson, whilst their colleagues followed the instruction and duly ensured Gompertz was not appointed to the Public Assistance Committee – albeit by one vote (although he was allocated a place on the uninfluential Markets and Quays Committee!) – someone had leaked the scabrous document to Gompertz before the Annual Council meeting.

Whilst in the normal operation of politics it is not unusual to operate a 'slate' of preferred candidates, indeed Gompertz and his colleagues had their own slate, what lit the fuse was the fact that the circular had clearly been typed and duplicated within the Town Hall and further on South Shields Corporation paper because the watermark identified the source. Again, in today's political environment it was hardly a scandal on the scale of the local government corruption scandals that rocked the country in the 1960s, but in the 1930s, Councillors simply would not have had access to such typing and duplicating equipment in the Town Hall – the scandal was that the circular had clearly been prepared by a Council official.

The affair would probably have run its course after Gompertz made his initial protest at the Council's Annual Meeting on Friday 11 November 1932, but there were three crucial by-elections being held to elect Councillors following appointments to the Aldermanic Bench in the Tyne Dock, Simonside and Beacon Wards in late November and the Labour Party was determined to use the controversy – now dubbed '*The Secret Document*' scandal by the *Shields Gazette* – to full effect and to help them achieve the majority they so desperately needed in the Chamber. Gompertz demanded a full Public Inquiry into how Corporation papers, not available to Councillors, had been used by the Moderates for political purposes and wrote to the Mayor and Town Clerk. The public were certainly gripped by the affair, with lively exchanges in the letters page of the *Shields Gazette*, either expressing indignation at the arrogance of the Moderates, or the pointless mudslinging by the Labour Party, depending upon your political persuasion.

The Labour Party held a public meeting in Tyne Dock to support their Council by-election candidate, Margaret Gallagher, at which the keynote speaker was the other local Tyne Dock Member, Ernie Gompertz who spoke to the packed meeting with populist outrage at the way he had been treated. Gompertz thundered, '*When you sent me to the Town Council … you considered I was a proper person to sit on any and all the committees according to the number allowed to a Councillor, and I contend there was no committee that the people of Tyne Dock desired me to sit on more than the Public Assistance Committee and the Moderates knew that.*'

The correspondence pages of the *Shields Gazette* indicated a clear divide over the issue, but some also displayed antipathy to Gompertz over his World War I conscientious objection.

One anonymous correspondent wrote:

> '*Sir – So the writer of the "secret document" is known and the town have to thank Councillors Bainbridge and Thompson and the members who voted as the document said, for keeping Coun. Gompertz off the P.A.C.*
>
> *All honour to them all, but Coun Gompertz will never be satisfied till he is on the P.A.C. that is what is worrying him.*
>
> *I hope these two young Councillors who have done so much for the town and the unemployed will continue to be successful in keeping Coun Gompertz off the P.A.C.*
>
> *Coun Gompertz wouldn't fight for anybody during the War, he rather went to prison. If he wouldn't fight with us, then why should he want to fight for us now!*
> **1914–1918**'

But Gompertz also had his admirers:

> '*Sir –*
>
> *I would like to express my disgust at the empty remarks made by "1914–1918" in reference to the controversy brought about the underhanded way certain members of the South Shields Council are trying to exploit a very live and capable gentlemen like Coun Gompertz.*
>
> *His attitude during the war was in the opinion of myself and thousands more the correct attitude.*

The people who were instrumental in putting Coun Gompertz where he is, will be well satisfied with their bargain. He is of a fighting nature when the correct fight comes along.

I only wish I had been a Gompertz or a Hopper, of Jarrow (another gentleman who was exploited) I might have been in better health. I was seriously gassed during the war, and I am totally disabled with no pension from an ungrateful country.

I extend the hand of friendship to both Councillors Hopper and Gompertz in their fight against heavy odds.

Old Contemptible'

The *Shields Gazette* in an editorial claimed that the Margaret Gallagher and the Labour Party wanted control of the Public Assistance Committee so that '... *they could dole out public money more lavishly to applicants for poor relief. That supplies a very sound reason for keeping her Party off the Committee in the best interests of the ratepayer.'* The Council by-elections held on Thursday 29 November saw Labour hold their seats in Simonside and Tyne Dock whilst the Moderates retained the Beacon Ward.

The following day, the Town Clerk, in an obvious attempt to draw a line under the 'secret document' affair which had paralysed civic affairs, wrote to Gompertz, advising he had conducted a full internal inquiry. In summary, the Town Clerk's investigations had established that, Bainbridge and Thompson had prepared a circular; unfortunately, the duplicating machine in Thompson's business premises was defective so they sought a machine in the Town Hall; a Council Official used three stencils for the duplicating machine to print the circular; the Councillors had supplied the paper, but it was too thick for the duplicating machine, so they used Corporation paper. The Town Clerk insisted that his officer did not peruse the document so did not know it was of a private nature and noted that the Councillors had left their own paper for the department to use as required in future. The Town Clerk could see no reason for a full-scale public inquiry.

To add insult to injury, the Councillors had sought an official in the Public Assistance Department to help prepare the offending circular, one can only imagine the fury in Labour ranks.

The Borough Council meeting on 7 December prepared itself for Gompertz's wrath. He tabled a motion to censure Edwin Thompson and Robert Bainbridge and to instruct Council Officials not to use Corporation time or materials for the private business of members. Initial attempts were made to prevent a debate, that motion was defeated by thirty-two votes to nineteen. The ensuring debate was lively although in reading the *Shields Gazette* transcript one cannot help feeling the event was pure theatre and attempts were made by both sides to 'play to gallery' since the *Shields Gazette* reported that the public gallery was indeed full, with members of the public standing in the gangways to listen to the debate. Gompertz, forever a political animal scented political blood but also felt he had a genuine grievance at having been singled out by the opposition in the Moderate Party circular. His failure to secure a place on the important Public Assistance Committee clearly rankled with him. He accused the Moderates of '*being instrumental in cutting relief to the bone*' and Bainbridge and Thompson of '*Throwing sand in the eyes of the public*' and further, he believed their excuses were so thin that he could prove to the Council that they had been telling untruths. Gompertz had even sought to establish how much money had been spent in preparing the document, which had urged Moderate Councillors not to place him on the Public Assistance Committee, the cost 10s 6d.

Thompson accused the Labour Party of making a '*Mountain out of a molehill*' and advised the Council: '*I have no unhappy conscience in this matter at all.*' He queried why Labour members sent their casework to him, if he had indeed '*cut relief to the bone.*' Meanwhile, an exasperated Bainbridge protested that the whole affair was '*puerile*', and that Gompertz was seeking nothing more than cheap notoriety. '*Talk about a storm in the teacup*', protested Bainbridge, '*The tiniest thimble possesses a prodigious capacity for such an infinitesimal thing as this. "The secret document," a sinister plot by A. E., Gompertz, the season's best thriller!*'

The Council eventually rejected Gompertz's motion of censure in Thompson and Bainbridge by thirty votes to twenty-three, preferring to see the whole matter as maladroit behaviour by the Moderates with even Gompertz's old Labour mentor, Jim Curbison, refusing to support him on this occasion, declaring in the meeting that he felt '*Theirs's was a mistake that might occur to any man or any two men who were prominent in any organisation.*'

The saga laid bare the simmering tensions that existed at the time, augmented by the arrival in the Chamber of Gompertz, one of Labour's key election strategists who held the Moderates in contempt and was determined to achieve a Labour working majority in the Council. The Moderates were principally businesspeople who although fought elections under the Moderate Party banner, perceived themselves as independent, refusing to be whipped into a voting bloc and believing that they acted on each issue as their conscience dictated. They had controlled the Council's affairs uninterrupted since its inception in 1850, but now found themselves faced with a solid bloc of Labour Party activists who wanted change.

Two editorials in the *Shields Gazette* highlighted the paradox for those in the town who opposed the Labour Party. On 14 November 1923, following the Council's Annual Meeting when Gompertz first raised the issue of the Moderate circular, the *Gazette* Editorial described the tactics of Bainbridge and Thompson as '*An error of judgement*' whilst acknowledging some manoeuvres to secure an anti-Labour majority on Council committees was inevitable, the Editorial believed that to '... *issue instructions that one individual of the other party must be kept off the committee is another and very different thing.*' It was, the Editorial believed, bringing a '*vicious element*' into municipal politics. Yet a week later on 22 November, in an apparent volte-face the *Shields Gazette* editorial lamented that the Labour Party was – '... *an organisation which runs smoothly, it has a programme that is well defined and effectively aimed at, its representatives on the Council are under the orders of the junta and usually do as they are told.*' Against this, were the Moderates, described as a collection of individuals – '... *which centres a collection of disunited elements of uncertain purpose and individualistic tendencies.*' Unfortunately for the *Shields Gazette*, this meant the tactical advantage in the Town Hall was with the Labour Party.

It was, the Editor believed a one-sided situation that needed the careful attention of the Moderate Party leadership.

II

Tensions simmered over into 1933 when at the February meeting of the Borough Council Curbison was again forcibly restrained by colleagues in the Chamber as he left his chair and advanced to one of the Moderate Councillors.

The episode centred around compensation payments to the owner of a butcher's shop as part of the slum clearance proposals for the Thames Street area. Curbison objected to the payment as being excessive on the grounds that the owners had been offered alternative accommodation to which Councillor Lamb retorted, '*What if it had been a cobblers shop?*', Curbison, a cobbler by trade, reacted angrily stating that he was not ashamed to be a cobbler and advanced towards the stunned Councillor. Gompertz and Pearson held back Curbison who struggled so violently his jacket was half off, it took another two Councillors to restrain him. Lamb was urged to withdraw the remark which he agreed to, but Curbison refused to accept the withdrawal. Order was restored, and the compensation agreed.

Lamb resigned from the Council in early July, the circumstances recorded were for business reasons, but one cannot help speculating that the incident, together with the resulting media interest probably encouraged the decision. The subsequent by election in Holborn, which would have given the Labour Group a majority of Councillors in the Chamber was won by the Moderates.

In a further tempestuous debate in March, Labour Councillors moved that the Education Committee should be instructed to make the necessary arrangements for extending the provision of free meals to the various elementary schools across the borough. The 1930s economic depression was hitting urban areas like the North East hard, no more so than in South Shields where there were over 15,000 unemployed adults, over 12,000 of whom had dependent children. However, less than 800 of these children were being provided with a meal which the mover of the motion, Labour's Councillor Harris regarded as '*alarming.*' Whilst the Public Assistance Committee had supported children by providing 'free meals centres', these were placed in the Riverside areas resulting in children not resident along the Riverside having to walk long distances to receive subsistence.

For Gompertz, seconding the motion, it was a moral obligation for the Council to support the extension of free meals within or near the vicinity of schools elsewhere in the borough, he argued that the town had: '... *deteriorated in citizenship physically because the youngsters were not being properly fed.*' Even more disturbing for Gompertz, were the claims that the parents of those children who received meals from the centres provided by PAC had the cost of the meal deducted when assessing the family's financial resources under the Means Test. The claim was disputed by the Chair of the PAC, Cllr Thompson.

The Moderates were reluctant to support the provision of free meals at schools. The Chair of the Education Committee, Ald Richardson said that if there was a need for more food centres operated by the PAC then logic would suggest they should open more centres, but there had no increase in applications. Moderate Cllr Brock disagreed with the motion advising the Chamber that: '*The reason no centres have been provided at Harton and Cleadon Park was that there had been no been applications.*'

The Council split 25–25 with the Mayor, Councillor Linney, giving his casting vote to motion for the Labour motion.

The Labour Group continued to maintain pressure at future Council meetings, but the continuing popularity of the National Government affected their efforts at the 1933 November municipal polls. The Moderates secured victories in two of Labour's traditional seats, St Hilda and Tyne Dock, albeit by small majorities. It was though a bitter blow for the local Party, with Gompertz unable to secure even his own power base of Tyne Dock for the Party. The Council balance now saw twenty-five Moderates Councillors and ten Alderman, with Labour down to twenty Councillors and five Aldermen, although some of the notional Labour Alderman were outside the Whip, such as Dunlop and Curbison.

III

The workload Gompertz was undertaking without secretarial support was substantial. He was a Councillor, still involved with the Shopworkers Union and he was responsible as the Labour and Trades Council Organising Secretary for all aspects of the organisation's administration. He maintained regular dialogue with affiliated Unions and Labour's headquarters in London, prepared the election campaigns, organised the May Day Rally and other regular public meetings which in 1933 saw Manny Shinwell and Ald W Dobbie MP visit the town. Gompertz oversaw fundraising drives and communicated with Ede so that he was always aware of developments in the town. He was also Chair of the local Free Speech Society and was required to deal with the media on all requests for comment, added to this would have been managing the Labour Hall and Office, with its constant stream of visits by constituents who turned to the Labour Party for support.

His diplomatic skills would have been required to deal with the endless complaints from affiliates about rival unions poaching their members and frequent missives from the Labour Group in relation to Councillors not following the Labour Group Whip and it was Gompertz, recognising how close Labour were to gaining municipal power, who tried to encourage Ald Dunlop to return to the Labour Group.

It was though the frequent attempts by the Communists to exert some influence over the Labour and Trades Council which saw Gompertz deploy a ruthless streak. In June 1933 he ensured the Chair ruled out of order a motion from a Boldon miners' delegate to a create 'A united front' of left-wing organisations in the town, and he demanded that Councillors who had associated themselves with a local group called the Winter Relief Campaign (organised by the local Communists) should renounce their membership. All did except the avowed left-wing miners delegate Councillor Pearson (who was closely associated with Will Lawther and would eventually become a full-time DMA Official). By November 1933 he asked the Party to endorse a rule that due to the workload at Party meetings, they would not read out at meetings communication from organisations opposed to the Labour Party. At the 1934 Annual Meeting when Gompertz refused to accept a member of the Boldon miners' delegation because he was associated with the National Unemployed Workers' Union (a subsidiary of the Communist Party) the Boldon miners promptly walked out.

He was determined to create a Labour Party that was social democratic in outlook, and one very much that would be in his (and unquestionably Ede's) image. He spent time in 1933 and 1934 restructuring the Women's branches in the town, as well as merging the individual Labour Party branches based on Council wards into a joint-ward structure (on the grounds individual branches did not attract large attendance at meetings, but of course joint ward structures would be easier to control and those wards without a Labour Councillor would in future have access to one at their meetings), and he refocused the work of Labour League of Youth, urging affiliates to ensure younger Union Members became involved in their meetings. The creation of an individual Men's Section in February 1933 saw the section gain six delegates to the Party meetings, and a member of the Executive Committee. Whilst the minutes do not recall the driving force behind the establishment of the Branch, we could speculate that it was a tactic by Gompertz to secure further support for him within the Party apparatus. The Men's Section though was declared unconstitutional and was closed down in 1934 on the orders of the Labour National Executive Committee.

Within all these machinations, Gompertz and the wider Party were not insulated against events occurring on continental Europe. The appointment of Adolf Hitler as German Chancellor in January 1933, led rapidly to attacks on German Jewry which in April 1933 saw Gompertz ask the Party to make protests to the German Embassy in London. The Party agreed to hold a public meeting on the issue and in August they were supporting proposals from the TUC to support a ban on German goods on the grounds of the oppression of trade unionists in Germany. In February 1934 they agreed to raise a collection in support of Austrian Socialists following the decision of Engelbert Dollfuss to declare an autocratic regime which leaned towards Italian Fascism (Dollfuss had outlawed the Social Democrat Schutzbund) and in June they were writing again in protest to the German Ambassador in London demanding the release of political prisoners or that they be brought to trial in a public legal tribunal, going so far as to organise further public meetings to demonstrate their own determination to resist Fascism and tyranny.

Bizarrely in June, Gompertz was writing to the Police in protest against a thirty-four-year-old German sailor called Wilhelm Hacker who was in the practice of parading around the town approaching the public with a 'Heil Hitler' and Nazi salute, and propagating Fascist beliefs, he was eventually imprisoned for a month after leaving a café without paying for his glass of milk. Gompertz asked the Chester-le-Street Labour MP to raise the matter with the Home Secretary on the grounds that Social Democrats fleeing Germany were barred entry into the country, yet a Fascist sympathiser was allowed to remain.

The Labour Party nationally was also starting to take the threat of Fascism seriously with their local branches being asked to complete a questionnaire in early 1934 as to Fascist activity in their area. Gompertz reported that in South Shields Fascists were utilising the correspondence columns of the local press but advised he could offer no evidence of the Fascists organising women, youth or seeking to infiltrate the local trade union branches.

IV Unemployment Bill

Internationally the National Government was consumed by several issues: the questions of India and whether to grant some form of Home Rule short of full independence; pursuing an Imperial Preference System in trade with the Empire and attending International Conferences aimed at disarmament. But domestically it was still the high unemployment rate, particularly in the northern industrial areas which dominated Parliamentary considerations.

The rate of insured unemployment had peaked at 22 per cent in 1932/33, it had fallen nationally to 16 per cent by mid-1934 but there were regional imbalances with Durham still facing an unemployment rate of over 30 per cent. Figures for December 1934 indicate that 952,000 workers were drawing insurance benefit, and 728,000 were subject to the local Means Test. The Government's response, led by the new Chancellor, Neville Chamberlain, was the Unemployment Act of 1934, which created a centralised bureaucracy, transferring the work of the local Public Assistance Committees (PACs) to a new Unemployment Assistance Board. Chamberlain had long been concerned that different rates were being paid depending upon the political make-up of the local PACs, with Labour Councils more likely to be lenient in their application of the Means Test. The remit of the new Board was too depoliticise unemployment relief by establishing a national scale to replace the various local scales of the PACs, with the Government claiming that there would be increased payments to the majority of the unemployed, although a significant proportion of the expenditure would still be borne by ratepayers.

When the Act was implemented in January 1935, hundreds of thousands of unemployed people found their subsistence was reduced, with the worst effects being felt in the areas of the heaviest long-term unemployment. The Means Test was implemented more harshly and for Labour Parliamentarians it seemed that the Government believed unemployment was an individual's problem, when in fact they asserted, it was Society's problem.

The consequences of the Act's implication, led to the Communist dominated National Unemployed Workers' Movement organising a series of hunger marches to London. Militant demonstrations were also organised outside town halls where, either worried or sympathetic, the local authority would pass resolutions urging modification or withdrawal of the Act. To appreciate the wide-scale opposition to the Act, we should recall Michael Foot's comments in his biography of Nye Bevan, Foot described the effects as: '... *the biggest explosion of popular anger in the whole of the inter-war period, second only to the General Strike itself*'.

Curbison's refusal at the Borough Council in December 1933 to support Labour Councillors in their demand for the Mayor to call a Town Meeting on the question of the Unemployment Bill was the final crossing of the Rubicon. Curbison now resided in Elmsleigh Gardens in Cleadon and as such was required to join the Houghton-le-Spring Labour Party, the South Shields Labour Party agreed that they should bring to the attention of their colleagues in Houghton Curbison's 'anti-Labour activities' and persistent refusal to support the Labour Group on South Shields Council. Curbison responded by making a complaint to Labour's Head Office in London, with the National Chairman of the Party, Walter Smith, visiting the South Shields Labour Hall in May 1934 to hold an inquiry into the affair at which Gompertz and the Labour Group Secretary, Councillor Harris represented the local Party. The conclusion was clear – the decision as to whether Curbison should be expelled would rest with the Houghton-le-Spring Labour Party.

In July, Houghton-le-Spring had concluded their own inquiry and had recommended that the South Shields Labour Group allow Curbison a final opportunity to accept the Labour whip in the Town Hall, a resolve endorsed by Walter Smith. Curbison was adamant, he refused to take the Whip or to associate himself with the local Party. The die was cast, correspondence sent to Gompertz in September from the Secretary of Houghton-le-Spring Labour Party confirmed that they had expelled Curbison from membership.

We cannot know for certain the reason for Curbison's intransigence, he had certainly become divorced from the local Party over a number of years, and perhaps the bitterness of his original expulsion in 1931 still caused him some anguish. We cannot though dismiss the fact that since his elevation to the Aldermanic Bench his voting record with the Labour Group became extremely erratic, and he was not the only one. Aldermen Dunlop and Charles Henderson, stalwarts of the pioneering days when the South Shields Labour Party was first formed, became more detached from their Labour Council colleagues once their assumed a seat on the Aldermanic Bench, and even more so when they were appointed to the Mayoralty.

V 'Good old Gompy'

The expulsion of Curbison should also be seen as an indication that the Labour Group, notwithstanding poor election results in 1933, felt strong enough to begin to exert its discipline on those refusing to support collective decision making. Curbison and Gompertz were clearly at one time close, they were both in the Shop Assistants' Union, both ILPers and both had taken positions of responsibility at the first Annual Meeting of the South Shields Labour Party. For Gompertz though, loyalty to the Labour Party was predominant. Unless there was discipline and an agreement to accept collective responsibility, then it was pointless seeking to win control of the Council Chamber, or Parliament.

As the local Party came to terms with the removal of Curbison, Gompertz turned their attentions to campaign work across South Shields, the first centred around Wright's Biscuits factory, located in the heart of Gompertz's Tyne Dock ward. Established in 1790, by the 1930s Wright's had become a national supplier of biscuits, cakes and groceries with a workforce which made the company one of the largest employers on Tyneside. Gompertz, in September 1933, had become aware that the company was allegedly paying abnormally low wages, £1.30 per week for men, women were being required to work 8 am until noon and young girls of fourteen years from 7 am until 8 pm. Gompertz raised complaints with both the Labour Exchange Committee, of which he was a member, and the local Labour and Trades Council, the latter of whom empowered Gompertz to take any action necessary to resolve the situation. With his usual tenacious enthusiasm Gompertz worked over the next few months highlighting the appalling wages being paid at Wright's and organised picketing at the factory gates with a view to encouraging employees to become members of a Union.

Gompertz encouraged the Co-op Wholesale Society, which had a significant retail outreach across the North East of England, to place pressure on Wright's and to ensure all their commercial bodies were aware of the problem at Wright's. Gompertz was able to report to the Trades Council in April that several Co-op divisions had agreed to remove the 'sweated products' of Wright's from their Society's shops. Within the Council, Gompertz endeavoured at the November 1933 Council meeting to halt the sale of land to Wright's as part of the nearby Stanley Terrace housing scheme, the attempt was heavily defeated, with three dissent Labour Aldermen, Curbison, Dunlop and Henderson voting against the Labour Group.

Gompertz's actions came to the attention of employees at Greenwoods Printers who complained that they were also required to work beyond legal hours. Gompertz's next move was to take Wright's and Greenwoods to Court for breaching the 1901 Factory and Workshop Act. He was successful but reported to the May Trades Council meeting that in giving a small fine for the breach, the Chairman of Bench, in convicting both Wright's and Greenwoods had expressed sympathy for the employers, a position which saw the Trades Council make a formal complaint to the Lord Chancellor. The working conditions at Wright's would continue to be of concern because in January 1936 the Boldon Miners' Lodge sought assurances that the workers at the factory were being organised given reports of unsatisfactory wage conditions that still prevailed at the Tyne Dock factory.

Whilst campaigning against Wright's, Gompertz also successfully appeared before the local Assessment Committee in February 1934 to argue a case against increasing the rateable value of municipal housing. Whilst he failed to secure any alteration to an increase for the new Cleadon Park estate, he did successfully persuade the Committee not to increase rates in areas undergoing extensive slum clearance. Unfortunately, the Council's Rating Committee decided to contest the decision with an Appeal to the Quarter Sessions. The decision led to Gompertz requesting the Party to organising open air meetings in the Market Place to protest at the decision. One open air meeting held on Sunday 11 March 1934, would see Gompertz in Court.

The principle for Gompertz was one of free speech and civil liberty. The local Party supported his claim for £25 damages against the Police and agreed to make a financial appeal to the wider movement if necessary. In South Shields County Court in May, Gompertz advised that whilst speaking from the steps of the Old Town Hall, two Police Constables approached and asked if he had a permit to speak in the Market Place. Gompertz informed them that he did but had left it in his Office. The Officers left, only for a Sgt McManus to approach and ask for his permit, when Gompertz explained it was in his Office he maintained McManus instructed him to cease the open-air meeting, when Gompertz refused McManus dragged him from the steps and marched him to the other side of the Market Place, with Gompertz advising a hostile crowd not to respond and telling McManus to '… *do your duty*'. Gompertz, advised the Court that he was arrested and assaulted. In Court, McManus insisted that Gompertz was excitable, attempted to ridicule him to the crowd and simply fell as opposed to being dragged from the steps, he was not, McManus told the Court, arrested. It was not a view shared by Councillor Purvis a member of the Council's Watch Committee who told the Court that as a member of audience, he felt Gompertz was being arrested. It was not a view shared by the Court either, who awarded Gompertz £5 with costs for the assault, but they advised that they felt no case had been made for wrongful imprisonment.

Gompertz had a pugnacious, populist streak, his disdain for the Moderates would come to the fore at every Council meeting, with frequent outbursts and indignation at the decisions arrived at by the controlling Group. In March 1934, Gompertz led a further walkout of the Chamber, after unruly scenes over the issue of appropriation of wards at Harton Institution as a public general hospital. The Council agreed to take no further action until Durham County Council had advised when they would take responsibility for their residents, residing in the Institution. Gompertz made several interjections, spurred on by a full public gallery. The exasperated Mayor called for Order and for the Public Gallery to be cleared, as the public left there were cries of '*Good old Gompy*' and '*Let's go to the market*', to which Gompertz replied, '*We will go with the public*' and duly led a walkout of the Labour members, although they were not joined, it was recorded in the *Shields Daily News* by Ald Curbison.

The October meeting of Borough Council saw Gompertz removed from the Chamber this time with a police escort, following his refusal to accept the Mayor's ruling that he '*no longer be heard*'. The Mayor expressed the view that he felt Gompertz was deploying facetious points of order and notices of amendments to Council reports purely to prevent Council business being completed. Gompertz made clear to the Mayor that he intended to speak in a recommendation relating to a school tender, and would also speak on further items, the Police were summoned and escorted Gompertz from the Town Hall.

Whilst Gompertz displayed on occasion an unorthodox approach to Council proceedings, he was well versed in the Council Standing Orders and clearly had a persuasive debating style as demonstrated at the September Council meeting, when proposals were brought forward to end the post-World War I ban on commercial trading with Germany and Austria. Given the rise of Fascism in both countries, and the brutal suppression of workers and trade unionists in those countries, Gompertz was adamant that there should be no change in the Constitution. He argued that you cannot put out the hand of friendship to people '… *who had disgraced the name of humanity*' and eloquently outlined his anti-Nazi arguments before pointing out that the Council's own Standing Orders made clear a preference for procuring goods made in the United Kingdom and the British Empire. Despite the Mayor complaining that it was '… *well to forget such things*' when it came to trade, the Council refused to change Standing Orders.

The local Party was always mindful that their key goal was to regain the South Shields Parliamentary seat. Following a unanimous invitation from the South Shields Labour Party to be their candidate, Ede wrote back to Gompertz in July 1934 accepting the nomination and made a visit to the town in September to address the Party and to be formally adopted as the candidate. Ede would return to South Shields to address a public meeting in support of Labour's municipal candidates on Sunday 28 October.

As the effects of the Unemployment Act took hold, and with dire unemployment figures, it was perhaps evitable that the municipal elections in November 1934 would be triumph for the Labour Party. They gained over 770 new Councillors across the country, whilst the Conservatives lost 635. The success was particularly stunning in London, where under the direction of Herbert Morrison Labour gained London County Council and fifteen of London boroughs, whilst across the country Labour gained twenty-one county boroughs and eighteen non-county boroughs. Although in South Shields Labour only gained back the Rekendyke ward the collective poll across the town did see Labour secure a majority of the votes cast across the town and their majorities in individual wards won were quite secure. It was a clear indication that their campaigning was resonating with the public as well as a feeling that the National Government was running out of steam.

Conservative MPs now spoken openly that it was time to remove MacDonald as Prime Minister and fight the next election under their own colours.

Chapter 11

Appeasement

I Appeasement and the Peace Ballot

For those who did not live through the 1930s, it is difficult to comprehend the appeal of the National Government's policy of appeasement. The economic crash in 1929, consequent mass unemployment and the continuing reparations on Germany because of the Versailles Treaty (1919), all contributed to social destabilisation in continental Europe, leading to a lack of confidence in the ability of democracies to provide a clear path to recovery. The horrors of World War I, still fresh in the public's eye, meant a fear of further war, with a call for world disarmament and a strengthening of the powers of the League of Nations to deal with international tensions. The Government undertook complex diplomatic negotiations to appease the demands of dictators and openly expressed admiration for Mussolini in order to prevent a Fascist alliance between Germany and Italy; whilst in the Soviet Union, Stalin was tightening his grip on power. At the Geneva Disarmament Conference in March 1935, MacDonald, presented Britain's proposals for a reduction in armaments, insisting in a reduction in the French Army, whilst the conference discussed an increase in that of Germany's. The British Government budgeted for a more extended defence production programme, whilst the League of Nations was proving ineffectual due to the refusal of the isolationist USA to join, and Germany, Italy and Japan eventually withdrawing from its remit.

The Labour Party was not insulated from public pressure for peace, despite their numerical weakness in the House of Commons. In 1934 the Party opposed strengthening the RAF and in 1935 opposed the Defence White Paper; the Communist Party was opposed to rearmament, the emerging and vocal British Union of Fascists were also opposed, whilst business leaders did not want an increase in taxes to fund rearmament, anti-war groups proliferated during the 1930s. Added to this would be the public themselves who expressed their incredulity to rearmament through the Peace Ballot.

The ballot was organised by the **National Declaration Committee** headed by the League of Nations supporter Lord Robert Cecil. Commencing in late 1934, volunteers canvassed electors asking them to vote on five questions (criticised by historians as being loaded), with the intention of convincing the Government to support the aims of the League of Nations. In South Shields, the local Labour Party had sent three delegates to a regional conference which discussed the mechanics of the ballot and in January 1935 the local Party was asking for support in helping to canvass and distribute the ballot papers. On 27 June in the Royal Albert Hall, the results were announced, ten million households to just under one million supported the League in its endeavours to secure disarmament and on the question of stopping an aggressor with the use of force, two million abstained, two million opposed and six million supported it. For Baldwin, who had assumed the Premiership from the ailing Ramsay MacDonald in May, the exercise reinforced his belief that he could fight no general election on the issue of rearmament.

II

Rearmament and peace were not the only policy consideration at the time. The South Shields MP Harcourt Johnstone, who as a Samuelite Liberal, had pledged to defend free trade, was becoming increasingly detached from the policies of the National Government. His Liberal faction was opposed to protectionism declaring the fiscal policy of the Government as '*wholly mischievous*' following the Ottawa Agreement in 1932 which had introduced a series of tariffs. The Samuelite Liberals withdrew from the National Government but continued to support the Government from the backbenches. In the absence of Lloyd George's campaign finance, Johnstone, as Liberal Chief Whip, was given the task of fundraising for what was left of the Liberal Party, but their declining influence meant there were fewer wealthy benefactors prepared to support them.

The decision by the National Liberals to withdraw from the Government allowed them to oppose measures contained in the Unemployment Bill. At a major rally held in North Shields in February 1935, Harcourt Johnstone was joined by Isaac Foot, the MP for Bodmin in explaining to Tyneside voters why they could no longer support the Government. Johnstone lambasted the Government over the work of the Unemployment Assistance Board, which he argued operated without Ministerial guidance, was centralised and removed local knowledge from its deliberations. The decision by the

Government a week earlier to withdraw the new Unemployment Assistance Board regulations (in the face of wide-scale public pressure) was, Johnstone declared, '*A sight to see*'.

Johnstone had won the South Shields seat in 1931 based on the basis of supporting the National Government. During that campaign he had ridiculed Labour's attempts to warn the electorate about the possibility of the Means Test returning producing his own posters declaring: '*There is **no** destitution test. Vote for Johnstone and truth in politics.*' The fact that the 1934 Unemployment Bill had indeed returned the Means Test, was not a point lost on Gompertz. Irrespective of Johnstone's comments at the North Shields rally in February, Gompertz was determined to hold Johnstone to account.

Following an approval from the local Labour Party in June 1935, which had endorsed a resolution demanding that the maintenance of the able-bodied unemployed should be the responsibility of Government, Gompertz wrote to the Prime Minister, the Minister for Labour and Harcourt Johnstone. The Prime Minister and Cabinet Minister responded, Johnstone did not. Gompertz had decorated the outside of his correspondence with a copy of Johnstone's 1931 poster which declared: 'There is no destitution test', Johnstone refused to respond. Gompertz wrote again to which Johnstone's secretary replied that any communication sent to the MP must, to receive attention, contain neither inside or outside any deliberately offensive or insulting matter. Gompertz tenaciously responded that the poster was indeed offensive because thousands of townsfolk had learned at first hand the effects of the Means Test, the Poor Law and the work of the Unemployment Assistance Board. As usual Gompertz ensured that the saga was highlighted in the local press.

During these exchanges Johnstone would have been acutely aware that MacDonald's National Labour faction of the Government had, in May, selected Frederick Burden to be the National Government supporting candidate for South Shields at the next General Election, a move endorsed by the local Conservative Association. Added to this, Johnstone was not the most assiduous of Constituency MPs. CR Coote records an anecdote of a fellow MP who saw Johnstone on a sleeper train travelling from King's Cross on an evening when a blizzard was raging.

'*What on earth are you doing?*' he asked.

'*I am going to my Constituency*' responded Johnstone.

'*That's bad luck on a night like this*'.

'*Yes …*' responded Johnstone, '*… and what makes it worse is that I shall probably have to go next year as well*'.

On every occasion the South Shields Labour and Trades Council made clear their opposition to the Employment Act. At the March 1935 meeting of the Borough Council, the Labour Group submitted a motion demanding an end to the Means Test and condemned the creation of an Unemployment Board outside the control of Parliament. The Unemployment Act should be repealed they asserted with the Government providing work and adequate support for all working people. The motion fell because Moderate Councillors began exiting the Chamber, requiring the Mayor to advise that the meeting was no longer quorate.

The local Party also reacted with fury when it was announced that the Moderate Councillor, Edwin Thompson, who had previously irked Gompertz over his missive to keep Gompertz off the PAC, had been appointed as the Chair of the local Appeals Panel. Protest letters from the local Party and affiliates were sent off to the Ministry of Labour demanding his removal. Regular public demonstrations protesting the Means Test were held with a large meeting organised for 17 March complete with a march from Westoe Parade into the Market Place accompanied by the colliery bands. Gompertz also represented the Party at regional meetings of the TUC called to coordinate opposition to the Means Test.

Opposition to the Means Test increased across the country, the offices of the Merthyr Unemployment Assistance Board were attacked and near riots occurred in major cities. Nervous Government Backbench MPs, who had won marginal seats in the 1931 election landslide reported outright opposition to the implementation of the Act, and not just from the left. Church groups and other civic bodies expressed outrage that the removal of former checks and balances in the local system had resulted in the full force of cuts hitting the unemployed who had been expecting an increase in their benefits under the Act. The Government, realising that the system was causing serve hardship, as noted above announced in early February 1935 a legal standstill for an indefinite period, during which UAB clients would receive either the Board's allowance or the amount they would have originally received under their local PAC, whichever was the highest. Conservative MPs were relieved, but the Means Test would remain in place leading to the Labour Party and other left-wing groups maintaining the pressure on the Government. William Beveridge, the Chair of the **Unemployment Insurance Statutory Commission** observed that the present crisis should lead to something beyond a mere increase in the scales, he wanted a new approach to the whole question of long-term unemployment.

In response to the unemployment crisis in the industrially decimated areas, the Government had implemented the Distress Areas Bill (renamed Special Areas) in 1934 which included Wales, Scotland, West Cumberland, Durham and Tyneside. £2m was allocated to a Commissioner for England who would be responsible for schemes to facilitate economic and social development. The leading Communist, Wal Hannington observed that the initiative was doomed to failure since the Commissioners were prohibited from providing subsidies to business or providing direct employment, they could not supplement any grants given by Government departments to the distressed areas and they were prohibited from financially supporting local authority initiatives. The local projects which were supported tendered to be sewerage treatment, harbour developments, hospital construction and land clearing for the potential establishment of trading estates. The long-term unemployed were also required to attend retraining and reconditioning centres in their area, contemptuously referred to as '*slave camps*' by opponents who regarded them as merely a means of reducing the unemployment statistics.

The Government measures were hopelessly inadequate, but with the economic situation improving in the more prosperous areas of the South, and wages for the employed increasing, the Government was reticent to do any more which might affect the fragile recovery taking place. In essence, outside the minor public works projects, Government policy was to encourage migration away from the worst affected industrial areas. Over time, and with unemployment nationally reducing, and the electorates' concerns more focused on whether there should be a huge rearmament programme, the National Government's non-interventionist strategy held sway.

Whilst opposition in South Shields – at least in Labour and trade union circles – to the Means Test continued, the question of whether a tunnel or bridge should be constructed over the River Tyne linking South and North Shields required a final decision. South Shields Labour Group, supported by the local Party maintained that a bridge was the more affordable solution, but in March 1935, the Council finally settled the matter. A heated Chamber debate centred around the corresponding costs of both solutions, and what amount would be borne by the rates given a full grant for the scheme would not be forthcoming from the Government. Gompertz proposed a series of amendments to the Council Report but the final vote was twenty-six to twenty in favour of the tunnel option with some Labour Members breaking ranks. Although both South Shields and Tynemouth Councils supported the tunnel option an appeal to the Government for financial support for the infrastructure works was not forthcoming.

In addition, the question of whether Tyneside would be better served by a single Council covering both sides of the river was considered by the Government when in March 1935 they announced that a Royal Commission would be established to gauge the views of the relevant stakeholders under the Chairmanship of Sir Sidney Rowlatt. The deliberations would take three years and would ultimately fail due to lack of support from the smaller Local Authorities, opposition from Durham and Northumberland County Councils and public apathy to the proposals. As early as May 1935, the South Shields Labour Party pledged to resist any proposals to create a single Authority across Tyneside and maintained their opposition as the Royal Commission visited the town, this was swiftly followed by both the Labour Group and the Council itself registering their opposition. Ede as a senior local government figure in his own right and with knowledge of Tyneside, had been asked to serve on the Royal Commission, but given his prospective candidature he declined, declaring during the 1935 General Election campaign that he had made clear his total opposition to a single Tyneside Authority.

The South Shields Labour Party were also concerned at this time with the operation of the Child Emigration Society scheme in the 1930s which saw children, with the support of the Government, relocated from South Shields to Australia. Although the Labour Party minutes are vague, it appears Gompertz had met with the Mayor and a representative from the Fairbridge Farm School in Western Australia where twelve children from South Shields had been sent since 1932. Rev West, a Member of the Fairbridge School Council was visiting South Shields in August with the intention of seeking the exportation of another hundred children from across Tyneside. A report in the *Shields Daily News* of 3 August 1935 gave the Child Emigration Society's justification for the removal of the children, namely that the economic position in areas like South Shields offered no prospects to the children, the continued unemployment of their parents rendered them incapable of providing any start in life to their children and they would have better prospects in the Dominions. Whatever was said in the actual meeting caused Gompertz alarm because he felt compelled to report the matter to the Party at their 6 August 1935 meeting and arrangements were made to hold a mass demonstration in South Shields Market Place. On 25 August over 2,000 residents attended and agreed to the resolution: '*That this mass meeting of South Shields citizens demands that no more children shall be exported*

*to Australia or anywhere overseas by the Local Authority and views with alarm
the absolute powers of exportation secured by the PAC and calls upon the Town
Council to revise these powers without necessary delay.'*

Representations by Labour Councillors were made at the August Borough
Council meeting and the matter referred to the Public Assistance Committee,
given no further mention of the issue was raised in local Labour Party meetings
or the Borough Council, we must assume that the practice was halted.

III Fighting Fascism

Gompertz had confidentially advised Labour's Head Office in 1934
that here was little Fascist activity in South Shields other than occasional
correspondence in the local newspaper. By 1935 however the British Union
of Fascists (BUF) had established a base at 208 Westoe Road and on 5
July held an open meeting at Boldon Colliery but following the arrival of
protesting miners, the Police closed the meeting. The local Fascist branch
were sufficiently well organised to invite the BUFs Director of Propaganda,
William Joyce, to address a public meeting in the Congregational Hall in
Ocean Road in May 1935. South Shields was seen as fertile recruiting ground
by the BUF not only because of the high unemployment figures but also
because they had misread the Mill Dam riot of 1930 believing it to have been
race related when in fact the episode had more to do with fair employment
practices.

Joyce's meeting was interrupted from the moment he rose to speak, with
protestors ejected from the meeting by up to forty meeting stewards, a Tory
woman supporter who appealed for free speech was heckled and put on
the defensive and Joyce baited the Communist supporters giving the usual
outpouring of venom against *'Jewish global financers'*.

The BUF although small in South Shields, were determined and held
regular open-air meetings at the Wouldhave Memorial on Ocean Road as
well as in the town's Market Place and were always inevitably challenged
by anti-Fascist demonstrators. Joyce himself, would make another visit
to South Shields on 20 March 1936, addressing a further meeting at the
Congregational Hall condemning Britain's *'interference'* in foreign quarrels.
Gompertz for his part would maintain regular correspondence in the *Shields
Gazette* attacking Fascism particularly in relation to their attitude to Trade
Unionism and tackling unemployment.

The Labour and trade union movement were sufficiently concerned at the Fascist activity that they organised a mass march and demonstration in September into the town's Market Place. Led by the Boldon Colliery miners' band, the march was supported by church groups, Co-operative Women Guilds, the local Labour Party, Trade Unions and was also joined by the local Communist Party. Over 6,000 people assembled on the Market Place to oppose Fascism and war. In October the local Trades Council raised a special collection in support of the plight of the dependents of political prisoners in Spain.

South Shields was not the only town in the North East to be subjected to significant Fascist activity at this time, in his well-researched book, *In Excited Times*, Nigel Todd chronicles in detail the activities of the BUF across the North East and the public's emphatic refusal to support them.

IV 1935 General Election

We cannot be certain why on 18 October 1935, Baldwin decided to call an early general election, he wrote no memoirs and spoke rarely of such matters in his retirement. The Government had a solid majority, and it had a year to run its mandate. Rumours of an early general election had been the subject of political gossip for most of 1935, with claims that Baldwin may seek a fresh mandate following the Jubilee celebrations for King George V's Jubilee in May, which had seen Baldwin assumed the Premiership from the ailing MacDonald. The considered view is that having secured the passage of the India Bill in August 1935 – which had aroused consistent opposition from a hard-core of Tory rebels – he was in a position to face the electorate with a united Party. Secondly, Baldwin was grappling with the diplomatic failure of the League of Nations to deal with Mussolini whose troops had invaded Abyssinia on the eve of the Conservative Party conference. Military experts advised that Abyssinia could probably hold out until June 1936 and might even defeat the Italians, but this intelligence was in no way infallible and the last thing Baldwin wanted was to fight an election with Britain's overseas diplomatic impotency being the cornerstone of the campaign. Far better, Baldwin judged, to go early and fight on the domestic agenda. Finally, he called an election early because he felt he could win, even if several key Northern seats which had fallen to the National Government in 1931 returned to the Labour fold, by-election results since 1931 had indicated the likelihood of a healthy National Government majority.

The election was set for 14 November and Ede returned to South Shields and was enthusiastically adopted at a large meeting of the South Shields Labour and Trades Council held on 20 October. The decision by MacDonald's renegade National Labour group to support a candidate against the Liberal's Harcourt Johnstone gave every succour to Labour's belief that they could win back the Parliamentary seat. Ede though like all candidates for public office was more circumspect, writing to Gompertz on 23 October he cautioned: '*Whilst the political cheerfulness of Sunday's meeting was very exhilarating, one cannot overlook the fact that a majority of over ten thousand, even with a third candidate, takes a great deal of wiping out and I trust that all our friends will realise that a great deal of hard work will have to be done if their cheerfulness is to be justified.*'

Gompertz, in preparing Ede's election material, highlighted on every occasion Johnstone's 1931 claim that there would be no destitution test and urging them not to be misled by any further claims from Johnstone. Labour organised the usual public meetings which proved so popular, that on at least one occasion an overflow meeting was held outdoors. Johnstone, furious that the Government had supported a rival candidate in South Shields responded by supporting Liberal candidates against National Government Ministers in key marginal seats, he opened his headquarters in the town at 28 Fowler Street and undertook several speaking engagements across the Constituency. Johnstone's guest speakers to Constituency – which in March included a visit by Lloyd George – did not worry Ede who told Gompertz in a letter dated 30 October that he did not think any of them '*… carry very heavy guns and certainly none of them are of the calibre of the people who were brought in during the 1931 Election*'. Twenty-nine-year-old Frederick Burden appealed to Ramsay MacDonald to visit South Shields to support his campaign, but MacDonald, facing a tight contest himself in Seaham Harbour, declined.

The General Election overlapped with the Council elections scheduled to take place on 1 November. Gompertz was due for re-election in his Tyne Dock ward, which he won convincingly. Whilst the election produced no changes to the composition to the overall political make-up of the Council, Gompertz would have been encouraged by the large majorities secured for returning Labour Councillors, with Gompertz himself receiving a majority of over 900.

In the autumn of 1935 as general election fever gripped the country, the BUF planned a series of meetings across the North East to be addressed by their leader, Sir Oswald Mosley. Arriving at High Shields Train Station in the heart of the Arab quarter of South Shields on 3 November 1935 Mosley, in black uniform and supported by stewards bussed in from other parts of the country endeavoured to address an audience at the Palace Cinema. There was uproar outside as thousands gathered to protest, with the evitable fighting breaking out between Blackshirts and the hecklers. The meeting was disrupted as mass walkouts occurred during Mosley's speech and fifty hecklers would eventually be ejected. At the end of the rally, as retiring Blackshirts endeavoured to return to their new headquarters at 109 Westoe Road, their buses were subjected to a volley of stones.

Mosley's visit to South Shields compelled Ede to write to the local newspapers on 7 November. Ignoring Mosley's visit and the resultant public disturbances that had occurred, he expressed his support for the '*coloured residents of South Shields*' and advised that during his previous period as the MP for the town he had '… *saw and helped many of the coloured population, if again returned I should welcome further similar chances of usefulness*'.

As Baldwin had hoped, the election was mainly fought on domestic issues, and tight discipline ensured all Ministers addressed the economic situation facing the country with only scant reference being made to international affairs and rearmament. Ede though made clear his opposition to Italian aggression in North Africa and declared his support for the League of Nations. With Clem Attlee acting as caretaker Leader of the Labour Party, following Lansbury's resignation, there was never any doubt that Labour would regain some of its electoral strength lost in 1931. On 8 November the *Yorkshire Post* in its assessment of the forthcoming election predicted that up to five Cabinet Members were in danger of losing their seats, including Ramsay MacDonald in Seaham. They also predicted that the Sir Herbert Samuel, the Leader of the Samuelite Liberals could lose his seat and acknowledged that Harcourt Johnstone was on a Liberal 'danger list' in South Shields.

Ede's campaign was again supported by a number of colleagues from Surrey. The local Branch of the National Unemployed Workers' Movement also offered their support, but records do not indicate if Gompertz availed himself to their services. Gompertz was required though to deal with the Public Assistance Committee who had ceased paying Mrs Mather of South Eldon Street her 5/- out relief because she had received a payment from the Labour Party for allowing a spare room in her home to be used as a Committee Room for the elections. The PAC were unmoved by Gompertz's intervention.

The election result, when it was declared, was a clear win for Ede. He received 22,031 votes, to Johnstone's 12,932 and Burden's 10,784.

Johnstone would eventually re-emerge as the MP for Middlesbrough and a respected hard-working Liberal Minister in Churchill's Wartime Coalition Government. Burden transferred his allegiance to the Conservatives and became the MP for Gillingham in 1950. Nationally Labour did recoup some of its former electoral strength mainly in the industrialised areas, but it was still a comfortable victory for Baldwin. The National Government secured 429 seats, Labour had won 105 seats new seats and now had a Parliamentary strength of 154 gaining over eight million votes. The loudest cheer for Labour supporters though was reserved for Ramsay MacDonald's stunning defeat at Seaham Harbour by Manny Shinwell.

V The Socialist League and Popular Front

1936 commenced with the death of one King and ended with the abdication of another. It was the year in which Italy realised its imperialist ambitions by overcoming Abyssinia; the left-wing Popular Front won the Spanish General Election only for the right-wing Nationalists to plunge the country into a bloody Civil War; Roosevelt won another landslide in the American Presidential Election and the African American Jesse Owens stormed to victory in the Berlin Olympics. Hitler would defy the Treaty of Versailles by invading the Rhineland and the radical militarist, Koki Hirota, would become Prime Minister of Japan; in Greece a right-wing coup would be successfully executed, and in the Soviet Union the first of the Moscow show trials began followed by the first of Stalin's Great Purges; Hitler would form the Rome–Berlin Axis followed by the Anti-Comintern Pact with Japan.

It was an unstable global environment. Historians continue to debate the British Government's attitude to rearmament, but without question it was preoccupied about international events and how to contain the rise of Fascism, with Churchill and others providing a siren voice as to the dangers of German militarisation. The British public on the other hand remained resolute in their determination to avoid war.

Following the decision of the ILP to disaffiliate from the national Labour Party in 1932, left-wing intellectuals established the **Socialist League** as a means of influencing Labour Party policy after the previous year's 'Great betrayal' by MacDonald, with the intention of giving the Party a more radical left-wing agenda. The League attracted support from a large minority of former ILP members who were not prepared to jettison their membership of the Labour Party and the League formally affiliated to the Labour Party in September 1933.

The League attracted support from Labour Constituency Delegates at that year's Labour Party Conference who were still reeling from the scale of their 1931 election defeat. The League's supporters achieved some early policy successes at the Labour Conferences of 1932 and 1933 but they had no lasting effect and the success was not repeated. Sections of the Labour movement leadership, principally Trade Union leaders, regarded the League as a divisive force with a reputation for extremism and dogmatism, and the decision by the League to allow into membership a former Communist in April 1933 served to confirm suspicions that the League was becoming a front to infiltrate the Labour Party for the purpose of turning it into a vehicle for Revolutionary Socialism. A rear-guard action was undertaken to not only curb the League's influence, but also to overturn their previous Conference policy successes.

In January 1937 the League joined with the ILP, Communist Party and other assorted left-wing groups to issue a *Unity Manifesto* calling for a joint front against '*Fascism, reaction and war and against the National Government*'. But their decision to work with the Communists was an act of political hara-kiri. The Labour Party responded immediately by proscribing the Socialist League and declaring that membership of the League was incompatible with membership of the Labour Party. By May, accepting that their membership of the Labour Party was in jeopardy a special conference of the Socialist League accepted its own leadership's recommendation and dissolved the organisation.

Within South Shields the Socialist League asked for permission to affiliate a local branch on the basis of fifteen members, but the influence of the League locally was negligible. Gompertz did attend one League Regional Conference in Newcastle in September 1935, the subject matter discussed was the need for action to create mass resistance to war, but given the radical agenda promoted by the League it is doubtful Gompertz, as Secretary of the local Party, would have given much leverage to correspondence received from them. There is no evidence that the local Party during the whole time of the League's existence undertook any joint campaigning or public meetings with them.

As a hardened anti-Communist, Gompertz maintained his opposition to any attempts to associate the Labour Party with the Communist Party. He was adamant that a planned demonstration on 16 August 1936 organised by the Labour Party against the UAB and the Means Test should not involve members of the local Communist Party or the Unemployed Workers' Movement. Pearson defiantly demanded that they should be included arguing that the Miners would not attend if the role of both organisations was not recognised. The meeting voted heavily against Pearson.

VI

The failure to provide new investment with the resultant new employment opportunities, meant that unemployment would continue to rise across Tyneside. By July 1932, with the failure to secure new Naval contracts, the Palmers Shipyard in Jarrow, which at its peak at the turn of the twentieth century employed over 10,000 men and boys, was insolvent and by June 1933 the company called in the receivers. The effect on Jarrow was devastating, unemployment reached over 80 per cent in the town and Ellen Wilkinson was moved to describe Jarrow as *The Town that was murdered*. As the Labour Party General Election candidate for Jarrow, Wilkinson led a deputation to see Ramsay MacDonald at his Seaham constituency in 1934 to no avail. When Baldwin's promise of a steelworks failed to materialise after the 1935 General Election, the town organised a petition to take to Parliament to press the Government for an interventionist strategy for the area.

South Shields Labour and Trades Council were asked to help with collecting names for a petition calling for '*The right to work*' and demanding that a promised new steelwork be built in Jarrow. The Jarrow Town Council had decided to send 200 men on the 291-mile march to London to present the Petition to Parliament. Appeals were made for donations to prevent the marchers being required to seek relief from the PAC during their absence from the town.

The Jarrow March took place between 5 October and 31 October 1936 beginning with a Church Service and was very much a cross-Party initiative with the Conservative Jarrow Councillor Suddick and the Labour Agent for the town, Harry Stoddart being the advance column seeking support from towns where the marchers would remain overnight. The March was not officially supported by the national Labour Party, who had become distrustful of hunger marches organised by the National Unemployed Workers' Union. However, the Jarrow March was not Communist inspired, indeed it is unlikely any of the marchers were Communist, there were no political slogans nor red flags and it was most definitely **not** a hunger march, these were proud Jarrow men demanding support from the Government for the right to provide for their families. Over 20,000 of their townsfolk turned out to wish them well as they started on their journey.

Whether the Jarrow Crusade was a success is open to conjecture, Government Ministers refused to meet the men when they arrived into central London led by their fiery red-headed MP, but their principled and well-disciplined march to London had raised the plight of the town throughout the country. In a Parliamentary debate on 4 November when Wilkinson presented their petition to Parliament she cautioned that given world events, the Nation would regret the dismantling of an important shipbuilding facility, whilst Chuter Ede replied that the Government's inaction was an affront to the national conscience.

Ironically it would take a war to change the town's employment fortunes.

VII Gompertz under attack

Gompertz faced challenge within the South Shields Labour and Trades Council in early 1936 when the local Trade Union branches insisted that 'card votes' should continue to operate when contentious issues were being debated in Labour and Trades Council meetings. The card vote enabled a Union branch to cast a bloc vote of its entire membership affiliated to the local Party. Gompertz was anxious to end the practice preferring a delegate system which afforded fair representation between the Unions and the Individual Labour Party branches. He sought advice from Labour headquarters as to the local Party's Constitution and was advised that 'card votes' were unconstitutional and the operation of such should cease immediately. Union delegates were in uproar. Procedural points of order dominated proceedings at every meeting the issue was discussed, and a demand that if card votes ceased, then the trade union branches should be entitled to additional delegates. The Party agreed to the request.

The growing Labour Group continued to face its own challenges in maintaining discipline and encouraging Councillors to attend their meetings to agree a common line for Council meetings. Dunlop's continued refusal to attend either the Labour Group or vote with them resulted in his expulsion from the Labour Group in July, he promptly wrote to Gompertz resigning from the Labour Party. The split was made permanent when Dunlop refused to vote for Gompertz to become the Chair of the Council's Finance Committee following the local elections in November 1936, Gompertz lost ten votes to eleven. Gompertz, the political tribalist would have regarded Dunlop's actions as treacherous.

Gompertz himself could be prone to theatrics, he was stubborn and forthright. Complaints from the Tenants' Defence League to Ede in September 1936 that Gompertz had been '*discourteous*' to them in a meeting, saw Ede ask two senior Councillors to review the matter on his behalf. Attempts were made at the September meeting to have Gompertz send a letter of apology to the Tenants' Defence League, but the motion was decisively defeated, and the matter was dropped. In October Gompertz caused a further stir when he advised the local Party that he was resigning from both the Labour Group of Councillors and the Council unless the Group gave an apology and a satisfactory explanation for not supporting him in the September Borough Council meeting. Gompertz had initially received the Labour Group's support to question the expenses of his nemesis Moderate Councillor Bainbridge, but when Gompertz raised the issue in the Council meeting he failed to find a seconder. Given Gompertz was frequently in the Moderate Group's firing line, and he usually undertook to harass the Moderates on controversial issues, he viewed the failure of the Labour Group to support him as a slight and an embarrassment. The Group Officers duly met the Party, pleaded that there had been no intended insult to Gompertz and explained that the Group usually left it to mover of a motion to find their own seconder. Gompertz rescinded his resignation threat.

The Royal Commission examining whether there should be a single Tyneside Authority continued its deliberations with Public Hearings being held in Newcastle over the course of 31 March until 2 April 1936. Gompertz was asked by South Shields Council if he would give evidence on behalf of the Labour and Trades Council. Appearing before the Commissioners, Gompertz was his usual combative self, and argued that a single Tyneside Authority with an administration based in Newcastle would create '*Vassal Boroughs*' and would be viewed with the utmost abhorrence by the organisations he represented. Commissioners advised that they could not look at the politics of the new arrangements, only whether public services would be more efficiently delivered with one single Authority, Gompertz accused the Commissioners of being biased against South Shields to which his comment was ruled out of order. Whilst one Local Government Commission was in progress, another came to an end with the creation of new Urban District Councils across the country which saw the South Shields Rural Council abolished and Boldon

UDC created with the resultant change in boundary between South Shields County Borough and Boldon.

Gompertz was recognised as the face of the South Shields and Trades Council but his formal position as Agent to Ede required approval from the Party at election time, and his Secretaryship of the Party and Trades Council was always subject to potential challenge at their respective Annual Meetings. In 1936, Gompertz and his allies sought to consolidate his position by merging the roles and appointing him as the full-time organiser of the local Party under the terms of employment applicable to National Agents of the Labour Party.

The move was supported by Ede who in February advised the Party that he would contribute £100 to the annual salary of the organiser, so long as the Agent and Secretary's positions were merged. The Executive supported the move, but the proposal was rejected at the subsequent meeting of the Party delegates who were not prepared to forego any control over the Secretaryship. Ede wrote to the Party withdrawing the £100 annual grant proposal in March at which the Miners' delegate, Bill Blyton moved that the correspondence be duly noted.

There were clear tensions in the local Party. The Miners' Lodges evidently took exception to Gompertz's growing influence even to the point of rejecting his attempts to establish an approved list of potential candidates for Municipal office. A Marsden Miners' delegate called Mr Ramsey certainly disapproved of Gompertz's style. Minutes note Ramsey's frequent querulous interventions with repeated attempts by him to overturn decisions of the Executive Committee. In June as the Party noted with thanks a £25 grant from the DMA, Ramsey advised that the grant had been late arriving because his own Marsden Lodge had resisted it, and that the Party should not expect to receive such a sum of money in the future. By July Gompertz was advising the Party that the Marsden Miners' Lodge's affiliation fees had still to be paid.

A Round Table Conference in September was convened between the Marsden, Boldon and Harton Miners' Lodges, the National Agent of the Labour Party together with senior Officers of the local Party, including Gompertz but the meeting did not resolve matters, with Ramsey being warned that his disruptive behaviour would be conveyed to his Union Lodge.

By October, the National Union of Labour Organisers and Agents requested permission to meet the Constituency Party and Ede wrote to the Party encouraging them to resume negotiations with regards financial matters. The saga continued into 1937, with the January Annual Meeting of the Party agreeing that they would conform to the regulations and wages governing the employment of a full-time Agent, that they would accept Ede's offer of a £100 annual grant towards the cost and that Gompertz would be appointed Secretary and Agent. Only two delegates opposed the move, but crucially before the debate commenced, the Miners' delegates walked out of the meeting. Union delegates were so incensed that the decision had been taken in their absence that at the February 1937 Labour Executive meeting a branch of the National Union of Railwaymen (NUR) gave notice of a motion seeking a full delegates' meeting with the intention of reversing the decision.

Gompertz was not quiescent and frantically organised support to resist the NUR motion and at a heavily attended delegates' meeting in March he was required to intervene in a heated meeting to correct what he regarded as some misunderstandings. The Miners' delegates including Blyton and Ramsey demanded that the decision be reversed, Gompertz in retaliation arranged for a series of supporters to oppose the motion. Following an extension of Standing Orders to allow the debate to continue, Gompertz and his allies convincingly defeated the NUR motion.

The manoeuvrings were not without rancour or bitterness, with Gompertz feeling compelled in December 1937 to make a personal statement to the Party that: *'I will tolerate no longer these constant attacks upon my veracity and integrity, I demand that the vendetta against me shall cease'*.

Critically, negotiations with the National Union of Labour Organisers and Agents must have agreed that the appointment of a full-time Agent did not mean Gompertz would automatically be the Constituency Party Secretary because at the January 1938 Annual Meeting he was opposed for the Secretary's position by the Boldon miners' delegate, McAnany. Gompertz easily won the election, fifty-seven votes to eighteen and until the fatal 1960 Annual Meeting of the South Shields Labour and Trades Council, he was never again opposed for the Secretary's post.

With the constant constitutional navel gazing occurring within Labour's ranks, it was with some astonishment that the November 1936 municipal election produced their most impressive electoral performance to date. Nationally, Labour suffered net losses, but in South Shields they overturned the Moderates in four wards, with Bill Blyton securing Tyne Dock, leading to them holding a Labour Group strength of twenty-five Councillors to the Moderates' twenty. This was offset by the Moderates holding ten Aldermanic seats to Labour's five, a statistical stalemate. The retirement though of any Aldermen would give Labour control since Aldermen could not vote on such appointments. In a show of strength and recognising the Mayor had a casting vote in the event of a tied vote on the floor of the Chamber, the Labour Group broke with the 'gentleman's agreement' on the Mayoralty (which asserted it should be rotated between the political groups) and nominated Charles Smith against their bête noire the Moderate Edwin Thompson. In a shock result, Labour won the Mayoralty (and the crucial Mayor's casting vote in the event of tied vote) courtesy of a renegade vote from a Moderate Councillor John Openshaw. Within days Openshaw was expelled from the Moderate Municipal Association and would eventually seek membership of the Labour Party. Gompertz secured the Vice Chairmanship of the Watch Committee.

With the political arithmetic in disarray, Gompertz took the opportunity to change one previous decision of the Moderate-led Council, a new housing scheme for Horsley Hill. The Council had previously agreed to sell the land to the Northeastern Housing Company but Gompertz was anxious for the Council to build the homes. In December, in a close vote – twenty-eight votes to twenty-five – the Council overturned the previous commitment and agreed that 650 homes would be constructed, maintained and managed by the Council.

In the face of a well-organised Labour group, fatal cracks were beginning to appear in the Moderate Association's ranks.

Chapter 12

The Road to War

I

Following the abdication crisis and the Coronation of George VI, Baldwin, by now worn out, stood down as Prime Minister in May 1937 and was replaced by Neville Chamberlain. In domestic policy Chamberlain was determined to pursue the social reform agenda which had optimised his time as Health Secretary. Modest reforms followed, the 1937 Factories Act which improved working conditions and limited the working hours of women and children; the 1938 Coal Act which allowed for the nationalisation of coal deposits; the Holidays with Pay Act of 1938 and the Housing Act of the same year which encouraged further slum clearance and maintained rent controls. Attempts to raise the school leaving age and reform local government further were shelved on the outbreak of war.

It was foreign policy which would define his Premiership; with the country still fearful of war, he continued a policy of appeasement, seeking to develop diplomatic relations with the European dictators, believing that the restoration of some of Germany's former colonies would pacify Hitler and encourage the Third Reich to become a stable partner in Europe. It was a strategy which had immense public support and was lauded in the media with Chamberlain being showered with gifts from a grateful public.

As history records, it would prove to be a mis-guided policy which would lead to a military ill-equipped Great Britain declaring war on Germany in September 1939.

II

As earlier recorded, the South Shields Labour and Trades Council spent most of 1937 concerned with internal constitutional issues over whether to merge the Agent and Secretary's role and whether to accept Ede's financial support for the full-time position. However, the ongoing Spanish Civil War did see them register a protest to the Government against any attempts to recognise Franco as the Spanish Head of State and demand that Britain should break diplomatic links with Italy given its decision to send troops to Spain. The Communist inspired *International Brigade* recruited volunteers to fight for the Republican Government in Spain, and although local Party Minutes do not record any discussion on this point, the author Nigel Todd records in his book, *In Excited Times*, that at least two South Shields men died in battle in Spain.

Within the Town Hall – given his own experiences of birching during his imprisonment as a conscientious objector – Gompertz used his new Council position as Vice Chair of the Watch Committee to press for the abolition of the birching of juveniles. In March 1937 the Party agreed to write to the Government supporting the Home Secretary's Departmental Committee under Edward Cadogan which was investigating the use of corporal punishment in the penal system. Arguing that the practice should be banned, the Council maintained that the punishment did not act as a deterrent and the physical torture created an '*anti-social feeling in the boy*'. The motion had been precipitated by the so called '*birching error*' case in which a nine-year-old boy was ordered to be birched by South Shields Magistrates in October 1936 leading to a Home Office Inquiry. The Report raised the issue that the boy's body was marked with an old appendicitis scar of only twelve months' standing, as a weal occurred across the scar during birching, questions were asked of the doctor's present whether this was likely to cause any serious injury, they advised it would not.

Gompertz was horrified by the incident, in an interview with the *Daily Herald* in April 1937 he remarked: '*Whether any serious injury has been caused is a matter which only time will reveal. One thing is definite, and that is that greater pain than was warranted was caused through this birching error.*' He demanded, and received assurances, that measures would be implemented to prevent the recurrence of such an event, but Gompertz was adamant that birching, as a form of punishment, should be outlawed. On 25 October 1937 he journeyed to London to appear before Cadogan's Committee urging them to ban the birch, whilst the Committee's finding did indeed conclude that birching did not act as a deterrent, Parliamentary time, during the War, meant that the practice would not be abolished for juveniles in the UK until 1948 when Ede was Home Secretary.

Regionally, the Royal Commission examining whether to create a single Tyneside Authority reported their deliberations to the Government in early

1937. The recommendation was very much of the view that the Tyneside conurbation would be better served with a single Authority, the South Shields Labour Party made clear their opposition to the proposals to the Minister of Health and Ede. The onset of War would prevent the proposals being fully debated in Parliament and the post-war Labour Government, probably understandably given Ede was the Home Secretary, did not pursue the matter further.

III The Moderate citadel falls

The elevation of the Mayor, Labour's Charles Smith to the Aldermanic Bench necessitated a by-election in his Deans Ward seat. The election in early July 1937 saw Frank Lawrence comfortably retain the seat for the Labour Party. With the victory in the Deans Ward and the erratic voting record of the renegade Moderate Councillor Openshaw from the Harton Ward, the Labour Group now had the numerical majority in the Chamber, but until the Annual Council meeting met in November, they would not be able to make any radical changes to the Chairmanships of the powerful Council Committees. They faced the 1937 November municipal poll with extreme confidence and Gompertz encouraged the Party to establish an election fund which raised financial support from their Trade Union and Women Section affiliates during the year to cover the cost of the election. When the polls closed, with a 51 per cent turnout across the town, Labour had secured a further gain in the Deans Ward, with the successful candidate being the Party Chairman James Hardwick. Although the renegade Moderate, Openshaw, seeking election as an Independent lost in his Harton Ward, Labour's position was strengthened by the prolonged absence of a Moderate Councillor from the town. Further, the death of long-serving Moderate Alderman Lawlan, meant that Labour was able to nominate one of their own, (Councillor Bradley) to the Aldermanic Bench at the November Council meeting giving them a clear majority on the floor of the Chamber.

It had been a long journey to secure municipal victory.

Since the election of the first working-class man to the Council, the early ILP pioneer, John Lisle in Laygate in 1892, they had sought to encourage candidates, maintain the momentum for victory in the face of decades of defeat, dealt with repeated internal difficulties, endeavoured to create a Labour Group which would act cohesively, and encouraged supporters to see themselves as Labour Party representatives, as opposed to representing their individual Trade Union. In so doing, they had smashed the glass ceiling by supporting the election of the first woman Councillor and ensured working-class representatives could ascend to the Aldermanic Bench and the Mayoralty. During those decades stalwarts had come and gone, many never to see either Ede's Parliamentary victory or Labour emerge victorious in the Municipal battle for control of the Council Chamber. The local stalwarts could allow themselves a brief period of rejoicing with a victory dance held at the Crown Rooms.

The Labour Group needed to reinforce their dominance in the Chamber and did so by nominating Bob Bradley, a miner, as Mayor, ignoring repeated calls from the Moderates to adhere to an unwritten agreement to rota the Mayoralty between the two Parties. Labour argued that Bradley had been a member of the Council since 1919 and to deny him the Mayoralty would be churlish. Bradley easily defeated the Moderate nominee. As the spoils of war were debated, Gompertz became Chair of the powerful Finance Committee and a Member of the influential Parliamentary, Trade and Commerce Committee and was proposed as the Council's representative to future regional meetings discussing the Royal Commission on the Unification of Tyneside Areas. The Moderates, still reeling from their loss of power were determined to block Gompertz saying his name was '... *a laughing stock ...*' amongst regional delegates and suggested that the Moderate Ald Chapman should attend future meetings instead. Gompertz was comfortably elected to the new post.

Gompertz was justifiably proud of Labour's electoral success. As the Secretary/Agent he had coordinated the campaign, raised the finance, developed the strategy, ensured candidates were in place and maintained effective dialogue with Trade Union affiliates so that they felt ownership of the process. Gompertz however was clear that in controlling the levers of power in the Town Hall, the Labour Party needed to be above reproach and his uncompromising views on the recruitment practices in the Council led to further disagreement between Gompertz and leading Labour Councillors.

The continuing Municipal success for the Labour Party across the country, saw them assume control of a number of Councils for the first time, and nationally, the Leadership wanted to ensure that such control was exercised in an open and transparent fashion. Central to this was the appointment of Public Officials. Concerned to always maintain probity, the Labour MP Herbert Morrison, the recognised force behind Labour's stunning success on the London County Council and the corresponding London Boroughs, issued a memo in early 1937 giving salutary counsel to his colleagues against arrogance and inappropriate conduct in the appointment of Public Officials. Cautioning against '*jobbery*' he insisted that there should be no undue influence in appointments and that relatives of Councillors, however worthy their merit, should not be appointed to any post within the Town Hall lest any such appointment be misinterpreted by the public.

South Shields Council was not insulated from allegations of malpractice. At the Council's meeting in October 1937, Moderate Alderman Chapman, with one eye on the Municipal polls in November, in an act of calumny alleged that Labour Councillors were using their influence to secure employment for friends and family members. Gompertz was furious, given the Moderates had controlled the Authority for decades he responded that: '… *if a list of corporation employees could be drawn up the ears of most members of the Council would burn.*'

Whilst Chapman's attacks did not affect Labour's election success in the November poll, the fact that the Party had secured a majority in the Chamber spurred Gompertz to seek changes to the Council's Constitution in relation to public appointments. At the November 1937 Labour Party Executive Committee immediately following the elections Gompertz proposed a new Council Standing Order which would prevent any relative of a Member of the Council being eligible for appointment to employment within the Council and that the canvassing for or by any candidate seeking employment would be prohibited. The proposal was agreed but needed ratification by a meeting of all the Party delegates. The subsequent Party delegates' meeting, whilst sympathetic to the intention behind the proposal, believed it was intrinsically unfair to Councillors relatives who may be well qualified for employment and would actually discourage Labour members from seeking elective Office. A compromise was agreed that no Councillor should serve on an appointment panel at which a relative was being interviewed and canvassing by either the applicant or Councillors would be prohibited.

The compromise did not satisfy Gompertz. At the next Party meeting in December, he presented correspondence from Labour's General Secretary JS Middleton complete with a memo in line with one produced by Herbert Morrison, making clear the Party's expectations of local Councils in Labour control in relation to the appointment of Councillors' relatives. The local Party was unmoved and rejected by a heavy majority an Executive recommendation that the Labour Group should follow the instruction from Head Office. Acrimony followed with some delegates accusing Gompertz of artifice by conspiring against the previously agreed compromise by writing to the General Secretary, Gompertz denied the allegation and made several comments which infuriated some delegates who demanded he apologise.

Gompertz during 1937 was under sustained attack from some delegates over his attempts to create the full-time role of Agent/Secretary and briefings against him were almost constant during the year to such an extent that he was moved to make a personal statement at the December Labour Party meeting, referred to earlier, at which he demanded that the vendetta against him must cease. He apologised if he had offended anyone at the previous meeting but maintained he would continue to protest nepotism in the Labour Party, it had, he stated, become '*intensified*' since they assumed control of the Council and he would take every endeavour to '*stamp it out.*'

Gompertz's firmness on the recruitment issue would see the March 1938 meeting of the Borough Council agreed the changes to Council Standing Orders as recommended by the local Labour Party.

IV 'To save Spain is to save Britain'

By 1937 Germany and its allies were leading the world into war, in March 1938 it annexed Austria into the Third Reich, in 1937 Japan invaded China, Italy consolidated its hold on Abyssinia whilst Franco and the Nationalists continued their onslaught against the Republican Government in Spain.

Ede, who had visited Austria in 1937, warned the Commons that following the Anschluss Czechoslovakia would be next, whilst the DMA with the Labour Party's support organised a rally in the South Shields Market Place in March on the question of 'Peace and Security'.

The brutal suppression of democracy in Spain was the issue which preoccupied left-wing activists across the country. With daily news of brutal murders and indiscriminate bombing of Republican-supporting towns, activists organised campaigns to provide food and medical aid for Spain. During the whole of 1938, the South Shields Labour and Trades Council undertook efforts to support the Republican cause. In January they were engaged in a '*Milk for Spain*' campaign which involved the purchase of tokens through the Co-operative Societies; they raised a collection in February for medical aid; a mass rally was organised for Easter Sunday in April which '*condemned the unjust, iniquitous and intolerable policy of non-intervention in Spain. We are in full agreement with the appeal of the Spanish Government to the British people to end non-intervention which ensures that the German and Italian armies of invasion shall decide the fate of Spain*'; in July they were organising with the local Picture Hall to screen the pro-democracy film *Blockade*, whilst an appeal in the *Shields Gazette* for '*Food for Spain*' saw townsfolk donating over 400 tins of supplies to the Labour Hall in Laygate Lane.

Rank and file members of the Labour Party across the country were valiant in their efforts to raise vital aid for Spain, but their national leadership was more ambivalent in its support with elements within the leadership concerned that the United Kingdom was not ready for war, leading to an ambiguous position being adopted at the 1936 Labour Party Conference in Edinburgh which supported non-intervention and an arms embargo for either side of the civil war. As the situation became more desperate for the Republicans in Spain Herbert Morrison attempted to have the Labour Party's position changed at the January 1937 meeting of the National Executive Committee, with a proposal that the British Government should be pressed to allow the exportation of arms to the Republican forces – the proposal was defeated. With the country still opposed to rearmament at home, the Labour Party gambled that they could not argue '*arms for Spain, but no arms for Great Britain*'. In the face of rank-and-file pressure, and with Attlee himself believing that Spanish democracy needed to be saved, Labour's conference in the summer of 1938 in Bournemouth agreed that if there were further violations of League of Nations resolutions by the Nationalists in Spain then they would support an end to the non-intervention policy and support direct aid to the Republican Government.

Sir Stafford Cripps the MP for Bristol, a former Solicitor General and a member of Labour's National Executive Committee began calling for a **United Front**, which would unite centre and left-wing factions into joint action to defend Spain and defeat Chamberlain's National Government. The proposals met with decisive rejection from the Labour leadership, principally because such a move would require cooperation with the Communist Party. Nevertheless, Cripps Chaired a conference in defence of Spain in the Queens Hall, London on 23 April attended by over 1,800 delegates representing over 1,200 affiliated organisations issuing the rallying cry: '*To save Spain is to save Britain*'. Gompertz attended the Conference on behalf of the South Shields Labour and Trades Council. The Conference demanded that both the Labour Party and TUC convene emergency conferences in order to raise the plight of Spanish Republicans. In an agreed conference resolution, they stated that the strategic safety of France, Great Britain, the Commonwealth as well as democracy itself depended upon the defeat of Franco's Fascists.

They demanded that the Government supply food, medical equipment and anti-aircraft guns to the Republicans whilst also insisting the Republicans should be allowed to purchase arms from Great Britain in the defence of their citizens.

Following the conference, the South Shields Labour and Trades Council wrote to both the Labour Party and the TUC supporting calls to convene respective conferences of their organisations – both organisations refused the request, the National Government maintained its non-intervention strategy, despite Franco receiving military aid from Germany and Italy. The local Party held a further town meeting in the Market Place on 29 May on the question of Spain with Republican flags fluttering from the Town Hall steps. Gompertz also maintained correspondence to the local newspaper attacking Fascism, on 23 May 1938, he wrote in response to the BUF supporting Olive Hawks' claim that under Fascism there would be equality of opportunity. '*Great inequalities of wealth still persist (in Nazi Germany) while the mass of the German workers suffer a lower standard of living. Men like Krupp von Bohleu [sic], the armaments manufacturer, Fritz Thyssen, steel manufacturer and Carl Bosch, the dye trust millionaire, continue to amass high fortunes*'. But in reality, with the public's antipathy to both war and rearmament both the Labour Party and the National Government were equally as torpid as they were ambivalent.

V

The Nazi invasion of Austria in March was followed by the swift oppression of Social Democracy. The persecution of opponents by the Nazi Party would see Gompertz campaign to save three Austrian Jews from deportation in July 1938. Otto Deutsch (29), his brother Walter (31) and their friend Alfred Mandle (26) were Social Democrats wanted by the Gestapo for crimes against the Nazi state. Smuggled out of Vienna they had crossed Europe to reach Le Havre in France where they were stowed away on the steamer Bloomfield heading for South Shields. Their arrival into the Tyne resulted in them being immediately arrested and detained for a week, with orders issued from the Home Office that they should be escorted to Seaham Harbour to rejoin the Bloomfield, where it was due to sail for Bristol and whereupon the men would be re-arrested before being deported back to Austria.

Their plight aroused the sympathy of the Jewish community in South Shields who urged Gompertz to do all he could to prevent the men being deported. As the three men waited anxiously in custody in Bristol, Gompertz encouraged Ede to raise the issue with the Government, whilst he also reached out to the Jewish community in Bristol. Stafford Cripps, supported by Ede, made urgent representations to the Government not to deport the men. The Home Office was initially unmoved, but with the Jewish community in Bristol assuring the Government that they would financially support the three fugitives until they were able to arrange for their safe passage to another country, the Home Secretary, Sir Samuel Hoare relented.

By the summer of 1938, as Ede had forewarned, Hitler began pressing claims for the Sudetenland in Czechoslovakia. No amount of shuttle diplomacy by Prime Minister Chamberlain would satisfy Hitler's insatiable appetite for more territory. Returning from Munich on 30 September, waving his piece of paper which had agreed the German takeover of the Sudetenland and declaring '*Peace in our time*' Chamberlain was hailed as a national hero for averting war, but the public mood was slowly changing, 15,000 people demonstrated later that day in Trafalgar Square protesting against the Agreement. As history will recall, Chamberlain's time in Number 10 would be at first obsequiously praised and then severely denounced.

Ede asked Gompertz to organise a public meeting at the Pavilion Cinema in Derby Street for Sunday 2 October so that he could speak directly to his constituents on the international situation, such was the demand for tickets that a further 'overspill' meeting was held on the same evening at the St Hilda's Miners Hall in Maxwell Street. To an apprehensive audience of over 2,000 people Ede remarked: '*If we meet here tonight in safety, let us remember that the people of Czechoslovakia paid the price*', the audience burst into applause. Ede's speech, covered extensively by the *Shields Gazette*, was probably the most important he had ever given, in a calm manner, he explained that no one should believe that Britain's issues with Hitler were over, the Munich Agreement would only be binding so long as it suited Hitler. He turned his thoughts to the defence of the realm; he expressed outrage that if war did break out no preparations were being made for the evacuation of children in the North East despite plans being put in place for London.

VI

International affairs may have dominated the attentions of the local Labour Party activists during 1938, but they did still have a Council to guide following their outright victory in the November 1937 Municipal polls. Civic attention was focused on plans for a wholesale slum clearance of the Holborn Riverside, with new emerging housing estates being created on the urban fringe of South Shields. Gompertz travelled to London in November as part of a civic delegation to the Ministry of Transport to discuss once again the issue of a tunnel or bridge across the River Tyne but officials were not only unmoved in relation to financially supporting the scheme they were now suggesting that Jarrow would be a more central location for a Tyne crossing, much to the chagrin of the South Shields delegation.

The need for new housing was always uppermost in the work of the Council with 1938 witnessing a slum clearance programme agreed for Adelaide Street area, Waterloo Vale and Heugh Street as well as further properties across the waterfront Holborn area. There was also the requirement to build schools at Harton for the new Council housing estates, and the Council signed off plans to build 652 new houses at 'Little Horsley Hill' at a cost of £231,689, 3s 0d.

The 1938 November municipal election was a lacklustre and somewhat mundane campaign, surprisingly so given the Moderates were keen to seize back control of the Council. Gompertz once again faced the electors of Tyne Dock, but not before his Labour candidacy was called into question. At the September meeting of the local Party, as candidates were recommended for selection, Gompertz, as he had done so in 1932 and 1935, reasserted that he would follow the Labour whip, but could not, as a conscientious objector, vote for or support war. An attempt by two delegates to remove Gompertz as the candidate for Tyne Dock was rebuffed when the matter went to a full vote of the meeting. Gompertz would go on to comfortably win his seat on the Council and at the Annual Meeting of the Council following the elections Gompertz was once again appointed Chair of the Finance Committee. But it was on the question of the appointment of new Aldermen that caused a storm, and solidified Labour's majority in the Chamber.

In November eight Aldermen were due for reappointment. The local Labour Party wanted to remove all eight and replace them with Labour nominees, a compromise appears to have been reached with the Labour Group to initially appoint only four new Aldermen with the remaining vacancies being completed later in the year. Even so, it meant the removal four long serving Moderate Aldermen. Tactically, the Labour Councillors elevated to the Aldermanic Bench represented safe Labour seats, Simonside, Victoria, Laygate and Rekendyke, and the Labour Group were confident that resultant by-elections would see four new Labour Councillors elected. Despite the Moderate Municipal Association reacting with dismay and threatening to field candidates in the by-elections, they only contested one, Simonside, with the former Labour Party Chairman, Robert Morgan winning a Council seat at his 14th attempt. His victory gave the Labour Group a combined strength of thirty-four, as opposed to the Moderates Group of twenty-four.

Although they would not know it at the time, this would be the last municipal poll the respective parties would contest until November 1945. The South Shields Labour Party would be required to guide the town during war.

VII Popular Front

With the apparent success of the Munich Agreement, Chamberlain's position as Prime Minister was for the moment secure, but world events as they unfolded in 1939 made clear that the country was on a collision course with Nazi Germany. In January Hitler ordered Plan Z which involved a massive increase in German Naval power with the intention to outstrip the Royal Navy by 1944, Franco's Fascist Government was officially recognised by Britain in February, further German territorial demands saw Czechoslovakia cease to exist in March, with Germany demanding and receiving the Memel Territory from Lithuania, Italy invaded Albania in April and Hitler signed a Non-Aggression Pact with the Soviet Union in August. The League of Nations was impotent and weakened even further when Hungary resigned its membership in April, followed by Spain in May. Chamberlain was forced to act, telling a Birmingham audience in March that Britain would not allow German domination in Europe, and in the Commons on 31 March made a pledge that Britain would stand by Poland. In August as tension mounted, Parliament passed the Emergency Powers (Defence) Act, put the Royal Navy on war footing and cancelled all military leave. As the public began to realise conflict was inevitable posters began to emerge around London asking: '*What price Churchill?*' and Chamberlain was pressed to bring him back into Government whilst at the same time Attlee and senior Labour leaders began making clandestine overtures to anti-appeasers within the Conservative Party who accepted that Chamberlain would have to go.

The country awaited Hitler's next egregious move.

During January 1939, to seize the initiative, Sir Stafford Cripps once again resurrected proposals to unite the country against Chamberlain and the National Government, this time though rather than attempting just to unite the left and centre, he called for a **Popular Front** which would include those on the right and dissident Conservatives, with the aim of defeating Fascism and defending democracy. After launching a national petition in *Tribune* newspaper to support the moves, the Labour leaderships response was swift. Cripps, Nye Bevan and George Strauss, the leading Parliamentary lights of the agitation were suspended from the Party and finally expelled. General Election rumours were circulating, and the Labour Party was not prepared to countenance deviance in its electoral strategy with suggestions of links with wayward Conservatives, Liberals and the Communists. The Labour Party front bench also began taking defence issues seriously, urging a firm alliance with France and the USSR as the bulwarks against German aggression.

Ede was totally opposed to the expulsions of those associated with the Popular Front, he wrote to the South Shields Labour Party advising he had made objections to Labour's General Secretary, and the Constituency Party dutifully followed their MP's line in objecting to Cripps expulsion and demanded that Cripps should be given the right of Appeal to Labour's next Annual Conference. Gompertz would have opposed any suggestion of a Popular Front with the Communists, but the support given by Cripps to the three Jewish fugitives from Austria a year earlier would have compelled him to give his personal support to his readmittance into the Labour Party. Bevan and Strauss would within months be back within the Labour fold after giving assurances as to their future conduct, Cripps would not be readmitted until 1945.

Gompertz was elected Chair of the then highly influential North-East Federation of Trades Councils in March 1939, a further indication of his growing standing amongst regional colleagues, but as war became inevitable, Gompertz would once again encourage the local Party to respect the rights of conscientious objectors. In February the Trades Council agreed that their motion to their Annual Conference that year should make clear their opposition to any form of 'industrial conscription' being imposed upon working people. Attempts by Gompertz to have the South Shields Trades Council affiliate to the **No-Conscription League** was defeated at their April meeting, a rare defeat for Gompertz, but he subsequently advised the local Labour Party that he was anxious about conscription and had, without their sanction, arranged a meeting of his own in the Market Place for 30 April. Following the rally, the local press reported that Gompertz had '*caught a chill*' and was required to take some leave of absence.

Gompertz by now fifty-one years old, was clearly under immense mental strain. He continued his work for the Labour and Trades Council, worked full time for Ede and had own civic duties to perform all undertaken prodigiously. In May his workload increased again as Chairman of the Council's Finance Committee when he led a delegation to London appearing in front of Tax Commissioners, contesting a complex Test Case on behalf of more than 200 local authorities into how income tax for Councils should be assessed and whether income tax should be paid with interest paid from borrowed money. Sir Stafford Cripps was engaged to present the case on behalf of the Council.

Adding to the mental strain, Gompertz had fallen badly in King Street in the town centre, in late December 1938 injuring his left leg and shoulder. During a Council meeting in Tynemouth a few days later (discussing the ongoing saga of a proposed Tyne Tunnel), Gompertz felt unwell, staggered back to South Shields Town Hall and was immediately taken home in a car. In March 1939 he was confined to bed for three days and in June, following a visit to the town by the King and Queen, he was required to undergo an operation, the details of the procedure are unknown, but Gompertz advised it was to resolve a *recurring problem* that had remained with him since his fall in December. Following the operation Gompertz recuperated at home during the whole of July and did not return to official duties until mid-August.

The news that Parliament had approved the Military Training Act in 1939 requiring men between the age of twenty and twenty-two to undertake six months' military training would have distressed Gompertz, the invasion of Poland by Germany on 1 September and Britain's declaration of war on the 3 September even more so.

Chapter 13

Defending the Town

I

South Shields was remarkably calm when the outbreak of war was declared. Despite the implementation of the 'blackout' which had been prepared for some months earlier, townsfolk took the news of war with resigned acceptance. When South Shields Trades Council met on 12 September 1939, Minutes record that they merely noted that they would meet every four weeks (as opposed to fortnightly) during hostilities. The passing of the Emergency Powers (Defence) Act, meant that the Government was given almost dictatorial powers over civil life, including censorship, internment powers and the bugging of telephones. A new Ministry took responsibility for supply and food, with local Councils being authorised to organise food distribution locally. Gompertz became Chairman of the pertinent Committee on the Council supervising this work, and by November he felt it necessary to press the Regional Controller to consider establishing early rationing in the town because of the shortage of bacon, butter and ham.

There were two main areas of defence work which required immediate action by the local authorities – and South Shields Council was not lacking in its execution of either duty – Air Raid Precautions (ARP) work and the evacuation of children from urban centres. Over 12,000 school children were to be evacuated to Cumberland and Westmorland, arrangements were swift. On 8 September, parents were instructed to prepare their children for removal from the town with special trains leaving South Shields, High Shields and Tyne Dock stations. On the first day 5,500 children left, followed by over 2,500 the next day. It was a huge logistical operation, but many parents were reluctant to allow their children to leave, resulting in South Shields having one of the lowest percentage of evacuees on Tyneside.

The arrival of urban children to the countryside and the cultural shock which occurred as their hosts were greeted by the poor condition of inner-city children is well documented in other books and does not need to be recorded here, but South Shields Council made an appeal to townsfolk to provide clothing and boots for the evacuees with local collection centres being opened and the Mayor establishing a fund to purchase items of necessary clothing for the children. Being parted from their children was clearly an emotional strain to such a point that many parents, as aerial bombing failed to materialise during the 'phoney war' insisted that their children should be returned. Evacuation arrangements took up a lot of Gompertz's time and in November he visited Workington and reported back that he had contacted over 200 South Shields children who were happy, well cared for and were being treated kindly by the people of Workington. The children were well-fed and receiving full-time education – '*Parents would be very ill-advised to remove them from the safety of Workington and the kindly sympathetic atmosphere which exists there*' Gompertz advised the *Evening Chronicle*. Ede for his part urged the Government to subside rail travel for parents to visit their siblings in the event of the child's illness.

The ARP Emergency Committee under the guidance of the borough's Chief Engineer, John Reid (before he himself signed up for military service), endeavoured to prepare households for potential aerial attack with advice on how to convert outside washhouses and coal sheds into bomb shelters. The Committee commandeered public buildings to be used as first aid centres, canteen facilities and temporary housing accommodation in the event of bombing. The location of South Shields and its industrial base meant that bombardment from the Luftwaffe needed to be taken seriously. The Committee also undertook extensive publicity campaigns seeking volunteers to act as wardens, medical orderlies and ambulance drivers. Gompertz maintained his objection to industrial or military conscription. In May 1939, following objections at an ARP meeting from the Moderate, Col Robert Chapman, that the Council was appointing men of military age to ARP Posts, Gompertz retorted that he would not stand for conscription, prompting Chapman to leave the meeting, he resigned his post as the Chief Air Raid warden for South Shields the following day.

The cost of the defence preparations was of concern not just for South Shields but Local Authorities across the country who were faced with the burden of finding the financial resource to pay for the new equipment such as ambulances as well as items such as uniforms for the new auxiliary volunteers. It was a situation raised in Parliament by Ede as early as August 1939 giving indication of how much preparatory work was being undertaken to defend towns like South Shields even before hostilities had commenced.

II Peace Aims

Chamberlain, who wrote that he believed the war would be over by the following spring, achieved approval ratings in September 1939 of near 70 per cent as the public rallied to him. With Britain entering an exceptionally chilly winter, Labour's leadership was receiving prolonged criticism from its own membership that in the absence of a clear strategy on the terms of a peace settlement they were giving the impression that Attlee and his front bench were supinely supporting the National Government.

South Shields Labour Party shared those concerns, approving a motion circulated by twenty MPs on the need for a clear Labour Party policy on the terms for a negotiated peace. In order to steady the position, and to speak to the country, the national Labour Party held a special Conference in Durham on Saturday 16 December. Gompertz along with Fitzsimmons the Party's Vice Chairman attended the Conference at which Attlee was clear, they were not supporting the National Government – certainly not one led by Chamberlain – but they were supportive of its attitude against aggression. Labour had not forgotten the Government's past failures; nor had it become converted to an unquestioning trust in the same Minister's future intentions. The conference met as the Soviet Union, under the terms of Soviet-Nazi Pact continued its invasion of Finland, which the British Cabinet discussed and considered whether to declare war on the Soviet Union. Attlee was opposed to all aggression whether from the Communists or Fascists and had urged the Government to send military aid to Finland.

For Attlee, and the Labour Party, the publication of their **Peace Aims document** following the Conference was designed to show leadership in a modern age, with a route-map for world peace once the war had been won. The six aims included the principle of abandoning imperialism; European democratic federation; the rights of racial and religious minorities; the right to self-determination and the abandonment of armed force as an instrument of policy, but the war needed to be won first, and there must be no 'dictated peace'. The following day, Ede visited South Shields to address Labour Party members, and whilst condemning the Government for its foreign policy failures, supported the war effort and commended to the local delegates the Peace Aims as set out by Attlee the previous day.

Local Labour activists were incensed when the left-wing *Labour Leader* newspaper in February 1940 included the South Shields Labour Party in a list of organisations opposed to the war, the local Party demanded that the newspaper withdraw their name in a future publication. How the *Labour Leader* came to include South Shields Labour Party in their list was never clarified but some delegates were no doubt suspicious that Gompertz was behind the confusion.

There could be no confusion that the phoney war for townsfolk was at an end when on 11 January 1940 enemy aircraft, probably on reconnaissance over Tyneside, were sighted over the town shortly after 10am. RAF fighters were scrambled and in the ensuring engagement shrapnel fell, damaging at least one house.

It was not South Shields, or even Britain which was to witness the next stage of the German Blitzkrieg. As the British Cabinet dithered over how to execute the war, Norway, within weeks had their ports and airports seized and the neutral country would be on the defensive against German invasion troops. Britain sent military aid, but the invasion was an unmitigated disaster since the Nazis' success would allow the Axis powers vital access to steel supplies. By 5 May, as the Norwegian Government fled to London, Parliament debated the Norwegian crisis during two debates on 7 and 8 May. The Government's seemingly incoherent strategy in conducting the war saw Chamberlain's nominal majority of 213 in a confidence vote reduced to 81 as swathes of backbench Tory MPs vented their anger. On 10 May, unable to command the confidence of the House of Commons; with the Labour Party refusing to serve under him and with the Nazis now attacking the Netherlands, Belgium and Luxembourg, Chamberlain resigned to be replaced by Winston Churchill. Within days, the Labour Party joined a Government of National Unity, Attlee became Deputy Prime Minister and Ede, joining Government for the first time, became the Parliamentary Secretary to the Board of Education.

III

A change of Government could not overnight change the course of war. By 25 June France had fallen, and frantic efforts were made to evacuate what remained of the British Expeditionary Force from the beaches of Dunkirk between 26 May and 4 June. Britain braced itself for possible invasion and faced a Blitzkrieg by the German Luftwaffe during the Battle of Britain. Over the course of two nights, on 21 and 22 June, bombs fell on South Shields landing in Centenary Avenue and Marsden Road, the attack was followed on 2 July with a Dornier bomber releasing bombs over Tyneside, destroying housing and St Bede's School in Jarrow. The resulting fatalities led to criticism as to the lack of air defence for Tyneside and also saw the forced closure of local dance halls at 10pm with a warning that under no circumstances would extensions be granted by the local Council. Still the raids continued, over the course of the evenings of 24 and 25 August fifteen bombs fell across South Shields. Claypath Lane, Derby Terrace, Ponton Street, Redhead Street and Percy Street were heavily affected with hundreds of residents being made homeless, utility services disrupted, and the local gasworks catching fire. Residents opened their homes to their homeless neighbours, whilst the local Council ensured 'feeding centres' were opened – but there would be more devastation to come during the 1941 Blitz.

To Gompertz, as a conscientious objector, war may have been an anathema, but he was determined to defend the residents of South Shields and insisted that more needed to be done to evacuate the high number of children who had not already been transferred to the safety of Cumberland and Westmorland, he also demanded that the Authorities increase their efforts to ensure residents had access to strong shelters from the bombing. The Council undertook a series of meetings across the town urging parents to evacuate their children with the expectation that all children would be transferred by the second week of June. Gompertz spoke at Laygate Lane school, with the Mayor attending every meeting to plead with parents to evacuate their children.

The local newspaper records that during the panic, correspondents were critical of food rationing which had been introduced in January 1940 and in particular the poor quality and high prices of food. As Chair of the local Food Control Committee Gompertz met with officials in almost constant session and was not averse to firing off letters and telegrams to the Minister of Food, Lord Woolton to appraise him of developments in South Shields. When in July 1940 the tea ration in Britain was reduced to just two ounces per week, Gompertz demanded from the Ministry of Food an investigation into the apparent leakage of the news before the official announcement in South Shields, which had resulted in panic-buying across the town. Gompertz also pleaded for the ability to increase the tea ration to three ounces for larger households and those with special diets, but the request was denied.

Gompertz did not always judge the public mood correctly, he supported moves to close the South Shields Market for the duration on the war on the grounds that not to do so would place people in danger and encourage them to purchase commodities they did not need at wartime. His suggestion was heavily outvoted at the August Council meeting with Bill Blyton arguing that until such time as the big shopping centres, cinemas and the dog track were closed it was ludicrous to single out the town's market. By December, the Council voted to support, with opposition from the local churches, the Sunday opening of cinemas in an attempt to maintain the morale of townsfolk.

In August 1940 it was announced by the Harton Coal Company that due to a slump in demand for coal exports – particularly since the fall of France – they would be closing St. Hilda's Colliery, rendering it 'uneconomic', with the loss of 1,000 jobs. Following the closure of St. Hilda's Colliery the men were prevented from undertaking other work of national importance or to seek work in other trades with recommendations from the Local Labour Exchange that they should move to Yorkshire or transfer to other Collieries in the region where there was a shortage of mineworkers. Both Ede and Gompertz raised the matter in mid 1940 with the new Minister of Mines, the Labour MP David Grenfell, in Gompertz's case when the Minister visited Newcastle in October. The Government agreed to instruct Local Labour Exchange's to be flexible in their attitude, but the problem was compounded in September 1941 when Union Official, Bill Blyton, complained that men from the former St. Hilda's Colliery, who had initially found work in munitions factories with a weekly wage of between £5 and £6, had been instructed to report for work at Harton Colliery with a guaranteed weekly wage of £3 9s, despite Blyton claimed, there being no work for them.

IV

Gompertz was anxious that local democratic government should still be maintained and function during the hostilities. Although municipal elections were cancelled with vacancies appointed by Borough Council on the understanding that the retiring members respective Party would be able to fill the vacancy unopposed, the normal running of the Council continued, with new Committees created to ensure the Council could fulfil its obligations in wartime. Gompertz spent more time in the Town Hall in continuous discussions with Officials and in meetings with Regional Civil Servants, determined to secure the best ARP preparations possible for the town and he was involved in bringing together key teams of Officials to execute defence aims for the town. Regular reports in the local media described Gompertz as the '*Leader of the Socialist Group*', and whilst there was no such formal position (nor indeed was there Constitutionally a Leader of the Council), he was clearly seen as the driving force in the Council given his Chairmanship of the predominant Finance Committee and his predominance as the official Council spokesman.

He was also desirous to ensure that the local Labour and Trades Council still functioned effectively, regular meetings were held with full reports and request for guidance on a whole series of issues. He dealt with the thorny issue of Cleadon Park Labour members who – although in the Houghton constituency were under South Shields County Borough for local government purposes – wanted to affiliate their members to South Shields Labour and Trades Council. The local Party agreed, but not before Gompertz (with one eye constantly on the Party's financial position) insisted all Cleadon Park members must pay their fees to South Shields not just a proportion of them, much to the chagrin of the Houghton Party. Gompertz was also in the Police Court in July 1940 when Wright's Biscuits factory was again in front of Magistrates, for a further breach of the Factory Act. A boy had been injured due to their failure to fit a proper gate to a lift, they were fined £20 with costs, and Gompertz immediately requested assurances that the General Workers' Union were taking seriously the unionisation of the employees at the factory, and he even tried, unsuccessfully to ban the purchase of Wright's products by the local Council. Gompertz also demanded and received a commitment from the Ministry of Information that they would establish a local committee in South Shields to coordinate their activities with the local authority; and in relation to fundraising the Party raised funds for new X-ray equipment at the local hospital and gave a donation to Bermondsey Labour Party, whose offices had been badly damaged in a bombing raid. Nearer home, the Landlord of the South Shields Labour and Trades Council, Martins Bank, received support from the Party who established a rota of volunteers to undertake 'fire watch' duties and as a consequence of the growing displacement of families because of the early bombing raids, they asked Ede to press for Local Authorities to receive Parliamentary powers to requisition empty properties to convert into families' homes for those residents affected.

Gompertz's workload for Ede would have increased considerably as war-weary concerned constituents seeking advice and support would have made their way to the Laygate Lane Offices to meet with Gompertz. Of the seventeen Parliamentary seats in the Durham Coalfield only four had full-time agents, of which Gompertz was one. Ede, now a Minister, maintained regular dialogue with Gompertz to appreciate how the town was coping and to raise any issues of concern direct with Ministerial colleagues and he made a further visit to the constituency to address the local Party personally in October. Gompertz's influence was unrivalled, and behind him giving emotional support and encouragement was his wife Annie, who accepted her husband's long absences from home with strict stoicism and devoted recognition that the Labour movement and public service was his life.

V 'All behind you Winston'

Churchill's wartime Ministry has been described by Roy Jenkins as '*One for winning*', with the Labour Party being appointed to senior roles for the duration of war, including Attlee as Deputy Prime Minister, Arthur Greenwood as Minister without Portfolio, AV Alexander as First Lord of the Admiralty, Herbert Morrison as Home Secretary, Ernest Bevin as Minister of Labour and National Service and Hugh Dalton as Minister of Economic Warfare. Although still outside the Labour Party, Sir Stafford Cripps would be appointed Leader of the House in February 1942. Along with Ede, there was also a place for Ellen Wilkinson, as Private Secretary to the Department of Pensions.

The Labour leadership, with one eye on the experiences of Ramsay MacDonald's National Government, was anxious to ensure that the wartime Government had the support of the entire Labour movement. Fortuitously, the Labour Party Conference was due to meet in Bournemouth on 13 May 1940 just days after Churchill's elevation to the Premiership, Attlee received unanimous support. Whatever misgivings the Labour movement may have had about Churchill's past, the defeat of Fascism and Nazism and the defence of the Country took priority.

As history records, at the dawn of 1941, Britain stood alone, the Soviet Union would not enter the war until 22 June when Hitler ordered the invasion of the USSR, and the USA would not declare war until the Japanese attack on Pearl Harbor on 7 December. Defending civilians from air attack, maintaining food supplies and securing a lend lease agreement with the USA to ensure Britain had access to military hardware dominated the work of the Government.

South Shields as a merchant port had over 3,000 men serving in the Merchant Navy whose work was vital in keeping the country supplied. Between 1940 and 1942, 779 British merchant ships were sunk, with the loss of 16,654 lives nearly 49 per cent of the available crews, the losses were staggering, but the bravery of the seamen ensured supplies still arrived. By the end of the war, they had suffered the highest ratio of casualties of any of the armed forces. In recognition of the sacrifice, South Shields to this day continues to hold an annual memorial service to the seafarers at a statue unveiled in their honour at Mill Dam at the mouth of the River Tyne.

VI The Blitz continues

During 1941 almost no area of the town was immune from the bombing, as outlined in Craig Armstrong's book, *South Shields at War 1939–45*, a sustained air raid over Tyneside took place in February as over 100 bombers attacked, a Heinkel bomber was brought down in Beach Road, the blast was so powerful it was heard in Newcastle, devastation befell Brodrick Street, Lawe Road and St Aidan's Road. In April bombs fell on Tyne Dock, commercial sites along the waterfront including the Brigham and Cowan's store, John Readhead's shipyard and Tyne Dock Engineering. Cleadon and Clyvedon Rise received direct hits, but the town centre was hit hardest, fire broke out at South Shields railway station; Westoe Road, Fawcett Street, Mile End Road, Robertson Street and Fort Street were ablaze, with sometimes whole families losing their lives. Harper Street was completely flattened.

Townsfolk rallied as best they could, opening their homes, volunteering to assist at the feeding centres which had opened across the town, supporting the medical services and giving emotional support to those who had lost loved ones. The military services also had to deal with several unexploded bombs, enhancing still further the fear and panic which must have taken hold.

By late April, houses at the junction of King George Road and Lascelles Avenue were destroyed, Green Lane and the Sea Hotel were hit. The authorities had to frantically reorganise how they managed public services in response to the raids and in particular the feeding centres and Gompertz again demanded Parliamentary approval to requisition vacant properties to provide emergency accommodation for homeless residents, while the ARP Committee discussed plans to increase the capacity of the emergency feeding centres to accommodate 10,000 people.

But still the bombing continued, on the night of 30 September and 1 October, bombs fell at Simonside, whilst the waterfront again sustained direct hits with Middle Docks hit by two bombs, Union Alley adjacent to the Market Place was set ablaze, the east side of the Market itself destroyed. Morton Street and Livingstone Street suffered severe property damage and the Shields Gazette offices in Chapter Row had a direct hit, ironically so did the ARP headquarters in Barrington Street. Residents in George Potts Street and Chichester Road lost their lives. Over 300 people were made homeless in this one raid alone.

There was no let-up in the aerial bombardment, the worst attack would come on the following nights during 2 and 3 October. Blanket bombing witnessed South Taylor Street and South Eldon Street suffered a number of fatalities, whilst the docks were again targeted. Oxford Street and Marlborough Street sustained direct hits; Thrift Street was badly damaged the Market Place was the omphalos of confusion following the raid. A number of those sheltering in the Market Place air raid shelters lost their lives, flames spread to the shopping districts as gas mains exploded and overhead wires were brought down, requiring the ARP to call on neighbouring authorities for support. The bombing was indiscriminate, houses in Candlish Street were flattened, in Selbourne Street properties destroyed and there were casualties in Hyde Street and Wharton Street. Street names now long gone suffered bombing, Challoner Terrace East and West, Isabella Street and Derby Terrace as well as Anderson Street, Ogle Terrace and Winchester Street. Over 2,000 people were made homeless, sixty-eight people were killed, the youngest four months, the oldest eighty-seven, scores of townsfolk were injured.

As Craig Armstrong observed, wartime censorship meant news of the raid was muted, but the Northern Regional Commissioner, Sir Arthur Lambert, was advised that the morale of townsfolk was high and industrial output would not be affected.

It seems incredible that in the face of such carnage and destruction, the South Shields Labour and Trades Councils continued to meet, debate and at times argue over procedural points, but such was the wartime spirit and the resilience of the country in the face of bombing, they simply rolled up their sleeves and were determined to continue as normal as possible. Bomb damaged shops proudly announced that they were '*Open for business*' and the Local Authorities endeavoured to clear the debris as quickly as possible and maintain some resemblance of normality.

The local Party refused to support the Communist newspaper, *The Daily Worker* after the Government had imposed a ban on the publication in March, although the Trades Council delegates (not always Labour Party members) registered their disapproval at the censorship, and both organisations made clear that they opposed the enforced Industrial Conscription of women in April. In August after some months of wrangling and repeated reference back to the Constituency Executive, the local Party eventually agreed to adopt a requirement by the national Labour Party that full-time Agents such as Gompertz should be superannuated with the cost borne by the local Party. In September they organised a highly successful public meeting for the left-wing activist Prof Harold Laski, a member of Labour's National Executive Committee who was Secretary to the Party's Committee on Reconstruction. Laski was an unusual choice for such a moderate Constituency Labour Party given his somewhat unorthodox views on the need for a revolution, but Ede had struck up a friendship with Laski particularly around issues on education policy and was no doubt a prime mover in the invite.

In August Gompertz travelled to London for a Trades Council meeting and took the opportunity to meet with Ede to arrange the MPs next visit to the Constituency planned for September, and in October he was back in London at the High Court to present the local authority's continuing case on behalf of 200 Councils in relation to the payment of tax on income Council's received, the judgement went against the Council, with Gompertz immediately announcing they would refer the matter for final decision to the House of Lords.

Despite the bombing, Gompertz was determined his work would continue.

VII Trouble and strife

The loss of so many merchant and naval ships meant that there was huge pressure on the country to replace those lost at sea. There was no shortage of men willing to serve as sailors, but the ships needed to be replaced as a matter of some urgency. The Government encouraged communities to buy into a National Savings Campaign to cover the costs. South Shields unsurprisingly rose to the challenge in January 1942 with the Mayor, Alderman McAnany opening an appeal to raise the sum of £500,000, it was an astonishing sum, and given the demographic make-up of the town, it is with some credit that within weeks they had raised the money and were able to adopt the HMS *Maori*.

As if to remind Tyneside that the Luftwaffe was still able to penetrate their air defences, Westoe Village would suffer enemy attack in April when four bombs fell, one on Fairfield, one on Eastgarth and another in the garden of Chapel House, the final bomb failed to detonate. Thankfully, there were no casualties but there was significant damage to properties.

In May 1942 Gompertz journeyed to Manchester as a member of the national Trades Councils Joint Consultative Committee – a position to which he was formally elected by North East Trades Council. The theme of the Conference was post-war reconstruction and a determination that the mistakes of the peace following World War I should not be repeated. The *Manchester Evening News* carried a frontpage story of the conference with a photograph of Gompertz stood alongside future TUC General Secretary Vic Feather.

Battling for an honourable peace seems to have occupied Gompertz's mind at this time. Following the Trades Council Conference in Manchester and exploiting his Chairmanship of the Government's Ministry of Information Committee in South Shields he began encouraging residents to think about the future.

In July Gompertz chaired a meeting at the Palladium Cinema in Harton under the auspices of the Ministry of Information at which Naomi Jacob, the novelist and actress, gave a talk on *Looking backward and looking forward*, the theme of which was that the mistakes of the peace following World War I should not be repeated at the end of World War II. Given the meeting was sponsored by the Government it was a strictly non-Party political event, but Jacob wanted people to start thinking about how the country should be organised after the war, and that meant ensuring local MPs appreciated the priorities of their constituents. In reference to the seafaring community, she praised the Merchant Navy without whom the country would not have food on the table.

Industrial tensions though surfaced both in the shipyards and within the mining industry. Men were being asked to work longer, and at times their pay did not reflect their commitment to the war effort. For shipyard workers, there was a lack of trust with their employers whom they felt were deliberately misinterpreting official wage agreements, and they also mistrusted their own Union officials to the extent that they simply walked out on an unofficial strike in the Spring 1942, Bevin as Minister of Labour demanded that all sides enter into a binding arbitration at which a compromise on pay rates was agreed. At Whitburn Colliery, 1,500 men and boys walked out in May over their pay and poor working conditions. Once again, the Ministry of Labour insisted on binding arbitration, but it was less successful with the Miners. By June with the men still on strike, Harton Coal Company announced it was impossible for them to maintain operations at Whitburn due to poor production levels and they intended to close down the Colliery.

Whilst production was indeed down, this was the case for Collieries across the country as the industry faced the fatigue of an ageing workforce and there was a lack of nutritional food to sustain energy for such hard manual work.

Although Whitburn was within the Houghton constituency, the men were predominately residents of South Shields – the Marsden Lodge being based in Imeary Street in the heart of the town. Ede on a visit to the town in June met the DMA and was prepared to also meet the Communist Party, Parliamentary questions followed, and an inquiry under the Ministry of Labour was established which dragged on through the summer months until a final resolve was reached in September with the men agreeing to increase production on the strict understanding that their pay rates would be renegotiated by the DMA with the Harton Coal Company. The Colliery remained productive until its eventual closure in 1960.

Whilst the above two disputes were not the only instances of a breakdown in industrial relations in the region – on 5 October the so-called 'Lying on strike' would see 18,000 men from the engineering trades on strike across Tyneside over the calculation of the working week and would not return to work until 12 October – they do give a sense of the frustration of the home workforce – and indeed an ageing workforce – who felt they were not being given due regard when the exigencies of the economy demanded it.

Gompertz himself was frequently in dispute with officialdom. The Ministry of Food would find itself challenged by him following the passing through Parliament of the Food Control Committees (Constitutional) Order 1942 in August. The Order made clear that nominations to local Food Committees – previously the preserve of Local Councils, would in future be subject to final approval by the Ministry of Food. In fairness to the Ministry, Councils across the country were operating different procedures as to who could serve on local Food Committees and the Order endeavoured to remove various anomalies in the appointments procedure. For Gompertz the Order was egregious and an affront to local decision making since he continued to assert it removed the right of the Local Council to determine their own membership free of interference by Government.

South Shields Council in November 1942 agreed to protest to the Government and Gompertz requested that other Councils in the region should be contacted to engage their support. Not only did other Councils in the North East join the protest, but the campaign gained traction across the Country with scores of Councils objecting to their nominations being subjected to final Government sign-off. The dispute would continue into

1943 with Gompertz using his influence within the regional Trade Union movement to encourage them to make their own protests, warning that direct Trade Union representation on the Food Committees could be jeopardised.

The War Office also came under metaphorical fire from Gompertz following their decision to withhold payments of dependants' allowances where employers were voluntarily making up the service pay of employees in the Forces to the amount of their civil pay. At the October 1942 Borough Council meeting Gompertz condemned the Government's actions. He castigated the War Office for the hardship they were causing to the dependants and argued that the employers (including South Shields Council) were carrying a burden which should be borne by the Exchequer. Someone in the town was clearly grateful for Gompertz's support for the service personnel, since at the late October Labour Party meeting it was reported that the Party had received a £5 (worth around £250 in today's prices) anonymous donation in recognition of the work performed by him on behalf of the armed services.

The war of course affected the Labour and Trades Council finances, more so the Trades Council because the Labour Party still received an annual grant of £100 from both the DMA and Ede. The Labour Party Accounts show that Gompertz was receiving a £271 year salary (around £13,100 at today's money) no contribution was made from the Trades Council towards this. The traditional fundraising activities had ceased due to the war, and there was a suspicion that some trade union branches were deliberately affiliating the minimum number of members up to their maximum amount of delegate entitlement, whilst others affiliated a greater number of members even though they received no additional delegates with voting rights at meetings.

During October and November Gompertz was instructed to discuss the matter with those branches believed to be under-affiliating with the main culprits identified as being the AEU and a branch of the Boilermakers' Union. Gompertz was inexorable, in the face of defiance from the Branches to increase their affiliation, the AEU Number 6 branch was expelled from the Trades Council, the Boilermakers Number 3 branch was next, while the AEU number 3 branch resigned from membership before suffering a similar fate, other AEU branches sent letters of protest. The Trades Council was unmoved and Gompertz encouraged Councillors and Alderman to seek a resolve with their respective Trade Union branches. The tactic worked, by April 1943 the expelled Unions had sought readmission to the Trades Council complete with an increase in their branch's financial affiliation fees.

Consequently, Gompertz was able to report to the February 1943 Annual Meeting of the South Shields Labour and Trades Council that there had been a substantial increase in affiliation fees from the Trade Unions, and that he was now turning his attention to increasing individual membership of the Labour Party which currently stood at 186 men and 112 women. He also clearly felt politically secure, since the Minute book now records that he was elected Secretary/Agent of the Labour and Trades Council, the first time such a description appeared at an Annual Meeting, and if any delegate raised an objection, it was certainly not recorded in the Minutes.

Earlier, in December 1942, South Shields Labour Party received the news that the redoubtable William Pearson, was resigning from the Council following his appointment as an Official with the Ministry of Mines; meanwhile another servant, 'Job back' Purvis, who had served in the Boer War and received the DCM as a member of the Royal Army Medical Corps in World War I, died as the New Year unfolded, he had been a Councillor for over twenty years and colleagues had appointed him to the Aldermanic Bench in recognition of his long service to the Council just weeks before his passing. In a sign of the growing influence of women members, Laura Glover would eventually be chosen to fill the St Hilda's Council vacancy in the Town Hall.

VIII Beveridge Report

With the invasion of the USSR and USA entering the war after Pearl Harbor, 1943 would see the tide slowly but inexorably turning as both powers utilised their industrial and military might against the Axis powers. With the Americans landing in Southern Europe, and the Russians defending Stalingrad, the Allied powers would begin their discussions at Casablanca on the eventual invasion of mainland Europe and the defeat of Nazi Germany, which President Roosevelt had agreed was the main priority. Reichsmarshall Göring's once proud boast that no air raid shelters were necessary for the German capital because the Allies would never be able to reach Berlin would hold him up to ridicule as RAF bombers pounded the City on nightly bombing raids. Britain would capture Tripoli; the US Navy would arrive in the Pacific Theater; and the Jews in the Warsaw Ghetto would fight.

Intellectuals began to debate the future of a post-war Britain, on the Left, Victor Gollancz continued to promote manuscripts under his **Left Book Club** publishing group. Before the war books like Orwell's *The Road to Wigan*

Pier and Ellen Wilkinson's *The Town that was Murdered*, graphically illustrated Britain as it was. During the War GDH Cole with his *The Means to Full Employment* and John Strachey, *A Faith to Fight For*, spoke of how the country should be organised, with no return to the Depression of the 1920s and 1930s.

William Beveridge, a senior Civil Servant, published his report on *Social Insurance and Allied Services* in November 1942. Declaring war on the five 'giant evils' of want, disease, ignorance, squalor and idleness, Beveridge recommended that all people of working age should pay a weekly National Insurance contribution which in return would guarantee benefits to people who were sick, unemployed, retired or widowed. He assumed that a National Health Service would underpin the welfare system and followed up his Report with his book, *Full Employment in a Free Society (1944)* which outlined that at the heart of the State's plans should be full employment and that it was the State's responsibility to ensure people's right to work which might require some form of state control of the means of production.

The ideas were radical, and extremely popular, and the public rallied to a blueprint which they felt would secure for them a better future, the TUC demanded Beveridge's Report should be immediately implemented. When the Report was debated in the House of Commons in February 1943, there was uproar on Labour's backbenches as Ministers endeavoured to curtail some of the recommendations contained in the Report. Churchill insisted that no firm commitment could be given until after the war and Herbert Morrison, the Home Secretary, despite his own support for the Beveridge Report, was required to submit to Cabinet collective responsibility and advised the Commons that the Government could, at this time, only commit to sixteen of the twenty-three recommendations in the Report. A rebellion followed with 119 MPs voting against the Government, the biggest rebellion it had faced during the war. Not for the first time, Attlee's Leadership of the Labour Party seemed in peril, a call for unity at a meeting of the Parliamentary Labour Party led Ede to later remark that Attlee, '… *did not make much impression*'.

In South Shields, activists were unimpressed by the behaviour of their national leadership, in February 1943 they endorsed the views of the TUC that the Beveridge Report should be implemented in full, supported those Labour MPs who had rebelled for refusing to countenance any watering down of the proposals and accordingly registered their support by writing to the TUC General Council and the Parliamentary Labour Party. No criticism was levelled at Ede, who as a Minister, would have been required to support the Government.

IX Anglo-Soviet Committee

The Communist USSR may have been Britain's ally in the war against Fascism but the Labour Party always maintained a fervent mistrust of the true intentions of the British Communist Party. As recorded earlier any attempt to link any Communist activity with the Labour Party was ruthlessly supressed by the Labour Leadership, whether it be the Socialist League, the Popular Front, or on the question of the Communist Party being allowed to affiliate to the Labour Party. No one was immune from sanction if they transgressed, even the status of leading and popular figures like Cripps and Bevan did not protect them from being expelled from the Labour Party until assurances given as to their future conduct.

There was always a belief, occasionally genuine, frequently paranoid, that any new political initiative was a Communist subversive plot to infiltrate the Labour Party. The Labour Party made clear to its local Constituency parties that correspondence from the Communist Party should be placed in the waste basket, resolutions which may seek to follow a Communist line should be ruled out of order, the local Party should carefully check any delegation list from a Trade Union least it contained the name of a Communist and any potential subversive activity should be reported immediately to Labour's head office. As we have seen, Gompertz, a hardened anti-Communist followed such instructions with ruthless efficiency.

As the war progressed, there was no let-up in the Labour Party's intolerance of Communist influence, the *People's Vigilance Committee* was denounced as a Communist Front and placed on Labour's proscribed list of organisations ineligible for affiliation, the Labour leadership were keen advocates of the ban on the Communist newspaper *The Daily Worker* (although the 1942 Labour Conference narrowly passed a motion demanding an end of the censorship), and viewed with some concern that by 1941 Communist Party membership had increased to 56,000. An attempt a year later by the AEU Trade Union to have a ban on Communists being delegates to Trades Councils lifted failed, as did annual manoeuvrings to allow the Communist Party the right of affiliation to the Labour Party, even when large Unions like the AEU and the Miners supported such affiliation.

In 1943 Labour's opposition turned to the **Anglo-Soviet Committee**, which the National Agent of the Labour Party, George Shepherd denounced as another Communist-front and advised London Labour Officials that they '... *ought not to be mealy-mouthed in dealing with the Communists*'. When attempts were made to have the South Shields Trades Council affiliate to the South Shields branch of the Anglo-Soviet Committee, the Trades Council Executive recommended no action should be taken, the main delegates' meeting saw a lengthy discussion and the Chair's ruling challenged, but the recommendation of the Executive stood. Next it was the South Shields Labour Party itself who at their February Executive Committee were advised by Gompertz that due to a 1942 Labour Party Conference decision, it was not permitted to associate with the Anglo-Soviet Committee movement and demanded that those Labour Party members in the town associated with it, should take appropriate action to close the branch down. Although supporters of the Committee tried to overturn the Executive's recommendation at their main delegates' meeting, Gompertz, with correspondence in hand from George Shepherd, explained no association was possible, the decision of the Executive was agreed decisively.

The South Shields Anglo-Soviet Committee was not a particularly large membership, it is known that Councillors Hymers, Sutton, Stoker, Brady and Mrs Sutton were members, and they were at pains to explain that the local Committee was not part of any national network and was merely established to show support and raise money for a wartime coalition ally. Gompertz refused to be pacified, the Labour Party Conference was brokering no connection with any organisation that could link the Labour Party to Communists, the NEC report to the 1942 Conference declaring: *'The Communist Party of Great Britain ever ready to create trouble whatever the conditions, has not hesitated to exploit friendly Anglo-Russian relations for purely Party aims.'* Organisations like the Anglo-Soviet Committee were ancillary organisations designed by the Communists to '... *lure all and sundry into their net*'. Clear instructions were given that friendship with Russia did not require friendship with the Communist Party.

The Councillors agreed to sever their links and the branch folded.

Bill Blyton from the Harton Miners' Lodge was also held to account at the September Labour Party meeting over his association with a South Shields Communist Party public meeting called to discuss *'The health of the people'*. Blyton, who was now seeking a Parliamentary seat for himself, was careful not to fall foul of the Labour Party constitution, explained that the DMA's support for Communist Party affiliation to the Labour Party at the 1943 Labour Party Conference, led him to believe it was acceptable to address such a meeting, but given sensitivities he was prepared to withdraw his name. Councillor Garnett thought the move out of order, remarking that the Communists were active, the Labour Party seemed dormant and advised he had every intention of attending the meeting and allowing his name to be associated with the event.

The year 1943 would prove to be the high-water mark of Communist potential within the Labour Party, subsequent Conference rule changes meant that the issue of their affiliation could not be debated for a further three years, and Labour's leadership tightened their grip on Constituency Parties allowing no cooperation or any form of electoral pact with local Communist Party branches.

X

The tenacious Gompertz would continue his opposition to the Food Control Committee 1942 Order which allowed the Ministry of Food to have oversight of nominations submitted for membership. In March 1943 at a meeting of the North-East Federation of Trades Councils he lambasted Lord Woolton for seeking to have 'dictatorial powers' and urged the TUC General Council to intervene fearing that attempts would be made in future to exclude Trade Union representation. The representations the Food Ministry were receiving from Councils across the country clearly had some impact since they were forced to clarify their position. The Ministry pointed out that the reasoning behind the Order was to prevent any recurrence of the difficulties which had arisen previously when persons had been appointed either as trade or consumer members and were not eligible to act in those capacities. Consequently, it had been necessary for the Ministry to issue a direction for their removal from the affected Food Committee. The Minister explained that he had therefore thought it desirable that before any person was formally appointed, every possible step should be taken to ensure that the names of nominees who are ineligible would be eliminated from the lists before appointments were made. In all such cases, the local authority concerned, not the Ministry, would be given the opportunity to substitute the names of persons qualified to fill the vacancies. The Minister also pointed out the Food Committees were not a Committee of the local Council, rather they were a devolved administration acting under the powers assigned to them by the Government.

This was one battle Gompertz would not win, but he was more successful in the House of Lords in August 1943 over the campaign he was waging on behalf of 200 Councils over the issue of whether Municipal trading undertakings should be assessed separately or as a whole for the purpose of

Income Tax. The Councils maintained they should be assessed collectively. The Lords upheld Gompertz's Appeal against the Crown, which would save the Councils £500,000. Gompertz graciously congratulated the Council's Town Clerk, Harold Ayrey, who he explained had undertaken the necessary detailed work in connection with what had become a long drawn-out point of Law. Nevertheless, Gompertz was the political driving force and had encouraged other Councils to join in the legal action leading the *Newcastle Journal* to observe that since his election in 1932, Gompertz, '... *has proved himself to be a tough opponent and a most candid critic on several occasions. Civic affairs in the Borough have felt the impulse of his energy.'* In recognition of their work the Town Clerk was awarded 500 guineas and the Treasurer 250 guineas by the Council, Gompertz received a vote of thanks.

South Shields suffered its final major raid over the night of 23 and 24 May 1943, as Craig Armstrong records the raid came at 3 am with bombs falling on Dean Road, Hepscott Terrace, Marsden and Stevenson Streets. Marsden Street suffered the worst damage, a close-knit community on the built-up John Clay Street housing estate, 300 people were made homeless with twenty-eight residents losing their lives, including members of the emergency services.

XI

Papers released by the United Nations in 2017 confirmed that as early as December 1942, the US, UK and USSR authorities were aware not only of the scale of persecution of European Jews but also of the methods being deployed by the Nazis under their 'Final Solution' plans. Papers released showed that the Allies estimated two million Jews had perished and another five million were at risk. In March 1943 Cabinet Member Viscount Cranborne said that Jews could not be considered a special case and that the British Empire was already too full of refugees to offer a safe haven to any more. The Independent MP Eleanor Rathbone, an ardent anti-appeaser was harassing Ministers in early 1942 to publish evidence of the Holocaust to make the public aware and the BBC in June 1942 reported on the mass slaughter of Polish Jews; but the sheer brutality and scale of the systematic extermination of European Jews would not be fully appreciated until after the defeat of Nazi Germany. The political and military response to the intelligence reports they were receiving from occupied Europe is not a subject for this book, it has been well documented elsewhere, but by December 1942 a Committee headed by Rathbone and Jewish representatives formed themselves into the *National Committee for Rescue from Nazi Terror*. The Committee aimed to raise the plight of refugees and to highlight the atrocities being undertaken across Europe.

By July 1943, in response to a circular from the Committee, the South Shields Labour and Trades Council agreed unanimously the motion: '*That we call upon the Government to adopt the boldest possible measures of rescue of Jews from the Nazi terrors and to provide shelter for refugees in suitable territories under British control*'. Copies were sent to the Government and Ede imploring the authorities to act.

The Allied powers made clear to Nazi Germany that they would be held to account for war crimes, but until the war was won, the Holocaust would continue.

Church Way, site of the Brown's Cocoa Rooms (on the left) where the South Shields Labour Party was formed (now the site of the town's library). (*Copyright the Francis Frith Collection*)

Early pioneers ready for a General Election campaign, *c.*1920/30s. (*South Shields Labour Party collection*)

Women activists marching into South Shields Market Place, *c.*1920/30s. (*South Shields Labour Party collection*)

Chuter Ede with South Shields Labour Party activists. Gompertz is on the far left, Cuth Barrass stands on the far right, third row, *c.*1920/30s. (*South Shields Labour Party collection*)

General Election 1929, Chuter Ede (centre) with William Nunn speaking, behind him stands William McAnany and Harold Robson is on the right. (*Courtesy of South Tyneside Libraries*)

Mayor's Sunday 1953, Gompertz enters St Hilda's Church accompanied by Labour Leader Clem Attlee, Chuter Ede and Town Clerk J Moore Hayton. (*Courtesy of South Tyneside Libraries*)

Aaron Ernest Gompertz with his wife, Annie Gompertz (nee Thompson), *c.*1954. (*Courtesy of Melville Goldbaum*)

First Chair of the South Shields Labour Party, Jim Curbison, during his Mayoral Year 1925/26. (*Courtesy of South Tyneside Council*)

Sarah Noble, the first female JP in South Shields, photographed during her husband's Mayoral Year, 1943. (*Courtesy of South Tyneside Council*)

Jane Peel, the first female Mayor of South Shields County Borough, 1947/48. (*Courtesy of South Tyneside Council*)

Ernest Mackley in his Mayoral Year 1965/66. (*Courtesy of South Tyneside Council*)

Jim Florence, who became the South Shields Labour Party Secretary following the demise of Gompertz. (*Author's private collection*)

The final farewell, Gompertz, Chuter Ede and McAnany at the Armstrong Hall, 1963. (*Author's private collection*)

Chapter 14

Securing the Peace

I

Preparations for D-Day and the long-awaited second front against Nazi Germany were progressing at some speed as Attlee issued his own New Year message to the country in 1944 warning that the peace had still not be achieved and '... *there is always a danger of slackening when things go well'*. By February Bevan was arguing that the Labour Party leadership must demonstrate its radicalism by agreeing to implement the Beveridge Report in full and was almost excluded from the Parliamentary Party for his constant public criticism of their strategy, whilst in March, Attlee announced that the wartime coalition would cease as soon as the war in Europe was over. Later that month, the Government suffered its first defeat when it tried to delay a motion on equal pay for women schoolteachers – a furious Churchill demanded that the vote be retaken as a 'Confidence vote' with a promise of a Royal Commission on Equal Pay, the Commons duly obliged.

The 1944 Education Bill was one of the major pieces of Government Legislation during the war and laid the foundations of how the education system would operate in a post-war Britain. It endeavoured to improve inequality of opportunity by ensuring all Maintained Schooling would be free, established a tripartite secondary schooling system (Grammar, Modern and Technical), provided for the establishment of Further Education Colleges for school leavers, removed the complexity of local education oversight by creating Local Education Authorities (LEAs) and strengthened the role of the Education Ministry. The Education Bill recommended raising the school leaving age to fifteen, which gave Local Authorities the ability to establish nursery provision, it also provided midday meals in Maintained Schools and ensured compulsory medical and dental services for all children, free of charge. It was classic Disraeli 'One-Nation' conservatism, but as President of the Board of Education, Rab Butler would acknowledge that many of the proposals were hard fought for against sectoral and religious interests,

Churchill himself needing loquacious persuading on some elements of the Bill, but all proposals were enthusiastically promoted by Ede.

Ostensibly the Bill was piloted by Butler, but it was very much a Coalition effort, with Ede as Minister of Education undertaking more than his fair share of steering the proposals through Parliament. South Shields Labour Party was certainly in no doubt of Ede's influence on the Education Bill and when it finally secured Parliamentary Approval, Gompertz sent a telegram to Ede congratulating him on his '*Great achievement we are proud of our Member, Gompertz*', although they were later to protest that plans to increase the school leaving age would not be implemented until after the war.

II

As Parliamentary debate raged over the future landscape of Britain in a post-war era, Gompertz was required to focus the South Shields Labour Party on the electoral battles which would undoubtedly come once the war had been won. For all the challenges of wartime, the local Party was in remarkably good shape, it was dominant in the Town Hall, Ede was the local MP, they had their own political base, (still at Martins Bank in Laygate Lane) and by the 1944 Annual Meeting Gompertz was able to report to the Trades Council that due to his work, they had increased the Trade Union affiliated membership to 8,600. Ever mindful of the need to raise finance, Gompertz, under instructions from the Party, met with Labour Councillors and Aldermen and advised that in future they were being asked to donate to the Election Fighting Fund. Given there had been no municipal elections since 1938, the Government may require an 'all out election' which would place considerable strain on the Party's finances.

The Home Secretary, Herbert Morrison also established a Speakers' Conference which led to the beginnings of regular Parliamentary boundary reviews. The aim was to achieve Constituencies of equal population sizes, up for discussion were proposals to end dual member Constituencies and reviewing the reserved Universities and City of London Parliamentary seats. Although the Legislation would not come into force until a 1947/48 Review (by which time Ede was Home Secretary) they did interest the South Shields Labour Party because it placed the principle of equal Constituency sizes over respect for local government boundaries – South Shields could expect to be finally enlarged with the incorporation of Cleadon Park and other outlining areas within its Parliamentary influence.

As the long-anticipated invasion of mainland Europe took place on the beaches of Normandy on 6 June 1944, at home the blackouts, rationing and shortages continued, together with the need to remove bomb damage from the previous years. As Allied forces began their march across Europe and into the heart of Hitler's Germany, at home residents began to turn their attentions to returning to some kind of normality. There were calls for the beaches at Marsden and Shields to be reopened, the Trades Council supported a resolution to their Annual Conference that the Government should repeal the 1927 Trade Disputes and Trade Union Act as a condition for the wartime coalition continuing, and there were calls – rather uncharacteristically for the local Party – for the NEC of the Labour Party to campaign for a Union of Socialist States in Europe after the war. South Shields Council, desperately seeking to provide new homes quickly for displaced families decided to construct new prefabricated homes across the town, much to the opposition of the Woodworkers' Union at Trades Council meetings.

In July Gompertz organised a further meeting for the Ministry of Information at the Palladium Cinema, where following the screening of the film – *Eve of Battle* – a talk was given by Captain Donald Leslie, a native of South Shields, who was an Officer-Observer at the D-Day landing with the 50th (Northumbrian) Division. They had, Leslie explained, been pelted with flowers by a grateful French public, with troops being effusively kissed and cheered as they made their way across France.

There would be no effusive kissing with Council colleagues in Tynemouth though, who in November 1944 made the decision not to continue discussions on a Tyne link between South Shields and Tynemouth. Several factors influenced their decision, not least that the Government had grown lukewarm on the idea (preferring a Jarrow–Howdon Tunnel) and accordingly no financial support would be given to the project. Tynemouth Council also argued that following the war they would not be able to finance such an ambitious project, and even if a bridge or tunnel was constructed, toll charges would be applied to pay for it. Gompertz, a member of the Joint Committee reviewing the proposals was incandescent in his outrage at the decision accusing Tynemouth of '... *treachery and cupidity* ...' and for good measure they were also '*traitors*'. Rather strong language to use against civic counterparts, Gompertz may have believed he was being veracious, but it earned him the rebuke of being '... *a little dictator* ...' when Tynemouth Council met in December.

III Let us face the future together

1945 beckoned with the march of the Allies towards Berlin, it was evident that the war in Europe would soon be over, and with it the wartime Coalition. On 30 April with the Russian Red Army less than 500 miles from the Führerbunker, Hitler killed himself, by 7 May the new German President, Admiral Dönitz authorised the unconditional surrender of the armed forces of Nazi Germany. The following day the country celebrated VE Day; South Shields Town Hall was decorated in flags and bunting, the Mayor, Alderman Mitchell, spoke to the crowds gathered on Westoe Road and gave thanks that the war was at an end, street parties and celebrations continued long into the evening. The following week as Attlee prepared to travel to Blackpool for a Labour Party Conference, Churchill gave him two choices, an early dissolution of Parliament, or a continuation of the Coalition until victory over Japan had been secured. Attlee was content to wait until final victory in the Far East, he feared a repeat of the 1918 General Election in which Lloyd George ruthlessly capitalised upon his status as the *man who had won the war*. Herbert Morrison, Labour's election supremo was concerned that an early election would use out of date electoral registers, but the Labour Party Conference, under guidance from the National Executive Committee refused to endorse the proposal, further there were rumblings about Attlee's leadership with Ellen Wilkinson acting as a cheerleader amongst North East Labour MPs for Morrison to assume the leadership. Churchill responded on 22 May by ending the Coalition Government and announcing the next day that a General Election would be held on 5 July.

Gompertz was again in London for an annual meeting of Trades Councils at the end of May and secured election to the Trades Union Congress Committee as the representative of the North East, North Riding and Cumberland area. The position would see Gompertz spend further time in London on Trades Council business. Following his national appointment Gompertz returned to South Shields to oversee a meeting on 3 June, where the South Shields Labour Party met to formally adopt Ede as the Labour Party candidate for the General Election and to suspend all meetings until after the General Election. The following evening Churchill gave his infamous radio broadcast in which he claimed a Labour Government would see *some form of Gestapo* to underpin its programme of introducing Socialism, the broadcast was not well received by the public, senior Conservative colleagues nor the mainstream media who criticised the extremism language levelled at wartime Coalition partners. Gompertz pressed on with his election planning. Labour's election address to the people of South Shields displayed, by modern standards, a rather pompous photograph of Ede in his Epsom robes of office complete with his Mayoral chain and described him as '*Your tried and trusted friend*', advising the electorate that '*The most important place in Britain on July 5th is The Polling Booth*'.

As nomination day approached it was clear that Ede would face a challenge from the Liberal Nationals (who were aligned with the Conservatives), they had chosen as their candidate Captain Donald Parry a young Scots Guards officer who flew into the region from Italy in order to accept the nomination. There were strong rumours that the local Liberal Association would contest the seat and they had approached a serving army Captain to be their standard bearer but delays in the candidate travelling from Austria to accept the nomination rendered it a straight two-way contest between Parry and Ede. Ede was cautious but confident, advising the local media that he was leaving the conduct of the campaign to his 'Mr Berthier', Ernest Gompertz, '… *Berthier really won the battles not Napoleon*'.

The local Party was in buoyant mood, Ede arrived on Tyneside to issue a *cri de coeur* for Grace Coleman in Tynemouth on 19 June, where he ridiculed Churchill's 'Gestapo' broadcast asking '… *was there anything more like it than the way the Tory Party from 1931 onwards administered unemployment benefit in this area* …' And by 25 June was addressing the first in a series of rallies organised by Gompertz in South Shields and spoke on 29 June in Jarrow to support Ellen Wilkinson's re-election bid.

Nationally the Labour Party was cautious as to their chances of victory, their manifesto title was, '*Let us face the future together*', but given the Conservative majority in the Commons, and Churchill's popularity as a war leader, they feared that the best they could hope for was to improve upon the 155 seats won at the 1935 General Election. But the mood of the country had changed and a feeling that there should be no return to the 1920s and 30s Depression. Labour fully supported the popular Beveridge Report, would work towards full employment, wanted affordable housing, social security and health for all free at the point of need. In contrast, Churchill endeavoured to lead on his popularity, a promise of lower taxes, maintaining defence spending, encouraging private business interests. If there was a need for social reform, the private sector rather than the State should take the lead. As the polling stations closed on the evening of 5 July, Ede journeyed home the following day. There was a lull across the country as they awaited the return of the armed services' votes to Britain and in Lancashire there was a so-called 'little Election' because 5 July fell in the religious celebratory 'Wakes Week' which necessitated some twenty constituencies having their polling day postponed until 12 July. The *Manchester Guardian* believed that the election would be a stalemate but that the Conservatives would just edge to a majority.

Gompertz wrote to Ede advising his assessment was that Labour had won South Shields by between 1,500 and 2,000 votes and Ellen Wilkinson would be returned with a 4,000-vote majority. Gompertz was proved wrong on both accounts. As the sealed ballot boxes were opened and counted in South Shields Town Hall on the morning of 26 July, Ede had won by 7,114, Wilkinson had secured Jarrow by over 11,000. Grace Coleman would seize the Tory Tyneside bastion of Tynemouth by just over 3,000 votes and Bill Blyton secured Houghton with a majority of over 20,000, he would resign from South Shields Council in September. Another South Shields former Councillor was elected for Labour in Sunderland, Richard Ewart secured victory in the two-member seat. The speed at which they had counted the votes in South Shields meant that the expected midday result was announced at 11 am from the Town Hall steps, where only a small crowd had assembled joined by inquisitive members of the public walking past the forecourt.

Across the country it would be a landslide for the Labour Party, with Cabinet Ministers such as Brendan Bracken, the First Lord of the Admiralty out in North Paddington, Harold Macmillan, Minister of Air, ousted in Stockton and Leo Amery the Secretary of State for India and Burma felled in Birmingham Sparkbrook. The scale of the victory was revealed by 7 pm, with Labour gaining 225 seats, and the Conservatives down to 195 seats, the Liberals limped back with twelve seats.

Ede immediately travelled back to London to be advised that the new Premier wished him to be Home Secretary in the new Cabinet, Ede's constituency neighbour, Ellen Wilkinson would serve with him in Cabinet as the Education Secretary.

IV Municipal defeat

The war in the Far East was over on 15 August, the ships on the Tyne sounded their hooters, fireworks were lit, and church bells pealed with the joyous news. The Town Hall once again saw crowds gather as spontaneous bonfires were lit across the borough and colliery bands led parades into the town centre. With Ede secure, and the Labour Government turning its attentions to the post-war settlement in Europe and winning the peace at home, local activists would turn their own attentions to the November municipal contest, the first since November 1938.

Attempts in September by the Communist Party to seek a conference to discuss the local elections were swiftly rebuffed by Gompertz who advised no useful purpose would be served in such a meeting. Gompertz was clearly feeling confident about the municipal elections, the Moderate Group of Councillors was becoming fragmented, encouraged by a local optician Sidney Walton who in May had launched a **South Shields Rent and Ratepayers' Association** (RRA) and was seeking candidates to contest seats under the new banner. The Moderates, always a loose Coalition of Liberals, Conservatives and assorted independent interests, agreed to meet with the RRA in order not to split the anti-Labour vote in the elections. A compromise was partially reached with the Moderates being allocated the Westoe, Holborn and Harton wards, but no agreement was found for the Bents or West Park.

The election held on 1 November was a disaster for the local Labour Party. In total they lost nine seats with the RRA seizing ten of the sixteen seats they contested. St Hilda's, Holborn and the Deans all saw Labour candidates defeated leaving Labour with only twenty-six Council seats as opposed to twenty-two Moderate Councillors, eleven RRA and one independent. The anti-Labour majority would be used to appoint anti-Labour Aldermen as terms of office expired increasing the Moderate/RRA hold on power further.

For Gompertz, who declined to speak to the press after the counting of votes, the silver linings would have been the defeat of his nemesis, Edwin Thompson in the Bents ward (losing his seat to an RRA candidate) and the poor electoral showing of the Communist Party's two candidates. One new addition to the Council was a young Harton miner from South Frederick Street, Ernest Mackley, regarded as one of the Party's leading candidates. Unopposed in Simonside, Mackley would eventually become in the 1960s the Leader of South Shields Council and would retain his Simonside seat until his defeat in May 1978.

Labour's shock and unexpected defeat in South Shields was not replicated elsewhere, London saw Labour hold its sixteen Councils and gain another six, Newcastle City went Labour for the first time as did Chamberlain's former powerbase Birmingham, Leeds returned Labour to power and regionally Gateshead, Sunderland and Hartlepool were solid for the Party even in Windsor the Labour Party managed eleven Council seat gains. The result in South Shields was a devastating disappointment to local activists, the defeat is not easily explained. One factor could have been that as the majority Party implementing sometimes unpopular decisions during wartime (such as rationing and the closure of local amenities) the public may have vented their disapproval at the ballot, but then other Labour Councils were in a similar predicament and retained control. One crucial factor would have been the ward boundaries themselves. There had been no local government boundary review for some time, areas like the expanding Cleadon Park estate were still grouped with the Harton ward even though its electorate was substantially more than the combined population of the riverside areas like Holborn, St Hilda's and Shields wards which had experienced significant slum clearance before the war. To reinforce the point, the Moderate victor in the Shields ward received just 250 votes the Moderate victor in Harton 2993; further the Moderate victor in Holborn won with only 329 votes, but his counterpart in West Park won with 1,798 votes. There was a clear disproportionate representational imbalance which needed to be addressed.

The Mayor, Ald Mitchell, alluded to this when he advised the local press after the results that he expected the Labour Party to regain control once a boundary review had been conducted. The Constituency Party discussed the situation at their November meeting following the elections, at which Minutes record, a number of opinions were expressed and the Executive empowered to ensure that any by-elections called, following the elevation of any Councillors to the Aldermanic Bench, should be contested. Inevitably the local media received criticism with Alex Stephenson alleging that the *Shields Gazette* correspondence column had been deliberately manipulated to promote the RRA, with pro-Labour correspondence being 'spiked'. Stephenson wanted a formal complaint sent to the Editor, but Gompertz urged caution.

The Moderate/RRA alliance struck with force when the Annual Council meeting was held in November after the local elections. Labour reacted with fury when their nominee for Mayor, Longstaff, who had served on the Council since 1927, was defeated by a relative newcomer to the Council, Malcolm Barbour by twenty-seven votes to twenty-four, given Labour's own ruthlessness in ensuring their own nominees had assumed the Civic Chair for the past decade, they could hardly have expected the Moderate/RRA alliance to act magnanimously. In scenes reminiscent of pre-war years, the Labour Group, led by Gompertz, harangued, and berated the new ruling Group over their appointments to Committees which saw Gompertz lose the Chair of the Finance Committee. There was no let-up in the attacks when the Council debated the appointment of Aldermen, only two of the retiring Aldermen were reappointed to Office, both Moderates; Labour's nominees for the Bench, which included Gompertz and long-serving Alderman Brady, were soundly defeated. By midnight Council business had still not been completed when an exhausted Mayor moved that the Council adjourn.

The five by-elections held in December to contest vacancies caused by the elevation of Councillors to the Bench held only one surprise. Whilst opposition parties held four seats, the vote-splitting antics of the RRA resulted in Ede's mentor, Cuth Barrass – recently retired as a headmaster – securing election for the West Park ward. The result was a warning to the RRA and Moderates. The Moderates would spend the early part of 1946 seeking to regroup under a new '*Progressive Party*' banner to counter the Labour Party offensive and to stem the RRA advance, for the moment the RRA would spurn any attempt to unite opposition forces.

V

Herbert Morrison once remarked that '*Socialism is whatever a Labour Government does*'. The legislative record of the 1945–51 Labour Governments is not a subject for this book, but it is worth pointing out for reference that given the devastation that had been wrecked upon Britain by the war and the dire condition of the British economy, the legislative programme which delivered a social democratic consensus which lasted until Margaret Thatcher's election in 1979 was truly impressive. Twenty per cent of the economy, including the Bank of England, the mines, iron and steel as well as transport were nationalised; a welfare state was created providing a comprehensive cradle-to-grave health care package, with unemployment and other insurance benefits underpinning a compassionate society. Britain slowly withdrew from its Empire and the country's shattered infrastructure meant almost full employment. There was a new Towns Act to grow the suburbs in order to reduce overcrowding in the inner cities, an ambitious housing building programme saw four out of every five houses constructed being built by Councils and the infamous 1927 Trade Disputes and Trade Union Act was abolished.

It was an impressive social democratic transformation rather than a Socialist revolution, whilst the left rejoiced in domestic policy initiatives, they looked on with some trepidation as Labour's Foreign Secretary aligned the country's foreign policy aims to the USA with the development of NATO being the cornerstone of a new defence strategy. As if to reinforce Britain's weakened new standing in the World, the US would only agree to a £3.5bn loan to Britain with a string of conditions which included the ending of the Sterling Area which had protected British manufacturers from US competition (even the Lend-Lease plan introduced to support Britain's lone stand during the war was conditional on Britain surrendering some of her markets in Latin America). With the rebuilding of its own economy taking priority, Britain, no longer able to afford its intervention in Greece, withdrew and supported the US taking its place through the Truman Doctrine.

VI Happy warrior

The war may have ended, but food rationing remained in place in Britain (it would not actually end completely until July 1954). The new Moderate/RRA administration in the town moved to remove Labour nominees on the local Food Committee replacing them with their own supporters. The Labour Party protested but it was to no avail. Gompertz, who had been Chair throughout the war years was not going to go quietly. In March 1946 as the new Committee assembled for their first meeting, Gompertz arrived early and placed himself in the Chairman's seat. A furious row ensued with Gompertz refusing to yield, arguing that he had been appointed by the previous members as Chair for the year at their 10 January meeting and accordingly the Committee should ignore items one and two on the Agenda which dealt with the appointment of the Chair and Vice Chair and move to the main business of the meeting. An exacerbated Food Executive Officer endeavoured to maintain order, advising that since it was a new Committee, they had a duty to appoint a new Chair. Gompertz stubbornly refused to move, the Committee voted to summon the Police, but upon arrival Gompertz's persuasive manner convinced the Officers they had been called unnecessarily so they left. Further procedural arguments followed for two hours before the meeting eventually adjourned. The fractious encounter was not helped by the fact that the Moderates had appointed as the new Chairman James Ockleton from the Seaman's Union, a long-standing member but one who had initially been recommended for appointment to the Food Control Committee by Gompertz in May 1942.

Gompertz was adopting his usual tactics of seeking to thwart and frustrate the new Council administration even when the procedural argument, such as over the Food Committee Chairmanship, was tenuous to say the least. They may have succeeded in removing him as Chair of the Committee and also as a Council nominee to the Committee itself, but he merely arranged to be appointed as the Trades Council Consumer Representative and continued to hold the Committee to account for their actions.

It was predictable Gompertz who continued to live up to his stormy petrel mantra and was very much William Wordsworth's *The Happy Warrior*. In February 1946 he objected to any attempt by the Council to use their powers to restrict free school meals only to those in need, rather than providing the meals as a universal service, in the same month he was supporting the Tyne Improvement Commissioners over their concerns that they would lose control of providing the cross Tyne ferry services if proposals by Northumberland and Durham County Councils to construct a Tyne Tunnel between Jarrow and Howdon were agreed by Parliament. March saw him react with indignation to attempts to close down local communal British Restaurants created during the war to help people bombed out of their homes arguing that they guaranteed a nourishing diet to the poorest in society. In June he was organising a public meeting of Council tenants at the Nook Assembly Rooms protesting at excessive increases in their rents and in July he was speaking out in support of Sunday opening of cinemas which had proven so popular during the war. Even the Sunderland and South Shields Water felt Gompertz's ire when he criticised publicly their proposals in August to decrease rebates to consumers from 20 per cent to just 5 per cent.

Complaining from the side lines about decisions he had little control over vexed Gompertz, he had exercised executive responsibility during the war years and witnessed the improvements Labour could make when it held civic power and as a consequence, he was determined that the November 1945 elections would be a temporary setback.

No Labour Party meeting was complete without Gompertz announcing how much had been raised for the 1946 Municipal Election Fund, individuals, affiliates, the Women Sections and Councillors were all gently cajoled to dig deep for the Labour Party cause. He wanted candidates selected early so that they were able to campaign much earlier introducing themselves to the electorate and he kept a close watching brief on the Moderate/RRA manoeuvrings appreciating that there were clear tensions developing between the long-serving Moderate Councillors and their new energetic RRA counterparts.

Gompertz at this time encouraged the formation of a League of Youth branch in the town. An attempt to create such a body before the war had met with only marginal success, but Labour's General Election victory had very much revived enthusiasm amongst the young and there is evidence through the Minute Book that the League grew in membership. Richard Ewart MP would return to the town to address their inaugural meeting in the Labour Hall.

Ever watchful and ambitious to extend Labour's reach, when criticism was made that the Jarrow and Hebburn Co-operative Society were being difficult and sometimes obstructive, Gompertz worked with the Jarrow Labour Party to successfully ensure that there was greater Labour representation on the Co-operative Society Board, and his vigilance against Communist influence was never far from his mind, including in February 1946 at Gateshead Town Hall, when at a regional Food Committee meeting Joe Waters, the North East District Secretary of the Communist Party rose to speak, only for Gompertz to object to his presence because he was not a member of the Committee. Waters resumed his seat.

VII Boundary challenges

Neither Parliamentary nor local government boundaries had been reviewed since before 1935, it was clear that regional and population imbalances could not continue. As mentioned earlier in this book, a Speakers' Conference had been convened in 1944 recommending the establishment of an Independent Commission which would review Parliamentary Boundaries on a regular basis, with a recommendation that plural voting should be abolished along with the reserved University and City of London seats. By October 1946 the Independent Boundary Commission had outlined their initial plans for new Parliamentary constituencies. Within what we now know as the South Tyneside administrative area, South Shields would retain the town centre wards, but in an east/west demarcation line it would lose Harton, Cleadon Park and Simonside to the Jarrow constituency which itself would also comprise Jarrow UDC and Boldon UDC area (which included the Whiteleas and Biddick Hall communities). Hebburn would form a new separate constituency with Felling. The effect would result in South Shields having 47,575 electors, Jarrow 49,481 and Hebburn and Felling 52,420.

The proposals were not well received either locally or nationally given the scale of the redistribution. There was a general view that the Commission had rushed the proposals and had not taken account of population upheaval during wartime. In the face of protests from all sides of the political spectrum, Ede was required to instruct the Commission to revisit the proposals. The new proposals were still drastic, all but eighty of the Parliamentary Constituencies faced some change, and in over 190 cases, the redistribution required the name of the Constituency to be changed completely. The Prime Minister himself was affected, Attlee's Limehouse Constituency was abolished and another seat needed to be found for him. Across South Tyneside, the Commission respected Council boundaries, South Shields would not be split as previously feared, and the Cleadon Park estate would transfer from the Houghton Constituency into South Shields. Jarrow would be grouped with Hebburn and Felling to form a separate constituency. Even with the changes, including the creation of seventeen new Constituencies, the redrawn boundaries across the Country would be a contributing factor in Labour's near defeat in the 1950 General Election.

The corresponding period also saw moves to re-examine local government boundaries which previously had not been coordinated nationally or locally. There was no procedure for adjusting boundaries between various administrative authorities nor indeed for amalgamating them. The January 1945 White Paper on *Local Government in England and Wales during the Period of Reconstruction* was designed to give order, provide some form of uniformity to local decision-making and was required to consider the role of local government as central Government began to centralise some of its functions – the creation of the NHS for example removed any role for local Government and the nationalisation of energy saw local councils lose the right to provide energy solutions for the local area.

The Review's work was extensive, taking nearly five years to complete, and during that time there were the inevitable arguments between competing local government interests. Newcastle endeavoured to resurrect the 'One Authority' for Tyneside option, and in the face of opposition began advocating for a *Greater Newcastle* option of expanding its boundaries to take Gosforth; Tynemouth Council eyed Wallsend; Sunderland wanted Washington as well as land to the south, South Shields made arguments for housing land in Marsden and commenced talks with Jarrow Council about a possible merger.

The Commission's initial recommendations were in the main logical, Newcastle and Sunderland would remain as a stand-alone single-tier Councils responsible for the execution of all local government functions in their area. However, Tynemouth, Gateshead and South Shields Councils who as County Boroughs had managed all their own functions would in future become two-tier Councils. Tynemouth would link with Northumberland County Council; South Shields and Gateshead with Durham County

Council. Key functions like the fire and police would be transferred to the respective County Council, residents in future would elect Councillors to represent them on the respective County Council. Whilst South Shields would cease to be a single-tier County Borough, it would in future extend its boundaries to Boldon, Jarrow, Hebburn, Felling and parts of Washington. A significant extension of its boundary, but it would have to accept that some key services like Fire and the Police would be managed regionally by Durham County Council.

The proposals, perhaps not unexpectedly, were met with open hostility from County Boroughs like South Shields who viewed the removal of key strategic functions from within their remit as unsatisfactory. Despite the extensive work undertaken by the Commission, in March 1949 the Health Minister, Nye Bevan, announced to the Commons that '...*it will not be practicable to introduce comprehensive legislation on local government reconstruction in the future.*' By June the Commission was abolished, with claims they did not have the powers under the 1945 Local Government Act to alter the structure or vary the functions of local government.

Whilst there would be no major local government reorganisation, South Shields County Borough did see its boundaries increase in April 1950 when Whiteleas, Marsden and parts of East Jarrow were moved within its borders principally to enable new housing provision to be provided.

Major local government reform would not be implemented for another twenty-five years.

VIII

As discussion over the Parliamentary and local government boundaries continued, in the summer of 1946 Gompertz was mindful of the need to have candidates in place for the November municipal elections. As he did so, Gompertz would have viewed with interest the opposition Parties descending into fratricide. Tension was escalating between the Moderates and the Rent and Ratepayers' Association (RRA) as to who was the dominant partner, and failure to reach agreement on which of their candidates should contest the various wards in the November poll.

The formation of the RRA had caused a stir not only within South Shields – where their spectacular success in 1945 had deprived Labour of a majority – but also within the wider region. Originally formed to contest Durham County Council's elections, the movement gained traction with numerous towns forming similar bodies across the region. Their claim to be strictly non-political (whereas the Moderates were Conservative and Liberal political activists fighting under a non-descript banner to appeal to working-class voters) and free of any political allegiances brought them widespread support with an underlining ethos that party politics should play no part in municipal affairs.

Despite being in a formal alliance to control South Shields Council, the Moderates and RRA simply could not reach agreement as to who should challenge Labour in the various wards across the town in November 1946. The failure to reach a settlement was mortiferous and resulted in Labour facing a split anti-opposition vote. As the results were announced on the evening of 3 November, the Labour Party had regained control of the Council, but victory was by no means certain. In the fifteen South Shields wards, the Progressives and RRA both challenged Labour in five wards, Labour seized them all including areas where they had never experienced significant success previously – the Beacon (by just six votes), Hadrian (by four votes) and the Bents (by five votes). It was a disaster for the anti-Labour opposition, more so for the RRA who failed to gain a single seat, Labour gained six. Within the Council Chamber, the Labour Group now had thirty-one Councillors, the Progressives sixteen and RRA thirteen. A two-seat majority for the Labour Party, but enough to install their own onto the Aldermanic Bench should any vacancy arise.

The victories for Labour saw several women activists seize municipal honours, Rose Ann Hart, Beatrice Cunningham, Margaret Sutton and Jane Fry (who only defeated the Communist by fifteen votes in the Holborn ward). Ede sent Gompertz a telegram offering '*Hearty congratulations to all concerned in obtaining victory*'; for Gompertz himself he acknowledged that they had been fighting three enemies, (RRA, the Progressives and the Communists) but felt it was a source of satisfaction that the Council would once again be under Labour control.

Gompertz used Labour's new majority to secure for himself a place on the Aldermanic Bench and resigned his seat as a Councillor for Tyne Dock. His next ambition for himself was to secure the Mayoralty.

Chapter 15

Consolidating Control

I 1947, a year of crisis

The 1945 Labour Government lives on in Labour movement folklore as one of the greatest reforming Governments in British history, typified by the creation of the NHS and the development of a social consensus. By January 1947 with the nationalisation of the coal industry, low inflation, a balanced budget, industrial recovery and almost full employment (although there were still 1.5 million men in the armed forces) an improved balance of payments position the nationalisation of the Bank of England and Civil aviation, Attlee's stock was rising high with the public. Events though would shake the confidence of the Government during 1947, leading to further speculation as to Attlee's future as Leader of the Labour Party with the US Ambassador to the UK reporting to Washington that there was a real danger the Government could fall.

A number of factors precipitated the crisis.

During 1946/47 a harsh winter descended over Europe but its adverse effects were felt more severely in Britain with 15 ft of snow drifts in some places. Towns and whole communities were cut off for days with offices and factories closing, there was a fear of food shortages and a fuel crisis, as supplies were affected, and vegetables were frozen in the ground. The warmer weather brought the thawing of the snow with widespread flooding affecting many parts of the country. Dissent broke out within the Cabinet as the shortage of coal inevitably brought down industrial output, unemployment began to rise, and food supplies were cut short. The Government was unprepared for the crisis and struggled to keep supplies moving. They survived a motion of censure in the Commons in March, but further problems followed. The terms of a US loan to Britain negotiated by John Maynard Keynes had the unintended effect of worsening the country's economic problems. The loan had come with a string of conditions, one of which was the convertibility of sterling into dollars which resulted in the demise of Britain's ability to exercise economic control over its Empire colonies who in future could convert their earnings into other currencies such as the US dollar and allow these earnings to be spent outside the sterling area. Convertibility led to a financial crisis with the Chancellor, Hugh Dalton, forced to introduce austerity measures including wage restraint, reductions in imports (including food) and an extension of the working day – an air of panic engulfed the Cabinet.

The left wing within the Parliamentary Labour Party were determined that the Government should remain firm to its manifesto commitments, not least the nationalisation of the iron and steel industries leading to Michael Foot launching the *Keep Left Group* to maintain pressure on the Cabinet. The Government faced further backbench rebellion as it implemented the National Service Act for eighteen year olds (intended to compensate for the loss of Indian army personnel after their independence). A further two-day Commons debate in early August followed as the national emergency grew; Attlee's personal approval ratings plummeted in the wake of further austerity measures, leading to an attempted coup to replace him with Morrison. The coup failed when Cripps, facing Attlee and telling him to go, left the Downing Street meeting with an enhanced role in Government as Minister for Economic Affairs. Further problems followed when six weeks later Dalton was forced to resign as Chancellor after inadvertently leaking elements of his budget speech to a journalist as he walked to the House of Commons on Budget Day, he was replaced by Cripps.

The US, appreciating the serious financial situation facing Britain, agreed to postpone convertibility temporarily, Britain accepting its economic fate, accelerated the independence of its Colonies and bid for its share of the Marshall Aid plan designed to help with the post-war industrial reconstruction of Europe's shattered economy.

Building the new Jerusalem was proving more difficult than imagined.

II

As the local MP and a member of the Cabinet, Ede religiously kept in close contact with the local Party providing regular reports both in correspondence and physically when he was in the Constituency. With the Labour Party in control of the Council, Gompertz was able to regain the Chairmanship of the Food Control Committee, a position which consumed more of his time due to fears of food shortages. Concerns were raised in Party meetings that the public could not choose their own coal merchants, with delegates alleging the procedure was unsatisfactory given concerns that some coal merchants were not operating within the rules. There was further bad news when in July the Trades Council were advised by the Ministry of Health that their nominees for the new NHS Steering Committee had all been rejected, protests to the Ministry brokered no concessions.

At the Party's Annual 1947 Dinner Dance in April, Ede sought to keep the local faithful firm in their support for the Government. In his address he led on the appalling winter, '... *the worst for 100 years, and the weather had presented problems which had never before been experienced by anyone now alive.*' Commenting on the fuel crisis he advised dinner guests that the country was better off with a Labour Government since following the nationalisation of the coal industry four million tons of coal were being mined every week: '*I defy anyone to say that a Conservative Government working the mines under the old system would get anything like that.*' In an indication of the hold Gompertz exerted over the Party on behalf of Ede, attempts to support Manny Shinwell, the Energy Minister when he was dismissed by Attlee in October were rebuffed. Gompertz though would always hold true to his own convictions, voting against the Government's National Service Act at the May Labour Party Conference in Margate because it enforced the principle of conscription.

The antics of far-right groups, often virulently anti-Semitic were causing local activists some concern. Although there is no recorded activity in South Shields, large meetings had again been organised in London's East End usually ending in street violence. In September with Fascist groups operating under the guise of ex-Servicemen Associations, the South Shields Labour Party wrote to the Government urging them to curb the influence of such groups, if necessary, through new legalisation. By November Manchester Gorton Labour Party had circulated a motion condemning the growth and spread of propaganda activities aimed at racial discrimination describing them as not only inciting racial hatred but also were a '*cloak behind which Fascist reactionary organisations are seeking to disrupt our democratic way of life.*'

As a libertarian, Ede was cautious about using Government legislation to restrict the activities of emerging hard right-wing groups. Speaking to a Labour League of Youth conference organised in South Shields in November 1947 he asserted that: '... *you do not kill ideas by attempting to say "... you shall not utter them". Ideas are only killed by stronger ideas and we believe we have a better idea than Fascism*'. Ede maintained that anyone could advocate any doctrine as long as it did not incite violence, or hold up to hatred, ridicule or contempt, masses of groups of people or individuals. Speaking alongside Ede was the Coventry West MP, Maurice Edelman, who explained that if the former BUF Leader, Oswald Mosley took steps which constituted an active threat to democracy then the Home Secretary would need to take action. By 1948 Mosely would go on to unite over fifty far-right groups under his leadership of a new **Union Movement**.

III Municipal triumph

The 1947 municipal elections would witness two developments which would provide challenges to Labour's rule within South Shields Town Hall.

Firstly, the election disaster of November 1946 had forced both the Moderates and the Rent and Ratepayers' Association to re-examine tactics. Their response was to merge the two organisations into the **Rent and Ratepayers' Municipal Association** (RARAMA), the new body recognised that individuals could be members of a political party, but they would contest Council seats as RARAMA and under no circumstances would Party politics be allowed to infiltrate their Group discussions.

Secondly, the anticipated boundary review of Council wards was taking place, small wards along the waterfront such as St Hilda's, Holborn, the Shields ward and Laygate would be abolished, new wards would be created to recognise the expanding housing estates on the urban fringe, Cleadon Park, Brinkburn, Marsden and Horsley Hill, the Council would have fifteen wards in total across the town. Gompertz had high hopes of securing Brinkburn, Marsden and Horsley Hill; Cleadon Park, due to its demographic make-up would prove a greater challenge.

The results when declared on the evening of Tuesday 4 November 1947 confirmed Labour's hold on the town, the decision to merge and create RARAMA allowed the opposition Parties to maintain their dominance in areas like the Beacon, Bents, West Park and Westoe, but the redrawn boundaries saw Labour seize the new Brinkburn and Marsden wards. Cleadon Park, as Gompertz expected proved a Ward too far for Labour, and Labour failed to gain Horsley Hill by just twenty-one votes, the intervention of a Communist candidate proving decisive. Nevertheless, Labour held the Town Hall albeit by just two seats. A new rising star called Jack Clark was elected in Marsden, whilst the election would see a railwayman, Bill Malcolm, make an unsuccessful bid for Harton. Labour's majority would enable them to again break the mould, when at the Council's Annual Meeting they would elect Jane Peel as the first woman Mayor of South Shields.

Across the country, it was to prove a disappointing evening for the Labour Government, probably not surprisingly given the events of 1947, losing nearly 700 Council seats with even Manchester falling from Labour control.

IV

With the *Annus Horribilis* 1947 behind them, the Labour Government pursued in 1948 its relentless agenda of reform with gas and electricity being nationalised along with the railways. The NHS, after protracted discussions with the British Medical Council would come into being on 5 July, an institution which epitomised the Welfare State more than any other social reform, it proved hugely popular, benefitted all sections of society in its embrace. Britain continued its moves in dismantling the expensive Empire with the formation of the Commonwealth. India granted independence in August 1947 was swiftly followed in 1948 by Burma and Ceylon.

It was international affairs which would cause the Government difficulty in the middle of the 1948 Parliament. The main focal point being members of the far left within the Parliamentary Labour Party being concerned at the Government's reaction to a series of annexations by the USSR in Eastern Europe, in particular Czechoslovakia. The Labour leadership's Cold War intransigence towards the totalitarian USSR regime and its own developing closer links with US foreign policy objectives saw a number of Labour MPs expelled from the Party for their open dissent from the official line, including the Gateshead MP, Konni Zilliacus.

1948 was not a good one for Gompertz. In May he fell again in the street, this time breaking his right arm, but despite his incapacity he maintained a firm grip on the Labour and Trades Council. In July he encouraged the Trades Council to reject as a delegate to the Trades Council Mr W Summerfield from the Boldon Miners' Lodge because he was a Communist. Protests and threats by the Lodge that they would disaffiliate from the Trades Council were met with the curt response that they could disaffiliate if they wished, but Summerfield would not be accepted as a delegate. Attempts by James Ockleton the Regional Seamen's Leader to join the local Labour Party were also rejected, Gompertz had still not forgiven Ockleton for replacing him as the Chair of the local Food Committee. Ockleton later faced calls to resign his position in the Union after allegations he was attempting to introduce a '*coloured bar*' in the shipping industry when he spoke at that year's NUS conference alleging '*gate crashing by coloured seamen in the industry*'. The Muslim League of Great Britain described Ockleton as '… *occupying the same place as Oswald Mosley*'.

In June the South Shields Labour Party welcomed the appointment of a new young activist, Len Rumney as the Secretary of the growing local branch of the Labour League of Youth. Rumney would go on to have a long and distinguished career in local government, becoming a well-respected, if a somewhat officious Solicitor and Returning Officer to South Tyneside Council. In July, news reached the town that Ede's wife Lilian had passed away, they stood in respectful silence, and allowed Ede time to grieve before formally re-adopting him in October as the Parliamentary candidate for the next General Election.

As he came to terms with his loss, Ede was still working, securing the passage of his Representation of the People Act in July which radically altered the Parliamentary Boundaries and made significant changes in the way in which elections would be conducted; postal voting was introduced and in future local elections would be fought in the spring month of May, thus there would be no local elections for South Shields Council in November 1948. As a result of the new boundary changes, Cleadon Park would be transferred into South Shields for Parliamentary purposes. Gompertz, who resided in the ward, would now be able to vote for Ede in Parliamentary elections rather than be part of the Houghton Constituency.

V

As plans for a new Marine and Technical College in the town progressed in 1949, Gompertz was fastidious in ensuring that the Trades Council had representation on the new Board and would himself be one the nominees, he was also nominated and became the Vice Chair of the Local Employment Committee which oversaw the work of the Employment Exchange. In January 1949, Gompertz safely back in the Chair of the local Food Control Committee was once again haranguing officials this time over the appointment of a retired Major-General as the new Divisional Food Officer for the District, with a generous renumeration as part of the package. It was, he felt improper to secure the services of someone from the War Office for such a role when they were enjoying a substantial pension. The Major-General was not without his supporters, the *Bellshill Speaker* newspaper pointing out that Gompertz himself was sixty years old and the Major-General had been a former Director of Supplies and Transport at the War Office.

Nothing demonstrated Gompertz's loyalty to the Labour Party more than his decision in February to resign his seat on the Aldermanic Bench to contest the marginal Horsley Hill ward. Gompertz was without question aggrieved that the Party had not taken the new seat in the 1947 municipal elections, he regarded it as fertile Labour territory and given the small majority the Party enjoyed in the Council Chamber, felt personally compelled to leave the safety of the unelected Aldermanic Bench to stand as a candidate in the ward, believing he had the best chance to secure victory. It was an act of stoicism which very few others would have done.

Whilst preparing for a fresh election battle, Gompertz was manoeuvring to secure new activists to become involved in the Party and in March announced he had encouraged two new members, Jim Ireland and Vincent Fitzpatrick to stand in the Westoe and Beacon wards respectively. Fitzpatrick, who would be recommended by Gompertz as the Party's new Press Office in June, would in time become a long-serving Leader of the new South Tyneside Council created following the 1972 Local Government Act.

As preparations were made for the 1949 Council elections, now to take place in May of each year, Gompertz organised a public meeting in March for Ede, Morgan Phillips the Party's National Secretary and Hugh Gaitskell, the new Energy Minister. The meeting, in the Marsden Miners' Hall saw Ede implore the electors to use their vote in the local elections. Phillips described local government as '... *the crucial cornerstone of British democracy*'; further public meetings followed with NEC Member Michael Foot MP addressing the faithful in the reception room of the Town Hall and the Government Chief Whip William Whiteley the key speaker at that year's May Day Rally. Ede was delivering the national figures; it would be up to Gompertz to secure victory in the May elections.

Gompertz would not disappoint.

When the election results were announced, the Labour Party had gained three seats, Gompertz converted a twenty-one-vote defeat in Horsley Hill in 1947, into a 173 vote Labour majority. It gave Labour a solid majority in the Town Hall, thirty-four seats to RARAMA's twenty-six, increased even further when Labour were able to appoint eight of their own to the Aldermanic Bench.

The South Shields Labour and Trades Council had much to be proud, but Gompertz's ruthlessness in controlling the Party machine would, following the May elections, irk the man who would do much to eventually bring him down in 1960.

Safely returned in Simonside was Ernest Mackley who would eventually become Secretary of the Harton Miners' Lodge, and the Leader of South Shields Council. In 1949 he was a relatively young man, but one who, like Gompertz, could bear grudges against those who crossed him. Gompertz did just that after the celebrations of election glory had eclipsed.

To a political outsider it may seem rather mundane, perhaps even officious, but Mackley's crime was to print his own election literature, and encouraged two other colleagues to do the same, Joe Abbott and Alex Stephenson. Gompertz who had always managed the publication of election literature centrally viewed it as a direct challenge to his authority. He insisted that the three Councillors apologise and that the Party reaffirm that all literature must be signed off by himself to ensure they complied with Party policy and were within the Law. Abbott immediately apologised, he had little choice, during the election 4,000 of his leaflets had to be destroyed because Gompertz highlighted they contained statements outside agreed policy and were potentially outside the Law (possibly no electoral imprint had been included). Mackley and Stephenson were stronger characters.

The local Party reaffirmed at their May meeting that Gompertz must sign off on all election literature, the matter could have ended there, but as if to rile Gompertz, Stephenson and Mackley circulated to all delegates a copy of their May election literature. Stephenson raised the game by verbally attacking Gompertz at the 28 July meeting of the Borough Council. Inevitably, the matter was considered further at the September meeting of the local Party where it was agreed to 'condemn the action of Councillors Stephenson and Mackley' and again insisted all literature in future must be signed off by the Secretary. The whole matter became drawn out in procedural arguments and counterarguments, Stephenson's union, the General and Municipal Workers demanded that the Minute be rescinded, Mackley's Harton Miners' Lodge did the same – Gompertz held fast but was under sustained attack. He eventually relented at the November meeting and agreed that to be diaphanous in future a subcommittee of the Chair, Vice Chair and himself would sign off on all literature. Stephenson for his part apologised for circulating delegates to his leaflet, Mackley did not.

But Gompertz was nothing if tenacious and stubborn. By late November he requested the local Labour Party to agree a further motion that anyone issuing circulars to delegates in future without formal permission would face expulsion, attempts by Mackley at the next Labour Party meeting to have the Motion changed to merely '*Disciplinary action*' was sounded defeated.

Gompertz had reasserted this authority – Mackley would bear the grudge.

VI Rebuilding the town

The death in May 1949 of Mary Sutton left a great lacuna in the local Party ranks, depriving it of one of its founding stalwarts. A member for over forty years, she was a driving force within the Women's movement and Chaired the West End Women's Section for over twenty-five years. A member of the Co-operative Movement she had also previously been co-opted onto the Council's Education and Children's Committees. Her death at the age of sixty-four, was a huge blow to the Movement in the town.

With Labour now back in control of the local Council, and with a respectable majority, Gompertz would without fear hold colleagues to account if he felt they fell short of the standards expected by the local Party. He complained at the Labour Party Delegates meeting in August 1949 that poor attendance at Council meetings in July had seen the Labour Party lose votes on the floor of the Chamber, and on one occasion only secure a Labour nominee to a co-opted Committee courtesy of the Mayor's casting vote, the absenteeism could not be tolerated. Gompertz also took to task in late May 1949 two Councillors, Hardwick and Clark, who had attended a public meeting of the RARAMA and had spoken in the meeting, Members were advised that they should refrain from attending the public meetings, even if it was to chastise the opposition.

The new Labour administration though had as a priority the rebuilding of the town after the war years, as well as tackling poor housing conditions that existed before 1939. In fairness to the previous Opposition a lot of groundwork had already been undertaken. Just **one** report submitted by the Borough Engineer to the Council in February 1947 gives an overview of the scale of change proposed. The submission outlined the need for the Council to seek to acquire land from adjacent Councils for housebuilding, with the Engineer assessing that the town would increase its population by 120,000 as the exigencies of the war passed. Plans were submitted to demolish whole areas around Mile End Road and River Drive, the Woodbine as well as High Shields. Land would be acquired from the Deans Hospital to develop new housing and a building licence awarded for new bungalows in Hemsley Road. The Engineer recommended entering negotiations with the Ministry of Housing to construct new housing at Whiteleas – but the land would need to be transferred from Boldon Council.

As new housing was developed, new schools and other social amenities would need to be built including Horsley Hill Primary, Marsden and Harton Downhill Schools, Redwell Secondary and Wenlock Primary School in Simonside with a new Community Centre in Broughton Road. This would be followed by extensive road network improvements around Waterloo Vale, road widening of Sunderland Road, Westoe Road and Fowler Street, and with better road connections to new housing estates outside the town centre in Mortimer Road and Horsley Hill Road. Green Street and Cuthbert Street areas would be demolished with new housing and retail being provided. There was also talk of the need to move South Shields Football Club to either a site at Simonside Hall or Leam Lane, with a crowd capacity of 10,000, whilst Commercial Road land would be developed for industry and manufacturing.

VII 1949 Devaluation

As Britain's balance of payments were brought under control in 1949, a mild recession in the US delivered bleak economic forecasts for the Labour Government. US demand for British exports collapsed. With Marshall Aid already fully committed to the domestic agenda and defence spending, the Chancellor, Stafford Cripps advocated cuts in social spending to balance the budget and advised Attlee that a 30 per cent devaluation of the pound was perhaps inevitable to counter the dip in exports caused by the depression in the US, although he preferred greater cuts in public expenditure. If neither option was pursued, the reserves would disappear, sterling could collapse. The press mendaciously claimed the country was facing a 1931 situation all over again. The advantage of devaluation of course is that British goods would be cheaper to the US consumer, the disadvantage was that British consumer would pay more for American imports. The Government devalued the pound on 18 September with cuts of up to 8 per cent in public expenditure following.

Attlee was lobbied to go to the country for a fresh mandate in 1949 before the full effect of devaluation was felt by the British public, he rejected the tactic as dishonest, a move which endeared his integrity to certain sections of the British media, but the crisis was hardly auspicious for Labour supporters with a general election required within nine months, but in reality, barely three months away.

Following the Christmas recess, Attlee announced that the General Election would indeed be held on 23 February 1950. Gompertz organised Ede's formal adoption meeting in the town but pressure of Ministerial work necessitated Ede remaining in London. He sent a handwritten note to, '*My dear friends ...*' apologised for not being there in person and explained that the Government had maintained full employment and had laid the foundations of a Socialist Britain by extending social justice. The 1950 Manifesto, **Let us win through together**, was an inspiring call for the coming contest with a pledge to continue and strengthen the good work already achieved by the Labour Government. He concluded: '*This is no time for complacency or over confidence. We deserve to win, let us make certain that we do*'. Ede was resoundingly readopted.

Gompertz undertook the election preparation with his usual enthusiasm and diligence. Party members opened their spare rooms across the town to enable Committee rooms to be established, in an age before mass car ownership, Gompertz received support from businesses like Sparks Radio of Westoe Road and Masons Shoe Repairs of Frederick Street who placed at his disposal their motor vehicles, a financial appeal to the Labour movement netted the required donations – although Ockleton of the Seamen's Union advised no finance would be forthcoming until he was admitted into the Labour Party – and in days before the internet, billboards were secured for Ede's posters across the town.

Ede advised Gompertz that the national Party had requested that he undertake speaking engagements across the country, Ede was happy to do so but only if Gompertz consented and on the condition that the Party sent a high-profile speaker to South Shields to address a public meeting. Ede also agreed to advance Gompertz £400 for the campaign which would be provided by his union, the NUT. Confident of success in the town, Gompertz agreed to release Ede and the Lord Chancellor, William Jowitt was despatched to South Shields as part of the agreement.

The close of nominations would see Ede challenged by a prominent local Conservative and dental surgeon John Chalmers, with a Communist FO Smith entering the fray. The Liberal Party for the first time since 1935 fielded their own candidate, John George. Gompertz was not complacent, it was a high-profile campaign with the local Party leading on Ede's legislative achievements as Home Secretary and describing him on their literature as – '*The best Member you have ever had*'. The electorate had increased principally due to redrawn Parliamentary Boundaries with Cleadon Park included for the first time, the result, when polls closed on 23 February saw Ede returned with 33,452 votes, to the Conservatives 15,897. The Liberal candidate mustered 9,446 votes whilst the Communist a derisory 415.

Across the country, boundary changes championed by Ede saw the Labour Party suffer a net loss of seventy-eight seats, including Tynemouth, despite its national vote increasing to 13,226,176 to the Conservatives 12,494,404. The Labour Government limped back into Office with an overall majority of five seats. In the new Cabinet, Ede remained as Home Secretary, but it was clear that the Party would have trouble implementing some of its more radical policies, such as further nationalisation and could in some cases be held to hostage by their own backbenchers. Attlee would be required to seek a fresh mandate within months.

VIII Gompertz's 1950 Mayoral bid

No sooner had the General Election concluded, than local activists were faced with the May municipal elections. Gompertz had good reason to be insouciant, Ede's vote was the highest ever recorded for Labour at a general election in the town, and the Labour Party would again face a divided opposition. In June 1949 following the local elections, Alderman Hardisty had resigned from RARAMA claiming that not enough young men were being encouraged to stand for Municipal office and formed the **People's Party**. One Labour member, Mr G Elliott, resigned to join the new grouping. At the May 1950 meeting of Council, Gompertz was nominated for the Mayoralty defeating RARAMA's Candidate Councillor Robert Bainbridge twenty-six votes to eighteen. His appointment though was dependent upon the Labour Party retaining control of the Council in the local elections. Given 1950 was also the Centenary of the creation of South Shields as a County Borough, it would have been a sweet victory for the Labour Party to hold the Civic Office in such a momentous year.

The turnout by the electorate on polling day was down, and one new candidate to emerge was Stella Lloyd in the Westoe Ward, the niece of one of the Party's founding members Joe Batey but the Labour Party would go on to suffer six stinging defeats with Gompertz unable to secure the election of Labour's candidate in Horsley Hill by just forty-seven votes. The People's Party in the end contested just three seats, their intervention having no effect on the overall voting. The election resulted in a stalemate; Labour had twenty-nine seats to Ramara's thirty with Alderman Hardisty's one vote in effect holding the balance of power.

As Councillors met for their Annual Meeting on 22 May, Bainbridge was unwell, he advised he was suffering from a recurrence of old issues due to being gassed on active service in World War I. Remaining for the meeting, he defeated Gompertz for the Mayoralty by thirty votes to twenty-eight, Alderman Hardisty voting for Bainbridge. Drama unfolded as Bainbridge, wrapped in a blanket was escorted out of the Chamber by Councillor Dr John McKee to be carried on a stretcher into an ambulance waiting outside the Town Hall. It was later confirmed Bainbridge had had a haemorrhage.

Although Gompertz had been defeated for the Mayoralty, he could take pride that the Labour Group remained firm, set aside any personal differences and voted as a bloc for their nominee. It had been a long and sometimes tortuous journey to achieve such discipline, but Gompertz himself was the leading driving force to achieve it. RARAMA's discipline also held, for a Grouping which always argued they were non-Party political, they displayed a remarkable consistency in voting against every Labour proposal before the Council. Gompertz emerged from the meeting with his usual pugnaciousness reporting to the next meeting of the local Party that election preparations for 1951 must commence immediately. He started with reorganisation of the Party structures. The Local Ward Committees, based around the Council wards, were not functioning effectively, attendance, particularly in those wards without Labour Councillors was sparse. Gompertz recommended that four joint ward branches should be created:

South Joint Wards: to cover Cleadon Park, Horsley Hill Marsden and Harton
West Joint Wards: to cover Tyne Dock, Simonside, West Park and Brinkburn
East Joint Wards: to cover Westoe, Beacon, Hadrian and The Bents
Central Joint Wards: to cover Rekendyke, Deans and Victoria

Next Gompertz proposed holding a monthly '*Open Meeting*' of all Members so that they could discuss policy, campaigning and fundraising, and he encouraged the Labour League of Youth to seek new recruits within the Trade Unions to expand their reach.

The Party agreed to the Joint Wards and also further work with the League of Youth but they would not accept Open Meetings. Trade Union delegates jealously guarded their influence in the decision-making process and wanted to retain delegate-only meetings. The position was not unique to South Shields, and in fact until John Smith's One Member, One Vote proposals at the 1993 Labour Party Conference, '*Delegates only*' meetings remained the norm. By December, Gompertz gave a full report to the Executive of his discussions with the Labour Group, Executive Committee, Ward Officials and Council candidates as to how the May 1951 elections would be executed, including a central team of workers prepared to devote time in marginal seats. Gompertz was determined to lay the groundwork for victory in 1951.

In September Ede celebrated his sixty-eighth birthday, still a member of the Cabinet, he relinquished though his positions in local government including resigning as an Alderman on Surrey County Council. Gompertz was sixty-two, and attended once again the Labour Party Annual Conference, this time held in Margate during 2–6 October. Whether Annie escorted her husband to the Annual Conference records do not indicate, but there is every likelihood that she did even if she did not physically attend the conference hall itself.

South Shields County Borough celebrated its Centenary in modest pride with the Lord Lieutenant of Durham, Lord Lawson, opening an exhibition in August which compared South Shields of 1850 with its progress in 1950, displaying the town's industrial products and the town's history as a borough. Ede spoke of the town's determination over the years to retain their independence and not be subservient to either Newcastle or Durham – they had, he said, '… *maintained this struggle*'.

Two further events would prove significant for the South Shields Council Centenary, one ceremonial, the other administrative. Ede was to be made a Freeman of the Borough on 6 September in recognition of his distinguished service to the town and the **South Shields Extension Pact** would see boundaries change once again from 1 April 1951, transferring from Boldon UDC the whole of Whiteleas and the Farding Lake Farmland in Marsden into the South Shields County Borough boundary. Gompertz argued that Whiteleas should be a 'stand alone' ward given that new housing proposals would see the area populated by up-to 8,000 new electors within a few years. The proposal was rejected with RARAMA maintaining that the area only have 500 electors at present and that the Whiteleas area should be assimilated into existing surrounding wards.

IX

When once asked what knocks Governments off-course, Harold Macmillan is quoted as saying, '*Events dear boy, events*'. That was certainly the case with Attlee's Government as it limped into 1951 with a small Government majority.

Attlee was now sixty-eight years old and had served in Government since joining Churchill's Coalition Government in 1940. The war years and the great reforms and challenges of post-war reconstruction had taken a toll on his health. Other big beasts within the Labour Government were also ageing, suffering frequent illness and stress and spending prolonged periods in hospital. Dalton was on medication, the Chancellor Stafford Cripps had resigned in October 1950 due to his stomach cancer and in April 1951 Ernest Bevin would die. There was the inevitable power struggle amongst younger Parliamentarians as to who would assume the leadership of the Labour Party once Attlee resigned with the new Chancellor, Hugh Gaitskell repeatedly facing down Nye Bevan in the Cabinet.

With the nationalisation of the iron and steel industries, doubts were emerging within the Parliamentary Labour Party as to the effectiveness of nationalisation and whether other industries should be corporately managed by the State. Morrison had his reservations and wanted to consolidate rather than attempt further nationalisation, going so far as to urge the Labour Party to rethink its strategy in light of the changing World stage rather than be tied to any policy objective set by Keir Hardie fifty years previous. It was radical thinking, but too radical for Labour's left wing who through their newspaper, *Tribune* asserted that the real lesson of Labour in power since 1945 was that '*reformism*' was not enough. The debate would fatally weaken the Labour Party during the remaining 1950s and early 1960s as the left coalesced around Bevan opposed by revisionist thinkers like Anthony Crosland who would group around Hugh Gaitskell.

The battle lines between a new generation of Labour Party leaders commenced on 22 April 1951 when Bevan resigned from the Cabinet. The issue centred around Chancellor Gaitskell's proposals to make savings of £13m in the NHS budget which would come from new charges on treatment of teeth, eyesight and prescriptions. Bevan objected, not only because the proposals undermined the principle of a free National Health Service, but also that the £13m saving was part of a larger package of cost reductions to meet the Government's obligations to fighting the Korean War. The Prime

Minister received the news of Bevan's departure whilst still recuperating in his hospital bed.

As Labour MPs were being carried from their sick beds to defend the Government's small majority, Bevan and his supporters relentlessly pursued an alternative agenda from the backbenches, and a rejuvenated Conservative opposition forced the Government into all-night sittings and Divisions, an exhausted Attlee called a General Election for 25 October 1951.

X

As the Labour Government neared its end, Gompertz would be required to spend more time himself in hospital on three occasions during July, August and December, records do not indicate the reasons but we cannot discount that he was feeling the strain of an increasing workload, even though the opposition controlled the Council and he had lost the Chair of the Finance Committee and the Local Food Control Committee. No time was lost in lamentations, there would be two difficult sets of elections to face once again with a General Election in October 1951 and the local elections in May 1952.

Failing health would not prevent Gompertz arranging both election battles with his usual determination and undefeatability. The Moderates were again using their numerical strength to pursue a policy of selling Council housing, bitterly opposed by the local Labour Party. Gompertz organised a public meeting for Ede and the Newcastle MP, Arthur Blenkinsop at the Nook Assembly Rooms in early April, the public were greeted by the Communist Party selling literature at the entrance and Ede's whole address was taken up with the issue of the Korean War – (which he asserted was a United Nations issue) – and the question of rearmament – (advising his audience that Britain would never use weapons of destruction first in a conflict).

Meanwhile, the decision of the National Negotiating Committee of Town Clerks to agree new salary scales for Town Clerks would have seen the South Shields Councils Town Clerk's salary increase from £1,570 to between £2,250 and £2,750, in addition Harold Ayrey, the Town Clerk, asked for his conditions of service to be amended. The salary increases were opposed by other Councils, and with South Shields Council refusing to accept the salary increase, Gompertz, although Labour was not in control of the Council, was delegated to head to the High Court in London in October to lead a test case on behalf of more than forty other Councils who had agreed to cover the cost of the Hearing. By November the Lord Chief Justice had ruled in favour of the Councils – on a point of technicality – that the Town Clerks' National Negotiating Committee's proposals were not binding. Gompertz had scored another victory.

The Opposition may have been in control of the Council and may even have been prepared to use Gompertz's undoubted debating skill in the High Court, but Gompertz was determined to oust them. In an indication of how fraught the May 1951 election campaign would be just days before the municipal elections, Labour members stormed out of the Council Chamber forcing the Mayor to adjourn the meeting since there was no quorum for business to be transacted. Essentially the walkout followed alleged remarks by a RARAMA Councillor RR Robson, in their Group meeting that the Council had previously been 'buying land by back door methods', the Labour members demanded a retraction, but with no apology forthcoming Ald Garnett led an exodus of his Group from the Chamber. One cannot help summarising that the event was pure theatrics, the accused RARAMA Councillor was seeking re-election in Horsley Hill one of the key election battlegrounds, Gompertz as a fellow Horsley Hill Councillor was determined to win the seat. The tactics played off, since following the close of poll Labour won Horsley Hill by a majority of over 300. It was the only change during the election resulting in a stalemate of Councillors between Labour and RARAMA, thirty members each.

As elected Members made their way into the Council Chamber for the 1951 Annual Meeting of the Borough Council it was clear the vote for the Mayoralty would be on a knife-edge, not a single absence was recorded, Gompertz rose to propose Margaret Sutton as the Mayor with RARAMA nominating Councillor Oliver, both candidates received twenty-nine votes, two members clearly abstaining, the retiring Mayor, RARAMA's Bainbridge used his casting vote for Oliver, the appointment of the town's second woman Mayor would have to wait for another occasion.

With the levers of power in the hands of RARAMA for another municipal year, Gompertz turned his attention to his ward. A resident of Farne Avenue on the recently built Horsley Hill estate, Margaret Thompson, had cause to contact Gompertz in March following her arrest, overnight detention and fining of £5 by Borough Magistrates after she was caught picking three tulips in a public park. The punishment was unduly harsh, but the fact that the Magistrate was Edwin Thompson, who back in 1933 was a prime instigator in the Secret Document affair, resulted in Gompertz taking the matter further. Using his network in the press Gompertz ensured the case was highlighted first locally, and then as the story gained traction also nationally.

In what became known as the '*Tulip affair*', Mrs Thompson accepted she had done wrong but the overnight detention was excessive for the crime. She was inundated with flowers from well-wishers as Gompertz enlisted the support of Ede and demanded that Thompson should be censured by the Lord Chancellor and removed from the Bench.

Gompertz's forensic skill was on display once again, with the case eventually being considered by the Lord Chancellor. Although the Lord Chancellor had no power to overrule a decision of the Magistrates and he refused to censure the local Magistrates, his verdict was damning enough for Edwin Thompson. The punishment did not fit the crime, even if it was an '... *anti-social act which should not be passed over as a matter of no consequence*' he believed that to keep the mother in custody overnight and fine her a substantial sum of £5 looked like punishing her twice for the same offence. Following the ruling, South Shields Magistrates refunded Mrs Thompson £4.

XI 1951 General Election

The decision by the Liberal Party to only contest 109 seats (as opposed to 475 in 1950) at the October 1951 General Election resulted in political overtures by the Conservative Party to court extensively the Liberal vote. The Conservative manifesto centred around commitments not to roll-back on Labour's Welfare State agenda, a promise to end rationing, to denationalise the steel industry, not to introduce legislation which would affect Trade Union privileges gained under Labour and to build 300,000 dwellings each year. In contrast, Attlee stressed the achievements of the Labour Government asking the country to compare Britain of 1951 with the predominantly Conservative interwar years which had seen mass unemployment and poverty. There was a need to build upon the peace, to maintain full employment and to build a just society, but the Manifesto lacked vision with emphasis being placed on the Conservatives not being trusted with the reforms already introduced. As the historian Charmley observed the Government was '... *exhausted in mind, body and manifesto commitments.*'

Preparing once again for a General Election contest, Gompertz organised Ede's adoption meeting for 25 September at the Labour Hall. When nominations closed, Ede was opposed once again by the Conservatives John Chalmers with a Liberal candidate, schoolteacher Charles Kitchell, who had initially been the Liberal candidate for Sunderland South. Gompertz was able to advise Ede that everything was copacetic, with the usual rallies, leafleting, door knocking and fundraising, the campaign in South Shields appears to have been relatively without drama, although attending a campaign hustings for Grace Coleman in Tynemouth, Ede is reported to have stood wagging his finger like a schoolmaster at persistent hecklers.

The result in South Shields was never in doubt, Ede had increased his vote to 33,633, the Liberal lost his deposit. Nationally, Labour achieved the largest vote for a political party in history 13,948,385, a quarter of a million more than the Conservatives, but still lost the election. They may have won the popular vote, gaining larger majorities in their Constituencies but the Conservatives won the majority of seats, gaining narrow victories in more Constituencies, in part due to their assiduous courting of the middle-class Liberal vote. The Labour Government had fallen more like a whimper rather than through a financial crisis and break-up which had engulfed its period in office in 1931, there was certainly no electoral meltdown rather a small shifting of votes in key Constituencies.

At sixty-nine, Ede was out of Government and would not hold Ministerial Office again but astonishingly he would still contest two further General Elections in South Shields, but like his faithful Agent Gompertz, he had now become an Elder Statesman.

Chapter 16

The Elder Statesman

I

At seventy-seven years old Churchill faced the Opposition Leader, Attlee who at the age of sixty-eight showed no signs of relinquishing his hold on the Labour Party. Labour's Parliamentary Party stuck rigidly to its old guard with Hugh Dalton, Herbert Morrison and Chuter Ede retaining their seats in the Shadow Cabinet. Attlee's determination to hold on until his arch-rival Morrison would be considered too old for the Leadership, had the effect of depriving the Labour Party of valuable time in reassessing its manifesto commitments, rejuvenating and refreshing the Party, and clarifying its appeal to the public. Consequently, the Party became embroiled in a civil war between a new generation led from the left by Nye Bevan and from the centre right, by Hugh Gaitskell, neither able to remove Attlee, both frantically organising their supporters within the Constituency Parties and the Trade Unions with the drama played out in the full glare of the media.

Labour's Morecambe Conference in October 1952 saw the Bevanites oust Morrison from the National Executive Committee which led Gaitskell to describe it as *'not only an act of gross ingratitude but also a piece of blind stupidity'* and made clear he felt there had been Communist infiltration into the Party declaring it was time to end the mob rule and restore the authority and leadership of the movement. In November 1952 Bevan challenged Morrison for the Deputy Leadership, losing out by 194 to 82 votes. The gloves were off, right-wing Union Leaders keen to assist Morrison urged him to stand for the Treasurership of the Labour Party at the 1953 Conference, Morrison dithered over whether he could defeat the aged and popular Arthur Greenwood. At the last moment, infuriating his Union supporters, Morrison withdrew. In so doing he unknowingly closed the door on his future leadership prospects since at the 1954 Conference Hugh Gaitskell stood and defeated Bevan for the Treasurership of the Labour Party and secured the mantle as the heir-apparent to Attlee.

Gompertz was again the South Shields Labour Party's delegate to both the 1952 and 1953 Labour Party Conferences, records do not indicate who he supported either for the National Executive Committee in 1952 or for the Treasurership in 1954, he was certainly not mandated. Given his positioning very much on the centre-right of the Labour Party and his dislike for any faction with a hint of Communist sympathy, we can safely assume he would have supported Morrison in his bid to remain on the NEC and supported Gaitskell for the Treasurership over Bevan.

II Consolidating civic control

As political fratricide engulfed the Labour Party nationally, Gompertz continued to maintain a firm grip of the political levers of power loyally. Returning to work from illness which had affected him in the previous winter, in February 1952 he faced down an attempt by the General and Municipal Workers' Union (GMWU) who wanted future meetings of the Trades and Labour Council to be held on separate evenings. Normally both meetings were held on the same evening. The GMWU felt that not enough time was being devoted to Trades Union business with items being rushed in order to ensure Labour Party business took precedence. Gompertz successfully argued that any new arrangement would be impracticable to operate and the matter was not pursued by the GMW.

Gompertz wanted the local Party and Trade Unions to concentrate their efforts on the May 1952 elections, not retreat into insular navel gazing which had gripped the national Party. Candidates were in place by February, including Gompertz who would face re-election in Horsley Hill. Ernest Mackley, although not a Party officer made sure he was still part of a troika reviewing all election material produced with the Party Chairman and Gompertz. The political make-up of the Council was on a knife-edge, unity and discipline held firm in both Labour and RARAMA's camps with all fifteen Council seats challenged in straight battles, no independents emerged and no Communists entered the field.

Once again Ede made his customary visit to the Constituency to formally record his public support for Labour's candidates at a public meeting in the Market Place and once again Trade Union affiliates financially supported the local Party's election fund.

The result of the elections saw the Council swing back to Labour control, they gained two rather unexpected victories in hitherto RARAMA seats, with Sidney Walton, the election strategist for RARAMA being ousted in the Hadrian Ward by Joseph Dixon and Jack Maddison winning the Bents ward. Gompertz himself was safely returned with an impregnable 551 vote majority in Horsley Hill.

In March, before the Council elections, Gompertz had cause to caution the South Shields Labour Party in relation to unguarded talk as to who may assume the Aldermanic Bench if Labour regained civic control. Following the elections, in advance of a meeting of the Labour Group being held on Sunday 18 May, Gompertz was instructed by the Party Chairman, Jack Clark, to convene an urgent delegates' meeting to discuss rumours circulating that attempts would be made to renominate some RARAMA Aldermen whose terms of office were due to expire. Although the exact details cannot be confirmed, it seemed that some Labour councillors had been discussing whether as a political tactic, they should not remove all of the retiring Aldermen. Clark and Sid Jones as the Party Chairman and Vice Chairman were not prepared to acquiesce to the move. The delegates' meeting was unanimous in their decision that the Labour Group should be instructed to appoint seven new Labour Aldermen to give the Labour Party full advantage of their municipal victory.

Labour's Margaret Sutton would become the second woman to hold the position of Mayor of South Shields, whilst the Labour Group nominated seven new Labour Aldermen with by-elections being required in Rekendyke, Victoria, Deans, Tyne Dock and Horsley Hill to replace the Councillors elevated to the Aldermanic Bench. Railwaymen Bill Malcolm was chosen for the Deans ward, in preference to his NUR union colleague Ken Scrimger who would in time become the Parliamentary Agent. Vincent Fitzpatrick, initially supported by Gompertz for the Rekendyke ward, was replaced at the Labour Party Executive meeting at the request of his own AEU Union who favoured Fred Pringle. The Assistant Secretary of the Party, John Elliott who was holding the fort during Gompertz's frequent absences was rewarded with the second vacancy in the Rekendyke ward. The Chair of the Marsden Miners, Jimmy 'Lanky' Edmondson was allocated the vacancy in the Victoria ward. The power struggles for the new seats give a clear sense of the power still wielded by the Trade Unions with seats like Deans, Tyne Dock, Rekendyke and Victoria, being regarded as reserved seats for individual Union favourites with no involvement in the selection of candidates from individual Labour Party members in those wards.

III

In July an inappropriate comment to the local newspaper would see Gompertz demand that James Garnett appear before a disciplinary Committee of the local Labour Party Executive. The Council's Education Committee had recommended the appointment of Mr J Adjeitey as the Schools Dental Officer. Garnett, as the Education Committee Chairman had remarked that in the event of a 'white applicant' he would have preferred to give the job to him. Gompertz was incandescent with outrage, advising a meeting of the Borough Council who agreed to the appointment without dissent that Garnett's remarks '... *in no way reflect the view of the Party to which he owes allegiance*'. Further that: *'Far from accepting the Chairman's views we repudiate his statement. We are firmly of the opinion that a man's colour or creed or religion should not enter into a matter of this nature'*.

Garnett appeared in front of a Panel in September with an Official from his NUR Trade Union, he was contrite and accepted his remarks were ill-advised and inappropriate. The fact that Gompertz covered a record of the meeting with over two pages of formal Minutes is an indication of how annoyed he was at the offensive comments against Mr Adjeitey. The conclusion was to reaffirm that Garnett's remarks did not reflect the values of the Party he represented and that Gompertz's public repudiation of them in Borough Council was sufficient to draw a line under the affair.

Gompertz was tremendously proud of his Trade Union work and in September he was presented with a Silver Badge in recognition of twenty-one years' unbroken service to the Trades Council Movement, the first recipient of such an Award from the TUC. Sir Luke Fawcett, the Chairman of the Trades Council Joint Consultative Committee made the presentation in South Shields following which a celebratory dinner was organised at the Royal Grill.

With the failure of RARAMA to retain control of the Council, divisions once again surfaced within the opposition ranks. The local Conservative Association Chairman, John Chalmers had taken the lead in a campaign against the sacking of a Council labourer because he had refused to continue paying his Trade Union subscriptions. With the closed-shop arrangements legally operating at the time, the Council had little choice but to endorse the dismissal. Chalmers believed that RARAMA representatives should have been more assertive over the issue and endeavoured to have the dismissal raised in Parliament through the Tynemouth Conservative MP, Irene Ward.

By September the Conservative Association announced that they intended to contest future Council elections and required their members to disassociate themselves from the Rarama grouping. To enforce discipline, RARAMA called a meeting of their elected representatives seeking assurances that they would remain with the independent grouping, all did, although Douglas Marshall resigned from the Executive of both RARAMA and the local Conservative Association because he could not support the two Groups potentially splitting the anti-Labour vote in future elections. The infighting would lead to three young Conservatives contesting the May 1953 elections in direct opposition to RARAMA, including (a future Progressive Association member) the combative Stan Smith, who would eventually assume the Leadership of the Council in 1969.

Garnett would however attract Gompertz's irritation once again in December over the issue of free school meals for children during school holidays. Garnett's Education Committee had recommended, that no action should be taken, but Gompertz moved in Borough Council that the Committee should be instructed to resume the service following the advice of the South Shields Schoolmasters Association and the NUT. The motion was agreed.

IV Trainee Agent

1953 would see the departure of a number of pioneers of the South Shields Labour Party, James Ramsey of the Marsden Miners' Lodge retired from active politics in January whilst one of the Party's earliest pioneers, John Thompson a former coal miner who as an ILP member was one of the first working-class men elected to the Council in 1894 died. In March they received the news that Dick Ewart who had been a local Councillor in the town at the age of just twenty-eight before becoming the MP for Sunderland had tragically died at the age of just forty-eight, Gompertz already in London for Trades Council business represented the local Party at his funeral at Potters Bar; and in May Alderman Charles Smith, a boilermaker who had enthusiastically supported George Rowes' Parliamentary bid passed away. Smith had been associated with South Shields Council since 1918, Mayor in 1936, an Alderman in 1937 and appointed a Freeman of the Borough in the Councils Centenary Celebrations in 1950. As David Clark observed in his book – *We Do Not Want the Earth*: '*Many of the early pioneers were particularly strong characters who by their personalities and determination had overcome severe deprivation to attain high civic office.'*

The new generation emerging at this time included Ernest Mackley, Alex Stephenson, Vincent Fitzpatrick, Jack Maddison, Bill Malcolm, Ken Scrimger, Stella Lloyd, Jane Fry and a young man appointed to represent the local Party on the Hospital Board, Murtaugh Diamond.

In February, Gompertz journeyed to Keighley where he was the guest speaker at the Trades Council dinner in his capacity as a member of the national Trades Council Joint Consultative Committee. His address warned guests that Trades Council would be at the forefront of the campaign to protect wages and living standards and that they would need to be vigilant in defence of Trade Union rights. But Gompertz's attentions were also turning towards his desire to be the Mayor of the Borough of South Shields for the 1953/54 municipal year. It would be the Coronation Year of Queen Elizabeth and in preparation of his expected nomination he would need to be provided with administrative support for his Labour and Parliamentary responsibilities. In January, following discussions with Labour's Regional office, the NEC had agreed to support the appointment of a trainee Agent for the year, the NEC would fund £125 towards the salary, and Gompertz £175, presumably surrendering his own salary for the year. In March the Labour Party Executive met Philip Hodson of Ilford Essex, a young man of twenty-one who had been recommended for appointment by the NEC. Hodson impressed the Executive and they agreed terms of service making clear he would work under the direction of Gompertz and commence his duties on 13 April at the Labour Hall.

Unfortunately, the appointment did not go well. By July Gompertz advised the Executive that he had suspended Hodson from his duties for refusing to carry out reasonable orders, refusing to disclose funds received in connection with the League of Youth and for insolence. Gompertz reported to the Executive that on 29 July he had visited the Labour Hall at 8.30 am but Hodson did not arrive for work until 9.25 am. Gompertz asked whether anyone had visited the Labour Hall the previous day, Hodson replied that a woman from the League of Youth had attended, but despite a requirement, he had not entered the details into the 'Day book'. Hodson apparently advised Gompertz that the visit had nothing to do with Gompertz because it was 'League' business and that it was not a recognised section of the local Party. He refused to divulge how much money had been handed over, explaining details would be given to the Auditors, and asserted that the League could spend its finances how it wished. He became insolent to Gompertz when advised it had everything to do with the local Party, Hodson apparently responded that he wasn't prepared to take orders from Gompertz, because he wasn't a Clerk. Matters were compounded when Gompertz explained that he had asked Hodson to complete a letter, taking in Gompertz's view, an inordinate time to complete the simple task.

Meeting the Executive, Hodson gave little in way of his defence and his speech to the Executive was platitudinous merely reinforcing the point that the visit by the young woman was personal, and that the League of Youth was a separate organisation. Mackley and Stella Lloyd moved that the suspension should remain in place unless Hodson gave assurances to follow instructions from Gompertz in future and to disclose the finances of the League of Youth. Hodson agreed.

Hodson's attitude did not improve necessitating a further meeting with the Executive in late August, the Regional Office was informed that they wanted a discussion on the continence of the Trainee Agent programme. At this meeting, Hodson spoke at great length following which the Executive requested that he resign his post with the employment terminating on 3 October. The Party agreed to recruit some temporary office help to support Gompertz.

This was more than just a personality clash between Gompertz and a young apprentice, with the ageing stalwart jealously protecting his powerbase. The September Executive meeting, separate to Hodson's issue, reported that Gompertz had been advised that members of the local League of Youth had been found to have been selling Communist literature at the Durham Miners' Gala. Within days, Gompertz had completed his investigation and the Chair and Secretary of the South Shields League were expelled from the Labour Party. As a young man, Hodson had clearly struck up a friendship with members of the local League and had been aware of where the finance had been raised when the young woman had visited the Labour Hall and handed money to Hodson to deposit into the Bank. Loyalty to the young Labour League of Youth members had set him on a collision course with the local Party.

The May 1953 local elections saw Labour seize a further three seats from RARAMA. In the Hadrian ward another woman would be joining the Labour Group, Mrs Maddison, Eddie Brady seized Horsley Hill and J Bulmer took the Deans ward. The local Conservative Association stood three candidates, but none made much impression on the overall result, it would be the last time a serious bid by the Conservative Association was made for Council seats until the creation of the new Tyne and Wear County in 1973.

Gompertz was now assured of victory to become the borough's Mayor at the May Annual Council meeting.

V 'The first Jewish Mayor'

On Monday 18 May, Jack Richardson rose in the Council Chamber to nominate Gompertz as Mayor of the Borough for 1953/54. He referred to Gompertz as a humane, generous and able man whose work on behalf of the residents of the borough was '*legion*'. Gompertz was, Richardson asserted a '*man of people*' who had striven to do his duty with the greatest of grace and the greatest of ability. He made glowing reference to Annie who would support Gompertz ably, as she always had done, they were worthy of the honour of being the borough's first citizens. McAnany in seconding the motion spoke of Gompertz's work over the past twenty years as a Councillor in particular his work on securing a reduction in income tax payable for local authorities and his Chairmanship of the Emergency Food Committee during World War II. Gompertz's appointment as Mayor was by acclaim, the Progressives having previously advised that as a gesture of goodwill in Coronation Year they would not oppose the no doubt have reflected on the years Mayor at the Annual Meeting.

In responding, Gompertz remarked that as he took Civic Office, he was reminded of the early pioneers of the Labour Party in South Shields whose steadfast work and commitment had made it possible for him to reach the Mayoralty. In remembering them and their valiant work on behalf of the poor and downcast he wanted from the beginning of his Mayoral Year to be forever associated with their sacrifice. He thanked Ede for his inspiration and unfailing sense of humour which had encouraged him during the many trials and tribulations they had faced together, and he reminded his audience that he was the first Jew to hold the Office of Mayor of South Shields and he was immensely proud that as Mayor, he would be an observer at Westminster Abbey in London for the Coronation of Queen Elizabeth II.

The Whitsun bank holiday weekend was warm, dry and sunny – nationally the country was making preparations for the Queen's Coronation, locally on Sunday 24 May, the Mayor's Parade left the Town Hall to march the short distance down Fowler Street to the town's mother-Church, St Hilda's. Described by the *Shields Gazette* as one of the biggest parades for a Mayor's Sunday, Colliery Bands with banners gently fluttering in the light breeze led the Mayor resplendent in his Red Robes of Office, accompanied by his wife,

Annie, the Mayoress. Marching alongside them were the Civic Party, the Police Chief Constable and Fire Chief, the Town Clerk in his black gown and judge's wig, the Aldermen and then Members of the Council. His former Council colleague and now MP for Houghton, Bill Blyton turned out to give his support, while members of the public stood to greet the new Mayor on his way to the traditional Sunday Service which would Bless the Mayor and Mayoress and wish them well for a successful ceremonial year in Office.

Photographs of Gompertz entering St Hilda's Church show him beaming with evident pride at what his life's journey had achieved. Standing alongside him was Chuter Ede who had travelled from Surrey to join his faithful supporters' day of celebration, and in tribute to Gompertz's quarter of a century devotion to Ede, the Labour Leader, Clem Attlee, still recovering from an April appendicitis operation, had agreed to attend Mayor's Sunday to thank Gompertz and his wife personally, for all they had done for both the Labour movement and the people of South Shields. It was a gracious gesture by Ede to encourage Attlee to make the journey and following the church service Attlee would visit the seafront to meet the Volunteer Life Brigade, before being taken on a tour of the new housing estates being constructed on the outskirts of the town. Attlee then travelled back to the Town Hall to be greeted by Mayor Gompertz and a formal civic reception.

Later that evening, Attlee would address a Labour rally, Chaired by Gompertz, held at the Marsden Miners' Hall, townsfolk purchased tickets to hear the Leader of the Opposition. As he sat listening to Attlee, Gompertz would no doubt have reflected of the years he had spent helping to build the local Labour Party into the dominant political force it had become. The appalling poverty, poor working conditions and slum housing which led to the establishment of the ILP in the 1890s and then a Labour Party branch on Valentine's Day 1912, his own brutal treatment in prison during World War I, securing the Parliamentary seat in 1929, only to see the Labour Party shattered at the 1931 General Election, campaigning to rebuild the Party's trust with the electorate, Ede's victory in 1935, their Municipal success for the first time in 1937, guiding and then rebuilding the town through World War II, his constant endeavours internally to keep the Party united and focused on the challenges they faced.

With the Town Council firmly in Labour's control, the local Labour MP and the Leader of the Labour Party sitting alongside him on the platform, this was Gompertz at the zenith of his power.

In his long public service, Gompertz had never shown much enthusiasm for seeking membership of the Magistrates' Bench, although he was determined to ensure its membership should be as diverse as possible. Tradition at the time dictated that the Mayor automatically became a member of the local Magistrates' Bench, and on 28 May Gompertz was formally welcomed by the Chairman of the Bench, his old adversary Edwin Thompson, who advised that whilst Gompertz may find it a new experience, he was confident he would bring the same forensic qualities as he had displayed in his other roles.

Gompertz's next function was to attend the Coronation of Queen Elizabeth II at Westminster Abbey on 2 June, as the Mayor of a County Borough he would be given a privileged seat in the Abbey for the Ceremony. From there it was the established functions, ceremonies and other events which the First Citizen is required to lead. He hosted the Coronation Civic Ball at the Londonderry Hall in June, Annie fronted the Mayoress at Home afternoon tea in the Town Hall, he welcomed HMS *Duchess* on a goodwill visit to the Tyne, met Mr Walter Nash the New Zealand Opposition Leader who was visiting the area and travelled to Knaresborough to visit the 1st Cadet Battalion of the DLI on a camping training exercise in North Yorkshire before hosting a civic visit to the Town Hall by the Trinity House Social Centre who were taking fourteen children on a visit to Belgium.

Gompertz's elevation to the Mayoralty though raised eyebrows within certain sections of the Royal British Legion concerned with his conscientious objector beliefs during World War I. An emergency meeting of the Legion was arranged two days after Gompertz's investiture to determine whether he should be invited to their Annual Memorial Service to be held that year on 14 June in the West Park. Ede had already accepted the invitation but indicated he would not feel able to speak if the Mayor was prevented from attending. The Editor of the *Gazette* and Sir Robert Chapman also implored the Legion to accept that Gompertz would be acting as the borough's First Citizen, not as an individual and should be invited. The vote was twenty-seven to nine to issue an invitation to the Mayor. Accepting he was the First Citizen, Gompertz attended the event.

In September he was honoured by the South Shields Marine and Technical College with opening their new Building Department, which he described as: '… *the finest of its kind in the North East.*' He was invited, with Ede, to attend a black tie dinner at the Royal Hotel in September to celebrate the 50th Anniversary of the NUT in the town and in October celebrated United Nations Day unfurling their flag above the Town Hall and remarked that the UN was, '*The embodiment of the hopes of mankind.*' In October he also hosted a reception from USDAW, the Shopworkers Union, where he advised delegates that as a young man he was '*apprenticed*' to a shop receiving only two shillings for a sixty-five hour week and his request for an increase was rejected, one cannot help suspecting he was using poetic licence with this remark given he was working in the family business.

Gompertz inaugurated a new ceremony by planting a Mayoral tree on a proposed new Mayor's Walk which was to lead from West Park Road to the Bowling Greens in November but he would not attend the Annual Remembrance Service held in November, the Shields Gazette made no issue of his decision save simply to advise that '… *the Mayor would not be in attendance*', there was no outcry from the British Legion and no letters of complaint to the local newspaper, the public were clearly aware of Gompertz's view on war. He did though days before the Parade host a civic reception for servicemen who were former Prisoners of War from the Korean War.

The Mayor undertook the usual festive niceties, including a switch-on of the Christmas lights, but was also urging the public to financially support efforts to raise funds for the Westminster Abbey restoration fund. His 1954 New Year message led on the development of a new South Shields Marine and Technical College as well as the need to allow peace to flourish across the world. He also took the opportunity to visit his old school in Middlesbrough with the town's Mayor holding a reciprocal visit to South Shields in March. February saw him address the Royal Society for the Prevention of Accidents in the Town Hall, and in March he presented a Royal Humane Society medal to Dr Eugene O'Neill, the sixth recipient of such an Award in nine months leading Gompertz to ask, '*Can South Shields boast that it has more men who have been recognised for bravery during the last nine months than any other town?*'

By March, Gompertz was offering to mediate in an industrial dispute within the local coal industry which had seen since 26 February three collieries out on strike. The strike centred around the grievances about a '*tyrannical Overman*' at Whitburn, with the Whitburn Miners demanding he be suspended whilst an inquiry was held. The dispute saw Westoe and Harton strike in sympathy but not Boldon. The stoppage had an immediate impact on coal exports from Harton Staithes but was 'unofficial', the NUM President Sir Will Lawther accused the men of '*McCarthyism*' and ordered them back to work. They not only rebuffed the demand the strike threatened to overspill across the Durham Coalfield in defiance of the regional DMA Leaders. The miners did not return to work until 22 March following assurances that a full inquiry into the Overman's behaviour would be conducted.

Easter saw Gompertz give the traditional Good Friday address to the local churches' open-air service at the town's Market Place. Speaking to over 6,000 children and their families he implored the young people to carry on the traditions of '... *this worthwhile place*'. Following the Spring break, the political parties were in campaign mode for the May Council elections. Gompertz though found time to lead a delegation to London to meet with Ede and the Parliamentary Boundary Commission imploring them not to transfer several wards from South Shields into Jarrow as part of their review.

It was during his Mayoral Year that Gompertz began developing a keen interest in cultural issues, in the summer of 1953 he attended the Official opening of the Roman Fort Museum by archaeologist Sir Mortimer Wheeler, and in late November he gave a Civic Reception for Prof Ian A Richmond, an Oxford Academic and a leading authority on the Roman Empire, who was the President of the South Shields Archaeological and Historical Society and had undertaken extensive research at the town's Roman fort. By July, Gompertz was opening the 12th Photographic Society exhibition in July, where he spoke of the need for a Hall of Culture for South Shields. In February 1954 he met the French Counsel Monsieur Topres with the aim of developing cultural links between South Shields and La Rochelle, in the Bay of Biscay.

VI

As his Mayoral year ended, Gompertz kept an ever-vigilant eye on local election planning for the May 1954 Council elections with the usual negotiation between the Trade Union affiliates and the Labour Party Executive as to who would contest the various seats. The election was fought against a backdrop of Bevan's resignation from the Shadow Cabinet in April over the decision by the Shadow Cabinet to support German rearmament, a volte-face from previous Labour Party Conference decisions and one which saw the local Labour Party adopt a resolution to protest to the Party's national headquarters in London.

The Council election results though confirmed Labour's continuing dominance of the Council Chamber with two new women joining the Labour Group, Jane Craggs Knight who secured a seat in the Hadrian Ward and Stella Lloyd (niece of the early Labour pioneer Joe Batey) winning

Simonside. As Gompertz stood down from the Mayoralty, his successor Councillor Laybourn as tradition dictated, requested that Gompertz serve as deputy Mayor for the 1954/55 municipal year. In valedictions to the outgoing Mayor, Gompertz's old adversary, Bainbridge praised him for his strict impartiality as Mayor during Council debates and the fairness with which he had treated the opposition. With a solid majority for Labour in the Chamber of twenty-six, and no discernible improvement in RARAMA's electoral fortunes, there was the inevitable post-mortem by leading lights in the opposition ranks as to how they should conduct their campaigns in future. Their response, when it eventually came in October, was to agree to change their name from RARAMA to the Progressive Association. It was not a unique name change, other non-Party political Rent and Ratepayers' Association across the North East were adopting the name and for the sake of uniformity as well as providing a more modern outlook for the opposition within South Shields, it seemed a logical choice.

Vincent Fitzpatrick, who had waited patiently for a safe Labour seat, having failed previously to win the Bents Ward by just fourteen votes, was chosen to contest a June by-election in the Victoria ward caused by the elevation to the Aldermanic Bench of Jack Richardson. The recommendation was not without controversy, the seat was regarded as a fiefdom of the Marsden Miners, Fitzpatrick was an Engineer, and attempts were made to replace him with a Miners nominee at an all-delegates' meeting before the close of nominations. Gompertz though had long supported the young Fitzpatrick's desire for a Council seat and the Miners' manoeuvres were defeated albeit by only seven votes. Fitzpatrick would go on to win the by-election and as previously mentioned would assume the leadership of the new South Tyneside Council in 1973.

The Labour Party's national internal disputes over German rearmament, were soon interwoven with events in the Pacific and the development of the H-bomb which took humankind's potential for self-destruction to new heights. The Labour leadership's exasperation with the behaviour of Bevan and his supporters would lead to constant threats of expulsion for the Ebbw Vale MP and the leadership's determination to keep an iron grip on control of the Party apparatus. Locally Gompertz suffered a rare defeat in the Party when the NEC of the Labour Party proscribed the newspaper *Socialist Outlook* and advised that any person found associating with the newspaper would be ineligible for membership of the Labour Party. The ban provoked fury in the South Shields Labour Party. Members instructed Gompertz to protest to Labour's General Secretary on their behalf. The edict would have caused Gompertz some discomfort since the *Socialist Outlook* was controlled by the Trotskyist Gerry Healy but the local Party was concerned less at the political views of the newspaper, but more with the Labour Party instructing them what publications they could read. As if to reinforce the Party's moderate leanings, Gompertz advised the Party that all delegates (and their Partners) would be invited to '... *a privileged position at the Town Hall*' when the new Queen visited the Borough on 29 October 1954.

Two issues would require the detailed attention of Gompertz during 1954, one at the beginning of the year as his Mayoralty grew to as close, and the second in December.

The first was in response to proposals to alter Parliamentary Boundaries. It was the First Periodic Review following the Redistribution of Seats Act in 1949 and was no less controversial with furious and ill-tempered debates in the House of Commons and Judicial reviews brought by aggrieved local Councils resulting in new Legislation being proposed in 1958 on how the Boundary Commission would conduct its Reviews in future. The Commissioner's recommendations were certainly not welcomed across South Shields since they proposed culling the expanding electorate by transferring Simonside, Brinkburn, Cleadon Park and Marsden to the Jarrow Constituency, and placing Felling and Hebburn into Gateshead East. It was certainly a radical change which would have seen whole swathes of South Shields being administrated locally by South Shields Council but represented nationally by a Jarrow MP. There was the predictable uproar, cross-Party and cross-Council unity in opposing the recommendations with no arid polarisation evident. Gompertz represented the Constituency Party at a Boundary Commission inquiry in June, and Ede wrote the obligatory letter objecting to the proposals but it was not until November that he was able to report that the recommendations – insofar as they affected South Shields – would not go ahead, although Jarrow would still lose Felling to the Gateshead East Constituency.

The second issue would see Gompertz, a man whose political outlook was to maintain unity in Labour's ranks, defy a decision of the Labour Group in the Council Chamber along with seventeen other colleagues. The episode centred around the operations of the new Westoe Colliery (opened in 1940) with residents in Erskine Road petitioning the Town Improvement Committee in October alleging nuisance from noise attributable to the working of rail traffic running along past their properties and residents on the new Bents Park estate objecting to the Colliery with its associated dirt and noise. The Committee agreed to make representations to the National Coal Board (NCB) to examine what measures could be taken to ameliorate the prevailing conditions, but their decision needed to be approved by the Borough Council.

Sectoral interests came into play with Councillors who were mineworkers, led by Mackley, successfully moving at the Labour Group that when the request came before Borough Council it should be rejected. When the Borough Council met, Mackley moved the agreed amendment on behalf of the Labour Group that the resident's complaints should be noted but no further action taken. The amendment was agreed by nineteen votes to seventeen, but sixteen Alderman and Councillors abstained including Gompertz, Vincent Fitzpatrick, Bill Malcolm, Cuth Barrass and Jack Maddison. The issue was raised again at the November meeting of the Town Improvement Committee and the Committee again requested approval to meet with the NCB to examine local residents' complaints.

Mackley succeeded in mandating Labour Group members to reject the further request when it came to the next meeting of the Borough Council. This time in the Chamber the rebel Labour members voted with RARAMA against Mackley's motion by twenty-nine votes to twenty-two. Undeterred, Mackley then moved a further amendment, that should a Council delegation meet with the NCB then any environmental improvements should be implemented: *without interfering with the present activities* the Amendment was successful by thirty votes to twenty-three, but a few Labour Group members continued to defy Mackley and voted with RARAMA including Gompertz, Barrass, Malcolm, Ald McAnany and Ald Peel.

The mineworkers were not prepared to allow indiscipline within Labour's ranks. In January 1955 Mackley's Harton Miners' Lodge sent correspondence to the local Labour Party demanding that action be taken against Ald Peel and Mitchell who had voted with RARAMA against Mackley's motion and that those Councillors who had abstained, including Gompertz, should be censured. The meeting agreed to refer the matter to the Labour Group with the proviso that local Party Officers would meet with the Officials of the Harton Lodge in an endeavour to resolve the issue. It was a classic stalling tactic. The size of the rebellion in the Council Chamber meant that no real firm action could be taken, and since the Party was heading into the 1955 local election campaign as well as a General Election, it was not in the interests of the Party to have such a dispute spiralling out of control.

VII The dullest General Election of 1955

The Conservatives' small Parliamentary majority of only seventeen prevented the Government from altering Labour's post-war welfare state agenda, Churchill contented himself with foreign affairs. Stalin's death in 1953 offered the chance to unfreeze the developing Cold War between the East and West, but President Eisenhower vetoed any moves by Churchill to enter into negotiations with the new Soviet Leadership, and for Churchill closer involvement with continental Europe was less attractive than developing the '*special relationship*' with America. He was finally persuaded to retire in April 1955 making way for the man so-long his heir apparent, Anthony Eden. With the economy buoyant, food rationing relaxing, a promise of a '*property owning democracy*', a tax-cutting budget before the election and facing the seventy-two-year-old Attlee, the new debonair Prime Minister, with a perceived deftness in foreign affairs, sought a fresh mandate and called a snap election for 26 May 1955.

The General Election would follow the local Council elections for which Gompertz once again was his usual effervescent self, ensuring candidates were selected, finance raised and the various election paraphernalia produced. The national Party Leaders would scrutinise closely the local results to give any indication of how their respective Parties may perform at the General Election. Labour had cause to be confident, although an ageing war-horse, Attlee was still widely respected across the country, Eden was untried. The local election results when they were announced gave some hope, sweeping Labour gains across the country saw over 500 new Councillors and the Party controlling fifty-three of the eighty-three County Boroughs.

In South Shields, only seven seats were contested in the Council election, although, the decision not to contest areas considered 'safe' Progressive strongholds like Westoe, West Park and Harton was probably taken in order to save finance for the General Election campaign. Gompertz himself fighting his third election in Horsley Hill was returned unopposed a strong indication that the Progressives felt he was unmoveable, they themselves contested only five seats across the town, whilst the Communist Party were the only candidates against Labour in Simonside and Victoria. Labour suffered two defeats, in the Hadrian and Bents wards. The defeat in the Bents was not unexpected, Westoe Colliery was located in the heart of the ward and there was still significant public agitation about a new Colliery coal washer and Labour's refusal to lobby the NCB on the residents' behalf.

As attention turned to the General Election, Ede would once again face a single candidate, the Conservative John Chalmers. Under a campaign slogan of '*Your tried and trusted friend*' Ede led on his opposition to H-bomb testing in the Pacific – '*If these latest weapons are ever used in war their effect will be so terrible that little but minor salvage operations will be possible afterwards*'. He wrote of Labour's achievements in granting independence to former colonies and the creation of a Commonwealth, he maintained the need for Local Authorities to build more housing, that pensioners deserved their rightful share in national prosperity and the abolition of the eleven-plus examination and he promised that a Labour Government would renationalise the steel and road haulage industries. The General Election itself would be described by the BBC as one of the dullest with the public seemingly more interested in Princess Margaret's romance with Peter Townsend. The public impression of the Labour Party was of a divided Party epitomised by the near expulsion of Bevan from the Party at a March meeting of the NEC. Few doubted that Eden would win a new mandate, and when the ballot boxes were opened the Conservatives secured 13,310,891 votes to Labour's 12,405,254, Labour lost a further eighteen seats (including Michael Foot at Plymouth Devonport), Eden secured a comfortable majority of sixty seats. The result would finally see the changing of the old guard in the national Labour Party, Ede, safely returned in South Shields with a majority of over 10,000 was among them as he announced he would not seek re-election to the Shadow Cabinet and thus would return, for the first time since the 1930s, to the backbenches.

VIII

On 28 June 1955, Cuth Barrass, the man who had introduced Ede to South Shields, and had remained a devotee of the MP since his first election victory died aged seventy-six. A now largely forgotten figure he was a decorated World War I veteran, a retired Headmaster, a rather stern and at times unforgiving Magistrate (he resolutely enforced the use of the birch on juveniles much to Gompertz's displeasure) and a long-serving Councillor, his passing deprived Ede of a faithful liege and Gompertz of a dependable and powerful voice in local Party meetings. His replacement in the Brinkburn ward would be Jane Fry, strengthening the representation of women within the Labour Group still further and a sign of the growing influence the Women's Sections had within the local Constituency Party. One has only to visit the local Labour Party headquarters to see the South Women's Section original banner hanging in the main meeting hall that had originally been '*unfurled*' by Gompertz at their request in January 1955, an indication of the respect in which the women held Gompertz.

As Gompertz travelled to Margate for the Labour Party Conference being held over the course of the 10–14 October, he was mandated by the South Shields Labour Party to support moves to abolish conscription following a debate within the local Party which was described as being of: '… *exceptional quality*'. The motion though would be heavily defeated at the conference and Bevan would be comprehensively defeated in his second challenge for the Treasurership against Gaitskell confirming Gaitskell's place as the heir apparent to the ailing Attlee.

The result would provoke the demand from the Bevanites on the need for Party reform and criticism of the Trade Union bloc vote, but the conference hall was dominated by speeches on the need to develop new policies and electoral strategy for the next General Election and the conference fringe awash with rumours of Attlee's impending retirement to which he was at pains to explain to the *Daily Herald* that he had no intention of resigning. Six weeks later on 8 December, he did resign, claiming repeated speculation about his future made it impossible to lead the Party. Whether he tenaciously hung onto the Leadership in an attempt to thwart Herbert Morrison's bid for the leadership by allowing Hugh Gaitskell time to build up support with new MPs, or whether he genuinely remained because of his fear that the Labour Party would fracture between the Bevanites and Gaitskellites has been the subject of much conjecture but the outcome in the leadership battle on 14 December was a decisive win on the first ballot for the authentic and unapologetic figure of the right-wing Gaitskell with one hundred and fifty-seven votes, to Bevan's seventy and Morrison's forty. Morrison bitterly disappointed, removed himself from the front bench and refused to serve as Gaitskell's deputy.

As fratricide still engulfed the national Labour Party, Gompertz was anxious to maintain the Party's links with its perceived core support, the council house tenants. In November 1955 it was reported that since the end of the war, South Shields Council had built 4,729 council houses. It was a phenomenal achievement, although not unique across Tyneside as new housing estates were constructed as part of the slum clearance programme initiated before 1939. The Government, despite coming to power on a programme of supporting investment in housing, wanted to remove rent restrictions with the aim of giving encouragement to private construction firms to meet building targets rather than support Local Authorities in building social housing. In the spring of 1955 subsidies to Local Authorities from central Government were reduced necessitating rent increases. The Housing Minister, Duncan Sandys made clear that keeping rents down via subsidies from the Government was unfair to taxpayers generally, the aim was that rents on new dwellings should be increased to cover the shortfall with the expectation that Councils would be encouraged to drive slum clearance programmes at a faster rate through private construction.

The effect of course was that working people, on moderate incomes, found that their rents would increase significantly by February 1956. In Marsden and Simonside, tenants would see their current rent of 23s 9d increased by 3s 9d. At Cleadon Park rents of 11s 4d would rise to 13s 1d. There was the predictable uproar, with the local Labour Party anxious to ensure that residents understood that the increase was due to the Government reducing financial subsidies to South Shields Council.

Whilst some areas across the country experienced rent strikes, South Shields did not, due in part to the local Labour Party not encouraging such action with local Councillors rejecting any suggestion that public meetings should be organised, although they did undertake an extensive propaganda campaign through a nationally produced Labour leaflet called '*Home Truths*', to inform residents that any rent increase was due to Government policy, not the actions of the local Labour Council. The Progressives could not claim political mileage from Labour's lack of campaigning, due in part to their own support for the measures, and their desire to encourage more private housing building across the town.

IX The Tyne Improvement Commission (TIC)

Since his election in November 1932, Gompertz served intermittent terms as a Tyne Improvement Commissioner. The TIC was established in 1859 with the aim to maintain and develop the Tyne as a trading port. The TIC deepened the river, built the north and south piers, established docks such as the Northumberland, Tyne and Albert Edward and provided cross ferry links between North and South Shields. Until 1949 the TIC also maintained their own police force to protect their property. Its relationship with local authority partners was not always easy and frequently tempestuous, due in part to the TIC jealously guarding its legal rights to operate without Council interference. As an advocate of a bridge at the mouth of the Tyne, Gompertz clashed on numerous occasions with the TIC who opposed any proposals for either a bridge or a Tyne Tunnel, lest such a project might affect the commercial viability of the TIC's ferries.

As a Commissioner, Gompertz was assiduous, if sometimes populist, in defending the interests of the travelling public – mainly shipyard workers – opposing increases in tolls and on one occasion in 1954 objecting to proposals that only two watchmen would be employed to guard the two piers, by February 1955 he was demanding that all Minutes of the TIC Board should be made public and the press admitted to their meetings. During his Mayoral year in 1953, he broke with protocol that the Mayor should not comment on policy, to demand at the South Shields Chamber of Commerce Annual Dinner in October, that given a bridge across the Mouth of the Tyne was not supported, every step should be taken to ensure a new Tyne Tunnel was located between South Shields and North Shields and attacked proposals by the TIC to discontinue a direct ferry between South Shields town centre and North Shields. His frequent sometimes officious interventions at Board meetings would without question have made him a bête noire to the TIC.

It was classic Gompertz, always suspicious of officialdom, relentlessly speaking out, acting with integrity, occasionally pious. But as 1955 gave way to 1956, the times were changing. Gone was the annual May Day Rally and frequent open air Market Place meetings, as the public turned to new forms of media such as radio and television for political education. The South Shields Labour Party, safely ensconced in both the Parliamentary seat and Council Chamber settled down to implement change and manage public affairs rather than to agitate for reform as they had done over the previous half a century.

Gompertz was still maintaining his firm grip on power within the local Labour and Trades Council, his workload never decreasing, his ambition for the Party always unrelenting. But the years were now taking their toll on his health with frequent absences due to regular visits to hospital and the exuberance of his youth long gone. As new young political activists began to emerge it was perhaps inevitable that talk would begin, just a whisper at first, about Gompertz being antediluvian and thoughts of life in the Party without Gompertz and Ede.

Chapter 17

Journey's End

I

If the Labour Party was ever to return to Government, it would need first to reconcile the differences between its competing left and right factions within the Parliamentary Party. The election of Gaitskell's preferred candidate, Jim Griffiths, as the Party's Deputy Leader against Bevan in 1956 was only secured by one hundred and forty-one votes to one hundred and eleven, a smaller majority than the leadership had expected, but the PLP were sending a clear message, the division had to end. To restore peace, Gaitskell offered, and Bevan accepted a position in the shadow Cabinet as Colonial Secretary. By the time the Labour Party Conference met again later that year, Bevan was elected the Party Treasurer – the South Shields Labour Party mandating Gompertz to support the nomination at the Conference. As Labour began to enjoy a renaissance with opinion polls showing favourable rating for Gaitskell, the Conservative media began to make moves against Eden's leadership.

It was not though the movement in the opinion polls that ultimately derailed Eden's short premiership but international events.

The Hungarian Revolution broke out on 23 October with the country reacting to the repressive Stalinist regime of Mátyás Rákosi. Around 50,000 protestors marched on Budapest to demand multi-Party elections and the withdrawal of Soviet troops. Initially prepared to negotiate a withdrawal, the Politburo changed its mind and sent a large Soviet force to crush the uprising, 2,500 Hungarians were killed, 200,000 fled the country but by 10 November the Soviet Union had imposed its will and installed János Kádár to form a new Soviet supporting Government. The brutal suppression saw thousands of members of the Communist Party of Great Britain resign their membership and mass protests and 'Help Hungary' campaigns being organised across Britain.

The decision by Colonel Nasser's Government in Egypt to nationalise the Suez Canal, alongside his pan-Arabist rhetoric and courtship of the Soviet Bloc in July 1956 saw Britain with France take military action to regain the initiative in the Middle East. Encouraging Israel to attack Egypt on 29 October, two days later British and French troops landed at Port Said and Port Fuad much to the fury of the American President Eisenhower who (facing his own Presidential re-election bid) regarded it as an overreaction and colonial meddling by Britain and France. Eisenhower demanded a complete withdrawal and all military intervention by the British and French was halted by the beginning of December. Conservative backbenchers were furious at Eden's decision to acquiesce by 9 January 1957 Eden was gone and the following day Harold Macmillan entered Number 10.

The South Shields Labour and Trades Council discussed the events in Hungary and the Middle East with increasing alarm, their November meetings agreed two formal motions, the first describing the Governments actions in Suez as: '... *the denial of the principles of Law and humanity which the aggression involves*' and demanded that the Government adhere to United Nations obligations that military intervention must cease immediately. The second motion condemned the Soviet Union for its attack on Hungary and called for the immediate withdrawal of Soviet troops. Both resolutions were sent to the Prime Minister and Ede. Speaking to the local Party in January 1957, Ede remarked prophetically that it would take years to eradicate the shock of the actions of the British Government in relation to Suez.

II

Whilst the local Party could express its indignation at world events, it still had issues nearer home to contend with. The May elections, held well before the autumn international crisis, were a lacklustre affair, eight wards were unopposed and in the only change to the Council Chamber, the Labour Party lost its last remaining seat in the Hadrian ward, meanwhile long-serving Labour stalwart Alderman Alex Stephenson would serve as Mayor for the 1956/57 municipal year. The year would also see approval for a massive slum clearance programme with the Council signing off plans to demolish whole swathes of the town centre housing including Alderson Street, Sunny Terrace, Somerset Street, Raglan Street area, Laygate area (demolishing St Mark's Church and erecting new flats), Denmark Street, Portberry Street and Derby Terrace. The sheer scale of the proposals was an indication of the Council's determination to tackle housing declared unfit for human habitation with some speed. Meanwhile, the RC Church sold land at Cauldwell for housing to finance a new school for the Whiteleas estate.

In July Gompertz attended the Regional Labour Party Conference where a motion supporting re-organisation of Local Government in the region was discussed. The Conference agreed the motion by eighty-three to thirty-eight votes, Gompertz voted against. He advised the South Shields Labour Party that he felt it looked suspiciously like an attempt to re-create the '*Tory unification of Tyneside*' policy. At the same local meeting Jim Florence, an AEU Member become the new Political Education Officer for the local Party. Florence would emerge as a brilliant administrator in his own right, eventually becoming the South Shields Labour Party Secretary, a long-serving Secretary to the Trades Council and a local Councillor, had it not been for his unexpected defeat in the May 1968 elections he may well have assumed the leadership of the Council over Ernest Mackley. He had certainly caught Gompertz's eye who unquestionably encouraged Florence in his work.

III

By 1957 the world was coming to terms with the Cold War hostilities between the East and West. The West looked on as the Soviet Union inaugurated the space race launching Sputnik 1, the East viewed with concern Britain detonating the H-bomb and President Eisenhower announced his Doctrine of supporting any Country facing Communist Aggression. Western Europe, determined never to experience a war on its continent again created the Common Market to give mutual economic aid to its members whilst Britain continued its path from Imperialism to a new Commonwealth by granting Singapore its Independence. The ending of rationing, a young Monarch on the throne and greater consumer durables to purchase led the new Prime Minister Harold Macmillan to announce to a Conservative audience in Bedford that for most people, '… *they've never had it so good.*'

It was the year that Gaitskell faced down the dogma of the left-wing in his Party and convincingly defeated attempts to make unilateral nuclear disarmament Party policy, thanks in no small measure to Nye Bevan pleading with conference delegates not to send him '… *into the Conference Chamber naked*'.

Locally, South Shields Council was required to consider population shifts across the town. As new estates emerged, ward boundaries would need to be changed. Gompertz as a member of the influential Parliamentary Trade and

Commerce Committee was a key member during the deliberations. Hadrian and the Deans wards would be abolished, changes would be made to the remaining wards and two new electoral divisions would be created, Whiteleas and Biddick Hall wards. The proposals would take affect for the May 1958 elections with the Councillors for Hadrian being transferred to represent Whiteleas and the Deans Councillors to Biddick Hall. The result would prove electorally disastrous for the Hadrian Progressive Councillors who would each lose their seats in the new council-house-dominated Whiteleas ward as their term of office expired.

One cannot help acknowledging that by 1957 the local Party seems to have lost some of its earlier pugnacity. Trades Council meetings were shorter in duration, with less debate taking place. Labour Party meetings centred around correspondence, the request for donations for numerous worthwhile national causes and occasionally an item of Municipal concern would be raised invariably always by Gompertz himself, frequently the meetings' denouement would be ambiguous, but the Stalwarts were not complacent. A new Fundraising Committee spearheaded by the redoubtable Murtaugh and Liz Diamond ensured finance was available for election campaigning, but the near collapse of the opposition, with the Progressives failing to make inroads into Labour's now impregnable majority in the Council Chamber and no serious Liberal or Conservative Association threat, meant that the Party concentrated on its strategy of transforming the town without the need to counteract any serious challenge between elections. The change in outlook was probably inevitable, like their Labour counterparts in other areas, they had now become the Civic establishment and acted accordingly.

The May 1957 Council elections confirmed this fact, there were only six contests, Labour may have lost its last remaining seat in the Hadrian Ward, but they unexpectedly won Cleadon Park for the first time by only fifty-five votes. Labour's strength in the Town Hall remained forty, with twenty Progressives forming the opposition.

There were though two items of note which Gompertz felt the need to involve the local Party, one in relation to his ongoing battles with the TIC and another involving the proposal to lease Council land to a developer in Laygate.

The TIC had not endeared itself to Gompertz, who was still a Commissioner on their Board, following their decision to support the construction of a Tyne Tunnel on the grounds that a bridge may affect the commercial viability of the shipyards by potentially restricting their ability to build some of the world's largest ships. Consequently, Gompertz would become more garrulous in his criticism of the TIC particularly when they were required to suspend ferry crossings between South and North Shields, without providing alternative transport. A delegation from the South Shields Labour Party met with the TIC in May but the critical issue was that ferries themselves were becoming outdated and the TIC needed to allocate finance to replace the rolling stock. The problem was further compounded for shipyard workers when the Jarrow to Howdon ferry began to breakdown, although operated by Durham and Northumberland County Councils, Gompertz argued that the TIC had an obligation to ensure a replacement service was provided to ensure the shipyard workers could travel to work. Criticism of the TIC's handling of the cross Tyne Ferry services continued at regular intervals with Tynemouth and South Shields Councils making repeated objections and Gompertz using his membership of the TIC Board to remonstrance with TIC Officials. The response from the TIC was to offer in October 1958 to hand over the ferry landings and the operation of the service to the two Councils, presumably on the assumption that the Councils would finance new rolling stock. Both Councils firmly rejected the offer. In response Gompertz endeavoured to coordinate resistance by seeking to form a TIC Labour Group but it failed to materialise due to the refusal of Labour Councillors from neighbouring authorities (who were also Commissioners of the TIC) to join.

The second issue was more significant and involved an issue which would set Gompertz on a collision course with senior members of the Labour Group, and fatally Ernest Mackley, and would prove to be another catalyst around which Gompertz's growing number of detractors would be able to coalesce as moves began to challenge his powerbase within the Constituency Labour Party.

The controversy began over the proposed granting of a lease to a long established drapers' company called Allen and Co Ltd (who in time would become Hedley Young) who were desirous to purchase freehold of some 847 square yards of land adjoining their premises in Laygate adjacent to the new western Approach Road. The Town Improvement Committee, whilst having a rather narrow policy of not selling public land, were supportive and instructed Officers to negotiate with the Company. By 16 May 1957 the Town Improvement Committee agreed an Officer recommendation to grant a 999-year lease to the Company. Not surprisingly Gompertz was outraged, he arranged for the matter to be discussed at a special meeting of the local Labour Party who were adamant that the terms of the lease were unacceptable. A delegation was despatched to the Labour Group, including Jim Florence and Ken Scrimger to seek a resolve. It was agreed that the original recommendation should be referred back to the Town Improvement Committee for further consideration. As instructed, the following meeting of the Town Improvement Committee agreed to reduce the terms of the lease to ninety-nine years, but when the matter was subsequently debated at Borough Council in July it was agreed to sell the freehold to the Company at a price fixed by the District Auditor. Gompertz opposed the sale of municipal land and abstained from the vote.

The controversy was not over though and would resurface in 1958.

IV

Macmillan's Government was rocked by a series of resignations as the new year unfolded in January 1958 which included the Chancellor, Peter Thorneycroft and his two junior Treasury Ministers over the issue of increased Government expenditure. Thorneycroft wanted to reduce spending and prevent inflation rising further, his Prime Minister refused, describing the departure of his entire Treasury Team as '... *a little local difficulty*'. The event was the highlight of Ede's speech to the Constituency Labour Party when he addressed them in early January, stating that it was: '... *a conflict between those who believe in stopping inflation and those who don't*'.

The formation of the Campaign for Nuclear Disarmament (CND) in February 1958, would in time unravel the 1957 settled will of the Labour Conference policy decision against unilateralism. Gaitskell, a passionate Atlanticist and firm believer in the need for a British nuclear deterrent, would be obliged to spend considerable time organising within the Labour movement to prevent CND's growing influence. The policy debate though was not a straightforward left versus the right-wing battle within the Labour movement and there was certainly support for unilateralism amongst a wide section of the British public concerned about the destructive power of the nuclear bomb. Neither were the motions to the Labour Party Conference supporting unilateralism always submitted by the usual Left-wing constituency Labour Parties. In February, just days after the formation of CND, the South Shields Labour and Trades Council agreed a motion to protest at the Government's decision to allow US American military bases in Great Britain. As a pacifist Gompertz would have been an active advocate of unilateralism.

The debate over unilateralism would ingulf the whole Labour movement, and in many respects denied the Labour Party the full opportunity to come to terms, debate and then react to their election defeat of 1955. Anthony Crosland's book, *The Future of Socialism* published in 1956 was an attempt to offer a new argument for Social Democracy in the context of the political consensus that had been introduced by the Attlee Government, with an emphasis more on social equality as opposed to merely believing that nationalisation was the defining goal of Socialism. The book was certainly in contrast with Bevan's 1952 highly acclaimed tome, *In Place of Fear*, in which Bevan wrote of his political journey and reasserted his belief that you cannot achieve Democratic Socialism without common ownership of the means of production. It is evident that the Labour Party at the time were unable to reconcile its various factions into a collegiate set of aims and values to present to the British electorate.

Meanwhile the South Shields Labour and Trades Council February 1958 Annual Meeting would see the beginnings of a new era with Murtaugh Diamond assuming the Chairmanship of the Party whilst the death of Party stalwart Alderman James Garnett before the Council elections presented the Party with an opportunity to appoint a new Alderman. The automatic nominee, on seniority (given Gompertz had pledged to the electors of Horsley Hill not to serve on the unelected Bench in future) was Ernest Mackley. With Mackley due for re-election to the Council in his Simonside ward in the May election, Gompertz argued that in order to save on the inevitable by-election costs, Mackley should withdraw his nomination for the election and await his appointment to the Aldermanic Bench at the Council's Annual Meeting. Gompertz went so far as to recommend the appointment of a new candidate for Simonside, a Boilermaker Joseph Jackson. Despite the local Party supporting the moves, Mackley steadfastly refused to withdraw his nomination. To do so would have meant a gap in public service, and he probably wasn't prepared to take the risk that once not a member of the Labour Group, his colleagues could be relied upon to appoint him to the Aldermanic vacancy. It is difficult not to conclude that Mackley, as a supporter of the Allen and Co leasing agreement, felt that Gompertz was attempting to outmanoeuvre him. Mackley was subjected to a formal motion of censure from the Party for his actions, in return he gave Gompertz some of his recalcitrant tongue and was re-elected unopposed in the May council election. It was an astonishing rebuke for Gompertz and demonstrated that his hold on power within the Party was beginning to unravel.

The actual elections in May 1958 were for once competitively contested by the Progressive Association and turnout was one of the highest in recent years, there was the predictable Labour gain in the Whiteleas ward, the only change to the Council, and Gompertz, in the last election he would contest, was safely re-elected in Horsley Hill with a majority of 219.

As the Borough Council met after the May elections for its Annual Meeting several Labour Councillors and Alderman were absent, including Gompertz. Mackley secured the coveted Aldermanic vacancy by only eighteen votes to seventeen against the Progressive nominee Edmund Hill. Whether there was a deliberate strategy to stop Mackley becoming an Alderman is now lost to history, but the fact remains that the usual omnipresent Gompertz was not in attendance at the crucial meeting, his absence was noted by Mackley.

The resulting by-election in Simonside would not be contested by Joseph Jackson. In a further defeat for Gompertz, Mackley insisted that all affiliated organisations should be requested to submit potential candidates' names and the shortlist subject to a vote by the Labour Party delegates. The miners were clearly disgruntled that Simonside – regarded as a 'Mineworkers' seat – had been allocated by Gompertz to a Boilermaker. In the resultant ballot, Hugh Armstrong of Mackley's Harton Miners' Lodge, was selected to contest the Council vacancy.

The decision to sell municipal land to Allen and Co resurfaced with a vengeance in August. In May 1958, following protracted negotiations with the Company the Town Improvement Committee had agreed to sell the requested land at Laygate to the Company but now the Company wanted 950 square yards as opposed to the original 847. Attempts by the Progressive Association at the subsequent Borough Council to refer the sale back to Committee were rebuffed – Council Minutes do not indicate a named vote so we cannot be certain how Gompertz voted although given his previous opposition to the land sale he is likely to have abstained.

There was further controversy when in July following the sale of the Freehold, Allen and Co announced they were in talks for a buy-out by Great Universal Stores. Gompertz believed that the Company had acted in a duplicitous manner and for a second time called an emergency meeting of the Labour Party Executive to discuss the whole saga. Delegates were clearly in an agitated mood, those Councillors who had voted for the sale of Freehold did so in open faith that Allen and Co required the land to invest and expand their operations in the town, to commence talks for a buy-out within days of signing the purchase caused a storm.

Harry Donkin and Stella Lloyd moved that the Labour Group should be requested to meet immediately and that the matter needed to be discussed at Borough Council with Counsel's Opinion being sought on whether the legality of the sale of the land to Great Universal could be contested. Despite the outcry, the issue was not raised at a meeting of the Borough Council nor any of its Committees, and the *Shields Gazette* does not carry any article of the saga. One can only conclude that discussions with the Council's legal department had taken the view that the actions of Allen and Co were legal and no judicial challenge could be made. Gompertz's opposition though had caused a serious rift between himself and other senior Labour Councillors – in particular, Mackley.

As Labour Party delegates gathered in Scarborough for their Annual Conference during 29 September–3 October, it was clear that there was a mood for unity. Individual Trade Union delegations had made clear that they opposed any attempts to commit the Party to unilateralism despite 142 motions being submitted supporting the measure. South Shields Labour Party was one of the 142. In a further demonstration of unity, Gaitskell manoeuvred for Bevan to become the new Treasurer of the Labour Party, securing him a place once again on the NEC. The debate on Britain's nuclear deterrent reaffirmed by a large majority the Party's previous position, to end nuclear testing, and then to strive for multilateral disarmament. The conference debate, although lasting nearly five hours was less emotional than in 1957 and with Labour leaders sensing that Harold Macmillan may call a snap General Election, delegates were sent home by the new Party Treasurer, Nye Bevan with a rallying call to start campaigning and raise much needed finance for victory.

There was certainly no shortage of financial resources locally. The new Social Committee which included Ken Scrimger, Jim Florence, Murtaugh and Liz Diamond was fastidious in their work in building up Party resources. In July, Jim Florence wrote formally to the Party recommending that they consider purchasing their own headquarters which led to the local Labour Party establishing an Acquisition of Property Committee in October 1958. The timing was fortuitous, since by April the following year, Martins Bank wrote to Gompertz to advise that they were terminating the Party's lease on the upstairs room of weekly hours from 43.5 to 40 on 11 November 1959. Given the Labour and Trades Council had tenanted the building since 1929, it was an unforgiving timeline, particularly since the Party would have a General Election to contest that year. Legal threats by Gompertz followed, advising that the Party would take Martins Bank to Court if more time for a move was not granted. The Bank relented and agreed that the Lease would not be terminated until 1 May 1960.

Why the lease was terminated is unclear, Minutes do not record any ongoing dispute between tenant and landlord, but the likely explanation is that the Council was moving to demolish and regenerate the Green Street area which would have included the Martins Bank property. The decision by the Bank meant that local activists would have to seek new premises, whether for rent or purchase and time was not on their side. Gompertz endeavoured to take the lead in securing new premises, identifying the recently vacated St Mark's Vicarage in Laygate as an ideal new base for the Party. He worked with Ede to secure the support of the Diocese and prepared a Report for the Constituency Executive.

During this period South Shields Council was taking the first steps to remodel the town centre, severely damaged during the war. The Market Place itself had witnessed bombing that wiped out almost half the properties with hardly a building in the area escaping some form of damage. In October the Chief Engineer, John Reid, outlined ambitious plans to remodel the Market Place to create a modern area but maintaining a link with the past by retaining the old Town Hall in the Market Square and ensuring St Hilda's Church formed part of the feature of the new Square. Property and land around the Market Square had gradually been purchased by the Council since 1947 and the developments would see new Office and shops constructed with two new occupants being the National Assistance Board and Law Courts. Reid would go on to redevelop Keppel Street, Fowler Street and surrounding areas, during a long and distinguished career. Modern-day critics decried the 1960s architecture which replaced the Victorian and Edwardian buildings, but at the time Reid was praised for giving South Shields town centre a modern outlook more in keeping with the period.

V

The 1959 May Council elections would witness the beginning of a local government career of two rising stars of both the Labour Party and Progressive opposition. Ken Scrimger was elected for Whiteleas, the only change of the night, whilst Stan Smith, would be elected unopposed as a Progressive in the Westoe Ward. A family dynasty was also in the making when hairdresser Bill Malcolm (nephew of railwayman Councillor Billy Malcolm) sought election in Cleadon Park but was unsuccessful. Gompertz had also insisted that extra campaign resource should be provided to Horsley Hill, a wise move given the Labour Party held the seat by only eleven votes. Gompertz's comments in relation to Labour's near-miss in the mixed housing ward are interesting because in many respects they epitomised Labour's problem nationally in seeking to broaden its electoral appeal beyond its core working-class vote: '*While the result in Horsley Hill is satisfactory to us, the figures indicate that unfortunately many owner-occupiers of new houses, the very people who have been severely punished by the present Government, still suffer from the delusion that there is something undignified about voting Labour.*'

In July the Country was gripped when printers and ink manufacturing workers went on strike seeking a 10 per cent wage increase and a reduction in their weekly hours from 43.5 to 40 hours. The dispute was solid with the employers saying nearly 90 per cent of the workforce across the country were supporting their respective Trade Unions. The dispute affected print production, with newspapers being required at first to produce much reduced newspaper output, but as the strike dragged on, some media outlets were forced to cease producing their publications. Initially, newspapers sought to carry on, but the National Union of Journalists (NUJ) ordered their members not to give assistance in the production of so-called 'Black newspapers' and Labour Councils across the country ordered those journalists breaking the embargo to leave Council meetings, journalists refusing to support the production of their newspaper during the dispute were summarily dismissed by their employers.

In South Shields, the local newspaper, the *Shields Gazette*, terminated the employment of their 35 journalists in July leading to the NUJ appealing to the South Shields Trades Council for assistance. The response was predictable, all possible support was offered, affiliates and Labour Party members were urged not to purchase the 'black newspapers' and letters of support for the print workers were sent to Ede, the *Northern Press*, the Secretary of the local Newsagents Federation and the TUC. The printers' dispute would last six weeks, before arbitration resolved the matter with the printers securing a forty-two-hour week and a 4.5 per cent pay rise.

VI 1959 General Election

The 1950s were a relatively successful period in British history and later declinist narratives underplay the evidence: increased manufacturing exports, rising living standards, improved housing, full employment and a decline in class deference. Had the 1951 Labour Government been able to hold onto Office until at least 1952 they would have been the beneficiaries of the economic boom. As history records, it was the Conservatives who reaped the benefits and in their April 1959 Budget were able to present a cornucopia of electoral inducements, cuts in income tax, cuts in purchase tax, the releasing of post-war credits, the result was a consumer-spending spree as people rushed to buy the capital goods they had been denied for so long.

Britain was changing, the nature of the workplace was changing with an expansion of the white-collar sector (where Trade Unionism was weaker). The social reforms instigated by the reforming Labour Government of 1945 had not been dismantled by their Conservative successors, far from it, they could point to an increase of spending in education, building new universities and more spending on the health service. The Labour Party by 1959 was perceived as essentially a working-class Party, too obsessed with nationalisation whilst the children of their core supporters began perceiving themselves as aspiring middle class.

Against this background, Macmillan called an election for 8 October 1959. Labour entered the campaign certainly more optimistic than in 1955 – Hugh Gaitskell (if not his Party) seemed more in tune with the public mood, he looked better on the growing medium of television and one of his open-air meetings attracted 20,000 people. The Party was more united than at the previous General Election (Bevan had been elected Deputy Leader of the Party in May 1959), opinion polls were turning favourably to the Labour Party in the closing days of the election and reports to Labour headquarters from the Constituencies were positive.

In South Shields, safely re-adopted by the South Shields Labour Party on Sunday 13 September the seventy-seven-year-old Ede would fight his final General Election campaign with the ever-loyal Gompertz by his side. For the third time his opponent was the Conservative John Chalmers, no other candidates emerged. His leaflet declared he was the '*Faithful man of the people*', announced he favoured gradual nuclear disarmament, reducing school class sizes, ending the anxieties associated with the eleven plus examination and abolishing all NHS charges. The result when declared was never in doubt, he secured 32,577 votes to Chalmers 23,638.

Nationally, it would prove a disaster for the Labour Party, losing its third General Election in a row. Although there were swings to the Party in the North West and in Scotland; in the West Midlands, location of the new light industries (where voters became prone to seeing themselves as a consumer as opposed to a member of the working class) there was a swing to the Conservatives. In all the Conservatives gained twenty-eight seats, Macmillan's majority was over 100 seats in the House of Commons.

Between 28 and 29 November, Gompertz journeyed to Blackpool for the postponed Labour Party Conference, it would be the last conference he attended as the delegate from South Shields. Despite a fiery speech from the Party Chair, Barbara Castle, morale was low. Gaitskell told delegates that internal research by the Labour Party had shown that the electorate felt the Party remained deeply ideological at a time of immense social change and simply didn't like or trust the Party's commitment to wholesale nationalisation and served notice he wanted to change Clause IV of the Party constitution. Fierce opposition within the higher echelons of the Party would prevent him from pursuing the issue, in part because his second plan was to reduce the influence of the Trade Unions by introducing a federal structure with indirect elections to the NEC. Neither would there be a change in the Party's name, despite suggestions by a close Gaitskell acolyte Douglas Jay. Bevan gave the usual barnstorming speech at the conclusion of the conference and to his credit sought to keep the Party united and focused on the challenges ahead. But seven months later, Bevan would be dead and the Labour Party would erupt again over the issue of unilateral nuclear disarmament.

VII

A review of local government boundaries reared its head again in late 1959 as the Government implemented its manifesto and endeavoured to restructure the operation of local authority services across the country. Predictably, all local Councils endeavour to protect their own positions, and emotions can rise given the Civic pride members of the public have in their respective areas and this review was no different. Sedulously, Newcastle City once again raised the spectre of a Tyneside Council under the auspices of a '*Greater Newcastle*' conurbation, their proposals would have seen Gateshead, Hebburn, Jarrow, Felling, Wallsend, Gosforth and parts of Longbenton becoming part of the Newcastle administrative area, with Tynemouth, South Shields and Sunderland County Boroughs remaining single tier authorities. Accents of cajolery would though not pacify their neighbours. South Shields Council reacted by submitting their own proposals which retained South Shields as a standalone County Borough, but with Jarrow, Hebburn and Boldon

Councils being absorbed into its boundaries, it was a proposal encouraged by the South Shields Labour and Trades Council and Gompertz would appear in front of the Boundary Commissioners at a Public Inquiry to support the proposal.

There was the usual tourney, Jarrow denounced both Newcastle City Council and the South Shields County Borough plans as a land grab. Hebburn rejected Newcastle's proposals as '*unwieldy*', thought the South Shields proposal more reasonable but eventually made their own submission to create a Hebburn, Jarrow, Boldon and Felling Council. Surprisingly, the Conservative Party in Newcastle opposed any moves to create a Greater Newcastle Authority accusing their Labour counterparts of acting as '*dictatorial tyrants*' and betraying the trust of neighbouring authorities.

The Commission's final deliberations would not report until 1963, when it proposed a two-tier Tyneside Local Government structure, a County Council named Tyneside, divided into four Council Boroughs, South Shields would form one Borough with Jarrow, Hebburn and Boldon. The debate raged on until 1965 when the new Labour Local Government Minister, Richard Crossman proposed a one-tier structure – the County Borough of Tyneside which would make it the second largest Council in England (after Birmingham). Even the 'Crossman Plan' would eventually be rejected in 1966 with the issue of Local Government reorganisation across the Tyneside conurbation not being finally settled until the 1972 Local Government Act which created a two-tier structure, Tyne and Wear County Council, with five corresponding District Councils in the new county.

VIII

The move against Gompertz's long reign and control of the South Shields Labour and Trades Council when it came was swift, ruthless and executed with precision planning, Gompertz, caught by the speed of the execution, was powerless to stop the camarilla around Ernest Mackley.

The 1960 Annual Meeting of Delegates held in February ran smoothly, Gompertz's protégé, joiner Ken Scrimger was to be the new Chair for the year and Gompertz was unchallenged for the post of Secretary/Agent, they retained long-serving Jack Clark as the Assistant Secretary. The finances were healthy, nearly £330 had been raised by the Property Acquisition Committee charged with securing finance for the local Party to purchase their own headquarters and the Social Committee had raised nearly £128 to support campaign efforts. Delegates considered the rising unemployment figures in the town and expressed particular concern that the clothing firm Mary Harris Ltd had announced it was to close its South Shields operations. Deputations to the Council were agreed with the aim of sending a delegation to the Board of Trade in London to examine how to arrest the rise in unemployment. Ominously, Ernest Mackley raised questions at the meeting in relation to the position of the Chairman and Secretary and was advised that the matter required a Notice of Motion to be considered formally.

Three weeks later Ernest Mackley struck with venom.

Submitting a notice of motion to 26 February Executive Committee he sought to change the status of the Party hierarchy. His motion, in full, read:

'A: A Chairman to be elected for the current year in accordance with the model rules published by the Labour Party.

B: The present post of Secretary/Agent be abolished and a parttime Secretary be elected.

C: The Party Agent to continue as full time Agent so long as authorised by the Member for the Borough and the Labour Party.

D: A special sub Committee of the Party and Council be set up to discuss the duties and renumeration of the part time Secretary and present a Report not later than the July 1960 meeting of the Party and Council'.

The Minutes record that the Executive agreed to recommend to the delegates' meeting that the Motion be endorsed and submitted to a Standing Orders Committee consisting of Jim Florence, Ken Scrimger, Jack Clark and Thomas Bell. The meeting further proposed making a number of recommendations for candidates for the May Council elections and Minutes record that at the conclusion of the meeting Gompertz was asked to produce all relevant documents relating to his appointment as Secretary. Gompertz advised that he had secured two offers of Office space in line with the requirements to vacate their premises in Laygate Lane and urged the Party to consider the option of purchasing St Mark's Vicarage, the Executive rejected the suggestions.

The business of the local Party continued when three days later the Property Acquisitions subcommittee met to consider a vacant property in Westoe Road, they would though require a mortgage and substantial works would be required to the building. In the meantime, they agreed to recommend that the Party move its operations to a one room office in King Street with a lease renewable quarterly.

The Labour Party delegates again assembled for their monthly meeting on 1 March. Minutes are vague, Ken Scrimger as Chair of the meeting advised that given its significance, he would take Mackley's notice of motion as the first item of business for the meeting but insisted, perhaps to aid Gompertz, that he would accept amendments to the motion from delegates – procedurally a correct course of action. Uproar followed, Scrimger was subjected to asperity from delegates and his ruling was challenged. He vacated the Chair whilst delegates considered the matter. Following a lengthy, unrecorded philippic debate, they voted that no amendments to Mackley's motion should be taken and following further debate voted 47–18 in favour of Mackley's motion – Gompertz's hold on the Party was at an end. Adopting a phlegmatic attitude, Gompertz, wearing a mask of imperturbability made a brief statement to delegates, professionally carried on with the meeting and reported on the deliberations of the Property Acquisition Committee.

At the conclusion of the meeting, Ken Scrimger made a public statement to the waiting media – who had clearly been forewarned of Gompertz's impending downfall – and advised them that the Party had decided to abolish the role of Secretary/Agent. Gompertz was heard in the background making a call to the Mayor, Tom Peel, advising him that it was his intention to resign as a Councillor at the following day's Borough Council meeting. At the Party Chairman's insistence, Gompertz then telegraphed the news to Ede and advised he was standing down as his Agent. Mackley was reticent to talk to the *Shields Gazette* save only to comment that '... *things have gone on as far as I wanted them to go on*'. He would not elaborate stating that he did not '... *want to add fuel to the fire.*' Gompertz returned home, wrote the Minutes of his last Labour and Trades Council meeting, and signed them off with the poignant words, '*Goodbye Comrades*'.

The following day residents were greeted with the banner *Gazette* headline: '***Gompertz is thrown out – resigning from Council and all public offices***' acknowledging the scale of the vote against Gompertz, they advised their readers that relations in the local Party had been difficult for some time. Gompertz they observed could be a stubborn man, '... *some would say bigoted, but dedicated to the people of the town*'. As he left the stage the *Gazette* recorded that he left behind many able men of diverse talents, '... *but it is to be doubted whether there is among them a man of Gompertz's stature*'.

At the Borough Council, after the Mayor announced he had received correspondence from Gompertz resigning with immediate effect and wishing him well for the future, he allowed Gompertz to address the meeting. Gompertz was heard in respectful silence as he gave a short speech, thanking fellow Members and Officers for the support they had rendered to him over the years and gave a special mention to the residents of Horsley Hill who had persistently stood by him over the years. Mackley and his supporters sat passively as Gompertz turned to exit the Chamber for the final time. As he did so, opposition Councillor Ernest Dodds rose, walked across the Chamber and magnanimously took Gompertz by the hand and gave a hearty handshake to a man who had tormented and frustrated the opposition since his first Council meeting in 1932. Once he had left, it was, ironically another opposition member, this time his old adversary Robert Bainbridge, who stood and moved a vote of appreciation in Gompertz's public service, acknowledging their long service on the Council together. Bainbridge said that Gompertz had been a '… *foeman worthy of a man's steel*' and continued '*On more than one occasion I have described him as a most bellicose pacifist I ever encountered. He is indeed a strange amalgam of incompatible characteristics but there is one thing which no one can deny that his probity is unimpeachable.*' Jim Ireland, who Gompertz had mentored, rose to second the vote of thanks in the absence of any moves from his own Group Leadership.

There was the predictable backlash to Gompertz's departure amongst his constituents in Horsley Hill. In a vox pop article a few days after his resignation, residents in Horsley Hill were demanding that he should be made a Freeman of the Borough. '*He was one of the finest fighters for the working class that it has been my privilege to meet*', was a typical reaction from one Constituent, '*I wish that he had not felt himself forced to give up all his work. We in Horsley Hill were proud to have him as one of our Councillors*' another. There was unanimity that the Labour Party had dealt with Gompertz unfairly, even though he may be advancing in years, his long service merited a more conciliatory removal.

The scale of the vote in favour of Mackley's motion demonstrated that the local Party desired change, but the unforgiving way in which Gompertz's removal was orchestrated proved to be a source of contention amongst stalwarts at the time and is still referred to even to the present day. Mackley, as previously recorded, disapproved of Gompertz's management style and over the years hostility and a clash of personalities between the two men festered. But Mackley wasn't the only opponent Gompertz faced. Union Organiser Alex Stephenson was also determined to end Gompertz's grip on the Party. Like all long-serving political operators, Gompertz built up during his tenure a number of political enemies all waiting patiently for the right time to make their move, Mackley fired the bullet but the bullet was made by a new younger generation emerging, bringing fresh ideas and a desire for a new approach – with Gompertz rigid and uncompromising in his approach Mackley was able to encourage them to coalesce around his moves for change. Finally the Party was probably also sending a signal to Ede that it was time to move on. By 1960 Gompertz would be seventy-two, Ede seventy-eight, neither showed any public sign of retiring, the move against Gompertz made clear to Ede that it was time to go, by July he would announce that he would not be contesting the next General Election.

Whilst Mackley had designs on the South Shields Parliamentary nomination and his motion was in many respects designed to force Ede's hand, he cannot be allowed to shoulder the full blame for Gompertz's downfall. Delegates from across the political spectrum were of the view that the local Party needed new Leadership and that an era was inevitably coming to an end. Could they have dealt with Gompertz more diplomatically in view of his long service, probably not, he showed no signs of retiring or relinquishing his total control over the Party machine, he was a stubborn seasoned political operator who given any forewarning would have deployed every procedural tactic to thwart his opponent's moves, they were not prepared to take the risk. Whilst he could have remained as Ede's Agent and remained in public office as a Councillor, he chose not to.

Following his defeat Gompertz wrote to '*My Dear Friend Ede*', to give his personal view on his removal. '*Countless pin pricks both in the Town Council and at Party meetings have been going on since the General Election; they have a motive which I hesitate to write, but the plan is quite clear to me.*' Acknowledging the scale of his defeat he accepted the decision but advised he would not accept any part-time post Agent's post. Ede responded on 5 March advising he was '… *aggrieved at the situation*', he continued: '*It has been clear for a long time that a crisis could only be avoided with great difficulty, but I am none the less sorry that it has come in this particularly objectionable manner. Over thirty years devoted service on your part should not have been brought to an end in such a way*'.

Despite being a founder member of the South Shields Labour Party, the Parliamentary Agent in eight Parliamentary elections and a long-serving public figure, the treatment of Gompertz following his downfall by the local Party was unforgiving and spiteful. Within days the Party closed their

Laygate Lane base and established their new headquarters, temporarily, at 29 King Street, Gompertz took only three items home with him from the Office, a photograph of his father, a photograph of himself with Keir Hardie at a Labour Party conference and a private letter from Ede advising that he was considering resigning from Parliament.

In further correspondence to Gompertz in late March 1960, Ede confided that he was of the opinion he should resign from Parliament, Gompertz was adamant that he must continue until the General Election, to do otherwise would merely play into the hands of those with *'guilty consciences'*. He reassured Ede that his letter advising that he was considering resigning had not been shared with Party Officials. Gompertz also indicated that he had offered to assist the Party in the preparations for the May 1960 Council elections but that the Executive Committee rejected his overtures, leading Gompertz to write: *'Public opinion is against the Party, I am worried on this score and dread to think what is going to happen in Horsley Hill in the event of an early by-election. I cannot put into writing all my fears …'*

Jack Clark assumed the Secretary's duties but the Labour Party Regional Organiser, Mr Algar, was required to attend the Constituency Executive meeting to advise that Gompertz had a written contract with the Party which stipulated three months' notice must be given to terminate his employment. The Party agreed to pay three months' salary in lieu of notice, but advised this would be from 1 March, national officials insisted it must be from 1 April. The discussion concluded with *'Failure to agree'* on this point, and Mr Algar further cautioned the Party on making any changes to their model Standing Orders until he had received further clarification from the National Executive Committee.

Attempts by Chuter Ede to move the Party on the issue of the 1 March date were rebuffed, as were repeated approaches during the year from the Labour Party Agents' Union. The Constituency Party, despite Algar's plea, were also adamant they would not themselves employ a full-time Agent but would instead employ an elected part-time Secretary. By 1 July, Ede appeared in front of the South Shields Labour Party Executive Committee to advise that he would still contribute £50 a year to the local Party who could use it as they saw fit, he made no arrangements to appoint a new Agent, but within days, accepting a change in leadership in the local Party and having agreed with Gompertz to postpone his announcement until after the May elections, Ede announced that he was retiring at the next General Election. Ken Scrimger in the meantime was asked to support Ede whenever he visited the Constituency.

IX Aftermath

Gompertz retreated to his Quarry Lane home, grew hyacinth bulbs in bowls and cultivated his garden. John Murtha, a young devotee, would visit him frequently, where even though he was a teetotaller he would pour his guest a glass of wine and reminisce about the rise of the South Shields Labour Party. Urged by the *Shields Gazette* to comment he simply remarked: '*I have not resigned as Secretary/Agent, the post has been abolished and I have gone with it*'. Demonstrating his total devotion to the Labour Party, he advised that it was the future which counted, not the past, and that he would remain a member of the Labour Party. The one Committee Gompertz retained was his membership of the Board of the Marine and Technical College.

The local Party sought to make rapid changes in its organisation, Brian Howard was encouraged to form a Young Socialist branch, they redoubled their efforts at securing their own premises, but Jack Clark found replacing Gompertz too much of a challenge, by the 1961 Annual Meeting Jim Florence would emerge as the Secretary to the Labour and Trades Council.

Florence oversaw the selection of a new Parliamentary candidate in December 1961 to replace Ede. Six candidates were shortlisted, Arthur Blenkinsop, Ted Fletcher, Jimmy Johnson, Ted Garrett, D Chasworth and Ernest Mackley. The final vote when candidates had addressed delegates at the Armstrong Hall was:

Arthur Blenkinsop	63 votes
Ernest Mackley	21 votes
Ted Garrett	10 votes
Jimmy Johnson	9 votes
D Chasworth	7 votes
Ted Fletcher	7 votes

Fletcher would eventually become the MP for Darlington, Garrett in Wallsend and Johnson in Hull West. For Mackley, the quotation that '*The hand that wields the knife shall never wear the crown*' proved prophetic. Blenkinsop who had been the MP for Newcastle upon Tyne East since 1945, had lost his seat in the 1959 General Election debacle and was a former Parliamentary Secretary to the Minister of Pensions and then the Ministry of Health. He remained the town's Member of Parliament until 1979.

With the Parliamentary nomination resolved, Florence with force of character changed the Party's standing orders, renaming the monthly delegates' meeting the General Management Committee (GMC) and brought the local Constitution (with acrimony and dissent along the way) into line with the Labour Party's national rules. This meant that in future individual wards would be able to select their own Council candidate, breaking the Trade Union hold over wards they considered their own fiefdoms in the town. The first candidate selected under the new system was hairdresser and USDAW activist Billy Malcolm who was selected unopposed by Rekendyke members to be their candidate in a March 1962 by-election. Protests at the new GMC meeting by Miners' Representatives that they should have been allowed to allocate the seat were forcibly rebuffed by Florence. Jim Florence also encouraged the Labour Group of Councillors to elect a formal leader who would be the public face of the local Party as well as guiding the group's deliberations. It was a suggestion adopted by the Labour Councillors who appointed Ald Jack Clark. In addition, the first moves to consider ending the South Shields Labour and Trades Council's complex constitutional arrangements were mooted, although it was not until February 1970 that they agreed to formally disband the joint organisation and established themselves as two separate entities, the South Shields Constituency Labour Party and the South Shields Trades Union Council. Somewhat ironically, when Florence stood down as Secretary in 1965 the stalwarts considered, but then rejected reappointing a new full-time Secretary/Agent.

As the new leadership of the Constituency Labour and Trades Council came to terms with their new responsibilities, supporters of Gompertz would frequently enquire as to how they should recognise and honour Gompertz's long service to the town.

In June 1960 the North-East Federation of Trades Councils advised their South Shields counterparts that they were preparing a testimonial to present to Gompertz, delegates gave a £5 donation towards the cost, but the local Labour Party were more restrained. In September the Labour Party Executive recommended to the delegates meeting that a resolution requesting a presentation evening for Gompertz be arranged from the East Joint Wards should be deferred for three months. Given the Party was still being pressed by the Labour Party Agents Union to honour 1 April 1960 as the beginning of Gompertz's three-month notice period, feelings were proving raw on both sides. In December the Executive once again considered the resolution from the East Joint Wards Committee, this time the Young Socialists also demanded that the Party recognise and honour Gompertz's long service to the Party.

The Executive Committee sought to defer the matter again but at the January 1961 delegates meeting they were thwarted by Jack Maddison who demanded that the Party take a formal decision on whether to proceed with a presentation to Gompertz. By twenty-two to eleven votes they supported moves that Gompertz be made a Freeman of the Borough and instructed the Executive to set in motion plans for formal recognition of Gompertz's long service to the Party.

Despite a clear instruction, no immediate action was taken on the decision. The Labour Group made no attempts to elevate Gompertz to a Freeman, that would not occur until September 1967. By October 1961 the local Party agreed to prepare a testimonial and hold a presentation evening for Chuter Ede, Jack Maddison intervened again and demanded that Gompertz also be included in the presentation, the meeting agreed the request without dissent, but it was not until February 1962 that they formally created a subcommittee to begin making arrangements for a presentation evening to thank Ede and Gompertz, Maddison wisely demanded that he be appointed as a member of the subcommittee.

The obfuscation was brutal, private correspondence between Gompertz and Ede reveal their bitterness and grief at the way Gompertz had been treated to the extent that there were no cordial relations with key members of the new establishment with Gompertz frequently referring to their unprofessionalism and inept behaviour in his correspondence to Ede and lamenting that '… *everything is being allowed to drift, it is heart breaking*'. Ede responded sympathetically, '*I realise the anxiety you must feel about the future of the organisation you built up from nothing into a magnificent machine producing beneficial results.*' However the local stalwarts did arrange for both Ede and Gompertz to receive a joint presentation when they opened their new headquarters at Westoe Road which they had agreed to name 'Ede House'. They also secured the services of the Party Leader, Hugh Gaitskell who had agreed to visit South Shields on 19 January 1963 to formally make presentations to both Ede and Gompertz.

X The final farewell

Like most events in Gompertz's life, his Testimonial presentation from the South Shields Labour and Trades Council was surrounded by drama.

On 18 January Hugh Gaitskell died, struck down by a rare disease – disseminated lupus erythematosus – at short notice Ede secured the services of Douglas Jay, a former Financial Secretary to Board of Trade whom some commentators maintain would have been Chancellor in a Gaitskell-led Government.

The day began with a Civic Reception at the Town Hall hosted by the Mayor, Ald Paddy Brady. Neighbouring MPs Bill Blyton and Ernie Fernyhough attended, along with Arthur Blenkinsop. From there they made an official visit to the new Labour Party headquarters in Westoe Road where Douglas Jay officially opened 'Ede House' the new permanent home to the South Shields Labour and Trades Council.

In the evening, the Party's Deputy Leader, George Brown, despite the unfolding drama in London honoured his commitment to attend a formal presentation ceremony to Ede and Gompertz at the miners Armstrong Hall in Stanhope Road at which 300 guests assembled. Ald McAnany presented Ede with an illustrated and bound album of photographs, to Gompertz he presented a silver trophy, which Gompertz insisted should be given to the Education Authority and awarded annually to a child who excelled in music. In an evening of emotional reminiscing Ede recalled how in his first election in 1929, McAnany had asked him to meet twenty-one nurses who were going to vote for his Liberal opponent, following a meeting with Ede they all agreed to give Labour a chance, '*I won that election by only forty votes, their votes decided it!*'

Gompertz without any malice gave a heart-warming address to his audience, recalling the battles and campaigns they had fought together to win South Shields for the Labour Party cause, the improvements they had made in people's lives, the trials and tribulations they had encountered along the way. Ever local to Ede, faithful to the Labour movement, devoted to the townsfolk of South Shields, he ended his address, receiving a standing ovation, with a paean which today adorns his photograph in the local Labour Party headquarters:

'*South Shields is worthy of the greatest effort and sacrifice. It is a wonderful town with wonderful people. They have been kind to me and generous to the Party. We are now the foremost political party in the town and we intend to remain so.*'

His life's work had achieved all he wanted for the Labour Party in the town.
His legacy was secure, he had reached journey's end.

Chapter 18

Afterword

As the 1950s drew to a close, the British public, encouraged by the media, were gripped by moral panic over the apparent increase in crimes of violence. By January 1960, the Home Secretary, Rab Butler, was sufficiently concerned that he appointed Justice Barry to report on the desirability of reintroducing corporal punishment in penal institutions. This was one issue Gompertz, even in retirement, was prepared to fight against. He had long opposed corporal punishment, had witnessed and experienced it as a conscientious objector and had urged the Cadogan Committee in the late 1930s to abolish it and Gompertz celebrated when Ede himself, as Home Secretary, found time in the Parliamentary schedule, to present a Bill outlawing the practice in 1948.

In June 1960, Gompertz was back in London to appear before Justice Black. Gompertz advised the Committee that his views on the use of corporal punishment for offenders was the same as it had always been, that it was not, and never will be, a deterrent to crime. '*There is unfortunately a very vocal demand in some quarters for the re-introduction of the birch. This demand receives big headlines in some of the newspapers, but the view of those who oppose it do not receive similar publicity*' he told the *Shields Gazette*. As part of his evidence, Gompertz produced photographs taken in 1937 showing the extent of injuries sustained by a nine-year-old boy who received six strokes of the birch ordered by the South Shields Juvenile Court.

Barry's Committee reached the unanimous conclusion that judicial corporal punishment should not be reintroduced.

Ede's private papers, held at the Surrey History Centre reveal that following his ousting, Gompertz was still financially retained by Ede to undertake casework on his behalf and Gompertz maintained regular dialogue with Ede advising him on progress of Council meetings and sending regular newspaper reports which would be of interest. It was an arrangement which did not sit well with the new Labour Party officials in the town, who cutely advised Ede that correspondence on Constituency matters must go through his new Agent,

Ken Scrimger before making its way to Gompertz for action. Ede though continued to rely heavily upon Gompertz's judgement on all issues affecting the Constituency, and numerous correspondence between the two men bear testament to Ede accepting the advice given right up until Ede retired from Parliament. No visit to South Shields was complete without Ede entertaining Gompertz to dinner at the Sea Hotel and they both continued their interest in the local Archaeological and Historical Society with Gompertz forming a South Shields Branch of the Civic Trust which campaigned to make towns better places for people to live. He played however, no part in the 1964 General Election which saw Arthur Blenkinsop replace Ede as the town's Member of Parliament. Ede was elevated in December 1964 to the Peerage, it was not a position he would enjoy for long. His health as Stephen Hart has observed, was deteriorating rapidly, suffering a fall at home in September 1965, he moved into a nursing home, was found to have prostrate problems and died on Armistice Day.

In a moving tribute recorded in the *Shields Gazette*, Ede's faithful friend Gompertz noted that when Ede had first arrived in South Shields it was during the blackest years of the depression, as an MP he lobbied those with influence in London and the growth of the town, its advancement from poverty to affluence and the transformation of South Shields through slum clearance, was as much Ede's achievements as anyone else's. No official delegation to London was complete without Ede joining them. He was, Gompertz appreciated, a little difficult to approach, but everyone's troubles were his own, pursing a resolve with determination. Ede wasn't a particularly great orator in the spell-binding sense, noted Gompertz, but his speeches were logical and concise and although he did not show it, Ede was warm-hearted, he abhorred flattery and never expected gratitude.

Whether Gompertz travelled to St Martin's Parish Church in Epsom for Ede's funeral on 16 November, we do not know, but as Mayor of the Borough of South Shields Ernest Mackley attended the funeral in an official capacity. We do know that Gompertz attended a special church service for Ede held at St Hilda's Parish Church in South Shields on 20 December.

As for Gompertz's wife Annie, correspondence from Gompertz to Ede, reveals that she took the downfall of her husband badly and within weeks of the fateful meeting had been admitted to hospital: '*The shock has done her no good*' confided Gompertz. By June 1960 Annie was in hospital again for a further (not specified) operation and was again admitted to hospital in November. In March 1961 Gompertz was reporting to Ede that Annie was making '... *little progress*', and she was required to return to hospital in December, by October 1963 he was writing expressing concern that '... *she may have to have some toes amputated, we shall be lucky to save her foot.*' In February 1964 Gompertz was advising Ede that Annie had been required to have a further operation and that '... *her foot has been saved thanks to the attention of our General Hospital*', which suggests she may have suffered from acute diabetes. Annie died on 3 January 1967, leaving an estate valued at £1,578.

Gompertz himself died suddenly at his home on 5 April 1968, he had been in ill health and had experienced trouble with his eyes. His Will, written on 29 August 1958 had not been changed and still advised that Annie should receive his shares, stocks and two properties – 38 Bertram Street and 40/42 South Eldon Street – a total probate of £6,103.14.0. The High Court directed that the estate would be left to his brother Gabriel to administer in equal shares to Gabriel, Alexander and his sister Rosa. Gompertz left clear instructions that he should receive a Secular Service and Cremation, which his Will advised, he had already paid for.

On receiving the news of his friend's death, Ald Albert Newman paid tribute saying that he had dedicated his life to fight for those principles he adopted to the progress and improvement of South Shields. He was, Newman said, tenacious in support of those principles and scathing in condemnation of the opposition. '*He was a character in many ways and had some amusing eccentricities. He hated war and suffered for his opposition to military expeditions of any kind.*' Jack Clark observed that Gompertz's passing marked the end of an era of pioneer and militant Socialism, scrupulously carried out by a man who fought hard to abolish poverty and inequality in society.

The *Shields Gazette* editorial wrote that Gompertz was a man of considerable stature, formidable in the Council Chamber as many lesser men had found to their cost. He was ruthless in his determination to carry through his Socialist policies, never seeking popularity, but because of his inflexibility where a cause dear to his heart was at stake, he made enemies. But the editorial continued he was a modest man, who shunned money and liked to spend his holidays quietly in the Northumberland countryside. '*The people whom he helped in so many ways, whose rights he fought for are legion. These are the people who will really miss him.*'

His cremation took place in South Shields on 9 April, with an address given by Councillor Griffin of Newcastle who was the Secretary of both the Tyneside Humanist Society and the Rationalist Press Association, organisations of which Gompertz was a lifelong member. Newman with euphonious phrase spoke of Gompertz's life work, an able advocate, passionately eloquent and energetic, '… *let it be said because Ernie Gompertz was the last man to gild the lily he was often obstinate and aggressive but was never deliberately unfair*'. In reference to his removal as Secretary/Agent Newman observed that in his retirement he never criticised or condemned any person or body. Any defects or imperfections in his character should be forgotten Newman asserted, people should remember only the service he rendered in his day and generation to the Labour movement and the citizens of the town he loved so well.

By the standards of his generation, Gompertz had a secure and comfortable upbringing and a close family network, he could easily have settled into a life of business, but his reading of Socialist texts, and his admiration of Keir Hardie, led him to the Labour movement and the need for the creation of a Labour Party pledged to progress the interests of working-class people. As a pawnbroker's manager in the family business, he would have come into daily contact with those in grinding poverty, struggling to feed their families, handing over their meagre possessions to put food on the table or to pay the rent. He did not accept that this needed to be the established order there was a better way to organise society to the benefit of all. He became an active trade unionist in the infant Shopworkers Union, what was eventually to become USDAW. A founder member of the South Shields Labour Party, he must have cut a somewhat eccentric figure amongst the heavy industrial workers who formed the core base of Labour's support at the time. Nevertheless, no one could deny his energy, enthusiasm and total commitment in developing a branch of the emerging Labour Party in the town.

Gompertz had integrity, a tribal politician fiercely loyal to the Labour pack, he was pugnacious in defence of his ideals and uncompromising in maintaining the highest standards in public office and at times his humour could be of acrid quality. Stan Smith, a young Progressive Councillor at the time observed he was a forceful and eloquent speaker – '*You always knew where Gompertz was coming from, and it was invariably for our throats*'. He set a clear path on how Labour could win South Shields, in April 1929 he admonished those in the Labour Group who sought comfort in merely maintaining their own positions in Council wards regarded as 'working class' seats, making clear to the then small Labour Group that the aim was to seize control of the Council Chamber not merely to secure safe havens for respected trade unionists. The Labour Party, he argued, needed to win in seats hitherto seen as unwinnable since without victory in those seats Labour could not hope to make the changes in the town he believed essential to improving people's lives. As Labour assumed a majority in the Council Chamber, he was adamant – perhaps unfairly – in 1937 that family members of serving Councillors should not be allowed to apply for employment with the Council, least the charge of nepotism be levelled at the new controlling Labour administration.

He was unselfish, he devoted his life to the Labour and trade union movement, and his actions in resigning his seat on the unelected Aldermanic Bench in order to contest the Horsley Hill ward in 1949 because he feared Labour could lose the seat, and with it control of the Council, was typical Gompertz, putting the interests of the Labour movement well before his own personal ambitions. He identified those whom he felt would make effective public servants, encouraged them, supported them – even if at times it went against the vested interests of trade unions who had their own favoured sons for public office. His health suffered, frequently languid because of the long hours he worked particularly during World War II when he was Chair of the Local Food Committee and he took the lead within the Council in meeting the challenges of the home front in wartime. Although no such formal post existed, he was frequently described by the *Shields Gazette* as the Leader of the Socialist Group of Councillors.

The manner of his ousting deeply wounded and hurt Gompertz, arguments as to when his three-month notice period should take affect being a point of principle for him, but he never criticised his colleagues in public and as the great healer time, slowly moved on, he was magnanimous to his colleagues at his final Testimonial presentation in January 1963. Cruelly, the leading lights within the Labour Group held back nominating him as a Freeman of the Borough until September 1967, after the death of his beloved Annie. It would take a further thirty-five years before his portrait was hung in the South Shields Labour Party headquarters and the Secretary's office named in his honour, forty years before South Tyneside Council named a housing development, Gompertz Gardens after him and fifty years before a conference room in South Shields Town Hall would bear his name.

Without question he was consistent, perhaps too rigidly so at times, but he remained a lifelong conscientious objector, a virulent anti-Communist and throughout his political career rightly deserved the title the Stormy Petrel, from the Secret Document affair (when the opposition surreptitiously endeavoured to block his nomination to the PAC) through to his outrage at the behaviour of Allen and Co (who entered buy-out talks days after they had bought land from the Council) he maintained high moral standards and expected everyone else across the political spectrum to follow suit. His utter determination to challenge those forces waged against the working-class interests across South Shields saw him on frequent occasion forcibly removed from the Council Chamber and on one occasion arrested whilst addressing a public meeting in the Market Place. Throughout his life, even as a devoted active trade unionist, he made repeatedly clear, that Labour Councillors were required to vote as a bloc in the Council Chamber, owing allegiance via their constituents to the Labour Group. He was unmoving on this principle to the point that he was prepared to support the expulsion from the Labour Group of any member who refused to accept collective responsibility including his mentor, the first Chairman of the South Shields Labour Party, Jim Curbison and then James Dunlop.

No individual nor organisation was safe from Gompertz's scrutiny, whether it was the operation of the local Police, the Tyne Improvement Commissioners, Government Ministries, the local Magistrates, the Public Assistance Committee or the impartiality of the local media – even his own Council Town Clerk who sought, what Gompertz felt, was an excessive pay rise saw the issue considered under Judicial Review in the High Court – repeatedly Gompertz at one time or another had reason to confront their actions and behaviours, and following detailed research and preparation, he invariably won his argument. Even in retirement, with a Home Office Commission examining whether to reintroduce corporal punishment, Gompertz was riled enough to take the journey to London to argue his lifelong view that it did not deter offenders.

Chuter Ede, in days when Members of Parliament would make only the occasional, well-planned visit to their constituencies, relied totally on Gompertz to maintain his profile, defend his interests and undertake the constituency caseload as his Parliamentary aide within the town. Gompertz in over thirty years working with Ede never let him down. Relations were always formal, Ede in correspondence always addressed him as, '*My Dear Friend*', Gompertz in return, certainly in public never referring to Ede as anything other than '*Mr Ede*'. Their bond was never broken, politically aligned, both mainstream Democratic Socialists with a Fabian outlook, it was inevitable that when Gompertz was ousted, Ede's position would become untenable.

He was a staunch advocate of municipal housing, recognising that the only way to vanquish the appalling slum housing that existed within the town centre quickly was to exploit fully the Housing Acts that allowed Councils at the time to construct good quality housing and he remained steadfast in opposing – not private ownership – but to the selling of Council housing. He was fiercely defensive of maintaining the independence of the County Borough of South Shields.

Gompertz had his imperfections and idiosyncrasies, everyone has. He could be churlish and stubborn – threatening to resign in 1936 because he felt slighted and let down by Labour colleagues in the Council Chamber – he could be abrasive, caustic and dismissive even to his Labour Party colleagues and was prone to use every procedural trick in the rule book to secure the position he wanted the South Shields Labour and Trades Council to take. He brokered no opposition even on the seemingly mundane point of allowing Labour Party leaflets to printed by Labour candidates without his approval. He was prone to pure theatrics at times to reinforce his point as his actions over the *Secret Document* affair demonstrated. As he grew older, he became obstinate to fresh ideas on campaigning as a new generation began to emerge within the local Labour movements ranks and he became defensive of his control over the Party machine, refusing a young university graduate Brian Howard a membership card because, he told Howard '... *the Labour Party is full up.*'

Shakespeare wrote: '*He was a man, take him for all in all, I shall not look upon his like again.*' When Gompertz died, he was the last of the Victorian stalwarts who had formed the Labour Party in the town, which affiliated to the national Labour Party on Valentine's Day in 1912. During his life he lived through two World Wars, saw the election of the first Labour Government, witnessed the General Strike, the Great Depression, MacDonald's Great Betrayal of 1931 and the resulting near collapse of the Labour Party as a national electoral force, campaigned for the franchise to be extended to women, fought the rise of Fascism, experienced the election of the Labour reforming Government of 1945, saw Labour seize control of South Shields Council for the first time in 1937 and personally witnessed the Coronation of a new Monarch. He was pivotal in ensuring the glass ceiling was smashed with Labour securing the election of the first women Councillors, appointment of women JPs and the first woman to be the Mayor of South Shields. He witnessed the growth of South Shields from a small compact Constituency clustered along the mouth of the South Bank of the River Tyne surrounded by agricultural land and hedgerows with only Harton and Westoe villages separating it from Boldon into the town we know today. He was the leading light in the then hugely influential Regional Trades Council structure which saw him representing them to the TUC in London. From 1929 until 1960 he held the position of Secretary/Agent of the South Shields and Labour Trades Council, he organised every local election campaign during his tenure and acted as the Parliamentary Election Agent in eight general elections, he served as a Member of South Shields Council for twenty-eight years and during his lifetime met and discussed politics with the early pioneers of the Labour movement including Keir Hardie, Ramsay MacDonald, George Lansbury and Clem Attlee.

No, we will not see his like again.

Arise, shine, for thy light is come

Abbreviations

AEU	Amalgamated Engineering Union
ARP	Air Raid Precautions
ASRS	Amalgamated Society of Railway Servants
BSP	British Socialist Party
BUF	British Union of Fascists
CND	Campaign for Nuclear Disarmament
DMA	Durham Miners' Association
GMC	General Management Committee
GMWU	General and Municipal Workers' Union
ILP	Independent Labour Party
LEA	Labour Electoral Association
LEAs	Local Education Authorities
LRC	Labour Representation Committee
MLL	Municipal Labour League
MRL	Municipal Representation League
NCB	National Coal Board
NCF	No Conscription Fellowship
NEC	National Executive Committee (of the Labour Party)
NUJ	National Union of Journalists
NUR	National Union of Railwaymen
NUS	National Union of Seamen
NUT	National Union of Teachers
PAC	Public Assistance Committee
PEA	Parliamentary Electoral Association
PLP	Parliamentary Labour Party
RARAMA	Rent and Ratepayers' Municipal Association
RDC	Rural District Council
RRA	Rent and Ratepayers Association
SDF	Social Democratic Federation
SDP	Social Democratic Party (successor to the SDF)

TIC	Tyne Improvement Commission
TUC	Trade Union Congress
UDC	Urban District Council
USDAW	Union of Shop, Distributive and Allied Workers
WSPU	Women's Social and Political Union

Appendix 1

The Gompertz Family Tree

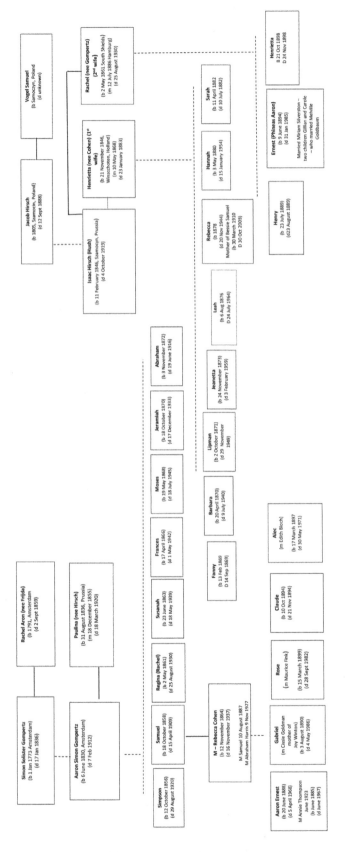

With thanks to Melville Goldbaum

Appendix 2

Aaron Ernest Gompertz Timeline

1888:   Born Middlesbrough, 20 June, 8 Gladstone Street

1895:   General Election, Liberal William Robson re-elected in South Shields

1900:   General Election, Liberal William Robson re-elected in South Shields

1902:   Ernie Gompertz's family move to South Shields

1906:   General Election, Liberal William Robson re-elected in South Shields

1909:   Death of Gompertz's father, Samuel

1910:   General Election (Jan), Liberal William Robson re-elected in South Shields, a by-election following his elevation to the Peerage sees Liberal Russell Rea elected, Rea is re-elected at the December General Election

1912:   Elected Asst Secretary of the South Shields Labour Party
Death of grandfather, Aaron Simon

1914:   Outbreak of World War I

1916:   Conscientious objector during World War I, Court-martialled and sentenced to hard labour
Parliamentary by-election in South Shields, Liberal Cecil Cochrane is unelected unopposed

1918:   August, Gompertz released from Prison on health grounds and returns to South Shields
Parliamentary by-election in South Shields, Havelock Wilson a TU-Coalition candidate is elected unopposed and goes on to defeat Labour's first Parliamentary candidate at the ensuring General Election

1919:   Death of great Uncle, Isaac Hush

1920:   Death of grandmother, Paulina

1922:   General Election, Labour contest South Shields, but Edward Harney, Liberal is elected

1923: General Election, Labour contest South Shields, but Edward Harney is re-elected
Marries Annie Thompson, Carlisle Civil Ceremony

1924: General Election, Edward Harney, Liberal is returned in South Shields

1928: Appointed James Chuter Ede's Election Agent

1929: General Election – Labour win South Shields for the first time with J Chuter Ede

1931: General Election – Labour lose South Shields in National Government Landslide
Gompertz unsuccessfully contests Westoe Ward in South Shields County Borough Council election

1932: Elected for the Tyne Dock ward – the so-called 'Secret Document Affair'

1934: Fights legal case to establish Freedom of Speech in Market Place

1935: General Election – Labour regains South Shields with James Chuter Ede
Re-elected to Council in Tyne Dock

1937: Labour takes control of South Shields Council for first time

1938: Gompertz re-elected in Tyne Dock

1939: World War II, Gompertz becomes Chair of Food Control Committee

1944: Death of mother, Rebecca

1945: General Election and the end of World War II, Labour loses control of South Shields Council

1946: Appointed to the Councils Aldermanic Bench, Labour regains control of South Shields Council

1949: Resigns as an Alderman to successfully contest Horsley Hill ward

1950: General Election, J Chuter Ede re-elected, Council falls to no overall control Gompertz fails in bid for Mayoralty

1951: General Election, J Chuter Ede re-elected

1952: Gompertz re-elected for Horsley Hill, Labour regains control of South Shields Council

1953: Elected Mayor of the County Borough of South Shields, former Prime Minister Attlee attends the Mayor's Sunday Parade, Gompertz attends Coronation of Queen Elizabeth II

1955: General Election, J Chuter Ede re-elected
Gompertz re-elected for Horsley Hill

1958:   Gompertz re-elected for Horsley Hill

1960:   Ousted as Secretary/Agent to the South Shields Labour Party, 1 March, resigns from public life at a meeting of the Borough Council the following day

1963:   January, Presented with Testimonial at formal Ceremony hosted by the South Shields Labour and Trades Council

1964:   General Election, Arthur Blenkinsop replaces James Chuter Ede as MP for South Shields

1965:   Death of James Chuter Ede, 11 November

1967:   Death of Annie Gompertz, 3 January
Appointed a Freeman of the County Borough of South Shields in September

1968:   Died suddenly at home, 5 April

Appendix 3

Gompertz Elective History to South Shields County Borough Council

1931 Westoe Ward

Samuel Lawlan (Moderate)	2,053	
AE Gompertz (Socialist)	329	
	maj 1,724 Moderate Hold	

1932 Tyne Dock Ward

AE Gompertz (Labour)	1,483	
D Fairbairn (Moderate)	634	
George Reay (Communist)	42	
	maj 849 Labour hold	

1935 Tyne Dock Ward

AE Gompertz (Labour)	1,570	
W Drummond (Moderate)	653	
	maj 917 Labour hold	

1938 Tyne Dock Ward

AE Gompertz (Labour)	1,149	
JH Smith (Moderate)	629	
	maj 520 Labour hold	

1946 Gompertz appointed to the Aldermanic Bench for the Bents Ward

1949 Gompertz resigns from Aldermanic Bench to contest Horsley Hill Ward

AE Gompertz (Labour)	1,069	
GI Coulthard (RARAMA)	896	
WP Scarth (Communist)	31	
	maj 173 Labour gain	

1952 Horsley Hill Ward

AE Gompertz (Labour)	1,321
H Marshall (RARAMA)	770
	maj 551 Labour hold

1955 Horsley Hill Ward

Returned unopposed

1958 Horsley Hill Ward

AE Gompertz (Labour)	1,169
S Lamb (Progressive)	949
	maj 220 Labour hold

Resigns from the Council, 2 March 1960

Bibliography and Notes

My main research references have been the Minute Books of the South Shields Labour and Trades Council, the Minutes of the South Shields Labour Group of Councillors, the *Shields Gazette*, the *Shields Daily News*, the *Newcastle Journal*, the *Northern Echo* and Minutes of meetings of South Shields County Borough Council. Through the former South Shields MP David Clark's efforts, there exists a range of items of interest originally stored on microfilm which I arranged to be converted onto JPEG, these include, the Minute Books, correspondence and letters relating to Gompertz's operation of the 1935 and 1950 Parliamentary Elections, the 1927 Annual Report of the South Shields Labour Party, Financial Accounts (1928–51) and other assorted campaign circulars. In any reference to *South Shields Labour Party Archives* the material can be found on the JPEG which has been donated to South Tyneside Libraries. For the early history of the South Shields Labour Party, the ILP *Labour Leader* and the SDF *Justice* newspapers have been invaluable. Chuter Ede's personal papers stored at the Surrey History Centre highlight the close bond between Gompertz and Chuter Ede. I have acknowledged sources as appropriate within each chapter. In addition, the following books, essays and manuscripts have assisted my research and where necessary acknowledged in individual chapters:

Karina Sonnenberg-Stern, *Emancipation and Poverty, the Ashkenazi Jews of Amsterdam 1796–1850*, Macmillan Press, 2000

Laura Tabili, *Global Migrants, Local Culture*, Palgrave Macmillan, 2011

Victoria Ann Brown, *Public Health Issues and General Practice in the Area of Middlesbrough, 1880–1980*, Durham Theses, Durham University

GW Keeton, *A Liberal Attorney General*, James Nisbet & Co, 1949

George B Hodgson, *The Borough of South Shields*, Reid and Company 1903

Andy Ward, *Conchies*, Matador, 2015

Havelock Wilson, *My stormy voyage through life*, Co-operative Press, 1925

Marsh and Ryan, *The Seamen: A History of the National Union of Seamen*, Malthouse Publishing, 1989

Matthew Worley, *Labour's Grass Roots: Essays on the Activities of Local Labour Parties and Members 1918–45*, Routledge, 2017

D Price, *Fighting like tigers*, Newcastle Polytechnic Paper, 1982

Keith Ewing, *The funding of political parties in Britain*, Cambridge University Press, 2009

Martin Pugh, *March of the Women*, Oxford University Press, 2011

Church and Outram, *Strikes and Solidarity*, Cambridge University Press, 1998

Herbert Tracey (edited), *The Book of the Labour Party,* Caxton, 1925

Peter Chapman, A Tyneside Heritage, The History Press, 2021

David Clark, *We do not want the Earth,* Bewick Press, 1992

Andrew Marr, *The Making of Modern Britain*, Macmillan, 2009

Asa Briggs and John Saville (ed), *Essays in Labour History 1886–1923*, Macmillan, 1971

Duncan Tanner, *Political change and the Labour Party 1900–1918*, Cambridge University Press, 1990

Norman McCord (ed), *Essays in Tyneside Labour History*, Newcastle Polytechnic, 1977

Henry Pelling, *Origins of the Labour Party*, Oxford University Press, 1966

Roy Jenkins, *Mr Balfour's Poodle*, Heinemann, 1954

D Morley Mathieson, *Medical Officers Report on Housing in the Borough*, 1914

South Shields Labour and Trades Council Minute Books – *stored in South Tyneside Libraries*

Brian Lund, *The housing crisis as the long-term casualty of austerity politics, 1918–2019*, King's College, London

Kevin Jefferys, *James Chuter Ede*, Oxford Dictionary of National Biography

Geoffrey Serle, *Arthur Lynch*, Australian Dictionary of Biography

Lynn Hollen Lees, *The Solidarities of Strangers*, Cambridge University Press, 1998

WR Garside, *The Durham Miners 1919–1960*, George Allen and Unwin, 1971

Roderick Martin, *Communism and the British Trade Unions, 1924–33, a study of the NMM*, Clarendon, 1969

Philip Williamson, *Safety First, Baldwin and the Conservative Party and the 1929 General Election, Cambridge Historical Journal*, 1982

Harold Wilson, *A Prime Minister on Prime Ministers,* Book Club Associates, 1977

Jaime Reynolds and Ian Hunter, *Crinks, Journal of Liberal History*, 2000

Stephen Hart, *James Chuter Ede*, Pen and Sword, 2021

W Campbell Lyons, *South Shields Medical Officers Report to Health Committee*, 1930

Fredric M Miller, *The Unemployment policy of the National Government, The History Journal*, 1976

James C Robertson, *The British General Election of 1935, Journal of Contemporary History*, 1974

Fredric M Miller, *The British Unemployment Assistance Crisis of 1935, Journal of Contemporary History*, 1979

Nigel Todd, *In Excited Times*, Bewick Press, 1995

Ben Pimlott, *The Socialist League: Intellectuals and the Labour Left in the 1930s, Journal of Contemporary History*, 1971

Ellen Wilkinson, *The Town that was murdered*, Gollancz, 1939

Wal Hannington, *The problem of the distressed areas*, Gollancz, 1937

Craig Armstrong, *South Shields at War 1939–45,* Pen and Sword, 2020

Andrew Thorpe, *'In a rather emotional state'? The Labour Party and British intervention in Greece, 1944–45,* Oxford University Press, 2006

Andrew Thorpe, *Locking out the Communists, 20th Century British History,* June 2014

Kevin Jeffreys, *RA Butler, the Board of Education and the 1944 Education Act,* Wiley, 1984

Labour Party, *Report of the NEC to the 41st Annual Conference,* Published by the Labour Party

Labour Party, *Report of the NEC to the 42nd Annual Conference,* Published by the Labour Party

Keith Middlemas, *Power, Competition and the State,* Macmillan, 1986

Bernard Donoughue and GW Jones, *Herbert Morrison, Portrait of a politician,* Weidenfeld and Nicolson, 1973

Michael Foot, *Aneurin Bevan 1946–1960,* Davis-Poynter Ltd, 1973

Michael Jago, *Clement Attlee the inevitable Prime Minister,* Biteback Publishing, 2014

Peter Shore, *Leading the Left,* Weidenfeld & Nicolson, 1993

Prof Vernon Bogdanor, *The General Election 1959,* Gresham College Lecture, 2014

Iain McLean, *Keir Hardie,* Penguin Books, 1975

Chapter 1 – The Early Years

Karina Sonnenberg-Stern, *Emancipation and Poverty*

Joy Winton, *article in Shields Gazette 15 July 2002*

South Shields Chief Medical Officers Report 1876

Laura Tabili, *Global Migrants, local culture*

Lewis Olsover, The Jewish Communities of the North East of England, 1980

Ministry of Health Report into South Shields 1902

Evening Gazette, AE Gompertz visit to Fleetham School, 23 January 1954

Personal correspondence from Leslie Price and Brenda Robinson

Catherine Cookson, *Our Kate*, 1969

Personal correspondence from Gillian Hush

Victoria Ann Brown, *Public health issues and general practice in the area of Middlesbrough*

UK Census Records

Evening Gazette, Profile of Ernest Hush, 22 August 1998

Samuel Smith, *Lives and Reminisces*, 1957

Shields Gazette, Opening of new South Shields Synagogue, 30 January 1933

Friendship Club Writers' Group, *Cannon Street Lest we forget*, 1993

Shields Gazette, Gompertz hosts Civic Reception for USDAW, 19 October 1953

Chapter 2 – The Struggle for Unity

Parliamentary Boundary Commissioners Report re: new South Shields Constituency – 1832

George Hodgson, Borough of South Shields

South Shields County Borough Chief Medical Officer's Report, 1903

Herbert Tracey, *The Book of the Labour Party*

South Shields Trades Council Minutes as referenced in *Shields Daily News* 1869

Shields Daily News, reference to Trades Council contesting Board of Guardians, 30 December 1891

Shields Daily News, reference to Fabian Society public meetings, 26 May 1892

Shields Daily News, reference to South Shields Debating Society, September 1893

Shields Daily News, Reynolds reference to the ILP in South Shields being 'dead', 25 April 1894

Shields Daily News, reference to ILP take-over of South Shields Trades Council, 26 April 1894

Shields Daily News, reference to Tom Mann's visit to South Shields, 14 June 1894

Shields Daily News, reference to selection meeting for Robson, 3July 1894

Shields Daily News, reference to Market Place rally for Threlfall, 3 August 1895

Labour Leader, article on Threlfall, 15 September 1894

Shields Daily News, Margaret Reynolds letter to newspaper, 18 July 1894

Shields Gazette, article on JC Stevenson standing down as MP, 6 August 1894

GW Keeton, *A Liberal Attorney General*

Chapter 3 – Growing Pains

Shields Daily News, Abbott calls a conference to oppose Board of Guardians, 7 November 1894

Shields Gazette, reference to Reynolds' election to Schools Board, 18 January 1895

Shields Daily News, Mass meeting of unemployed in Market Place, 29 January 1895

Shields Daily News, Lisle ousted as Trades Council Secretary, 11 September 1895

GW Keeton, *A Liberal Attorney General*

Shields Daily News, Municipal League founded, 1 April 1899

Shields Daily News, Batey on Board of Guardians elections, 17 March 1899

Shields Daily News, Fair wages clause defeated at Guardians Board meeting, 24 March 1899

Shields Daily News, Municipal Labour League formed, 1 April 1899

Shields Daily News, Calls to establish an LRC in South Shields, 7 September 1903

Shields Daily News, Unions oppose LRC formation in South Shields, 1 October 1903

Shields Daily News, Philip Snowden in South Shields, 31 July 1904

Shields Daily News, Keir Hardie visits Jarrow, 20 December 1904

Shields Daily News, Further attempts to form an LRC in South Shields, 22 August 1906

Shields Daily News, REL Vaughan chosen as Liberal Unionist Parliamentary candidate, 24 December 1909

Chief Medical Officer's Report into South Shields 1908

Labour Leader newspaper articles

SDF *Justice* newspaper articles

Shields Daily News, reference to South Shields Fabians' Market Place meeting, 26 May 1892

Roy Jenkins, *Mr Balfour's Poodle*

Interesting article outlining platform for municipal elections, *Shields Daily News*, 20 October 1899

Chapter 4 – Division and Unity

Shields Daily News, ILP form a Tyne Dock branch, 29 January 1909

Labour Leader, April 1909 report of ILP Edinburgh Conference

Shields Daily News, Town Hall seized 15th February 1909 (also *Labour Leader* 29 January 1909)

MacDonald's reference to South Shields Trades Council, *Shields Daily News*, 19 October 1910

Evening Chronicle, Labour will contest by-election, 10 October 1910

Shields Daily News, Interesting article on Russell Rea and Votes for Women, 12 October 1910

Daily Telegraph, Article on South Shields Labour selection meeting, 15 October 1910

Shields Daily News, Mrs Pankhurst in South Shields, 15 October 1910

Westminster Gazette, 'Why Labour will not run a candidate', 18 October 1910

Daily Telegraph, Article on failed Labour Party selection meeting, 19 October 1910

Labour Leader, South Shields by-election is test of Osborne Judgement, 21 October 1910

Votes for Women reference to 28 October 1910 visit of Christabel Pankhurst in South Shields

Shields Daily News, Reference to Cuth Barrass activities, 14 October 1911

Shields Daily News, ILP backs Votes for Women, 21 November 1911

Justice Newspaper, SDF becomes BSP and calls for joint branch with ILP, 16 March 1912

Newcastle Chronicle, South Shields Labour Party calls for a Parliamentary candidate, 19 April 1913

Newcastle Chronicle, Parliamentary selection conference of South Shields Labour Party called, 25 August 1913

Newcastle Chronicle, Arthur Peters, National Agent of the Labour Party in South Shields, 28 August 1913

Shields Daily News, Labour candidate sought, 1 November 1913

Shields Daily News, Joe Batey calls for improved housing in South Shields, 6 November 1913

Shields Daily News, Joe Batey selected as Labour Parliamentary candidate, 19 February 1914

Shields Daily News, Joe Batey endorsed by Trades Council, 18 April 1914
Shields Daily News, South Shields Council seeks extension of its boundaries, 4 June 1914
Chief Medical Officer's Report on housing in South Shields 1914
Journal newspaper, *The Eternal Rebel*, 18 December 1954
Keith Ewing, *The funding of political parties in Britain*
Martin Pugh, *March of the Women*

Chapter 5 – Conscientious Objector
Gompertz military records stored at the National Archives
Andy Ward, *Conchies*
Herbert Tracey, *The book of the Labour Party*
Church and Outram, *Strikes and Solidarity*
Hansard, William Anderson MP raises plight of Gompertz, 27 July 1916
Labour Leader, Report of mock Parliament in Leicester Prison, 23 November 1916
Labour Leader, Reference to Gompertz's mock trial at Leicester Prison, 23 November 1916
Tom Davie, *The Highway: Turbulent Times 1918–28*, published by the WEA
Herbert Tracey, *The history of the Labour Party*
Havelock Wilson, *My stormy voyage through life*
Duncan Tanner, *Political change and the Labour Party*
Newcastle Journal, article outlining Wilson's political thinking, 17 October 1918
Newcastle Journal, reports on General Election in South Shields, 16 December 1918

Chapter 6 – The Interwar Years
D Price, *Fighting like tigers* – gives an in-depth assessment of housing in South Shields and Mayor Anderson controversy
Lewis Mates, *The Syndicalist challenge in the Durham Coalfield before 1914*, Durham University – extensive research on Will Lawther
Shields Daily News, reference to Lawther's bid for South Shields, December 1919
South Shields Labour and Trades Council Minutes re: formation of Labour Group of Councillors
Shields Daily News, Gompertz as President of North East Federation of Shop Assistants, 12 March 1925
Andrew Marr, *The Making of Modern Britain*
Lynn Hollen Lees, *The Solidarities of Strangers*
Shields Daily News, May Day Rally in South Shields, 8 May 1921
South Shields Labour and Trades Council Minutes, Gompertz investigates Union complaint, October 1921

Chapter 7 – Unstable Times
Herbert Tracey, *The history of the Labour Party*
Ivan Yates, *Power in the Labour Party* (reference to Sidney Webb's view of Labour Constituency Parties) *Political Quarterly* 1960

Shields Daily News, Wilson heckled at public meeting in South Shields, 20 February 1922

Shields Daily News, reference to public meeting on increased water charges, 15 February 1922

Shields Daily News, Reference to Wilson Libel case, 31 August 1922

Shields Daily News, Liberal candidate for South Shields, 20 October 1922

Shields Daily News, Liberal await decision of Ald Brown, 25 October 1922

Shields Daily News, Unionists ask Wilson to be their candidate, 28 October 1922

Shields Daily News, South Shields Liberals meet to choose candidate, 1 November 1922

Shields Daily News, Article on 1922 General Election Campaign in South Shields, 11 November 1922

Shields Daily News, Wilson has bronchitis, 22 November 1922

Shields Daily News, Boxes under seal, 16 December 1922

Shields Daily News, Wilson Out, result of 1922 election in South Shields, 17 December 1922

Shields Daily News, Havelock Wilson and National Democratic Party reference, 8 November 1922

WR Garside, *The Durham Miners*

Guardian, Foreign Office and Zinoviev letter, 3 February 1999

Harold Laski, *Parliamentary Government in England*, reference to 'Insane miracle' Routledge

Chapter 8 – Victory …

Sir Arthur Griffith-Boscawen, *Oxford Dictionary of National Biography*, Oxford

Andrew Marr, *The Making of Modern Britain*

Patrick Renshaw, Black Friday 1921, *History Today*, Vol 22 Issue 6, 1971

Surrey Mirror, Mitcham by-election, 16 February 1923

Surrey Mirror, Mitcham by-election, 2 March 1923

Surrey Mirror, Mitcham by-election, 23 March 1923

Daily Herald, article on Ede, 15 March 1923

Kevin Jefferys, James Chuter Ede, *Oxford Dictionary of National Biography*, Oxford

Geoffrey Serle, Arthur Lynch, *Australian Dictionary of Biography*

Shields Daily News, Municipal Association meeting in South Shields to stop 'Communistic advance', 22 September 1923

Shields Daily News, Curbison is first Labour Mayor in South Shields, 9 October 1925

Shields Daily News, Curbison appointed Mayor, 10 November 1925

WR Garside, *The Durham Miners* – reference to Newcastle Workers' Chronicle and General Strike

Bedfordshire Times and Independent, reference to JH Thomas disapproving of General Strike, 14 May 1926

Hansard, Coal Mines Bill, including Harney's speech referencing South Shields, 28 June 1926

Yorkshire Post, reference to Chamberlain's views of Labour control of Board of Guardians, 30 March 1927

Surrey Mirror, Epsom by election, 15 June 1928

Philip Williamson, Safety First: Baldwin, the Conservative Party and the 1929 General Election, *Historical Journal*, 1982

Sunderland Echo, Harney to stand, 15 May 1929

Yorkshire Post, Article on TT Anderson potentially standing as Liberal in place of Harney, 16 May 1929

Sunderland Echo, Mr Harney dead, 17 May 1929

Western Mail, Ede's letter denying he is considering resigning, 30 January 1931

Shields Daily News, Labour expels South Shields rebels, 7 May 1931

Shields Daily News, Labour friction over magistrates appointments, 1 July 1931

Hartlepool Northern Daily Mail, Ede's letter to South Shields Labour Party from Penzance, 25 August 1931

Shields Gazette, Ede – 'Socialism is the only remedy', 25 August 1931

Shields Daily News, Labour rift at an end, 13 October 1931

Shields Daily News, Kearney's telegram to South Shields Liberals, 14 October 1931

Shields Daily News – Police called to PAC meeting following Gompertz's actions, 31 December 1931

Lynn Hollen Lees, *The Solidarities of Strangers*

Harold Wilson, *A Prime Minister on Prime Ministers*

Stephen Hart, *James Chuter Ede*

Chapter 9 – … And Defeat

Roderick Martin, *Communism and the British Trade Unions 1924–29*, a study of the NMM

Chief Medical Officer's Report to South Shields Health Committee, 1930

Shields Daily News, Report of Gompertz at Tyneside Federation of Trades Council, 21 December 1931

Peter Chapman, *A Tyneside Heritage*, The History Press, 2021

Herbert Tracey, *A history of the Labour Party*

Jaime Reynolds and Ian Hunter, *Crinks*

TD Nudds, *History of the Liberal Party*

Stephen Hart, *James Chuter Ede*

Shields Daily News, Council receives Labour delegation opposed to Means Test, 7 January 1932

Daily Herald, Mass protest against Means Test, 14 May 1932

Shields Daily News, Gompertz organises Tyne Dock public meetings against water charges, 15 June 1932

Shields Daily News, Gompertz attacks PAC, 24 December 1932

South Shields Labour Party Financial Records
Harold Wilson, *A Prime Minister on Prime Ministers*
Andrew Marr, *The Making of Modern Britain*

Chapter 10 – Municipal Honours
Shields Gazette, Editorial on Moderate Party tactics, 14 November 1932
Shields Gazette, Editorial on 'Political whipping' policy, 22 November 1932
Shields Gazette, 'Kept off the PAC' 24th November 1932
Shields Gazette, Editorial, 'A Councillor and a plot', 25 November 1932
Shields Gazette, Tyne Dock by-election held during Secret Document affair, 28 November 1932
Shields Gazette, Town Clerk's reply, 29 November 1932
Shields Gazette, Latest phase of Shields Controversy, 2 December 1932
Shields Gazette, Report on Council debate re 'Secret document', 8 December 1932
Shields Gazette, letters on Secret Document affairs, 6, 7, 8, 10, 12 December, 1932
Shields Gazette, Scuffle at Shields Council (re: Ald Curbison), 2 February 1932
Shields Gazette, Free meals at Shields schools, 2 February 1933
Shields Daily News, Gompertz attacks water companies, 7 March 1933
Shields Daily News, Mayor rebukes public following show of support for Gompertz, 4 January 1934
Shields Daily News, '*Good old Gompy*', 10 March 1934
Shields Daily News, Gompertz raises Tyne River crossing, 7 March 1935
Nigel Todd, *In Excited Times*
David Clark, *We do not want the earth*
Fredric M Miller, The unemployment policy of the National Government 1931–36, *Historical Journal*, 1976
Fredric M Miller, The British unemployment Assistance crisis of 1935, *Journal of Contemporary History*, 1979
Michael Foot, *Biography of Aneurin Bevan*

Chapter 11 – Appeasement
James C Robertson, The British General Election of 1935, *Journal of Contemporary History*, 1974
Michael Foot, *Biography of Aneurin Bevan*, outlines the mass opposition to the Means Test
Wal Hannington, *The Problem of the distressed areas*
Ernie Gompertz, correspondence to the national Labour Party re: Fascist activity in South Shields, Labour Party archives
Nigel Todd, *In Excited Times*
Ben Pimlott, The Socialist League: Intellectuals and the Labour Left in the 1930s, *Journal of Contemporary History*, 1971
Martin Pugh, The Liberal Party and the Popular Front, *The English Historical Review*, 2006

Ellen Wilkinson, *The Town that was murdered*

Herbert Tracy, *History of the Labour Party*

CR Coote, *The Other Club* (reference to anecdote of fellow MP re: Crinks), 1971

Daily Herald, Article on Gompertz letter to H Johnstone, 6 July 1935

Yorkshire Post, Tyneside Unification proposals, 20 November 1935

Ede, statement on his opposition to Tyneside Unification, South Shields Labour Party archives

Shields Daily News, Article on child emigration, 3 August 1935

Shields Daily News, Mosley in South Shields, 4 November 1935

Shields Daily News, William Joyce public meeting, 21 March 1936

Yorkshire Post, Gompertz reference to 'Vassal Boroughs', 3 April 1936

Sunderland Echo, South Shields Moderates walk out of Council Chamber, 16 June 1936

Shields Daily News, Gompertz seeks Chair of Finance Committee, 25 November 1936

Shields Daily News, Dunlop votes against Gompertz for Finance Chair, 27 November 1936

Ede, Correspondence to *Shields Gazette* on '*coloured residents of South Shields*', South Shields Labour Party archives

Correspondence to Gompertz from National Unemployed Workers' Movement, South Shields Labour Party archives

Chapter 12 – The Road to War

Harold Wilson, *A Prime Minister on Prime Ministers*

Daily Herald, Article quoting Gompertz opposition to birching, 5 April 1937

Newcastle Journal, Gompertz comment on Councillors relatives working in Town Hall, 28 October 1937

Newcastle Journal, Labour controls South Shields Council for first time, 3 November 1937

Newcastle Journal, Moderates claim Gompertz is a '*laughing stock*', 2 December 1937

Shields Daily News, Rally for Spain, 18 April 1938

Shields Daily News, Gompertz letter in response to BUF member Olive Hawks, 23 May 1938

Shields Daily News, Cripps assists Austrian Jewish fugitives, 15 July 1938

Sunderland Echo, Austrian Jewish fugitives, 16 July 1938

Reynolds News, Austrian Jewish fugitives, 17 July 1938

Daily Herald, Austrian Jewish fugitives, 18 and 19 July 1938

Shields Daily News, Tynemouth and South Shields Councils to meet Minister re Tyne Crossing, 6 August 1938

Shields Gazette, Ede's address to constituents on the Munich Agreement, 2 October 1938

Shields Daily News, Moderate Aldermen deposed, 14 November 1938

Newcastle Chronicle, Gompertz appointed Chair of North-East Federation of Trades Councils, 4 March 1939

Shields Daily News, London meeting on income tax, 8 March 1940

Andrew Marr, *The Making of Modern Britain*

Chapter 13 – Defending the Town

Shields Gazette, Gompertz makes clear his views on military conscription, 19 May 1939

New Leader, Includes South Shields Labour Party as opposed to war, 23 February 1940

Craig Armstrong, *South Shields at War 1939–45*

Newcastle Evening Chronicle, Article on Gompertz visit to Workington, 10 November 1939

Shields Daily News, Ede's Question in House of Commons on defence preparations, 3 August 1939

Sunderland Echo, Attlee and the Peace Aims Document, 18 December 1939

Shields Daily News, Gompertz writes to Lord Woolton as Chair of Food Control committee, 12 August 1940

Shields Daily News, St Hilda's colliery threatened closure, 1 August, 6 September 1940

Manchester Evening News, Photograph and article, Gompertz attendance at Trades Council conference, 30 May 1942

Shields Daily News, Naomi Jacob visits South Shields, 6 July 1942

Shields Daily News, Gompertz castigates War Office over service pay, 1 October 1942

John Bew, Clem Attlee, the Man who made modern Britain – Ede's comment about Attlee's performance in February PLP meeting

Shields Daily News, Income Tax case, 1 February 1943

Shields Daily News, Income Tax case, 13 March 1943

Yorkshire Post, Gompertz and Income Tax case, 6 August 1943

Newcastle Journal, Gompertz wins Income Tax case, 6 August 1943

Labour Party NEC Report to Labour Party Conference 1943

Andrew Marr, *The Making of Modern Britain*

Chapter 14 – Securing the Peace

Stephen Hart, *James Chuter Ede*

Donoughue and Jones, *Herbert Morrison, portrait of a politician*

Andrew Thorpe, 'In a rather emotional state', *The English Historical Review*, 2006

Andrew Thorpe, *Locking out the Communists, the Labour Party and Communist Party, 1939–46*

Kevin Jeffreys, *RA Butler, the Board of Education and the 1944 Education Act*

Shields Daily News, Gompertz reacts to Tynemouth decision not to proceed with Tyne Tunnel, 8 December 1944

Shields Daily News, Tynemouth responds to Gompertz's verbal attack, 14 December 1944

Chuter Ede 1945 election leaflet, author's private collection

Shields Daily News, Gompertz elected to represent Trades Council Federation to TUC, 29 May 1945

Newcastle Journal, Ede describes Gompertz as his 'Mr Berthier', 20 June 1945

Shields Daily News, Labour victory supper in Town Hall, 27 July 1945

Shields Daily News, Ede addresses public meeting for Grace Coleman, 20 June 1945

Shields Daily News, Labour loses control of South Shields Council, 2 November 1945

Shields Daily News, Gompertz objects to Communist speaking at Regional Food Committee, 27 February 1946

Sunderland Echo, Gompertz protests at his removal as Chair of Food Committee, 13 March 1946

The Times, Town and County boundaries, 2 May 1947

The Times, Local Government boundaries, 16 May 1947

The Times, Repeal of Local Boundary Act, 28 June 1949

Michael Foot, *Aneurin Bevan*

Chapter 15 – Consolidating Control

Keith Middlemas, *Power, competition and the State* (chapter 5: Crisis and Austerity 1947–49)

Thomas P Jenkin, *The British General Election of 1951*, University of California

Shields Daily News, Ede addresses Labour Party dinner in South Shields, 18 April 1947

Shields Daily News, Ede addresses Young Labour conference in South Shields, 1 December 1947

Shields Daily News, Ockleton accused of being like Mosley, 19 August 1948

Shields Daily News, Gompertz attacks appointed of retired Major-General to regional post, 7 January 1949

Shields Daily News, Ede launches South Shields Labour Party's local election campaign, 14 March 1949

Shields Daily News, Labour members walk-out over RR Robson's remarks, 5 May 1951

Ede's letter accepting nomination for the 1950 General Election is part of the South Shields Labour Party archives

Ockleton's letter to Gompertz, South Shields Labour Party Archives

Daily News (London) *Tulip Affair*, 4 June 1951

Shields Daily News, *Tulip Affair*, 6 June 1951

Sunderland Echo, *Tulip Affair*, 17 July 1951

Shields Daily News, Town Clerk's salary increase opposed, 3 October 1951

Liverpool Echo, Article on Court case on Town Clerk's salary increase, 3 October 1951

John Charmley, referenced in *The Fall of the Attlee Government 1951*, Crowcroft and Theakston

Chapter 16 – Elder Statesman
Peter Shore, *Leading from the Left*
Michael Jago, *Clement Attlee the inevitable Prime Minister* (reference Gaitskell's quote on Morrison's removal from NEC)
Ede 1955 Election leaflet, author's private collection
Prof Vernon Bogdanor, *The General Election of 1959*, Gresham College Lecture
Shields Daily News, Appointment of Mr Adjeitey, 31 July 1952
Shields Daily News, Gompertz receives award from TUC, 24 September 1952
Shields Daily News, Presentation to Ald Sutton, 6 November 1952
Shields Daily News, Conservative discontent with RARAMA, 17 September 1952
David Clark, *We do not want the earth*
Shields Daily News, Free School meals issues, 4 December 1952
Bradford Observer, Gompertz visits Keighley, 9 February 1953
Shields Gazette, Gompertz offers to mediate in Miners' strike, 10 March 1954
Shields Gazette, Miners dispute at Whitburn Colliery, 12 March 1954
Shields Gazette, Miners dispute ends, 22 March 1954
Shields Daily News, Parliamentary Boundary changes, 9 April 1954
Shields Daily News, Gompertz nominated for Mayoralty, 12 May 1953
Shields Daily News, Gompertz appointed Mayor, 19 May 1953
Shields Daily News, Royal British Legion concerned at Gompertz becoming Mayor, 21 May 1953
Shields Daily News, Article on Mayoral Sunday and Attlee addressing public meeting, 25 May 1953
Newcastle Evening Chronicle, *Shields Daily News*, Parliamentary Boundary changes, 29 June 1954
Newcastle Evening Chronicle, Parliamentary Boundary Review, 8 July 1954
Shields Daily News, RARAMA becomes Progressive Association, 14 October 1954
Shields Daily News, Parliamentary boundary review, 15 December 1954
Chuter Ede 1955 Election leaflet, private collection

Chapter 17 – Journey's End
Peter G Boyle, The Hungarian Revolution and the Suez Crisis, *History*, 2005
Conversation with Stan Smith
Shields Daily News, Reid outlines his plans for Market Place, 8 October 1958
Shields Gazette, 1958 Local Council election results, 8 May 1958
Tim Gopsill and Greg Neale, *100 years of the NUJ*, Profile Books, 2007
Prof Vernon Bogdanor, *The General Election 1959*, Gresham College Lecture 2014

Shields Gazette, Gompertz downfall, 2 March 1960
Shields Gazette, Gompertz downfall articles, 3 March 1960
Shields Gazette, Horsley Hill residents react to Gompertz departure, 4 March 1960
Shields Gazette, Ede and Gompertz presentation, 20 January 1960
Copy of Ernie Gompertz last Will via Leeds Probate Registry
Chuter Ede's personal papers stored at Surrey History Centre

Chapter 18 – Afterword
Shields Gazette, Gompertz speaks against birching, 17 June 1960
National Archives HO291/854, File on Gompertz's appearance in front of Justice
    Black Commission
Shields Gazette, Gompertz tribute to Ede, 11 November 1965
Shields Gazette, Article on death of Gompertz, 8 April 1968
Shields Gazette, Article on Gompertz funeral service, 10 April 1960
Chuter Ede's personal papers stored at Surrey History Centre
Recollections of Brian Howard

Index